Jean H. Merle d'Aubigné

History of the Reformation in the Sixteenth Century

Vol. 3

Jean H. Merle d'Aubigné

History of the Reformation in the Sixteenth Century
Vol. 3

ISBN/EAN: 9783337295653

Printed in Europe, USA, Canada, Australia, Japan

Cover: Foto ©ninafisch / pixelio.de

More available books at **www.hansebooks.com**

Collins's Select Library.

HISTORY

OF

THE REFORMATION

IN THE

SIXTEENTH CENTURY.

BY

J. H. MERLE D'AUBIGNE, D.D.

J'appelle accessoire, l'estat des affaires de ceste vie caduque et transitoire. J'appelle principal, le gouvernement spirituel auquel reluit souverninement la providence de Dieu.—*Theodore de Beze.*

By *accessory*, I mean the state of affairs in this fading and transitory life. By *principal*, I mean the spiritual government in which the providence of God is sovereignly displayed.—*Theodore Beza.*

A NEW TRANSLATION, CONTAINING THE AUTHOR'S LATEST IMPROVEMENTS.

BY

HENRY BEVERIDGE, ESQ., ADVOCATE.

VOL. III.

GLASGOW:
WILLIAM COLLINS, PUBLISHER & QUEEN'S PRINTER.
1862.

PREFACE TO VOLUME THIRD.

LITERARY men in France, Switzerland, Germany, and England, urged on by a spirit of examination and research, are constantly enquiring after the original documents on which modern history is founded. I wish to contribute my mite to the accomplishment of the important task which our age appears to have undertaken. Hitherto I have not deemed it enough to peruse contemporary historians. I have interrogated eye-witnesses, private letters, and original narratives, and made use of some manuscripts, particularly that of Bullinger, which has since been printed. (Frauenfield, 1838-1840.)

The necessity of having recourse to unpublished documents became more urgent on approaching, as I do in the twelfth book, the Reformation of France, with regard to which, in consequence of the continual turmoil in which the reformed church of that country has lived, we have only a few printed memoirs. In the spring of 1838, I endeavoured, as far as was in my power, to examine the manuscripts of the public libraries of Paris; it will be seen that a manuscript of the Royal Library, hitherto I believe unknown, throws great light on the first stages of the Reformation. In the autumn of 1839, I consulted the manuscripts in the library of the consistory of pastors of Neufchâtel, a collection which is very rich in regard to this period, from a bequest of the manuscripts of Farel's library, and through the kindness of the proprietor of Meuron, I obtained the use of the manuscript life of Farel by Choupard, into which the greater part of these documents have been transcribed. These manuscripts have enabled me to remodel one entire section of the Reformation in France. In addition to this assistance, and that furnished by the library of Geneva, I made an appeal, through the medium of the *Archives du Christianisme*, to all the friends of history and the Reformation, who may have any manuscripts at their disposal, and I here express my gratitude for different communications which have been made to me, in particular by the Rev. Mr. Ladevèze of Meaux. But though religious wars and persecutions have destroyed many precious documents, there doubtless still exist in different parts of France several which would be of essential service to the history of the Reformation, and I earnestly entreat all who may possess or have any knowledge of them to have the goodness to communicate with me on the subject. Documents of this nature are felt in our days to be common property, and, therefore, I hope that this appeal will not be in vain.

It will perhaps be thought that in writing a general history of the Reformation, I have entered too much into detail on its first beginnings in France. But these beginnings are little known: the events which form the subject of my twelfth book occupy only three or four pages in the 'Histoire Ecclesiastique des Eglises Reformées au Royaume de France,' by Theodore Beza, while other historians confine themselves almost entirely to political developments. It is true that in this part of my work I have not been able to describe scenes so imposing as the Diet of Worms. Nevertheless, independent of the religious interest attached to it, the humble but truly divine movement which I have attempted to describe, had perhaps more influence on the destinies of France than the celebrated wars of Charles V and Francis I. In a large machine the result is often produced not by the parts which make the greatest appearance, but by the most hidden springs.

Complaints have been made of the delay which has taken place in the publication of this third volume. Some would even have had me not to print the first before the whole was completed. There may be certain superior intellects to which conditions may be prescribed, but there are others whose feebleness must give conditions, and to this class I belong. To publish a volume at one time, at another time when I am able a second volume, and then a third, is the course which my primary duties and humble abilities allow me to take. Other circumstances, moreover, have interposed; severe afflictions have on two occasions interrupted the composition of this third volume, and concentrated all my affections and all my thoughts on the tomb of beloved children.

The thought that it was my duty to glorify the adorable Master, who addressed those powerful calls to me, and accompanied them with so much divine consolation, could alone have given me the courage necessary to prosecute my labours.

These explanations seemed due to the kindness with which this work has been received in France, and especially in England, where the fourth edition of a translation is about to appear, beside two others in smaller form, which I am told are in course of preparation. Owing to this, no doubt, the *Journal des Débats*, in an article signed M. Chasles, has announced this history of the Reformation as an English work. I set a high value on the approbation of the protestant Christians of Great Britain, the representatives of evangelical principles and doctrines in the most remote regions of the globe, and I beg to assure them that I feel it to be a most valuable encouragement to my labours. The first book of the fourth volume will be devoted (God willing) to the Reformation of England and Scotland.[1]

The cause of truth recompenses those who embrace and defend it; and so it has proved with the nations who embraced the Reformation. In the eighteenth century, at the moment when Rome was anticipating her triumph through her Jesuits and scaffolds, victory slipt through her hands. Rome, like Naples, Portugal, and Spain, fell into interminable difficulties, while at the same time two protestant kingdoms arose in Europe, and began to exercise an influence which till then had belonged to Roman Catholic states. England came forth victorious from the Spanish and French assaults, which the pope had so long stirred up against her, and the Elector of Brandenburg, in spite of the wrath of Clement XI, encircled his head with a royal crown. From that period England has extended her dominion in every quarter of the world, and Prussia has taken a new rank among continental states, while a third power also separated from Rome, *viz.* Russia was growing up in her immense deserts. In this way evangelical principles have exerted their influence on the countries which have received them, and *by righteousness nations have been exalted.* Let evangelical states be well assured that to protestantism they owe their greatness. Should

---

[1] The last book of the present ought, perhaps, to have formed the commencement of a succeeding volume. It seemed better, however, to introduce the Reformation of France into the third volume, though the effect has been to make it about 150 pages larger than each of the other two.

they abandon the position which God has given them, or incline anew towards Rome, that moment they lose their power and glory. Rome is now striving to gain them; alternately employing flattery and threatening, she would, like Delilah, lull them asleep upon her knees . . . but it is to rob them of their locks, that thus their enemies may be able to put out their eyes, and bind them with fetters of iron.

Herein, too, is a great lesson for France, with which the author feels himself so intimately connected through his forefathers. Should France, like her different governments, incline anew to the papacy, our belief is, that it will prove the signal of great disasters. Every one who attaches himself to the papacy will be compromised in its downfall. France has her only prospect of strength and greatness in turning towards the gospel. May this great truth be understood by rulers and people!

In our day, it is true, there is great activity in the papacy. Though attacked by an inevitable consumption, she would fain, by showy colours and feverish paroxysms, persuade others, and persuade herself, that she is still full of vigour. An attempt of this kind has been made by a theologian of Turin, in a treatise occasioned by this history, and in which it is pleasing to recognise a certain talent in presenting proofs, however feeble, with an air of candour to which we are little accustomed, and in a manner by no means offensive, notwithstanding of the sad and culpable facility with which the author, in his twelfth chapter, revives accusations against the Reformers, the falsehood of which has been completely demonstrated, and is generally acknowledged.[1]

We will give an example, referring to matters contained in the present volume. James le Vasseur, doctor of Sorbonne, and canon and dean of the church of Noyon, wrote Annals of the Church of Noyon, (1633,) in which he is at a loss for epithets against our Reformer, and only consoles himself by the thought that *Saint Eloi gave Calvin the mortal blow*, (p. 1164). After saying that the Reformer in early life held benefices in the Church of Noyon, the canon in proof of this quotes a declaration of James Desmay, also a doctor of theology, in his "Life of Calvin the heresiarch,"

---

[1] LA PAPAUTÉ *consideree dans son Origine et dans son Developpement au moyen age, ou Reponse aux Allegations de M. Merle d'Aubigne dans son Histoire de la Reformation au Seizieme Siecle, par l'abbe* C. MAGNIN, *docteur en theologie. Genev?, chez Berthier-Guers.* 1840.

who, after a very careful examination of every thing relating to the Reformer, says, "*I have been unable to discover* ANYTHING ELSE *in the same registers.*" (Annales de Noyon, p. 1162). Then the devout historian of the Church of Noyon, after pouring out all his wrath on Calvin and all the members of his family, without mentioning a single act of the Reformer at variance with morality, but contenting himself with simply observing, that *to call him heresiarch is to charge him with the sum of all crimes* (ib.) adds a XCVI chapter, entitled, "*Of another John Cauvin, chaplain Vicar of the same church of Noyon,* NOT A HERETIC," in which he says, "Another John Cauvin presented himself and was admitted to our choir at a vicarial chapel, but was shortly after dismissed *for his incontinence, punishment* having been repeatedly inflicted to no purpose. He was vicar for the diocese, and the belief of our old people is, that he served the cure of Trachy-le-Val in this diocese in the capacity of vicar, and then died *a good catholic.* He was, nevertheless, beaten with rods when in custody, as Desmay writes in his little book, pp. 39, 40, and yet he was a priest not subject to such discipline. He has, therefore, fallen into a blunder, taking this man for another vicar, also chaplain, named Baldwin le Jeune, doubly young in name and in manners, who had not then entered the priesthood or taken any holy orders. The conclusion of the capitulary is as follows :— . . . . *Quod Balduinus, le Jeune capellanus vicarialis, . . . pro scandalis commissis, ordinarunt præfati domini* IPSUM CÆDI VIRGIS, *quia puer et nondum in sacris constitutus.* I thought it my duty (continues the dean of Noyon) to add this chapter to the history of the first Calvin, *ad diluendam homonymiam,* (to guard against the similarity of names,) lest the one should be taken for the other, the catholic for the heretic." Thus speaks the canon and dean of Noyon, pp. 1170, 1171. Now what is done by Doctor Magnin and the writers of the papacy whom he quotes? They announce quite gravely that Calvin was banished from his native town for bad conduct ; that being convicted of a horrible crime, he would have been condemned to be publicly burnt had not the burning been commuted, at the prayer of the bishop, into scourging and branding with a hot iron, etc. (La Papauté, p. 109.) Thus, in spite of all the pains which the dean of Noyon took to add a chapter *for fear the one should be taken for the other, the catholic for the heretic,* the writers f the papacy uniformly attribute to the Reformer the misdeeds of his namesake. The thought uppermost with the canon of Noyon was the fair fame of this John Calvin *who died a good catholic*, and he trembled lest he should be charged with the heresy of Calvin. Accordingly he draws the distinction between them very clearly, giving the *heresies* to the one, and *the incontinence* to the other. But the result is the very opposite of what he anticipated. It is not "the heresy of Calvin" that has brought opprobrium on John Cauvin, but the incontinence and chastisement of John Cauvin are brought forward for the purpose of throwing opprobrium on the Reformer. And such is the way in which history is written!—such, we will not say the bad faith, but the levity and ignorance of the apologists of the papacy! These blunders occur in the writings of men otherwise respectable, and who ought to have nothing in common with the hateful name of calumniator. The present volume gives a true account of the early life of Calvin.

M. Audin, as a sequel to his History of Luther, has recently published a History of Calvin, written under the influence of deplorable prejudice, and in which it is difficult to recognise the Reformers and the Reformation.

Perhaps, on another occasion, we shall make some addition to what we have said in our first book on the origin of the papacy. It were out of place to do it here.

I will only remark in general, that the *human* and natural causes which so well explain its origin are precisely those to which the Papacy appeals in order to demonstrate its *divine* institution. Thus Christian antiquity declares, that the universal episcopate was committed to all the bishops, so that the bishops of Jerusalem, Alexandria, Antioch, Ephesus, Rome, Carthage, Lyons, Arles, Milan, Hippo, Cesarea, etc., took an interest in whatever occurred throughout the Christian world. Shortly after Rome appropriated to herself this duty, which was incumbent on all, and arguing as if it were her concern only, converts it into a demonstration of her primacy.

We give another example. The Christian churches established in the great towns of the empire sent missionaries to the countries to which they stood related. This was done first of all by Jerusalem, then by Antioch, Alexandria, Ephesus, and at length by Rome; and Rome forthwith concluded, from what she did after others and less than others, that she was entitled to set herself above all others. These examples will suffice.

Let us only observe further, that in the West Rome alone enjoyed the honour which in the East was shared by Corinth, Philippi, Thessalonica, Ephesus, Antioch, and in a far higher degree by Jerusalem,[1]—the honour of having had one or more apostles among her first teachers. Hence the Latin churches must naturally have had a certain degree of respect for Rome. But never would the eastern Christians, though they honoured her as the church of the political metropolis of the empire, acknowledge in her any ecclesiastical superiority. The celebrated general Council of Chalcedon assigned to Constantinople, previously the obscure Byzantium, the same privileges (τὰ ἴσα πρισβεῖα) as Rome, and declared that it was entitled to equal dignity. Accordingly, when the papacy was distinctly formed in Rome, the East showed no desire to acknowledge a master of whom it had never heard; and standing on the ancient territory of catholicity, abandoned the West to the domination of the new sect which had risen up within its bosom. The East still styles herself, by way of pre-eminence, *catholic and orthodox*, and when the question is asked at one of these eastern Christians, whom Rome has united to herself by means of numerous concessions, "Are you a Catholic?"—"No," he immediately replies, "I am *papistian*" (papist).—*Journal of the Rev. Joseph Wolf.* London, 1839, p. 225.

If this History has been subjected to criticism from the Romish party, it has also been subjected to it in a literary point of view. Individuals for whom I entertain great respect appear to attach more importance to a political or literary history of the Reformation, than to an exposition which points out its spiritual principles and moving springs. I can understand this manner of viewing the subject, but I cannot adopt it. In my opinion, the essentials of the Reformation are its doctrines and inward life. Any work in which these do not occupy the first place, may be brilliant, but will not be faithfully and candidly historical. It will resemble a philosopher, who, wishing to describe man, should with great accuracy and graphic beauty explain every thing that relates to his body,

---

[1] St. Epiphanius says that our Lord committed to James the greater at Jerusalem his *throne on earth* (τὸν θρόνον αὐτοῦ ἐπὶ τῆς γῆς); and speaking of bishops assembled at Jerusalem, he declares that the *whole world* (πάντα κόσμον) ought to submit to their authority. (Epiph. Hæres., 70, 10-78, 7.

but should give only a subordinate place to the divine inmate, the soul.

There are many defects, doubtless, in the feeble work of which I here present a new fragment to the Christian public, but the greatest defect I see in it is, that it does not breathe still more of the spirit of the Reformation. The more I succeed in calling attention to what manifests the glory of Christ, the more faithful I am to history. I willingly adopt as my law those words which a historian of the sixteenth century, still more celebrated as a warrior than a writer, after giving a part of the history of Protestantism, of which I do not purpose to treat, addresses to those who should think of completing his task,—"I give them the law which I take to myself, and it is, that while seeking the honour of this precious instrument, their principal aim should be the glory of the arm which prepared, employed, and wielded it at pleasure. For all the praises given to princes are unseasonable and misplaced, if they have not for their aim and foundation that of the living God, to whom belong honour and dominion for ever and ever."

Eaux-Vives, near Geneva, Feb. 1841.

CONTENTS.

BOOK NINTH.
FIRST REFORMS.—(1521, 1522.)

CHAP. I.
Progress of the Reformation—New Period—Advantages of Luther's Captivity—Agitation of Germany—Melancthon and Luther—Enthusiasm, - - - - - - - 11

CHAP. II.
Luther in the Wartburg—Object of his Captivity—Agonies—Sickness—Labour of Luther—On Confession—To Latomus—Walks. 17

CHAP. III.
Reformation begins—Marriage of Feldkirchen—Marriage of Monks—Theses—Writes against Monachism—Luther ceases to be a Monk. - - - - - - - 23

CHAP. IV.
Archbishop Albert—The Idol of Halle—Luther apears—Terror at the Court—Luther to the Archbishop—The Archbishop's Reply—Joachim of Brandenburg, - - - - - 27

CHAP. V.
Translation of the Bible—Wants of the Church—Principles of the Reformation—Alarm at Court—Luther to the Archbishop—Temptations of the Devil—Condemnation of the Sorbonne—Melancthon's Reply—Visit to Wittemberg. - - - 32

CHAP. VI.
New Reforms—Gabriel Zwilling on the Mass—The University—The Elector—Monachism attacked—Emancipation of the Monks—Disturbances—Chapter of the Augustins—The Mass and Carlstadt—First Supper—Importance of the Mass in the Roman System. - - - - - - - 37

CHAP. VII.
Spurious Reform—The new Prophets—The Prophets at Wittemberg—Melancthon—The Elector—Luther, Carlstadt, and Images—Disorders—Luther sent for—He hesitates not—Dangers. - 46

CHAP. VIII.
Departure from the Wartburg—New Position—Luther and Primitive Catholicism—Meeting at the Black Bear—Luther to the Elector—Return to Wittemberg—Discourses at Wittemberg—Charity—the Word—How the Reformation was effected—Faith in Christ—Effect—Didymus—Carlstadt—The Prophets—Conference with Luther—End of the Struggle. - - - 54

CONTENTS.

CHAP. IX.

Translation of the New Testament—Faith and Scripture—Opposition—Importance of Luther's Publication—Need of a Systematic Exposition—Melancthon's *Common Places*—Original Sin—Salvation—Free-will—Effect of the Common Places. - - 68

CHAP. X.

Opposition—Henry VIII—Wolsey—The Queen—Fisher—Thomas More—Luther's Books burnt—Henry attacks Luther—Presentation to the Pope—Effect on Luther—Force and violence—His book—Reply of the Bishop of Rochester—Reply by More—Step by the King. - - - - - - - 76

CHAP. XI.

General Movement—The Monks—How the Reformation is Accomplished—Ordinary Believers—The Old and the New Teachers—Printing and Literature—Booksellers and Hawkers. - - 86

CHAP. XII.

Luther at Zwickau—The Castle of Freyberg—Worms—Frankfort Universal movement—Wittemberg, the centre of the Reformation—Luther's sentiments. - - - - - - 92

BOOK TENTH.

AGITATION, REVERSES, AND PROGRESS.—(1522-1526.)

CHAP. I.

Political element—Want of Enthusiasm at Rome—Siege of Pampeluna—Courage of Inigo—Transformation—Luther and Loyola—Visions—The two principles. - - - - 98

CHAP. II.

Victory of the Pope—Death of Leo X—Oratory of Divine Love—Adrian VI—Schemes of Reform—Opposition. - - 105

CHAP. III.

Diet of Nuremberg—Invasion of Solyman—The Nuncio demands the Death of Luther—The Preachers of Nuremberg—Promise of Reform—National Grievances—Decree of the Diet—Thundering Letter of the Pope—Luther's Advice. - - - - 109

CHAP. IV.

Persecution—Efforts of Duke George—The Convent of Antwerp—Miltenberg—The three Monks of Antwerp—The Scaffold—Martyrdom at Brussels. - - - - - 116

CHAP. V.

New Pope—The Legate Campeggio—Diet of Nuremberg—Demand of the Legate—Reply of the Diet—Project of a Secular Council—Alarm and Efforts of the Pope—Bavaria—League of Ratisbon—Rigour and Reform—Political Schisms—Opposition—Intrigues of Rome—Edict of Bruges—Rupture. - - - 122

CONTENTS.

CHAP. VI.   PAGE
Persecution—Gaspard Tauber—A Bookseller—Cruelties in Wurtemberg, Salzburg, Bavaria, Pomerania—Henry of Zuphten,   - 128

CHAP. VII.
Divisions—Lord's Supper—Two Extremes—Carlstadt—Luther—Mysticism of the Anabaptists—Carlstadt at Orlamund—Mission of Luther—Interview at dinner—Conference of Orlamund—Carlstadt banished, - - - - - - 133

CHAP. VIII.
Progress—Resistance to the Leaguers—Meeting between Philip of Hesse and Melancthon—The Landgrave gained to the Gospel—The Palatinate, Luneburg, Holstein—The Grand Master at Wittemberg, 139

CHAP. IX.
Reformers—The Church of All Saints—Fall of the Mass—Literature—Christian Schools—Science offered to the Laity—Arts—Moral Religion, Esthetical Religion—Music—Poetry—Painting, 142

CHAP. X.
Political ferment—Luther against Revolution—Thomas Munzer—Agitation—The Black Forest—The Twelve Articles—Luther's Advice—Helfenstein—Advance of the Peasants—Advance of the Imperial Army—Defeat of the Peasants—Cruelty of the Princes, 149

CHAP. XI.
Munzer at Mulhausen—Appeal to the People—March of the Princes—End of the Revolt—Influence of the Reformers—Sufferings—Change, - - - - - - - 159

CHAP. XII.
Two Issues—Death of Frederick—The Prince and the Reformer—Catholic Alliance—Projects of Charles—Dangers, - - 165

CHAP. XIII.
The Nuns of Nimptsch—Luther's Feelings—End of the Convent—Luther's Marriage—Domestic Happiness, - - - 168

CHAP. XIV.
The Landgrave—The Elector—Prussia—Reformation—Secularisation—The Archbishop of Mentz—Conference of Friedewalt—Diet—Alliance of Torgau—Resistance of the Reformers—Alliance of Magdeburg—The Catholics redouble their efforts—Marriage of the Emperor—Threatening Letters—The two Parties, - - 173

BOOK ELEVENTH.
DIVISION—SWITZERLAND, GERMANY—(1523-1527).

CHAP. I.
Unity in Diversity—Primitive Faith and Liberty—Formation of Roman Unity—A Monk and Leo Juda—Theses of Zuinglius—The Discussion of January, - - - - - 181

CHAP. II.
Caresses of the Pope—Progress of the Reformation—The Image of Stadelhofen—Sacrilege—The Ornaments of the Saints, - - 186

CONTENTS.

CHAP. III.

The October Discussion—Zuinglius on the Church—The Church—First Outline of Presbyterianism—Discussion on the Mass—Enthusiasts—A Voice of Wisdom—Victory—A characteristic of the Swiss Reformation—Moderation—Oswald Myconius at Zurich—The Revival of Letters—Thomas Plater of the Valois, - 189

CHAP. IV.

Diet of Lucerne—Hottinger arrested—His Death—Deputation of the Diet to Zurich—Abolition of Processions—Abolition of Images—The two Reformations—Appeal to the People, - - 195

CHAP. V.

New Opposition—Œxlin carried off—The Family of the Wirths—The Mob at the Convent of Ittengen—The Diet of Zug—The Wirths seized and given up to the Diet—Condemnation, - 201

CHAP. VI.

Abolition of the Mass—Zuinglius' Dream—Celebration of the Lord's Supper—Brotherly Charity—Original Sin—The Oligarchs against the Reformation—Divers Attacks, - - - - 207

CHAP. VII.

Berne—The Provost of Watteville—First Successes of the Reformation—Haller at the Convent—Accusation and Deliverance—The Monastery of Königsfeld—Margaret of Watteville to Zuinglius—The Convent open—Two opposite Champions—Clara May and the Provost of Watteville, - - - - - 211

CHAP. VIII.

Basle—Œcolampadius—He goes to Augsburg—He enters the Convent—He returns to Sickingen—Returns to Basle—Ulric Von Hutten—His projects—Last Effort of Chivalry—Hutten dies at Uffnan, 217

CHAP. IX.

Erasmus and Luther—Uncertainty of Erasmus—Luther to Erasmus—Work of Erasmus against Luther on Free Will—Three Opinions—Effect on Luther—Luther on Free Will—The Jansenists and the Reformers—Homage to Erasmus—Rage of Erasmus—The Three Days, - - - - - - - 222

CHAP. X.

The Three Adversaries—Source of the Truth—Anabaptism—Anabaptism and Zuinglius—Constitution of the Church—Prison—The Prophet Blaurock—Anabaptism at St. Gall—An Anabaptist Family—Dispute at Zurich—The limits of the Reformation—Punishment of the Anabaptists, - - - - 232

CHAP. XI.

Popish Immobility—Protestant Progression—Zuinglius and Luther—Zuinglius and the Lord's Supper—Luther's great Principle—Carlstadt's Writings Prohibited—Zuinglius's Commentary—The Suabian Syngram—Capito and Bucer—Need of Unity in Diversity, - - - - - - - 238

CONTENTS.

CHAP. XII.
The Toekenburg—An Assembly of the People—Reformation—The Grisons—Discussion of Ilantz—Results—Reformation at Zurich, 245

CHAP. XIII.
Executions—Discussion at Baden—Rules of the Discussion—Riches and Poverty—Eck and Œcolampadius—Discussion—Part taken by Zuinglius—Boasting of the Romans—Insults of a Monk—End of the Discussion, - - - - - - 249

CHAP. XIV.
Consequences at Basle, Berne, St. Gall, and other places—Diet at Zurich—The Small Cantons—Menaces at Berne—Foreign Aid, 254

BOOK TWELFTH.
THE FRENCH.—(1500-1526.)

CHAP. I.
Universality of Christianity—Enemies of the Reformation in France—Heresy and Persecution in Dauphiny—A Gentleman's Family—The Family Farel—Pilgrimage to St. Croix—Immorality and Superstition—William desires to become a Student, - - 259

CHAP. II.
Louis XII, and the Assembly of Tours—Francis and Margaret—The Literati—Lefevre—His teaching at the University—Lefevre and Farel meet—Doubts and Inquiries of Farel—First awakening—Prophecy of Lefevre—He teaches Justification by Faith—Objections—Irregularities in Colleges—Effects on Farel—Election—Holiness of Life, - - - - - - 265

CHAP. III.
Farel and the Saints—The University—Conversion of Farel—Farel and Luther—Other Disciples—Date of the Reformation in France—The different Reformation spontaneous—Which is the First?—Place due to Lefevre, - - - - - - 274

CHAP. IV.
Character of Francis I—Beginning of Modern times—Liberty and Obedience—Margaret of Valois—The Court—Briçonnet, Count of Montbrun—Lefevre applies to the Bible—Francis I and his "Sons"—The Gospel brought to Margaret—A Conversion—Adoration—Character of Margaret. - - - - 278

CHAP V.
Enemies of the Reformation—Louisa—Duprat—Concordat at Bologna—Opposition of the Parliament and the University—The Sorbonne—Beda—His character—His Tyranny—Berquin, the most learned of the nobles—The Leaders of the Sorbonne—Heresy of the three Magdalenes—Luther Condemned at Paris—The Sorbonne addresses the King—Lefevre quits Paris for Meaux, - 286

CHAP. VI.
Briçonnet visits his Diocese—Reformation—The Reformers Prosecuted at Paris—Philibert of Savoy—Correspondence of Margaret and Briçonnet, - - - - - - 293

CHAP. VII.
First beginnings of the Church of Meaux—The Scriptures in French

CONTENTS.

—The Tradesmen and the Bishop—Evangelical Harvest—The Epistles of St. Paul sent to the King—Lefevre and Roma—The Monks before the Bishop—The Monks before the Parliament—Briçonnet yields, - - - - - 300

CHAP. VIII.

Lefevre and Farel Persecuted—Difference between the Lutheran and Reformed Churches—Leclerc puts up his Pancartes—Leclerc Branded—Zeal of Berquin—Berquin before the Parliament—Francis I saves him—Apostacy of Mazurier—Fall and grief of Pavanne—Metz—Chatelain—Peter Toussaint becomes attentive—Leclerc breaks Images—Condemnation and Torture of Leclerc—Martyrdom of Chatelain—Flight, - - - - 307

CHAP. IX.

Farel and his brothers—Farel driven from Gap—He preaches in the fields—Chevalier Anemond of Coct—The Minorite—Anemond quits France—Luther to the Duke of Savoy—Farel quits France, 318

CHAP. X.

Catholicity of the Reformation—Friendship of Farel and Œcolampadius—Farel and Erasmus—Altercation—Farel calls for a Discussion—Theses—Scripture and Faith—Discussion, - - 323

CHAP. XI

New Campaign—Calling of Farel to the Ministry—An advanced post—Lyons an Evangelical Focus—Sebville at Grenoble—Conventicles—Preaching at Lyons—Maigret in Prison—Margaret intimidated, - - - - - - - 329

CHAP. XII.

The French at Basle—Encouragement of the Swiss—Fear of disunion—Translations and Printing Presses at Basle—Bibles and Tracts circulated in France, - - - - - 335

CHAP. XIII.

Progress at Montbeliard—Opposition and Disturbance—Toussaint quits Œcolampadius—The day of the Bridge—Death of Anemond —Successive Defeats, - - - - - - 340

CHAP. XIV.

Francis taken at Pavia—Reaction against the Reformation—Louisa consults the Sorbonne—Commission against the Heretics—Briçonnet denounced—Appeal to the Assembled Parliament—Fall—Reconciliation—Lefevre accused—Condemnation and flight—Lefevre at Strasburg—Louis de Berquin incarcerated—Erasmus attacked—Schuch at Nantz—His Martyrdom—Contest with Caroli—Sadness of Pavanne—His Faggot Pile—A Christian Hermit —Concourse at Notre Dame. - - - - - 345

CHAP. XV.

A Scholar of Noyon—Character of young Calvin—Early Education—He is devoted to Theology—The bishop gives him the tonsure—He quits Noyon because of the Plague—The Reformation creates new languages—Persecution and terror—Toussaint put into prison—Persecution gives new strength—Death of Du Blet, Merlin, and Papillon—God saves the Church—Project of Margaret —Departure for Spain, - - - - - 305

HISTORY OF THE REFORMATION

OF THE

SIXTEENTH CENTURY.

BOOK NINTH.

FIRST REFORMS.

1521—1522.

CHAP. I.

Progress of the Reformation—New Period—Advantages of Luther's Captivity—Agitation of Germany—Melancthon and Luther—Enthusiasm. . . . .

FOUR years had elapsed since an ancient doctrine had again been preached in the church. The great doctrine of salvation by grace formerly published in Asia, Greece, and Italy, by Paul and his brethren, and again after several centuries discovered in the Bible by a monk of Wittemberg, had echoed from the plains of Saxony to Rome, Paris, and London, and the lofty mountains of Switzerland had repeated its energetic accents. The fountains of truth, liberty, and life had been again opened to humanity. Crowds had repaired thither and quaffed with joy, but those who had pressed forward and taken the draught had preserved their former appearance. All within was new, and yet all without seemed to have remained as before.

The constitution of the Church, its ritual, and discipline, had not undergone any change. In Saxony, at Wittemberg even, in every place where the new ideas had penetrated, the papal worship gravely continued its pomp; the priest at the foot of the altar, in offering the host to God, seemed to produce an ineffable transformation; monks and nuns entered convents to undertake obligations that were to bind them for ever; pastors lived not as heads of families, brotherhoods assembled, pilgrimages were performed; the faithful hung up their votive offerings on the pillars of chapels; and all ceremonies, even to the most insignificant formality of the sanctuary, were celebrated as before. There was a new doctrine in the world, but it had not given itself a new body. The language of the priest formed a striking contrast to the proceedings of the priest. He was heard thundering from the pulpit against the mass as an idolatrous worship, and then seen descending and taking his place before the altar, to celebrate this pompous ceremony with scrupulous exactness. Every where the new gospel resounded beside the ancient ritual. The priest himself did not perceive the strange inconsistency, and the people who listened with acclamation to the bold discourses of the new preachers, devoutly observed their ancient customs as if they were never to abandon them. At the domestic hearth and in social life, as in the house of God, every thing remained the same. There was a new faith in the world, but not new works. The season of spring had appeared, but winter seemed still to hold nature in chains; no flowers—no leaves—nothing external gave indication of the new season. But these appearances were illusory; a potent, though hidden sap was already circulating beneath, and on the eve of changing the world.

To this course, a course fraught with wisdom, the Reformation perhaps owes its triumphs. Prior to the actual accomplishment of any revolution there must be a revolution in thought. The inconsistency already alluded to did not even strike Luther at the first glance. He seemed to consider it quite natural that, while men were receiving his writings with enthusiasm, they should at the same time remain devotedly attached to the abuses which these writings attacked. It might even be thought that he had traced out his plan beforehand, and resolved to produce a change of minds before introducing a change of forms. This, however, were to ascribe to him a wisdom the honour of which belongs to a higher source. He executed a plan which was not of his own devising. These matters he was able at a later period to acknowledge and comprehend, but he had not imagined them, and accordingly had not regulated them. God took the lead; Luther's part was to follow.

Had Luther begun with an external reform: had he, immediately after he had spoken, attempted to abolish monastic vows, the mass, confession, and the existing forms of worship, he should undoubtedly have encountered the keenest opposition. Man must have time before he can adapt himself to great revolutions. Luther was by no means the violent, imprudent, rash innovator that some historians have represented.[1] The people seeing nothing changed in

---

[1] See Hume, etc.

the routine of their devotions, committed themselves without distrust to their new leader. They were even astonished at the attacks directed against a man who left them their mass, beads, and confessor, and attributed these attacks to the grovelling jealousy of obscure rivals, or the cruel injustice of powerful adversaries. Meanwhile Luther's ideas aroused the minds of men, improved their hearts, and so undermined the ancient edifice that it soon fell of its own accord, without any human hand. Ideas do not act instantaneously: they make their way in silence, like water which, filtering behind rocks, detaches them from the mountain on which they rest : all at once the work done in secret manifests itself, and a single day suffices to display the work of several years, perhaps several ages.

A new era in the reformation commences. The truth is already re-established in doctrine, and doctrine is now going to re-establish the truth in all the forms of the church and of society. The agitation is too great for men's minds to remain fixed and immovable at the point at which they have arrived. On those dogmas which have been so powerfully shaken depend customs which are beginning to give way, and which must disappear along with them. There is too much courage and life in the new generation to feel under constraint in the presence of error. Sacraments, ritual, hierarchy, vows, constitution, domestic life, public life, all are about to be modified. The ship which has been slowly and laboriously built is about to leave the dock and be launched on the vast ocean. We shall have to follow its track across numerous perils.

The captivity of the Wartburg separates these two periods. Providence, which designed to give a mighty impulse to the Reformation, had prepared its progress by leading him who was selected to be the instrument of it into profound retirement. For a time the work seemed buried with the workman ; but the seed must be deposited in the earth in order to produce fruit, and from the prison which seemed destined to be the Reformer's tomb the Reformation is going to come forth to make new conquests, and rapidly diffuse itself over the whole world.

Hitherto the Reformation had been concentrated in the person of the Reformer. His appearance before the Diet of Worms was undoubtedly the sublimest moment of his life. His character then appeared almost exempt from blemish, and hence it has been said, that if God who hid the Reformer during ten months within the walls of the Wartburg had, at that moment, withdrawn him for ever from the eye of the world, his end would have been a kind of apotheosis. But God wills not an apotheosis for his servants ; and Luther was preserved to the Church in order that he might show by his very faults that the faith of Christians must be founded on the word of God alone. He was abruptly transported far from the scene where the great revolution of the sixteenth century was in course of accomplishment; the truth which he had for four years so powerfully preached continued in his absence to act upon Christendom, and the work of which he was only a feeble instrument thenceforth bore not the impress of a man but the seal of God himself.

Germany was moved by the captivity of Luther. The most contradictory reports circulated throughout her provinces. Men's minds were more agitated by the absence of the Reformer than they would have been by his presence. Here it was affirmed that friends, who had come from France, had set him in safety on the other bank of the Rhine.[1] There it was said that assassins had put him to death. Even the smallest villages were anxious for information about Luther; the passing traveller was interrogated, and groups assembled in the market place. Sometimes an unknown orator gave the people an animated narrative of the manner in which the doctor had been carried off; he showed the barbarous horsemen binding fast the hands of their prisoner, hastening at full speed, dragging him on foot behind them, wearing out his strength, shutting their ears to his cries, causing the blood to spring from his fingers.[2] "The dead body of Luther," added he, "has been seen pierced with wounds."[3] Then cries of grief were heard. "Ah," said the multitude, "no more shall we see, no more shall we hear the noble-minded man whose voice stirred our hearts." The friends of Luther muttering wrath swore to avenge his death. Women and children, the lovers of peace, and the aged looked forward with alarm to new struggles. Nothing could equal the terror of the partisans of Rome. The priests and monks, thinking themselves sure of victory, because one man was dead, at first had been unable to conceal their joy, and had raised their heads with an insulting air of triumph, but now they would gladly have fled far away from the wrath and threats of the people.[4] These men, who, while Luther was at liberty, had given free vent to their fury, trembled now that he was captive.[5] Aleander especially was in consternation. "The only means of safety now left us," wrote a

---

[1] Hic ... invalescit opinio, me esse ab amicis captum Francia missis. (L. Ep. ii, 5.) Here an opinion gains ground that I was taken away by friends who had been sent from France. [2] Et iter festinantes cursu equitis ipsum pedestrem raptim, tractum fuisse ut sanguis e digitis erumperet.(Coch. 39.) And while the horsemen hastened on at speed, he was dragged behind on foot, so that the blood sprang from his fingers. [3] Fuit qui testatus sit, visum a se Lutheri cadaver transfossum. (Pallav. Hist. Conc. Trid. i, p. 122.) There was one who declared that he had seen Luther's body pierced with wounds. [4] Molem vulgi imminentes ferre non possunt. (L. Ep. ii, p. 13.) Are unable to withstand the threats of the common people. [5] Qui me libero insanierunt nunc, me captivo ita formidant ut incipiant mitigare. (Ibid.) They raged when I was free, but now that I am a captive begin to soften from terror.

Roman Catholic to the Archbishop of Mentz, "is to kindle torches and make a search for Luther over the whole world, in order to restore him to the wishes of the nation."[1] It might have been said that the Reformer's ghost, all pale, and clanking its chains, had appeared to spread terror and demand vengeance. The general exclamation was, " Luther's death will cause torrents of blood to flow!"[2]

No where were the minds of men more deeply agitated than at Worms itself; energetic measures were proposed both among people and princes. Ulrich von Hütten and Hermann Busch filled the country with their plaintive songs and warlike cries. Charles V and the nuncios were loudly accused. The nation took up the cause of the poor monk, who by the power of his faith had become its chief.

At Wittemberg, his colleagues and friends, Melancthon especially, were at first astounded with grief. Luther had imparted to this young scholar the treasures of that sacred theology which had thenceforth completely filled his soul. It was Luther who had given substance and life to the purely intellectual culture which Melancthon had brought to Wittemberg. The profundity of the Reformer's doctrine had struck the young Hellenist, and his courage in maintaining the rights of the eternal word against all human authority, had filled him with enthusiasm. He had been associated with him in his work; he had seized the pen, and in that admirable style which he had derived from the study of antiquity, had successfully, and with a powerful hand, lowered the authority of the Fathers and the authority of Councils before the sovereign Word of God.

The decision which Luther had in action Melancthon had in science. Never were more diversity and more unity exhibited in two individuals. " Scripture," said Melancthon, " imparts to the soul a holy and marvellous delight. It is a heavenly ambrosia."[3] " The Word of God," exclaimed Luther, " is a sword, a war, a destruction; it springs upon the children of Ephraim like the lioness in the forest." Thus, in Scripture, the one saw a power of consolation, and the other an energetic opposition to the corruption of the world. Both held it to be the greatest thing on earth, and hence they understood each other perfectly. " Melancthon," said Luther, " is a miracle: all now acknowledge this. He is the most formidable enemy of Satan and the schoolmen, for he knows their

[1] Nos vitam vix redempturos, nisi accensis candelis undique cum requiramus. (Ibid.) We shall scarcely ransom our lives unless we light candles and search for him every where. [2] GerbelL Ep. in MSS. Heckelianis Lindner Leb. Luth. p. 244. [3] Mirabilis in iis voluptas, immo ambrosia quædam cœlestis. (Corp. Ref. i, 128.) There is a wondrous pleasure in them (the Scriptures,) nay a kind of heavenly ambrosia.

folly, and the rock which is Christ. This little Greek surpasses me even in theology: he will be as useful to you as many Luthers." And he added, that he was ready to abandon an opinion if Philip did not approve of it. Melancthon, on his part, full of admiration for the knowledge which Luther had of Scripture, placed him far above the fathers of the Church. He had a wish to excuse the pleasantries for which Luther was sometimes upbraided, and compared him to a vessel of clay containing precious treasure under a coarse covering. " I will take good care not to blame him for them inconsiderately," said he.[1]

But these two souls so intimately united are now separated. These two valiant soldiers can no longer march together for the deliverance of the Church. Luther has disappeared, and is perhaps lost for ever. The consternation of Wittemberg was extreme: it might have been likened to an army standing with sullen and downcast look over the bloody remains of the general who was leading them on to victory.

Suddenly intelligence the most gratifying was received. " Our dearly beloved father lives,"[2] exclaimed Melancthon in the joy of his heart, " take courage and be strong." But grief soon resumed the ascendancy. Luther was alive but in prison. The edict of Worms with its cruel prescriptions,[3] had been circulated by thousands throughout the empire, and even in the mountains of the Tyrol.[4] Could the Reformation avoid being crushed by the iron hand which lay upon it? Melancthon's gentle spirit sank within him while he uttered a cry of grief.

But above the hand of man a more powerful hand was at work: God himself deprived the formidable edict of its force. The German princes who had always sought to humble the power of Rome in the empire, trembled on seeing the alliance of the emperor with the pope, and feared lest it should result in the destruction of all their liberties. Accordingly, though Charles, on his passage through the Low Countries, smiled ironically as he saluted the flames which some flatterers and fanatics were kindling in the public places with the writings of Luther, these writings were read in Germany with constantly increasing avidity, and every day new pamphlets appeared to support the Reformation, and make new assaults on the papacy. The nuncios were disconcerted out of measure on seeing that the edict, which had cost them so much injustice, produced so little effect. " The ink of the Emperor's signature," said some

[1] Spiritum Martini nolim tenere in hoc causa interpellare. (Corp. Ref. i, 211.) I would be unwilling in this matter to interdict Martin's humour. [2] Pater noster charissimus vivit. (Ibid, p. 389.) [3] Dicitur parari proscriptio horrenda. (Ibid.) It is said that a horrible proscription is being prepared. [4] Dicuntu signatae chartae proscriptiones bis mille missae quoque ad Insbruck. (Ibid.) Two thousand copies of the proscription were said to have been sent as far as Insbruck.

with bitterness, " was scarcely dry, before the decree itself was every where torn in pieces . . . The people become more and more attached to the wondrous man who unawed by the thunders of Charles and the pope, had confessed his faith with the courage of a martyr. "He offered to retract," observed others, "if he was refuted, but none ventured to undertake the refutation. Is not this a proof that what he teaches is true?" Accordingly, at Wittemberg and throughout the empire, the first movement of alarm was succeeded by a movement of enthusiasm. Even the Archbishop of Mentz, seeing how strongly the sympathy of the people was expressed, did not venture to give permission to the Cordeliers to preach against the Reformer. The university, which seemed on the eve of destruction, raised its head. There the new doctrines were two well established to be shaken by Luther's absence. In a short time the academic halls could scarcely contain the crowds of hearers.[1]

CHAP. II.

Luther in the Wartburg—Object of his Captivity—Agonies—Sickness—Labour of Luther—On Confession—To Latomus—Walks.

Meanwhile Knight George (this was Luther's name in the Wartburg) lived solitary and unknown. " If you saw me," wrote he to Melancthon, " you would take me for a knight, and would scarcely be able to recognise me."[2] Luther at first took some repose, enjoying a leisure which he had never tasted till this time. He moved freely within the fortress, but could not go beyond its walls.[3] All his wants were supplied, and he had never been better treated.[4] Many thoughts filled his soul, but none could trouble him. He cast his eyes alternately to the surrounding forests, and raised them towards heaven—" A singular captive !" exclaimed he, " captive both with and against my will."[5]

Writing to Spalatin, he says, " Pray for me ; your prayers are the only thing I want. I give myself no concern with all that is said and done with regard to me in the world. At length I am at rest."[6] . . . . This letter, as well as several others of the same

[1] Scholastici quorum supra millia ibi tunc fuerunt. (Spalatini Annales, 1521 Octo.) The students, of whom there were then above a thousand.
[2] Equitem videres ac ipse vix agnosceres. (L Ep. ii, 11.) You would see a knight, and would yourself scarcely recognise me. [3] Nunc sum hic otiosus, sicut inter captivos liber. (Ibid., p. 3, 12 May.) I am now at leisure—free, as it were, among captives.
[4] Quanquam et hilariter et libenter omnia mihi ministret. (Ibid., p. 13, Aug. 15.) Although he both willingly and cheerfully supplies me with every thing. [5] Ego mirabilis captivus qui et volens et nolens hic sedeo. (Ibid., p..4. May 12.) I am a strange captive, sitting here both willing and unwilling. [6] Tu fac ut pro me ores;

period, is dated from the isle of Patmos. Luther compared the Wartburg to the celebrated island to which the anger of the emperor Domitian banished the apostle John.

The Reformer reposed amid the dark forests of Thuringia from the violent struggles which had agitated his soul. Here he studied Christian truth, not for disputation, but as a means of regeneration and life. The commencement of the Reformation behoved to be polemical; new times demanded new exertions. After rooting up the thorns and brambles, it was necessary to sow the seed peacefully in men's hearts. Had Luther been obliged incessantly to fight new battles, he could not have accomplished a lasting work in the Church. By his captivity he escaped a danger which might perhaps have destroyed the Reformation—that of always attacking and destroying, without ever defending and building up.

This humble retreat produced a result still more precious. Raised as it were upon a pedestal by his countrymen, he was within a step of the abyss, and a moment of giddiness might have sufficed to throw him headlong into it. Some [of the first agents in the Reformation in Germany and Switzerland were dashed to pieces against the rock of spiritual pride and fanaticism. Luther was a man very subject to the infirmities of our nature, and he did not entirely escape these dangers. Still the hand of God delivered him from them for a time, by suddenly withdrawing him from intoxicating triumphs, and consigning him to the depth of an unknown retreat. His soul there communed with itself near to God; it was there bathed in the waters of adversity; his sufferings, his humiliations, constrained him at least for a time to walk with the humble, and the principles of the Christian life thenceforth were developed in his soul with new energy and freedom.

Luther's quiet was not of long duration. Seated on the walls of the Wartburg, he spent whole days absorbed in profound meditation. Sometimes the Church presented herself to his mind, and displayed all her miseries before him.[1] At other times turning his eye upwards with hope towards heaven, he exclaimed, "How, O Lord, couldst thou have made all men in vain!" (Ps. lxxxix, 47.) At other times, again abandoning this hope, he was downcast and exclaimed, "Alas, there is no one, in the last day of His wrath, who can stand as a wall before the Lord to save Israel! . . ."

Then returning to his own destiny, he feared lest he should be

---

hac una re opus mihi est. Quicquid de me fit in publico, nihil moror; ego in quiete tandem sedeo. (Ibid., p. 4, June 10, 1521.) Do you pray for me. As to what is done concerning me in public I care not: at length I sit in quietness.

[1] Ego hic sedens tota die faciem Ecclesiæ ante me constituo. (L. Ep. ii, 1.) I, sitting here a whole day, figure to myself the appearance of the Church.

accused of having abandoned the field of battle,[1] and the idea afflicted his soul. "I would far rather," said he, "be laid on burning coals than stagnate here half dead."[2]

Next transporting himself in imagination to Worms and Wittemberg to the midst of his enemies, he regretted that he had yielded to the counsels of his friends, instead of remaining in the world, and offering his breast to the fury of men.[3] "Ah," said he, "there is nothing I desire more than to present myself before my cruel enemies."[4]

Still some sweet thought arose, and gave a truce to these agonies. All was not torment to Luther; from time to time his agitated spirit found some degree of calmness and consolation. After the assurance of divine aid, his greatest solace in his grief was the remembrance of Melancthon. "If I perish," wrote he to him, "the gospel will lose nothing;[5] you will succeed me as Elisha did, with a double measure of my spirit." But calling to mind Philip's timidity, he cried to him aloud, "Minister of the word, guard the walls and towers of Jerusalem until the adversary strike you. We are still standing alone on the field of battle: after me they will next assail you."[6]

The thought of this last attack which Rome was going to make on the rising Church threw him into new anxiety. The poor monk, a solitary prisoner, had violent wrestling with himself. But suddenly he obtained a glimpse of his deliverance. It occurred to him that the attacks of the papacy would arouse the nations of Germany, and that the soldiers of the gospel, proving victorious, would surround the Wartburg and give liberty to the prisoner. "If the pope," said he, "lays hands on all who are for me, there will be a commotion in Germany; the more haste he makes to crush us, the more speedy will be the end both of him and his. And I . . . will be restored to you.[7] God awakening many minds, and stirring up the nations. Let our enemies only seize our cause in their arms and try to strangle it; it will grow under their grasp, and come forth ten times more formidable."

But sickness brought him down from those heights to which his courage and his faith had elevated him. He had already suffer-

[1] Verebar ego ne aciem deserere viderer. (L. Ep. ii, 1.) I feared lest I should seem to have deserted the field. [2] Mallem inter carbones vivos ardere, quam solus se mivivus, atque utinam non mortuus putere. (Ibid., 10.) I would rather burn among live coals than remain alone half alive; and I wish it may not prove a noisome carcase. (Ibid., p. 10.) [3] Cervicem esse objectandam publico furori. (Ibid., p. 89.) That I ought to expose my neck to the public fury. [4] Nihil magis opto quam furoribus adversariorum occurrere, objecto jugulo. (Ibid., p. 1.) I desire nothing more than to meet the fury of adversaries, offering them my neck. [5] Etiam si peream, nihil peribit Evangelio. (Ibid., p. 10.) Even if I perish, nothing will perish to the gospel. [6] Nos soli adhuc stamus in acie: te quærent post me. (L. Ep. ii, p. 2.)
[7] Quo citius id tentaverit, hoc citius et ipse et sui peribunt. (L. Ep. ii, p. 10.) The sooner he attempts it, the sooner he and his will perish

ed much at Worms, and his illness increased in solitude.¹ He could not digest the food of the Wartburg, which was somewhat less homely than that of his convent: it was necessary to return to the poor fare to which he had been accustomed. He passed whole nights without sleep. Anguish of mind was added to bodily suffering. No work is accomplished without pain and self-denial. Luther, alone upon his rock, endured in his powerful nature a passion which the emancipation of humanity rendered necessary. "Seated at night in my chamber," says he, " I sent forth cries like a woman in travail—torn, wounded, and bleeding."² Then, interrupting his complaints, and impressed with the thought that his sufferings were benefits from God, he gratefully exclaims, "Thanks be rendered unto thee, O Christ, in that thou hast been pleased not to leave me without the precious relics of thy holy cross!"³ He soon becomes indignant at himself, and exclaims, " Infatuated, hardened creature that I am! How grievous! I pray little, I wrestle little with the Lord, I do not groan for the church of God.⁴ Instead of being fervent in spirit, my passions only are inflamed; I remain in sloth, sleep, and indolence." Then, not knowing to what this state should be ascribed, and accustomed to expect every thing from the affection of his brethren, he exclaims, in the desolation of his soul, " O, my friends, is it because you forget to pray for me that God is thus estranged from me!"

Those about him, as well as his friends at Wittemberg and in the Elector's court, were uneasy and alarmed at this state of suffering. They trembled to think, that a life snatched from the scaffold of the pope and the sword of Charles V, should sadly wane and vanish away. Can the Wartburg be destined to be the tomb of Luther? "I fear," said Melancthon, "that the grief which he feels for the church will be his death. A torch has been kindled by him in Israel: if it is extinguished what hope will be left us? Would to God I were able, at the cost of my miserable life, to detain in the world one who is its brightest ornament."⁵ "O, what a man!" he exclaims, as if he were on the borders of the tomb, "we have not duly appreciated him."

What Luther called the unbecoming indolence of his prison was labour almost above man's utmost strength. "I am here every day," said he, (14th May,) "in idleness and luxury, (referring, doubtless, to his fare, which at first was not quite so coarse as he had been

---

[1] Auctum est malum, quo Wormatiæ laborabam. (Ibid., p. 17.) The illness with which I was attacked at Worms increased. [2] Sedeo dolens sicut puerpera, lacer, et saucius, et cruentus. (Ibid., p. 50, 9th Sept.) [3] Gratius Christo, qui me sine reliquiis sanctæ crucis non derelinquit. (Ibid.) [4] Nihil gemens pro ecclesiâ Dei. (Ibid. p. 22, 13th July.) [5] Utinam hac vili anima mea ipsius vitam emere queam (Corp. Ref. i, p. 415, 6th July.) I wish I were able, with this worthless life of mine, to purchase his life.

accustomed to.) I read the Bible in Hebrew and Greek: I am going to write a discourse in German on auricular confession: I will continue the translation of the Psalms, and compose a collection of sermons as soon as I get from Wittemberg what I require. I write without intermission;"[1] and yet these were only a part of Luther's labours.

His enemies thought that if he was not dead, at all events, his voice would not again be heard: but their joy was of short duration, and the world was not left long in doubt whether he were alive. A multitude of writings, composed in the Wartburg, appeared in rapid succession, and the cherished voice of the Reformer was every where received with enthusiasm. Luther published at once works fitted to edify the Church and polemical treatises, which interrupted the too hasty joy of his enemies. For nearly a year he instructed, exhorted, rebuked, and thundered from his mountain top, and his adversaries, confounded, asked whether there were not some supernatural mystery in this prodigious activity. "He could not rest," says Cochlœus.[2]

The only mystery was, the impudence of the partisans of Rome: They hastened to avail themselves of the Edict of Worms to give a mortal blow to the Reformation, while Luther, condemned, placed under the ban of the empire, and shut up in the Wartburg, stood forth to defend sound doctrine as if he had been still free and victorious. It was in the confessional especially that the priests strove to rivet the chains of their deluded parishioners, and accordingly confession was the object of Luther's first attack. "They found," says he, "on the words of St. James, '*Confess your sins one to another.*' Singular confession! He says, '*one to another*,' whence it should follow, that confessors ought also to confess to their penitents; that every Christian should, in his turn, be pope, bishop, priest, and that the pope himself should confess to all."[3]

Scarcely had Luther finished this small work, than he began another. Latomus a theologian of Louvain, already celebrated for his opposition to Reuchlin and Erasmus, had attacked the views of the Reformer. In twelve days Luther's refutation was ready, and it is one of his master-pieces. He vindicates himself from the charge of wanting moderation. "The moderation of the age," says he, "is to bend the knee before sacrilegious pontiffs, impious sophists, and address them as gracious lord! excellent master! Then when you have done so, you may put to death whomsoever you please; overturn the world, nay, you will still be a moderate man. Far from me be this moderation. I like better to be frank

---

[1] Sine intermissione scribo. (L. l!p. ii, pp. 6, 16.) [2] Cum quiescere non possset. (Cochlœus, Acta Lutheri, p. 39.) [3] Und der Papst müsse ihm beichten. (L. Op. xvii, p. 701.)

and deceive nobody. The shell, perhaps, is hard, but the kernel is sweet and tender."[1]

Luther's health continuing to decline, he thought of quitting the Wartburg. But how was he to do it? To appear in public was to risk his life. The back of the mountain on which the fortress stood was traversed by numerous paths, the sides of which were bordered with tufts of strawberries. The massy gate of the castle was opened, and the prisoner ventured, not without fear, stealthily to gather some of the fruit.[2] He became bolder by degrees, and began to survey the surrounding country in his knight's dress, and attended by a guard of the castle, a blunt but trustworthy man. One day having entered an inn he threw aside his sword, which encumbered him, and ran towards some book which happened to be lying. Nature was stronger than prudence. His attendant trembled fearing that a proceeding so unusual in a warrior would be regarded as a proof that the doctor was not a true knight. On another occasion the two warriors descended into the convent of Reichardsbrunn, where Luther had slept a few months before, on his way to Worms.[3] Suddenly a friar allowed a sign of surprise to escape from him Luther is recognised. His attendant perceives it, and, dragging him off in all haste, they gallop away far from the convent, before the poor friar has time to recover from his astonishment.

The chivalric life of the doctor occasionally partook strongly of the theological. One day the nets are prepared, the gates of the fortress are thrown open, and the dogs with long flapping ears rush forth. Luther had wished to taste the pleasures of the chace. The hunters soon become animated, the dogs dart along, and drive the brown hares among the brush-wood. In the midst of the turmoil the chevalier George, standing motionless, had his mind filled with serious thoughts; at the sight of the objects around him his heart is bursting with grief.[4] "Is it not," said he, "an image of the devil who arouses his dogs, in other words, the bishops, those messengers of antichrist, and hounds them on in pursuit of poor souls."[5] A young hare had just been caught, and Luther, happy to save it, wraps it carefully in his cloak, and places it under a bush. Before he proceeds many steps the dogs scent out the poor creature and kill it. Luther attracted by the noise, utters a cry of grief,—" O pope!" says he, " and thou Satan! it is thus you

---

[1] Cortex meus esse potest durior, sed nucleus meus mollis et dulcis est. (L. Op. xvii, Lat. ii, p. 213.) My husk may be somewhat hard, but my kernel is soft and sweet.
[2] Zu zeiten gehet er inn die Erdbeer am Schlossberg. (Mathesius, p. 33.) [3] See the Second Vol. [4] Theologisabar etiam ibi inter retia et canes . . tantum misericordiæ et doloris miscuit mysterium. (L. Ep. ii, p. 43.) I theologised them also among nets and dogs: it produced such a mixture of pity and grief.
[5] Quid enim ista imago, nisi Diabolum significat per insidias suas et impios magistros canes suos... (L. Ep. ii, p. 43.) For what does that represent but the devil with snares and the impious masters, his dogs.

strive to destroy even those souls which have been already saved from death"[1]

CHAP. III.

The Reformation begins—Marriage of Feldkirchen—Marriage of Monks—Theses— Writes against Monachism—Luther ceases to be a Monk.

While the doctor of Wittemberg, dead to the world, was relaxing himself by these sports in the environs of the Wartburg, the work was advancing as of itself; the Reformation had commenced. No longer confining itself to doctrine, it energetically advanced into act. Bernard Feldkirchen, pastor of Kemberg, who, under the direction of Luther, had first attacked the errors of Rome,[2] was also the first to throw off the yoke of her institutions. He married.

The German character delights in domestic life and the joys of home; accordingly of all the ordinances of the papacy, that of forced celibacy had produced the worst consequences. The imposition of this law on the heads of the clergy had prevented the fiefs of the Church from becoming hereditary. But when extended by Gregory VII to the lower clergy, it had led to deplorable results. Many priests had evaded the obligations imposed on them by shameful irregularities, and brought hatred and contempt on their order, while those who had submitted to Hildebrand's law felt inwardly indignant against the Church, because at the same time that it gave its high dignitaries so much power, wealth, and worldly enjoyment, it forced humble ministers, who were, however, its most useful supports, to sacrifices altogether contrary to the Gospel.

"Neither popes nor councils," said Feldkirchen and another pastor named Seidler, who followed his example, " can impose on the Church an ordinance which endangers soul and body. The obligation to maintain the law of God constrains us to violate the traditions of men."[3] The reestablishment of marriage in the sixteenth century was an act of homage to the moral law. The ecclesiastical authority, taking alarm, immediately launched its decrees against the two priests. Seidler, who was in the territories of duke George, was given up to his superiors, and died in prison. But the elector Frederick refused to give up Feldkirchen to the archbishop of Magdeburg. " His Highness," said Spalatin, " has no

---

[1] Sic sævit Papa et Satan ut servatas etiam animas perdat. (Ibid., p. 44.) So rage the Pope and Satan, in order to destroy even souls that have been saved.
[2] Volume First. [3] Coëgit me ergo ut humanas traditiones violarem, necessitas servandi juris divini. (Corp. Ref. i, p. 441.) The necessity of keeping the divine law compelled me to violate human traditions.

wish to act as a police officer." Feldkirchen, therefore, though he had become a husband and a father, continued pastor of his flock.

The first emotion of the Reformer on learning these things was to give expression to his joy. "I admire this new husband of Kemberg who fears nothing, and hastens into the midst of the tumult." Luther was convinced that priests ought to marry. But this question led to another—the marriage of monks, and here Luther had to maintain one of those internal combats of which his whole life was composed; for every reformation must be effected by an intellectual struggle. Melancthon and Carlstadt, the one a layman and the other a priest, thought that the liberty of entering into the bonds of marriage ought to belong to monks as well as to priests. Luther, a monk, did not think so at first. One day the governor of the Wartburg having brought him some theses of Carlstadt, on celibacy, "Good God!" exclaimed he, "will our Wittembergers give wives to monks even!" .... The idea astonished and confounded him; his mind was troubled. The liberty which he claimed for others he rejected for himself. "Ah!" exclaimed he with indignation, "at all events they will not force me to take a wife." [1] This saying is doubtless unknown to those who pretend that Luther effected the Reformation in order that he might be able to marry. Seeking the truth honestly, not through passion, he defended whatever presented itself to him as true, though it might be contrary to his system as a whole. He moved in a mixture of truth and error, waiting the time when all error would fall and truth alone remain.

There was in fact a great difference between the two questions. The marriage of the priests did not put an end to the priesthood; on the contrary, it alone could restore the secular clergy to the respect of the people; but the marriage of monks was the destruction of monachism. The question then was to determine whether it was necessary to break up and disband the mighty army which the popes held under their command. "The priests," wrote Luther to Melancthon, "are appointed of God, and consequently are free in regard to human commandments. But the monks have voluntarily chosen celibacy, and therefore are not free to withdraw themselves from the yoke of their own choice." [2]

The Reformer behoved to advance and carry this new position of the adversary by means of a new struggle. He had already put under his feet many abuses of Rome and Rome itself, but

---

[1] At mihi non obtrudent uxorem. (L. Ep. ii, p. 40.) But they should not obtrude a wife upon me. [2] Me inem vehementer movet, quod sacerdotum ordo, a Deo institutus, est liber, non autem monachorum qui sua sponte statum eligerunt. (Ibid. p. 34.) I am exceedingly moved by the thought, that the order of priests instituted by God is free, not so that of the monks who have spontaneously chosen their state.

monachism was still standing. Monachism, which of old carried life into so many deserts, and which after traversing many centuries, now filled so many cloisters with indolence and often with luxury, seemed to have personified itself and come to defend its rights in the castle of Thuringia, where was to be decided in the conscience of a single man the question of its life or its death. Luther wrestled with it. Sometimes he was on the point of overcoming it, and sometimes he was on the point of being overcome. At length, unable any longer to maintain the combat, he prostrated himself in prayer at the feet of Jesus Christ, and exclaimed, "Instruct us! deliver us! In thy mercy establish us in the liberty which belongs to us, for certainly we are thy people."[1]

He had not to wait for deliverance: an important revolution was produced in the Reformer's mind, and it was again the doctrine of justification by faith that gave him the victory. This weapon before which had fallen in the mind of Luther and of Christendom, indulgences, the discipline of Rome, and the pope himself, also effected the downfall of the monks. Luther saw that monachism and the doctrine of salvation by grace were in flagrant opposition, and that monastic life was founded entirely on the pretended merits of man. Thenceforth, convinced that the glory of Jesus Christ was at stake, he heard a voice within incessantly repeating, "Monachism must fall." "So long," said he, "as the doctrine of justification continues in the Church unimpaired, no man will become a monk."[2] This conviction always acquired more strength in his heart, and in the beginning of September he sent "to the bishops and deacons of the Church of Wittemberg" the following theses, which formed his declaration of war against monastic life.

"Whatsoever is not of faith is sin." (Rom. xiv, 23.)

"Whosoever makes a vow of virginity, chastity, or service to God without faith, makes an impious and idolatrous vow, and makes it to the devil himself.

"To make such vows is to be worse than the priests of Cybele, or the vestals of the heathen; for the monks pronounce their vows in the idea that they are to be faithful and saved by them, and what ought to be ascribed solely to the mercy of God, is thus attributed to the merit of works.

"Such convents should be completely overturned as houses of the devil.

"There is only one order which is holy and produces holiness, and that is Christianity or faith.[3]

[1] Dominus Jesus erudiat et liberet nos, per misericordiam suam, in libertatem nostram. (To Melancthon on Celibacy, 6th August, 1621, p. 40.) May the Lord Jesus instruct us, and in his mercy put us in possession of our freedom! [2] L. Op. (W.) xxii, p. 1466. [3] Es ist nicht mehr denn eine einige Geistlichkeit, die da heilig ist, und heilig macht. . . . (L. Op. xvii, p. 718.)

"Convents, to be useful, should be schools in which children might be trained to man's estate, whereas they are houses in which full grown men again become children, and so continue ever after."

We see that at this period Luther would still have tolerated convents as houses of education, but his attacks on these establishments soon became more energetic. The immorality of cloisters, and the shameful practices which prevailed in them, were vividly present to his mind. "I am desirous," wrote he to Spalatin on the 11th Nov. "to deliver young people from the infernal flames of celibacy."[1] Then he wrote a treatise against celibacy, and dedicated it to his father. "Are you desirous," said he in his dedication to the old man of Mansfield, "are you still desirous to snatch me from monasticism? You are entitled to do so: for you are still my father, and I am still your son; but it is no longer necessary; God has gone before you, and snatched me from it by his own power. What matters it whether I continue or lay aside the tonsure and monk's hood? Is it the hood, is it the tonsure that makes a monk? *All things are yours*, says St. Paul, *and you are Christ's*. I belong not to the hood, but the hood to me. I am a monk, and yet not a monk; I am a new creature, not of the pope but of Jesus Christ. Christ alone, and without any intermediate person, is my bishop, my abbot, my prior, my lord, my father, and I know no other. What matters it to me though the pope should condemn and butcher me? He will not be able to bring me forth from the tomb to do it a second time. The great day is approaching when the kingdom of abominations will be overthrown. Would to God we were worthy of being butchered by the pope. Our blood would cry to Heaven against him, and thus his judgment would be hastened, and his end brought near."[2]

The transformation had been produced in Luther himself; he was no longer a monk. This change was not the result of external causes, of human passions, of carnal precipitancy. There had been a struggle in it. Luther had at first been arrayed on the side of monachism; but truth also had entered the lists, and monachism had been vanquished. The victories which passion gains are ephemeral, whereas those of truth are durable and decisive.

[1] Adolescentes liberare ex isto inferno cœlibatus. (L. Op. ii, p. 95.) [2] Dass unser Blut möcht schreien und dringen sein Gericht, dass sein bald ein Ende würde (Ibid., p. 105.)

CHAP. IV.

Archbishop Albert—The Idol of Halle—Luther appears—Terror at the Court—Luther to the Archbishop—The Archbishop's Reply—Joachim of Brandenburg.

While Luther was thus making preparation for one of the greatest revolutions which was to be effected in the Church, and while the Reformation was beginning to act so powerfully on the state of society in Christendom, the partisans of Rome, blinded as those usually are who have long been in possession of power, imagined that because Luther was in the Wartburg, the Reformation was for ever dead and buried, and that henceforth they would be able in peace to resume their ancient practices after being momentarily disturbed by the monk of Wittemberg. Albert, the Archbishop-Elector of Mentz, was one of those feeble spirits, who, when all things are equal, are in favour of truth, but as soon as their interest is thrown into the balance, are ready to array themselves on the side of error. The great point with him was, that his court should be as brilliant as that of any prince in Germany, his equipage as rich, and his table as well supplied, and to this end the traffic in indulgences contributed admirably. Hence, no sooner had the decree condemning Luther and the Reformation issued from the imperial chancery, than Albert, who was then with his court at Halle, assembled the indulgence merchants who were still in alarm at the preaching of the Reformer, and tried to encourage them by such words as these,—" Fear no more; we have reduced him to silence; let us again begin to clip the flock; the monk is captive; he is under lock and key, and will this time be dexterous indeed if he again comes to disturb us." The market was opened anew, the merchandise exhibited, and the churches of Halle resounded once more with the harangues of the quacks.

But Luther was still alive, and his voice was powerful enough to pierce the walls and bars behind which he had been hid. Nothing could inflame his indignation to a higher degree. What! the fiercest battles have been fought, he has faced all dangers, the truth has come off victorious, and yet men dare to trample it under their feet as if it had been vanquished. . . . The doctrine which has already once overthrown this criminal traffic will again be heard. " I shall have no rest," wrote he to Spalatin, " till I have attacked the idol of Mentz, and its prostitutions at Halle." [1]

---

[1] Non continebor quin idolum Moguntinum invadam, cum suo lupanari Hallensi. (L. Ep. ii. p. 59, 7th Oct.) I shall not be prevented from attacking the idol of Mentz, with his brothel at Halle.

Luther forthwith set to work; he gave himself little concern about the mysteriousness with which it was sought to envelope his residence in the Wartburg. Elijah in the desert forges new thunderbolts against impious Ahab. On the 1st November he finished a tract *against the new idol of Halle.*

The archbishop received intelligence of Luther's design. Apprehensive and frightened at the thought, he, about the middle of October, sent two officials of his court, Capito and Auerbach, to Wittemberg to lay the storm. "It is necessary," said they to Melancthon, who most courteously received them, " it is necessary for Luther to moderate his impetuosity." But Melancthon, though mild himself, was not one of those who imagine that wisdom consists in always yielding, always equivocating, always holding one's peace. " It is God himself who calls him," replied he, " and our age stands in need of an acrid and pungent salt."[1] Capito then turned to Jonas and endeavoured through him, to act upon the court at which intelligence of Luther's design had already arrived, and produced the greatest consternation. " What!" said the courtiers, " revive the flames which there has been so much difficulty in extinguishing! Luther can only be saved by allowing himself to be forgotten, and here he is setting himself in opposition to the first prince of the empire." " I wont allow Luther, said the Elector, "to write against the Archbishop of Mentz, and thereby disturb the public peace."[2]

Luther felt indignant when these words were reported to him. It is not enough to imprison his body: they must also chain his mind, and truth herself. Do they imagine that he conceals himself from fear, and that his retirement is an acknowledgment of defeat? He, on the contrary, maintains that it is a victory. Who, then, at Worms, dared to rise up against him and to contradict the truth? Accordingly when the prisoner of the Wartburg had read the chaplain's letter, which made him aware of the prince's sentiments, he threw it from him, determined not to reply to it. But he could not long refrain, and he again lifted the letter. "The Elector will not permit!" . . . .—wrote he to Spalatin—" and I will not suffer the Elector not to permit me to write . . . Sooner ruin you for ever—you, the Elector—the whole world.[3] If I have resisted the pope who is the creature of your cardinal, why should I yield to his creature? It is really good to hear you say, that the public peace must not be disturbed, while you allow others to dis-

---

[1] Huic seculo opus esse acerrimo sale. (Corp. Ref. i. 463.) This age stands in need of a very pungent salt. [2] Non passurum principem, scribi in Moguntinum. (L. Ep. ii, p. 94.) That the prince will not allow any thing to be written against the archbishop of Mentz. [3] Potius te et principem ipsum perdam et omnem creaturam. (Ibid.) I will rather destroy you and the prince himself and every creature.

turb the eternal peace of God. It will not be so, O prince.[1] I send you a tract which I had already prepared against the cardinal, before I received your letter. Hand it to Melancthon...."

The perusal of this manuscript made Spalatin tremble. He again represented to the Reformer how imprudent it would be to publish a work which would compel the imperial government to lay aside its apparent ignorance of Luther's fate, and to punish a prisoner who dared to attack the first prince of the empire and the Church. If Luther persisted in this design, peace was again disturbed, and the Reformation perhaps lost. Luther consented to delay the publication of his treatise; he even allowed Melancthon to erase the strongest passages.[2] But indignant at the timidity of his friend, he wrote to the chaplain, "He lives, he reigns—the Lord in whom you court folks believe not, at least, if he does not so accommodate his works to your reason, that there is no longer occasion to believe any thing." He forthwith resolved on writing directly to the elector cardinal.

It is the whole episcopate that Luther brings to his bar in the person of the primate of Germany. His words are those of an intrepid man, burning with zeal for the truth, and under a consciousness of speaking in the name of God himself.

Writing from the depth of the retreat in which he was concealed, he says, "Your Electoral Highness has again set up in Halle the idol which devours the silver and the souls of poor Christians. You think, perhaps, that I am off the field, and that his imperial majesty will easily stifle the cries of the poor monk..... But know that I will discharge the duty which Christian charity imposes on me, without fearing the gates of hell and *a fortiori*, without fearing the pope, bishops, and cardinals.

"Wherefore, my most humble prayer is, that your Royal Highness will call to mind the commencement of this affair, and how one small spark produced a fearful conflagration. Then also the whole world felt secure. The thought was—the poor mendicant who is disposed, single-handed, to attack the pope, is too feeble for such a work. But God interposed, and has given the pope more toil and anxiety than he ever had since he seated himself in the temple of God, to domineer over the Church. The same God still lives: let no man doubt it.[3] He knows how to withstand a cardinal of Mentz, were he even supported by four emperors; for he loves above all things, to bow down the lofty cedars and humble proud Pharaohs.

---

[1] Non sic, Spalatine, non sic, princeps. (L. Ep. ii, p. 94.) 'Not so, O Spalatin! not so, O prince! [2] Ut acerbiora tradat. (Ibid., p. 110.) The reading should doubtless be *radat*. [3] Derselbig Gott lebet noch, da zweifel nur niemand an ... Ibid., p. 113.

"Wherefore, I hereby give your Highness to wit, that if the idol is not cast down, I must, in obedience to the command of God, publicly attack your Highness, as I have attacked the pope himself. Let your Highness act upon this notice; I expect a prompt and good answer within a fortnight. Given in my desert, Sunday after St. Catherine's day, 1521, by your Electoral Highness's humble and devoted, MARTIN LUTHER."

This letter was sent to Wittemberg, and from Wittemberg to Halle, where the cardinal elector then resided, no attempt was made to stop it in its course, as it was foreseen what a storm such an audacious proceeding would have called forth. But Melancthon accompanied it with a letter to the prudent Capito, with a view to bring this difficult affair to a good termination.

We cannot say what were the feelings of the young and feeble archbishop on receiving the Reformer's letter. The tract announced *against the idol of Halle* was like a sword suspended over his head. At the same time, what rage must have been kindled in his heart by the insolence of this peasant's son, this excommunicated monk, who dared to hold such language to a prince of the house of Brandenburg, the primate of the German Church? Capito implored the archbishop to satisfy the monk. Terror, pride, conscience whose voice he could not stifle, produced a fearful struggle in Albert's soul. At length, dread of the tract, and it may be also remorse, carried the day. He humbled himself and gathered together whatever he thought fitted to appease the man of the Wartburg; scarcely had the fortnight elapsed, when Luther received the following letter, which is still more astonishing than his formidable epistle.

"My dear Doctor,—I have received and read your letter, and taken it in good part. But I believe that for a long time the motive which led you to write me such a letter has not existed. I wish, with God's help, to conduct myself as a pious bishop and a Christian prince, and I acknowledge that I stand in need of the grace of God. I deny not that I am a sinful man, one who may sin and be mistaken, one even who sins and is mistaken every day. I know well that without the grace of God I am useless and filthy mire like other men, if not more so. In reply to your letter, I did not wish to conceal from you this gracious disposition; for, from the love of Christ, I am more than desirous to show you all sorts of kindness and favour. I know how to receive a Christian and fraternal reprimand.

"With my own hand, ALBERT."

Such was the language held to the excommunicated of the Wartburg by the Elector Archbishop of Mentz and Magdeburg, whose office it was to represent and maintain in Germany the constitution of the Church. Had Albert, in writing it, obeyed the generous inspirations of his conscience, or his servile fears? In the former view, this letter is noble; in the latter, it deserves contempt. We prefer supposing that it proceeded from a good emotion in his heart. Be this as it may, it shows the immense superiority of the servant of God over earthly grandeur. While Luther, single, captive, and condemned, found indomitable courage in his faith, the archbishop cardinal elector, surrounded by all the power and favour of the world, trembled in his chair. This contrast is constantly displayed, and it furnishes a key to the strange enigma with which we are presented in the history of the Reformation. The Christian is not called to sum up his forces and make an enumeration of his means of victory. The only thing which ought to give him any concern is, whether the cause which he maintains is indeed that of God, and whether his sole aim is the glory of his Master. He has doubtless an examination to make, but it is wholly spiritual; the Christian looks to the heart and not to the arm; to the justice of the cause and not to its strength. And when once this question is decided, his path is marked out. He must advance boldly, even should it be against the world and all its hosts, in the unwavering conviction that God himself will fight for him.

The enemies of the Reformation thus passed from extreme rigour to extreme feebleness. They had already done so at Worms, and these abrupt transitions are ever appearing in the war which error makes upon truth. Every cause destined to give way is affected with an inward dissatisfaction, which makes it vacillating and dubious, and pushes it by turns from one extreme to the other. Far better were consistency and energy. It might be, that thereby the fall would be precipitated, but at all events when it did come, it would come gloriously.

The Elector of Brandenburg, Joachim I, a brother of Albert, gave an example of this decision of character which is so rare, especially in our own age. Immovable in his principles, firm in his actions, knowing when necessary to resist the will of the pope, he opposed an iron hand to the progress of the Reformation. At Worms, he had insisted that Luther should not be heard, and even that he should be punished as a heretic, notwithstanding of his safe conduct. No sooner was the edict of Worms issued than he ordered it to be rigorously executed in all his states. Luther was able to estimate a character thus energetic, and distinguishing Joachim from his other opponents, said, "We can still pray for the Elector of Brandenburg."[1] The spirit of the prince seemed to have been communicated to his subjects. Berlin and Brandenburg

[1] Helwing, Gesch. der Brandeb. ii, p. 605.

long remained completely closed against the Reformation. But what was received slowly was kept faithfully, while countries which then received the gospel with joy, Belgium, for instance, and Westphalia, were soon to abandon it. Brandenburg, the last of the German states to enter on the paths of faith, was, at a latter period, to take its place in the foremost ranks of the Reformation.[1]

Luther did not receive the letter of the cardinal archbishop without some suspicion of its having been dictated by hypocrisy, or in compliance with the counsels of Capito. He was silent, however, contenting himself with a declaration to the latter, that so long as the archbishop, who was scarcely capable of managing a small parish, would not lay aside the mask of the cardinalate and pomp of the episcopate, and become a simple minister of the word, it was impossible he could be in the way of salvation.[2]

CHAP. V.

Translation of the Bible—Wants of the Church—Principles of the Reformation—Alarm at Court—Luther to the Archbishop—Temptations of the Devil—Condemnation of the Sorbonne—Melancthon's Reply—Visit to Wittemberg.

While Luther was thus combating error as if he had still been upon the field of battle, he was at work in his retreat as if he were a stranger to every thing that was taking place in the world. The moment had arrived when the Reformation was to pass from the speculations of theologians into common life, and yet the great instrument by which this transaction was to be effected was not yet in existence. This wondrous and mighty engine, destined to assail the edifice of Rome from all quarters, with bolts which would demolish its walls, to lift off the enormous weight under which the papacy held down the half-suffocated Church, and give to humanity itself an impulse which it should retain to the latest ages, was to come forth from the old castle of the Wartburg and enter the world with the Reformer the very day when his captivity should terminate.

The further the Church was removed from the period when Jesus Christ, the true light of the world, dwelt in it, the more need she had of the lamp of the Word of God, which was to transmit the brightness of Jesus Christ unimpaired to the latest ages. But this

---

[1] Hoc enim proprium est illorum hominum (ex March. Brandeburg) ut quam semel in religione sententiam approbaverint, non facile deserant. (Leutingeri, Op. i, 41.) This is a characteristic of those men (the Dukes of Brandenburg), that when once they have formed an opinion in religion, they do not easily abandon it. [2] Larvam cardinalatus et pompam episcopalem ablegare. (L. Ep. ii, p. 132.)

divine Word was then unknown to the people. Attempts at translation, from the vulgate in 1477, 1490, and 1518, had succeeded ill, were almost unintelligible, and, from their high price, beyond the reach of the people. It had even been prohibited to give the Bible to the Germanic Church in the vulgar tongue.[1] Besides, the number of those able to read was inconsiderable, so long as there was no work in the German tongue of deep and universal interest.

Luther was called to give the Scriptures to his country, Italy. The same God who withdrew St. John to Patmos there to write his Revelation, had shut up Luther in the Wartburg to translate his Word. This great work, which it would have been difficult for him to undertake amid the distractions and occupations of Wittemberg, was destined to establish the new edifice on the primitive rock, and bring back Christians, after so many ages of scholastic subtleties to the pure and primary source of redemption and salvation.

The wants of the Church pleaded strongly; they demanded this great work, and Luther was to be trained by his own deep experience for the performance of it. In fact, he had found in faith that spiritual repose which his agitated conscience and monastic ideas had long made him seek in his own merit and holiness. The doctrine of the Church, viz. scholastic theology, knew nothing of the consolations which faith gives, but these were forcibly announced in Scripture, and there he found them. Faith in the Word of God had made him free. By means of it, he felt himself emancipated from the dogmatical authority of the Church, its hierarchy, its traditions, scholastic opinions, powerful prejudices, and all tyranny of man. The numerous and powerful links which had for ages chained and bound Christendom, were broken, destroyed, and scattered in fragments around him, and he nobly raised his head, free of every thing save the Word. This independence of men, this submission to God, which he had learned in the Holy Scriptures, he wished the Church to possess. But in order to accomplish this, it was necessary to give her back the revelation of God. It was necessary that a mighty hand should throw back the ponderous gates of that arsenal of the Word of God, in which Luther himself had found his armour, and that those vaults and ancient halls which no foot had traversed for ages, should be again opened wide to the Christian people for the day of battle.

Luther had already translated different portions of the Holy Scriptures : the seven penitential Psalms had been his first labour.[2]

[1] Codex Diplom. Ecclesiæ Magunt, iv, p. 460. [2] Ps. vi, xxxii, xxxviii, li, cii, cxxx, cxlvii.

Jesus Christ, John Baptist, and the Reformation, alike began with the doctrine of repentance, which is the first beginning of renovation in the individual and in the race. These essays had been received with avidity: all wished for more, and this call from the people was to Luther a call from God himself. He formed the design of responding to it. He was a captive behind high walls. True! He will employ his leisure in transferring the Word of God into the language of his people. This Word will shortly descend with him from the Wartburg; it will circulate among the population of Germany, and put them in possession of spiritual treasures—treasures like them, shut up within the hearts of a few pious men. "Let this single book," exclaims he, "be in all tongues, in all hands, before all eyes, in all ears, and in all hearts."[1] Admirable words! which a distinguished society[2] for translating the Bible into the languages of all nations is now, after three centuries, engaged in carrying into effect. "The Scripture, without any commentary," says he on another occasion, "is the sun from which all teachers receive light."

Such are the principles of Christianity and of the Reformation. According to those venerable words, we are not to take the Fathers in order to throw light on Scripture, but Scripture to throw light on the Fathers. The Reformers and the Apostles held up the Word of God alone for light, just as they hold up the sacrifice of Christ alone for righteousness. To attempt to mix up human authority with this absolute authority of God, or human righteousness with this perfect righteousness of Christ, is to corrupt Christianity in its two foundations. Such are the two fundamental heresies of Rome, heresies moreover which some teachers would fain introduce, though, doubtless, in a modified form, into the bosom of the Reformation.

Luther opened the Greek text of the Evangelists and Apostles, and undertook the difficult task of making these inspired teachers speak his mother tongue—an important epoch in the history of the Reformation which was thenceforth no longer in the hand of the Reformer. The Bible came forward; Luther drew back; God showed himself, and man disappeared. The Reformer has placed THE BOOK in the hands of his contemporaries. Every one can now listen to God himself. As for Luther, he from this time mingles in the crowd, and takes his place among those who come to draw at the common fountain of light and life.

In the translation of the Holy Scriptures Luther found in abundance that consolation and strength which were most necessary to

---

[1] Et solus hic liber omnium linguâ, manû, oculis, auribus, cordibus, versaretur. (L. Ep. ii, p. 116.) [2] The Bible Society.

him. Sick, isolated, saddened by the efforts of his enemies and the errors of some of his partisans, seeing his life wasting away in the gloom of this old castle, he had many fearful combats to maintain. In those times there was an inclination to transfer to the visible world the struggles which the soul maintains with its spiritual foes. The lively imagination of Luther easily gave a bodily shape to the emotions of his heart, while the superstition of the middle ages had still some hold upon his intellect, so that in this respect it may be said of him as has been said of Calvin in the punishment of heretics—he had a remnant of popery.[1] In Luther's idea Satan was not merely an invisible though real being; he thought that this enemy of God appeared to man as he had appeared to Jesus Christ. Although the authenticity of several of the accounts given on this subject in the 'Table Talk,' and elsewhere, is more than doubtful, the historian is bound to point out this foible in the reformer. Never did these dark ideas assail him more than in the solitude of the Wartburg. He had defied the devil at Worms in the days of his strength; but now all the power of the Reformer seemed broken and his glory tarnished. He was thrown aside. Satan was victorious in his turn, and Luther, in the anguish of his spirit thought he saw him raising his gigantic figure before him, pointing his threatening finger, triumphing with bitter and infernal leer, and gnashing his teeth in frightful rage. One day among others it is said, when Luther was working at his translation of the New Testament, he thought he saw Satan, who, dreadfully terrified at this work, kept teazing him, and turning round and round him like a lion about to pounce upon his prey. Luther, frightened and irritated, seized his inkstand and threw it at the head of his enemy. The figure vanished and the inkstand struck against the wall.[2]

Luther's residence in the Wartburg began to be insupportable. He felt indignant at the pusillanimity of his protectors. Sometimes he remained a whole day absorbed in silent and profound meditation, and came out of it only to exclaim, "Oh that I were at Wittemberg!" At length he could hold out no longer: there has been enough of political management: he must see his friends again,—hear them and speak to them. True! he runs the risk of falling into the hands of his enemies, but nothing can stop him. Towards the end of November he secretly quits the Wartburg and sets out for Wittemberg.[3]

A new storm had just burst upon him. The Sorbonne had at

---

[1] M. Michelet, in his Memoires de Luther, devotes more than thirty pages to different accounts of the apparition of the devil. [2] The keeper of the Wartburg is still careful to show the traveller the mark made by Luther's inkstand.
[3] Machete er sich heimlich aus seiner Patmo auf. (L. Op. xviii, p. 238.)

length broken silence. This celebrated school of Paris, the first authority in the Church after the pope, the ancient and venerable fountain, whence theological dogmas had sprung, had just issued its verdict against the Reformation.

The following are some of the propositions which it condemned: Luther had said, "God always pardons and remits sins gratuitously, and asks nothing of us in return but only to live in future according to his will." He had added, "Of all mortal sins the most mortal is this,—for any one to believe that he is not guilty before God of mortal and damnable sin." He had further said, "To burn heretics is contrary to the will of the Holy Spirit."

To all these propositions, and many others which were quoted, the faculty of theology replied, "Heresy, anathema!" [1]

But a young man of twenty-four, of small stature, modest, and unostentatious, dared to take up the gauntlet which had been thrown down by the first school in the world. It was well known at Wittemberg what view ought to be taken of these pompous condemnations: it was known that Rome had yielded to the suggestion of the Dominicans, and that the Sorbonne was dragged along by two or three fanatical doctors, who were designated at Paris by derisive nicknames.[2] Accordingly, Melancthon, in his apology, did not confine himself to the defence of Luther, but with the boldness which characterises his writings, carried the assault into the camp of his adversaries. "You say he is a manichean, a montanist! let fire and flame repress his folly! Which, pray, is montanist? Luther who wishes men to believe in the Holy Scriptures, or yourselves who will have them to believe the views of men rather than the Word of God." [3]

To attribute more to man's word than to the Word of God was in fact the heresy of Montanus, as it is still that of the pope, and of all those who set the hierarchical authority of the Church, or the internal inspiration of mysticism above the positive declaration of the Sacred Writings. Accordingly, the young master of arts who had said, "I will lose my life sooner than my faith," [4] did not stop there He accused the Sorbonne of having obscured the gospel, extinguished faith, and substituted a vain philosophy for Christianity.[5] After the work of Melancthon the position of the question

---

[1] Determinatio theologorum Parisiensium super doctrina Lutherana. (Corp. Ret. i, p. 366—388.) [2] Damnarunt triumviri Beda, Quercus, et Christophorus. Nomina sunt horum monstrorum etiam vulgo nunc nota Belua, Stercus, Christotomus. (Zwing. Ep. i, p. 176.) He was condemned by the triumvirs *Beda, Quercus*, and *Christophorus*. These are the names of three monsters now commonly known as Bellua (beast) Stercus (dung) and *Christotomus* (Christ-slayer.) [3] Corp. Ref. i, p. 396.) [4] Scias me positurum animam citius quam fidem. (Ibid.) [5] Evangelium abscuratum est. fides extincta . . . Ex Christianismo, contra omnem sensum Spiritus, facta est quædam philosophica vivendi ratio. (Corp. Ref. i. p. 400.)

was changed; he proved to demonstration that heresy was at Paris and Rome, and catholic truth at Wittemberg.

Meanwhile, Luther giving himself little concern with the condemnation of the Sorbonne, repaired in his knight's dress to the university seat. On the way different reports reached him, that a spirit of impatience and independence was manifesting itself among his adherents, and he was grieved to the heart.[1] At length he arrived at Wittemberg without having been recognised, and stopped at the house of Amsdorff. Forthwith all his friends were secretly summoned,[2] Melancthon especially, who had often said, "If I must be deprived of him I prefer death.[3] On their arrival, what a meeting! what joy! The captive of the Wartburg seated amidst them enjoys all the sweets of Christian friendship. He learns the progress of the Reformation, and the hopes of his brethren; and, overjoyed at what he sees and hears,[4] prays, gives thanks, and then, after a short delay, returns to the Wartburg.

CHAP VI.

New Reforms—Gabriel Zwilling on the Mass—The University—The Elector—Monachism attacked—Emancipation of the Monks—Disturbances—Chapter of the Augustins—The Mass and Carlstadt—First Supper—Importance of the Mass in the Roman System.

Luther's joy was well founded—the Reformation was then advancing at an immense pace. Feldkirchen, always in the advanced guard, had first mounted to the assault: the main body was now shaken, and the power which carried the Reformation from doctrine which it had purified, into worship, common life, and the constitution of the Church now manifested itself by a new explosion still more formidable to the papacy than the former had been.

Rome, disencumbered of the Reformer, thought she had done with heresy. But in a short time all was changed. Death precipitated the man who had laid Luther under interdict from the pontifical throne. Disturbances arising in Spain, obliged Charles V to repair beyond the Pyrenees. War broke out between this prince and Francis I, and, as if this had not been

Instead of Christianity there was adopted allegiance contrary to the meaning of the Spirit, a certain philosophical mode of life. [1] Per viam vexatus rumore varis de nostrorum quorundam importunitate. (L. Ep. ii, p. 109.) He was grieved by the way, by various rumours as to the rashness of some of our people.
[2] Liess in der Stille seine Freunde fodern. (L. Op. xviii, p. 258.) [3] Quo si mihi carendum est, mortem fortius tulero. (Corp. Ref. i, p. 453—455.) I could bear death more easily than want him. [4] Omnia vehementer placent quæ video et audio. (L. Ep. ii, p. 109.) All that I see and hear pleases me exceedingly.

enough to occupy the Emperor, Solyman advanced into Hungary. Charles, attacked on all sides, saw himself constrained to forget the monk at Worms, and his religious innovations.

About the same time the vessel of the Reformation which, driven in all directions by contrary winds, had well nigh foundered, righted and floated firmly on the waves.

It was in the Augustin Convent of Wittemberg that the Reformation broke out. We must not be surprised at this: the Reformer was no longer there, but no power could banish the spirit which had animated him.

For some time the church in which Luther so often preached had resounded with strange doctrines. Gabriel Zwilling, the preacher of the convent, a monk full of zeal, preached with ardour in favour of the Reformation. As if Luther, whose name was everywhere proclaimed, had become too powerful and too illustrious, God selected feeble and obscure individuals to commence the Reformation which Luther had prepared. "Jesus Christ," said the preacher, "instituted the sacrament of the altar as a memorial of his death, not to make it an object of adoration. To adore it is real idolatry. The priest who communicates alone commits a sin. No prior is entitled to compel a monk to say mass alone. Let one, two, or three officiate and let all the others receive the sacrament in both kinds." [1]

Such was the demand of friar Gabriel, and these bold words were listened to with approbation by the other friars, especially by those who came from the Low Countries.[2] Being disciples of the gospel why should they not in everything conform themselves to its commands? Had not Luther himself, in the month of August, written to Melancthon, "Never more from this time will I say a private mass." [3] Thus the monks, those soldiers of the hierarchy, set free by the Word of God, boldly took part against Rome.

At Wittemberg they experienced an obstinate resistance on the part of the prior. Recollecting that all things ought to be done in order, they yielded, still declaring that to maintain the mass was to oppose the Gospel of God.

The prior had carried the day: one had proved stronger than all. It might therefore be supposed that the movement of the Augustins had only been one of those freaks of insubordination of which convents were so often the theatre. But it was in reality the Spirit of God that was then agitating Christendom. An isolated

---

[1] Einem 2 oder 3 befehlen Mess zu halten, und die andern 12 von denen, das Sacrament sub utraque specie mit empfahen. (Corp. Ref. i, p. 460.) [2] Der meiste Theil jener Parthœi Niederlænder seyn. (Ibid. 476.) [3] Sed et ego amplius non faciam missam privatim in æternum. (L. Ep. ii, p. 36.)

cry sent forth from the recess of a monastery found a thousand echoing voices, and that which it was wished to keep confined within the walls of a convent, came forth and assumed a distinct shape in the very heart of the city.

A rumour of the dissensions of the monks was soon noised in the town. The citizens and students of the University took part either for or against the mass. The electoral court was alarmed. Frederick, in astonishment, sent his chancellor Pontanus to Wittemberg, with orders, to tame the monks, by putting them, if necessary, on bread and water;[1] and on the 12th October, at seven in the morning, a deputation of professors, of whom Melancthon was one, repaired to the convent to exhort the monks not to make any innovation,[2] or at least to wait. On this all their zeal revived: unanimous in their belief, with the exception of the prior who combated them, they appealed to the Holy Scriptures, to the intelligence of the faithful, and the consciences of theologians, and two days after returned a written declaration.

The teachers now examined the question more closely, and perceived that truth was on the side of the monks. They went to convince, but were themselves convinced. What were they to do? Their conscience spake aloud; their distress continually increased: at last, after long hesitation, they adopted a bold resolution.

On the 20th October, the University gave in their report to the Elector. "Let your Electoral Highness," said they to him, after exposing the errors of the mass, "Let your Electoral Highness abolish all abuses, lest Christ, on the day of judgment, upbraid us as he once did Capernaum."

It is no longer some obscure monks who speak, but that University which all sober men have hailed for years as the national school. The very means employed to stifle the Reformation are going to contribute to its extension.

Melancthon, with the boldness which he showed in speculation, published fifty-five propositions with a view to enlighten the public mind:

"Just," says he, "as to look at a crucifix is not to do a good work, but simply to contemplate a sign which reminds us of the death of Christ.

"As to look at the sun is not to do a good work, but simply to contemplate a sign which reminds us of Christ and his gospel.

"So to partake of the table of the Lord is not to do a good

---

[1] Wollen die Mönche nicht Mess halten, sie werden's bald in der Küchen und Keller empfnnden. .... (Corp. Ref. i, p. 461.)   [2] Mit dem Mess halten kein Neuerung machen. (Ibid.)

work, but simply to make use of a sign which reminds of the grace given us by Christ.

"But herein is the difference. The symbols invented by men simply recall what they signify, whereas the signs given by God not only recall the things, but also make the heart sure of the will of God.

"As the sight of a cross does not justify, so the mass does not justify.

"As the sight of a cross is not a sacrifice for our own sins or for those of others, so the mass is not a sacrifice.

"There is only one sacrifice, only one satisfaction—Jesus Christ. Out of him there is none.

"Let the bishops who do not oppose the impiety of the mass be anathema." [1]

Thus spake the pious and gentle Philip.

The Elector was in consternation. His wish had been to repress some young monks, and lo! all the University, with Melancthon himself, rise up in their defence. To wait appeared to him to be in all things the surest means of success. He had no taste for sudden reforms, and wished every opinion to have full opportunity of showing itself. "Time," thought he, "throws light on all things, and brings them to maturity." And yet the Reformation advances in spite of him with rapid steps, and threatens to carry every thing along with it. Frederick used all his efforts to arrest it. His authority, the weight of his character, the arguments which appeared to him most decisive—every thing was put in requisition. He sent a message to the theologians, "Dont be in a haste; you are too few in number to carry out such a reformation. If it is founded on the holy Gospel, others will perceive it, and the whole Church will concur with you in abolishing these abuses. Speak, debate, preach as much on these subjects as you please; but preserve ancient customs."

Such was the struggle which took place on the subject of the mass. The monks had gone up courageously to the assault; the theologians, for a moment undecided, had soon supported them. The prince and his ministers alone defended the place. It has been said that the Reformation was effected by the power and authority of the Elector; but so far from this, the assailants were obliged to retire at the venerated voice of Frederick, and the mass was saved for some days.

Moreover, the hottest of the assault had already been directed to another point. Friar Gabriel continued his fervid harangues in

---

[1] Signa ab hominibus reperta admonent tantum; signa a Deo tradita, præterquam quod admonent, certificant etiam cor de voluntate Dei. (Corp. Ref. i, p. 478.)

the church of the Augustins. It was against monachism itself that he now directed those redoubled blows. If the mass constituted the strength of the Romish doctrine, monachism constituted the strength of the hierarchy. These, therefore, were the two first positions which required to be carried.

"Nobody," exclaimed Gabriel, according to the prior's account, "nobody in convents observes the commandments of God; nobody can be saved under the monk's cowl;[1] every man in a cloister must have entered it in the name of the devil. Vows of chastity, poverty, and obedience are contrary to the Gospel."

These strange addresses were reported to the prior, who took good care to keep away from the church, that he might not hear them.

"Gabriel," it was also said, "wishes every means to be taken to empty cloisters." If monks are met in the street, it is proper, according to him, to pull them by the frock, and point the finger at them; and if mockery does not succeed in making them quit the convent, they must be violently hunted out of it. "Break open, destroy, throw down the monasteries," said he, "so that not a vestige of them may remain, and on the site which they have so long occupied let it be impossible to find any one of the stones which served to shelter so much idleness and superstition."[2]

The monks were astonished; their conscience told them that what Gabriel said was only too true—that the life of a monk was not conformable to the will of God, and that none was enabled to dispose of them but themselves.

Thirteen Augustins left the convent at once, and, laying aside the dress of their order, assumed common clothes. Those of them who had some education attended the lectures in the University, that they might one day become useful to the Church, and those whose minds were little cultivated sought to gain their living by working with their own hands, according to the injunction of the apostle and the example of the worthy burghers of Wittemberg.[3] One of them, who was acquainted with the trade of carpenter, entered with the corporation, and resolved to marry.

If Luther's entrance into the convent of the Augustins of Erfurth was the first germ of the Reformation, the departure of these thirteen monks from the convent of the Augustins of Wittemberg was a sign that it was beginning to take possession of Christendom. For thirty years Erasmus had been exposing the uselessness, the

[1] Kein Mönch werde in der Kappe selig. Corp. Ref. i, p. 433.) [2] Dass man nicht oben Stück von einem Kloster da sey gestanden, merken möge. (Ibib., p. 483.)
[3] "Etliche unter den Bürgern, etliche unter den Studenten," says the Prior in his complaint to the Elector. (Ibid.)

follies, and vices of the monks, and with him all Europe had laughed or felt indignant. But it was no longer an affair of sarcasm. Thirteen spirited and brave men again appeared in the midst of their fellow-men to render themselves useful to society, and fulfil the orders of God. The marriage of Feldkirchen had been the first defeat of the hierarchy—the emancipation of these thirteen Augustins was the second. Monachism, which had been formed the moment the Church commenced her period of bondage and error, behoved to fall the moment she recovered liberty and truth.

This bold proceeding caused a general fermentation in Wittemberg. Admiration was felt for the men who came to share in the common toils, and they were received as brethren. At the same time, cries were heard against those who persisted in remaining idly hid behind the walls of a monastery. The monks who adhered to the prior trembled in their cells, and he, carried away by the universal movement, discontinued the celebration of low mass.

The smallest concession at so critical a moment could not but hasten the progress of events. This order by the prior caused a very lively sensation in the town and the University, and produced a sudden explosion. Among the students and citizens of Wittemberg were some turbulent men, whom the least excitement stirs up and hurries into culpable disorders. They were indignant at the idea that low mass, which was suspended even by the superstitious prior, should still be said in the parish church, and on Tuesday, the 3rd Dec., when mass was about to be chanted, they made a sudden rush towards the altar, carried off the books, and drove away the priests. The Council and the University were indignant, and met to punish the authors of these misdeeds. But the passions, when once roused, are not easily calmed. The Cordeliers had not taken part in the reform movement of the Augustins. The next day some students put up a threatening placard on the door of their monastery: thereafter forty students entered their church, and, without proceeding to actual violence, mocked the monks, who, in consequence, did not venture to say mass except in the choir. Towards evening, the fathers received intimation to be upon their guard. "The students," it was said, "intended to attack the monastery! . . ." The monks in alarm, not knowing how to defend themselves against these real or supposed attacks, hastily petitioned the Council to defend them. Some soldiers were sent, but the enemy did not appear. The University caused the students who had taken part in these disturbances to be arrested. They were discovered to be students from Erfurth, already marked for insubordination.[1] University penalties were inflicted on them.

Still it was felt necessary carefully to examine the lawfulness of monastic vows. A chapter, consisting of the Augustins of Thuringia and Misnia, met at Wittemberg in the month of December. Their views coincided with Luther's. They declared on the one hand that monastic vows were not sinful, but, on the other, that they were not obligatory. "In Christ," said they, "there is neither laic nor monk: every one is free to quit the monastery or to remain in it. Let him who departs, not abuse his liberty—let him who remains, obey his superiors and that from love." Then they abolished mendicancy and masses said for money: they also decreed that the most learned among them should apply themselves to the teaching of the Word of God, and that the others should support their brethren by the work of their hands.[2]

The question of vows thus seemed determined, but that of the mass remained undecided. The Elector continued to oppose the torrent, and protected an institution which was still standing in every part of Christendom. The orders of an indulgent prince were unable, however, long to restrain men's minds. The brain of Carlstadt especially, fermented amid the general fermentation. Full of zeal, honesty and intrepidity, and ready, like Luther, to sacrifice every thing for the truth, he had less wisdom and moderation than the Reformer. He was not free from a love of vain-glory, and, with a decided inclination to go to the bottom of every question, he had little judgment and little clearness in his ideas. Luther had drawn him from the midst of the schoolmen, and turned him towards the study of Scripture, but Carlstadt had not patience to study the original tongues, and had not perceived, like his friend, the full sufficiency of the Word of God. Accordingly he was often seen to fasten on the most singular interpretations. So long as Luther was at his side, the superiority of the master kept the scholar within due bounds. But Carlstadt was now at liberty, and this little man, of sallow tint, who had never been conspicuous for eloquence, was heard at the university and the church, especially in Wittemberg, giving eager expression to ideas which, though sometimes profound, were often enthusiastic and extravagant. "What folly," exclaimed he, "to think that the Reformation should be left to the agency of God alone! A new order of things begins. The hand of man must interpose. Wo to him who stays behind, and will not mount the breach in the cause of the mighty God . . ."

[1] In Summa es sollen die Aufruhr etliche Studenten von Erffurth erwerckt haben. Corp. Ref. i, p. 490.) [2] Ibid., p. 456.—The editors date this decree in October before the friars had left the convent of Wittemberg.

The words of the archdeacon communicated to others the impatience which animated himself. Following his example, individuals who were sincere and straightforward exclaimed, "All that the popes have ordained is impious. Let us not become accomplices in these abominations by allowing them to subsist. What is condemned by the word of God must be abolished in Christendom, whatever be the ordinances of men. If the heads of the State and Church will not do their duty, let us do ours. Let us renounce negotiations, conferences, theses, and debates, and have recourse to the true remedy for all these evils. There must be a second Elijah to destroy the altars of Baal."

The re-establishment of the Last Supper at this moment of fermentation and enthusiasm doubtless could not exhibit the solemnity and sacredness of its institution by the Son of God the evening before his death, and almost at the foot of his cross. But if God now made use of feeble, and perhaps passionate men, it was still his hand which re-established the feast of his love in the bosom of his Church.

As early as the month of October, Carlstadt, with twelve of his friends, had secretly celebrated the Lord's Supper, agreeably to its original institution. The Sunday before Christmas he intimated from the pulpit that, on the feast of the Circumcision, being new New-year's-day, he would dispense the Supper under the two kinds of bread and wine to all who should present themselves at the altar, that he would omit all useless ceremonies,[1] and in celebrating this mass would not put on either cope or chasuble.

The Council, in alarm, requested Counsellor Beyer to prevent so great an irregularity. On this Carlstadt resolved not to wait for the time he had appointed. On Christmas, 1521, he preaches in the parish church, on the necessity of abandoning the mass, and receiving the sacrament under the two kinds. After sermon he descends to the altar, pronounces the words of consecration in German, then turning to the people, who were all attention, he says in a solemn tone, " Whosoever feels the burden of his sins, and is hungering and thirsting for divine grace, let him come and receive the body and blood of the Lord."[2] Afterwards, without raising the host, he distributes the bread and wine to all, saying, "This is the cup of my blood, the blood of the new and everlasting covenant."

Different sentiments pervaded the audience. Some feeling that new grace from God was given to the church, came to the altar

---

[1] Und die anderen *Schirymstege* alle aussen lassen. (Corp. Ref. i, p. 512.)
[2] Wer mit Sünden beschwert und nach der Gnade Gottes hungrig und durstig. (Ibid., p. 540.)

under deep emotion and in silence. Others, attracted particularly by the novelty, approached with agitation and a certain degree of impatience. Only five communicants presented themselves at the confessional. The others simply took part in the public confession of sins. Carlstadt gave general absolution to all, enjoining no other penitence than this, "Sin no more." At the close they sang the hymn, *Lamb of God.*[1]

No opposition was made to Carlstadt: these reforms had already obtained the public consent. The archdeacon dispensed the Supper again on New-year's-day; then, on the following Sunday, and thereafter, the ordinance was regularly observed. Einsidlen, one of the Elector's counsellors, having upbraided Carlstadt with seeking his own glory rather than the salvation of his hearers, "Mighty Sir," replied he, "there is no death that can make me abandon Scripture. The word has come to me so readily . . . . . Wo to me if I preach not."[2] Carlstadt married soon after.

In the month of January the town council of Wittemberg and the university regulated the celebration of the Supper in accordance with the new form. At the same time the means were taken into consideration of restoring the moral influence of religion; for the Reformation behoved to re-establish simultaneously faith, worship, and manners. It was decreed that mendicants, whether lay or not, should no longer be tolerated, and that in each street a pious man should be charged to take care of the poor, and cite scandalous offenders before the university or the council.[3]

Thus fell the mass, the principal bulwark of Rome; thus the Reformation passed from doctrine to worship. Three ages before, the mass and transubstantiation had been definitively established,[4] and thereafter every thing in the Church had taken a new direction—the general tendency being to give glory to man and reverence to the priest. The holy sacrament had been worshipped; feasts had been instituted in honour of the greatest miracles; the adoration of Mary had obtained an important place; the priest who, in his consecration, received the strange power of "making the body of Christ," had been separated from the laity, and had become, according to Thomas Aquinas, a mediator between God and man;[5] celibacy had been proclaimed as an inviolable law; auricular confession had been imposed on the people, and the cup taken from them: for how could humble laity be placed on the same level with priests

---

[1] Wenn man communicirt hat, so singt man: *Agnus Dei* carmen. (Corp. Ref. i. p. 540.)   [2] Mir ist das Wort fast in grosser Geschwindigkeit eingefallen. (Ibid. p. 545.)   [3] Keinen offenbaren Sünder zu dulden . . . . (Ibid., p. 540.)   [4] By the Lateran Council, 1215.   [5] Sacerdos constituitur medius inter Deum et populum. (Th. Aquin. Summa, iii, 22.) The priest is appointed mediator between God and the people.

entrusted with the most august ministry? The mass was an insult to the Son of God; it was opposed to the perfect grace of his cross and the spotless glory of his eternal kingdom. But if it degraded our Lord, it exalted the priest whom it invested with the extraordinary power of reproducing in his hands, at will, his sovereign Creator. The Church appeared henceforth to exist, not in order to preach the gospel, but simply to reproduce Christ corporeally in the midst of her.[1] The pontiff of Rome, whose most humble servants at pleasure created the body of God himself, sat as God in the temple of God, and ascribed to himself a spiritual treasure out of which he drew unlimited indulgences for the pardon of sins.

Such were the gross errors which, together with the mass, had for three centuries been imposed on the Church. The Reformation, in abolishing this human institution, abolished all these abuses. The act of the Archdeacon of Wittemberg was therefore one of high consequence. The sumptuous festivals which amused the people, the worship of Mary, the pride of the priesthood, the power of the pope, all tottered with the mass. Glory was withdrawn from the priests and restored to Jesus Christ. The Reformation thus took an immense step in advance.

CHAP. VII.

Spurious Reform—The new Prophets—The Prophets at Wittemberg—Melancthon —The Elector—Luther, Carlstadt, and Images—Disorders—Luther sent for—He hesitates not—Dangers.

Still men under the influence of prejudice might have been unable to see in the work which was being accomplished more than the effect of vain enthusiasm. Facts themselves behoved to prove the contrary and demonstrate that there is a wide space between a reformation founded on the word of God and a giddy fanaticism.

When a great religious fermentation takes place in the Church, some impure elements always mingle with the manifestation of the truth. One or more false reforms proceeding from man rise to the surface, and serve as a testimony or countersign to true reform. Thus, in the days of Christ, several false Messiahs attested that the true Messiah had appeared. The Reformation of the sixteenth century could not be accomplished without exhibiting a similar phenomenon. The place where it appeared was the little town of Zwickau.

[1] Perfectio hujus sacramenti non est in usu fidelium, sed in consecratione materiæ. (Th. Aquin. Summa, Quæst. 80.) The perfection of this sacrament is not in its use to the faithful but in the consecration of the matter.

There were some men who, excited by the great events which then agitated Christendom, aspired to direct revelations from the Deity, instead of simply seeking sanctification of heart, and who pretended they had a call to complete the reformation which had been feebly sketched by Luther. "What use is there," said they, "in attaching oneself so strictly to the Bible? The Bible; always the Bible! Can the Bible speak to us? Is it not insufficient to instruct us? Had God designed to teach us by a book, would he not have sent a Bible from heaven? It is by the Spirit only that we can be illumined. God himself speaks to us. God himself reveals to us what we ought to do and what we ought to say." Thus, like the partisans of Rome, these fanatics attacked the fundamental principle on which the whole Reformation rests—the sufficiency of the Word of God.

A simple weaver, named Nicholas Storck, announced that the angel Gabriel had appeared to him during the night, and after having communicated to him things which he could not yet reveal, had said to him, "Thou, thou shalt sit upon my throne."[1] An old student of Wittemberg, named Mark Stubner, joined Storck, and forthwith abandoned his studies, having, as he said, received the gift of interpreting the Holy Scriptures immediately from God. Mark Thomas, also a weaver, added to their number and a new adept, Thomas Munzer, a man of a fanatical spirit, gave a regular organisation to this new sect. Storck, wishing to follow the example of Christ, chose among his adherents twelve apostles and seventy-two disciples. All of these openly announced, as a sect in our days has done, that apostles and prophets are at length restored to the Church of God.[2]

Shortly after the new prophets, pretending to walk in the footsteps of those of ancient times, delivered their message. "Woe! Woe!" said they. "A church governed by men so corrupt as the bishops cannot be the church of Christ. The wicked rulers of Christendom will ere long be overthrown. In five, six, or seven years, universal desolation will burst forth. The Turk will seize upon Germany: all the priests, even those who are married, will be put to death. No wicked man, no sinner will be left alive; and after the earth shall have been purified by blood, God will set up his kingdom in it: Storck will be put in possession of supreme authority, and will commit the government of the nations to saints."[3]

---

[1] Advolasse Gabrielem Angelum. (Camerarii Vita Melancth. p. 48.) [2] Breviter de sese prædicant, viros esse propheticos et apostolicos. (Corp. Ref, i, p. 514.) Briefly they declare that they are prophetical and apostolical men. [3] Ut rerum potiatur, et instauret sacra, et respublicas tradat sanctis viris tenendas. (Camerar. Vit. Mel. p. 45.) To become supreme renew sacred things, and entrust governments to the hands of holy men.

Henceforth there will be only one faith and one baptism. The day of the Lord is at hand, and we are touching on the end of the world. Woe! Woe! Woe!" Then declaring that the baptism received in infancy was of no value, the new prophets invited all men to come and receive the true baptism at their hands, as a sign of introduction into the new Church of God.

These discourses made a strong impression on the people. Some pious souls were moved at the idea that prophets were restored to the Church, and all who loved the marvellous threw themselves into the arms of the eccentric men of Zwickau.

But scarcely had this old heresy which had formerly existed in the times of Montanism, and in the middle ages, again found followers than it encountered a powerful opponent in the Reformation. Nicolas Haussman, to whom Luther bore this fine testimony, " What we teach, he practises,"[1] was pastor of Zwickau. This good man did not allow himself to be led astray by the pretensions of the false prophets. He laid an arrest on the innovations which Storck and his adherents wished to introduce, and in this his two deacons concurred with him. The fanatics, repulsed by the ministers of the Church, plunged into another excess. They formed assemblies, in which revolutionary doctrines were professed. The people were excited, and disturbances broke out; a priest, who was carrying the holy sacrament, was assailed with volleys of stones.[2] The civil authority interposed, and threw the most violent into prison.[3] Indignant at this proceeding, and impatient to justify themselves and state their complaint, Storck, Mark Thomas, and Stubner, repaired to Wittemberg.[4]

They arrived on the 27th December, 1521. Storck walked in front with the bearing and mien of a trooper.[5] Mark Thomas and Stubner followed him. The disquiet which prevailed in Wittemberg favoured their designs. The students and burghers deeply moved, and already in a state of fermentation, were a soil well fitted for the new prophets.

Thinking themselves sure of their support, they immediately repaired to the professors of the university, in order to obtain a testimony in their favour. "We," said they, "are sent by God to instruct the people. We hold familiar converse with the Lord; we know things to come[6]—in a word, we are apostles and

---

[1] Quod nos docemus, ille facit. (Seck. p. 482.) (Mel. Corp. Ref. i, p. 513.)
[2] Ein Priester der das Venerabile getragen mit Steinen geworfen.
[3] Sunt et illic in vincula conjecti.
[4] Huc advolarunt tres viri, duo lanifices, literarum rudes, literatus tertius est. (Ibid.) Three men hastened hither, two of them clothiers of no education, and the third educated.
[5] Incedens more et habitu militum, istorum quos *Lanzkyecht* dicimus. (L. Ep. ii, p. 245.)
[6] Esse sibi cum Deo familiaria colloquia, videre futura . . . . (Mel. Electori, 27th December, 1521. Corp. Ref. i, p. 514.)

prophets, and we appeal for the fact to Doctor Luther." This strange language astonished the professors.

"Who ordained you to preach?" asked Melancthon of Stubner, his old student, who had lodged in his house, "Our Lord God." "Have you written any books?—" Our Lord God has forbidden me." Melancthon is moved, astonished, and alarmed.

"There are extraordinary spirits in these men," says he, "but what kind of spirits? Luther alone can determine. On the one hand, let us beware of extinguishing the Spirit of God, and on the other, of being seduced by the spirit of the devil." Storck, who was of a restless temper, soon quitted Wittemberg. Stubner remained. Animated with an ardent spirit of proselytism, he went up and down the town, speaking sometimes to one, and sometimes to another. Several acknowledged him as a prophet of God. He applied particularly to a Suabian, named Cellarius, a friend of Melancthon, who kept a school, in which he instructed a great number of young people in literature, and who soon became a firm believer in the mission of the new apostles.

Melancthon became the more uncertain and perplexed. The visions of the new prophets did not disturb him so much as their new doctrine on baptism. It seemed to him agreeable to reason, and he considered it a subject worthy of examination; "for," said he, "it is not right either to admit or reject any thing lightly."[1]

Such is the spirit of the Reformation. Melancthon's hesitancy and anxiety are proofs of the uprightness of his heart, and perhaps do him more honour than a systematic opposition could have done.

The Elector, whom Melancthon named "*the lamp of Israel*,"[2] was also hesitating. Prophets and apostles in the electorate of Saxony, as formerly at Jerusalem! "This is an important affair," said he, "and as a layman I cannot comprehend it. But sooner than act against God, I will take my staff in my hand and quit my throne."

At last he desired his counsellors to say to the professors that they had enough of trouble on their hands at Wittemberg, that in all probability the pretensions of the men of Zwickau were only a delusion of the devil, and that the wisest course seemed to be to let the whole affair go off; that nevertheless, in every case where his Electoral Highness saw the will of God clearly, he would not take counsel, either of brother or mother, but would be ready to suffer every thing for the cause of truth.[3]

---

[1] Censebat enim neque admittendum neque rejiciendum quicquam temere. (Camer Vit. Mel. p. 49.) [2] Electori lucernæ Israel. (Ibid. p. 513.) [3] Darüber auch leiden was S. C. G. leiden sollt. Ibid. p. 537.)

Luther in the Wartburg was apprised of the agitation which prevailed at the court and at Wittemberg. Strange men had appeared, and it was difficult to say whence their message came. He instantly perceived that God had permitted these sad events to humble his servants, and urge them by trials to make greater endeavours after sanctification.

"Your Electoral Highness," wrote he to Frederick, "for many years made search for relics in all countries. God has listened to your desires, and sent you a *cross* quite entire, with nails, spears, and scourges . . . Grace and prosperity to the new relic! . . . . Only let your Highness extend your arms without fear, and allow the nails to sink into your flesh! . . . . I always expected that Satan would send us this sore plague . . . ."

But at the same time nothing appeared to him more urgent than to secure others in the liberty which he claimed for himself. He had not two weights and two measures." "Beware," wrote he to Spalatin, "of throwing them into prison; let not the prince embrue his hands in the blood of these new prophets."[1] Luther was far before his age, and even before several other Reformers, on the subject of religious liberty.

Circumstances continued to become more serious at Wittemberg.[2]

Carlstadt rejected several of the doctrines of the new prophets, and in particular their anabaptism; but there is in religious enthusiasm something contagious, from which a head like his could not easily defend itself. No sooner had the men of Zwickau arrived at Wittemberg than Carlstadt quickened his pace in the prosecution of violent reforms. "It is necessary," said he, "to make an assault on all impious customs, and overturn them in one day.[3] Calling to mind all the passages of Scripture against images, he declaimed with increasing energy against the idolatry of Rome. They bow and crouch before these idols," exclaimed he, "they kindle tapers to them, and present offerings to them. . . . Let us arise and pluck them from their altars!"

These words did not sound in vain in the ears of the people. They entered the churches, carried off the images, broke them in pieces, and burnt them.[4] It would have been better to wait till their abolition had been legally determined; but it was thought that the tardiness of the leaders was compromising the Reformation itself.

Shortly, to hear these enthusiasts, there were no longer any true

---

[1] Ne princeps manus cruentet in prophetis. (L. Epp. ii, p. 135.) [2] Ubi fiebant omnia in dies difficiliora. (Camer. Vit. Mel. p. 49.) [3] Irruendum et demoliendum statim. We must rush in and demolish them instantly. (Ibid.) [4] Die Bilder zu stürmen und aus den Kirchen zu werfen. (Math. p. 31.)

Christians in Wittemberg save those who did not confess, who assailed the priests, and ate flesh on forbidden days. Any one suspected of not rejecting all the observances of Rome as inventions of the devil was a worshipper of Baal. "It is necessary," exclaimed they, "to form a church composed only of saints."

The citizens of Wittemberg presented certain articles to the Council for their adoption. Several of these articles were conformable to evangelical morality. In particular, they asked that all places of public amusement should be shut.

But Carlstadt soon went still farther; he began to despise learning; and the old professor was heard from his chair counselling his students to return to their homes, resume the hoe, hold the plough, and quietly cultivate the ground, since it was by the sweat of his brow that man was to eat bread. George Mohr, master of the school-boys at Wittemberg, led astray by the same crotchet, called from his school window to the assembled citizens, to come and take away their children. What was the use of making them study? Storck and Stubner had never been at the university, and yet they were prophets. In preaching the gospel, therefore, a citizen was worth as much, perhaps worth more than all the teachers of the world.

Thus arose doctrines in direct opposition to the Reformation, which the revival of letters had prepared. It was with the armour of theological science that Luther had attacked Rome; and yet the enthusiasts of Wittemberg, like the fanatical monks, whom Erasmus and Reuchlin had combated, pretended to trample all human knowledge under their feet. Should Vandalism come to be established, the hope of the world was lost. A new invasion of barbarism would quench the light which God had again kindled in Christendom.

The effects of these strange harangues were soon seen. Men's minds were prejudiced, agitated, turned aside from the gospel; the university was disorganised, and the students becoming demoralised were dispersed—the governments of Germany recalling such as belonged to them.[1] Thus the men who wished to reform, and give life to every thing, were proceeding in a course of destruction. "One last effort more," exclaimed the friends of Rome, who were every where resuming courage—"one last effort more, and all will be gained."[2]

The only means of saving the Reformation was a prompt suppression of the excesses of the fanatics; but who could do it? Melancthon? He was too young, too feeble, too much agitated himself

[1] Etliche Fürsten ihre Bewandten abgefordert. (Corp. Ref. i, p. 560.) [2] Perdita et funditus diruta. (Cam. Vit. Mel. p. 52.)

by these strange apparitions. The Elector? He was the most pacific man of his age. To build the castles of Altenburg, Weimar, and Coburg, to adorn the churches with the fine paintings of Lucas Cranach, to perfect the music of his chapels, to promote the prosperity of his university, to render his people happy; to stop in the midst of the children whom he met playing on the road, and distribute little presents among them,—such were the sweetest occupations of his life. And now, as he advanced in life, would he come to close quarters with fanatics, and oppose violence to violence! How could the good, the pious Frederick resolve to do so?

Accordingly the evil continued, and none appeared to arrest it. Luther was away from Wittemberg. Trouble and ruin had invaded the city. The Reformation had seen an enemy arise in its bosom, more formidable than popes and emperors, and now stood on the brink of the precipice.

"Luther! Luther!" was the universal cry at Wittemberg. The burghers urgently called for him, the professors longed for his counsels; the prophets themselves appealed to him. All implored him to return.[1]

We can conceive what was passing in the mind of the Reformer. All the severities of Rome were nothing in comparison of the distress which now afflicted his soul. The enemies of the Reformation were coming forth from her own bosom. She was tearing her own vitals; and the doctrine, which alone gave peace to his agitated heart, was becoming an occasion of fatal disaster to the Church.

He had said, "If I knew that my doctrine was hurtful to man, to any one simple obscure man—(this it cannot be, since it is the gospel itself)—I would sooner die ten times than not retract it."[2]

And now a whole town, and this town Wittemberg, was falling into error. The doctrine was no way to blame; but from all quarters of Germany voices were raised to accuse him. Sorrows keener than any he had ever felt now assailed, and new temptations agitated him. "Can this, then," he asked himself, "be the end to which the work of the Reformation was to lead?" But he repels these doubts. God began, and God will accomplish. "I creep and keep dragging on towards the grace of the Eternal," exclaims he, "and entreat that His name may remain attached to this work, that if any thing impure has mingled with it, He would remember that I am but a sinful man."[3]

The account sent to Luther of the inspiration of the new prophets and their sublime converse with God did not shake him for

---

[1] Lutherum revocavimus ex heremo suo magnis de causis. (Corp. Ref. i, p. 566.) For strong reasons we recalled Luther from his hermitage. [2] Möchte ich ehe zehn Toden levden. (*Wieder Emser*, L. Op. xviii, p. 613.) [3] Ich krieche zu seiner Gnaden. (L. Op. xviii, p. 615.)

one moment. He knew the depths, the agonies, and humiliations of the spiritual life. At Erfurth and Wittemberg he had had experience of the power of God—experience which did not allow him to believe so easily that God should appear to the creature, and hold converse with him. "Ask them," wrote he to Melancthon, "if they have experienced those spiritual tortures, those creations of God, those deaths and hells which accompany a true regeneration.[1] And if they tell you only of enjoyment of what they call tranquil impressions of devotion and piety, believe them not, even should they pretend to have been carried to the third heaven. Christ, in order that he might arrive at his glory, behoved to pass through death; so must the believer pass through the anguish of sin before he arrive at peace. Would you know the time, the place, the manner in which God speaks with men? Listen: *He has broken all my bones like a lion; I am rejected before his face, and my soul is humbled to the lowest hell.* No! the divine majesty (as they term it) does not speak to man so directly, that man can visibly behold it; *for no man*, says He, *can see me and live.*"

But the conviction that the prophets were deluded only served to augment Luther's grief. Is it true, then, that the great doctrine of salvation by grace has so soon lost its attractions that men turn aside from it to attach themselves to fables? He begins to experience that the work is not so easy as he had at first supposed. He stumbles over this first stone which the wanderings of the human mind have placed in his path. Distressed and in anguish, he is willing, at the cost of his life, to take it out of the way of his people, and determines on returning to Wittemberg.

Many were the dangers which then threatened him. The enemies of the Reformation were confident of destroying it. George of Saxony, whose wish was neither for Rome nor Wittemberg, had written, 16th October, 1521, to Duke John the Elector's brother, advising him to join the ranks of the enemies of reform. "Some," said he, "deny the immortality of the soul. Others (and they are monks) drag the relics of St. Anthony with tinkling bells and swine, and cast them into the mire.[2] And all this comes of Luther's doctrine! Entreat your brother the Elector either to punish the impious authors of these innovations, or publicly to declare what his ultimate intentions are. The whitening of our locks warns us that we are drawing near the last stage of life, and urge us to put an end to all these evils."

After this, George departed to take his seat in the imperial go-

---

[1] Quæras num experti sint spirituales illas angustias et nativitates divinas, mortes infernosque. (L. Ep. ii, p. 215.) Ask whether they have experienced these spiritual straits and divine births, deaths, and hells. [2] Mit Schweinen und Schellen ... in Koth geworfen. (Weym. Ann. Seck. p. 482.)

vernment established at Nuremberg, and immediately on his arrival used every means he could to induce the adoption of severe measures. In fact, this body on the 21st January issued an edict, complaining bitterly that the priests said mass without being clothed in the sacerdotal dress, consecrated the holy sacrament in German, dispensed it without receiving the necessary confessions, placed it in the hands of laics, and did not even trouble themselves to inquire whether or not those who came forward to take it had broken their fast.[1]

The imperial government accordingly called upon the bishops to search out and rigorously punish all the innovators who might be found within their respective dioceses. The bishops hastened to comply with these orders.

Such was the moment which Luther chose to re-appear upon the scene. He saw the danger; he foresaw immense disasters. "In the empire," said he, "there will soon be a tumult, which will drag, pell mell, princes, magistrates, and bishops. The people have eyes: they neither will nor can be led by force. Germany will swim in blood.[2] Let us place ourselves in the breach, and save our country in this great and terrible day of the Lord."

CHAPTER VIII.

Departure from the Wartburg—New Position—Luther and Primitive Catholicism—Meeting at the Black Bear—Luther to the Elector—Return to Wittemberg—Discourses at Wittemberg—Charity—the Word—How the Reformation was effected—Faith in Christ—Effect—Didymus—Carlstadt—The Prophets—Conference with Luther—End of the Struggle.

Such was Luther's thought, but he saw a still more pressing danger. At Wittemberg the fire, far from being extinguished, was becoming more violent from day to day. From the heights of the Wartburg, Luther could discover in the horizon the signs of devastation—frightful blazes darting up suddenly into the air. Is not he the only one who can bring assistance in this extremity? Will he not throw himself into the midst of the flames, to extinguish the conflagration? In vain do his enemies prepare to strike the last blow; in vain does the Elector implore him to continue in the Wartburg, and prepare his defence for the next Diet. He has something more important to do, he has to defend the gospel itself. "More

---

[1] In ihre laïsche Hände reiche. (L. Op. xviii, p. 285.)   [2] Germaniam in sanguine natare. (L. Ep. ii, p. 157.)

serious news reach me from day to day," writes he. "I am preparing to depart; circumstances demand it."[1]

In fact, on the morning of the 3rd of March he rises with the determination to quit the Wartburg for ever. He bids adieu to its old towers and gloomy forests,—crosses the walls where the excommunication of Leo X and the sword of Charles V were unable to reach him, and descends the mountain. The world which extends at his feet, and in which he is going to re-appear, will perhaps raise a death-cry against him. But no matter: he advances joyfully, for it is in the name of the Lord that he is rejoining the society of his fellow-men.[2]

Time had moved onward. Luther came out of the Wartburg for a different cause from that for which he had entered it. He had entered as the assailant of ancient tradition and ancient doctors; he left it as a defender of the doctrine of the apostles against new adversaries. He had entered as an innovator and assailant of the ancient hierarchy: he came out as its preserver, and for the defence of the Christian faith. Till now, Luther had only one aim in his work, viz., the triumph of justification by faith; with this weapon, he had struck down powerful superstitions. But if there had been a time to pull down, there behoved also to be a time to build up. Behind those ruins with which his arm had strewed the ground—behind those tattered letters of indulgences—those broken tiaras and torn cowls—behind all the abuses and errors of Rome, which lay in confused heaps on the field of battle, he discerned and exhibited the primitive Catholic Church, re-appearing always the same, and coming forth, after a long trial, with its immutable doctrines and heavenly accents. He knew how to distinguish between it and Rome: he hailed it and embraced it with joy. Luther did not, as he has been falsely accused, bring a novelty into the world. He did not build up an edifice for the future that had no connection with the past. He discovered and brought to light the old foundation, overgrown with thorns and brambles, and merely continuing the structure of the temple, built on the foundation which the apostles had laid. Luther understood that the ancient and primitive Church of the apostles required on the one hand to be re-built in opposition to the papacy, which had so long oppressed it, and on the other, to be defended against enthusiasts and unbelievers, who pretended not to see it, and who, making no account of all that God had done in times past, wished to begin a work entirely new. Luther was no longer exclusively the apostle of a single doctrine, that of justification, though he always

---

[1] Ita enim res postulat ipsa. (L. Ep. ii, p. 135.)   [2] So machte er sich mit unglaublicher Freudigkeit des Geistes, im Namen Gottes auf den Weg. (Seck. p. 458.)

reserved the first place for it;—he became the apostle of the whole Christian system, and while believing that the Church consists essentially of the whole body of the saints, he by no means despised the visible Church, but recognised the assembly of all who are called, as the kingdom of God. Thus a great change now took place in Luther's soul, in his theology, and in the work of renovation which God was accomplishing in the world. The hierarchy of Rome might perhaps have urged the Reformer into an extreme: the sects which then raised their heads so boldly helped to bring him to the proper medium. His residence in the Wartburg divides the history of the Reformation into two periods.

Luther was trotting along the road to Wittemberg on the second day of his journey, which was Shrove Tuesday. Towards evening a dreadful storm arose and inundated the roads. Two young Swiss, who were proceeding in the same direction, hastened on in order to take shelter in the town of Jena. They had studied at Bale, but were on their way to Wittemberg, attracted by the great celebrity of its University. Travelling on foot, fatigued, and drenched, John Kessler of St. Gall, and his companion, quickened their pace. The town was in the full gayety of the carnival: dances, masquerades, and noisy feasts occupied all the inhabitants of Jena, and when the two travellers arrived, every inn was occupied. At last the *Black Bear*, in front of the town gate, was mentioned to them. Jaded and out of spirits, they sadly repaired to it. The host received them kindly,[1] and they sat down near the door opening into the public room, without presuming to enter, being ashamed of the state into which the storm had put them. At one of the tables sat a solitary individual in the dress of a knight; his head was covered with a red cap, and his underdress was covered by the skirts of his doublet; his right hand rested on the pommel of his sword, while his left held it by the hilt. A book was open before him, and he seemed to be reading with great attention.[2] At the noise made by the two youths, he raised his head, saluted them courteously, and invited them to come forward and take a seat at table with him; then offering them a glass of beer, and referring to their accent, he said to them, "You are Swiss, I see, but of what Canton?" "St. Gall."—"If you are going to Wittemberg you will find a countryman there, Dr. Schurff." Encouraged by this kind reception, they asked, "Sir, are you not able to tell us where Martin Luther now is?" "I know for certain," replied the knight, "that Luther is not at Wittemberg, but is

---

[1] See Kessler's narrative with all its details, in the simple language of the period in Bernet, Johann Kessler, p. 27. Hanhard Erzählungen, iii, p. 300, and Marheineck, Gesch. der Ref. ii, p. 321, 2nd edition. [2] In einem rothen Schlöpli, in blosser Hosen und Wamms. . . . (Ibid.)

to be soon. Philip Melancthon is there. Study Greek and Hebrew, that you may have a good understanding of the Holy Scriptures." "If God spares our lives," replied one of the youths of St. Gall, " we shall not return home till we have seen and heard doctor Luther, for it is on account of him we have undertaken this long journey. We know that he wishes to overthrow the priesthood and the mass, and as our parents have, from our infancy, intended us for priests, we would fain know on what he bottoms his enterprise." The knight was silent for a moment, and then said, " where have you studied hitherto ?" "At Bale." "Is Erasmus of Rotterdam still there ?—what is he about ?" They answered these questions, and there was a new pause. The two Swiss knew not what to think. " Is it not a strange thing," said they, " that this knight talks to us of Schurff, Melancthon, and Erasmus, and of the necessity of studying Greek and Hebrew." "Dear friends," said the stranger abruptly, "what is thought of Luther in Switzerland?" " Sir," replied Kessler, "opinions differ, as every where else; some cannot extol him sufficiently ; others condemn him as an abominable heretic." " Ah, the priests, no doubt," said the stranger.

The knight's affability had put the two students at their ease. They longed eagerly to know what book he was reading at the moment of their arrival. The knight had closed it and laid it down near him. Kessler's companion was at length emboldened to take it up. What was the astonishment of the two youths ! The Psalms in Hebrew. The student immediately laid down the book, and wishing to make his indiscretion be forgotten, said, " I would willingly give one of my fingers to know this language." " This you will certainly do," replied the stranger, " if you take the trouble to learn it."

Some moments after Kessler heard himself called by the host. The poor young Swiss feared something was wrong, but the host whispered to him, " I perceive you have a great desire to see and hear Luther; very well, he is sitting beside you." Kessler taking it for a joke said, " Ah, host, you want to hoax me." " It is he, certainly," replied the host, "only don't let it be seen that you know who he is." Kessler gave no answer, and returned to the table, burning with eagerness to repeat what he had heard to his companion. But how was he to do it ? At last it occurred to him to lean forward as if he were looking to the door, when, being close to his friend's ear, he whispered to him, " the host assures me that this is Luther." " He perhaps said Hütten," replied his companion, "you may have misunderstood him." " It is quite possible," replied Kessler, " the host may have said Hütten : the two sounds are not unlike, I may have mistaken the one for the other."

At this moment the trampling of horses was heard in front of the hotel; and two merchants, who wished to pass the night there, entered the room. After taking off their spurs, and laying aside their cloaks, one of them put down on the table beside him an unbound volume, which immediately caught the eye of the knight. "What book is that?" said he. "An exposition of some gospels and epistles by Dr. Luther," replied the merchant: "it has just appeared." "I shall soon have it," replied the knight.

The host at this moment announced supper. The two students, fearing the expence of a repast in company with the chevalier, Ulric Von Hütten and the rich merchants, took the host aside, and begged him to give them something by themselves. "Stay, my friends," replied the host of the Black Bear, "take your seat at table beside this gentleman; I will charge moderately." "Come," said the knight, "I will settle the charge."

During the repast the stranger knight made many simple and edifying observations. The merchants and students were riveted, and paid more attention to his conversation than to the dishes that were served up. "Luther must either be an angel from heaven or a devil of hell," said one of the merchants in the course of the conversation, and then added, "I would willingly give ten florins to meet Luther and be able to confess to him."

When the supper was ended the merchants rose up, and the two Swiss remained alone with the knight, who, taking a large glass of beer, lifted it and said gravely, according to the custom of the country, "Swiss, one glass more for thanks." As Kessler was going to take the glass, the stranger put it down and presented him with one filled with wine: "You are not accustomed to beer," said he.

He then rose up, threw a military cloak on his shoulders, shook hands with the students, and said to them, "When you arrive at Wittemberg, give my compliments to Doctor Jerôme Schurff."— "Willingly," replied they; "but from whom shall we say?" "Say simply," replied he, "He who is coming salutes you." On this he walked out, leaving them in admiration at his courtesy and meekness.

Luther, for it was indeed he, continued his journey. Be it remembered he had been put under the ban of the empire; whosoever met him and recognised him might lay hands upon him. But at the moment when he was executing an enterprise which exposed him to every risk, he discoursed gaily with those whom he met on his way.

It was not because he was under any illusion. He saw the future big with storms. "Satan," said he, "is transported with rage, and all around me meditate death and hell.[1] I advance, nevertheless, and throw myself in the way of the emperor and the pope, having none to defend me save God in heaven. On the part of man power has been given to every one to slay me wheresoever I am found. But Christ is the Lord of all: if it is his will that I be slain, so be it!"

The same day, being Ash Wednesday, Luther arrived at Borne, a small town near Leipsic. Feeling that he ought to give notice to his prince of the bold step which he was going to take, he wrote him the following letter from the Conductor Tavern where he had alighted:—

"Grace and peace from God our Father and from the Lord Jesus Christ.

"Most serene Elector! gracious lord! what has happened at Wittemberg to the great shame of the gospel has filled me with such grief that if I were not certain of the truth of our cause I would have despaired of it.

"Your Highness knows, or if not, please to be informed. I received the gospel not from men but from heaven, by our Lord Jesus Christ. If I have asked for conferences, it was not because I had doubts of the truth, but from humility, and for the purpose of winning others. But since my humility is turned against the gospel, my conscience now impels me to act in a different manner. I have yielded enough to your highness in exiling myself during this year. The devil knows it was not from fear I did it. I would have entered Worms though there had been as many devils in the town as there were tiles on the roofs. Now Duke George with whom your Highness tries so much to frighten me, is far less to be feared than a single devil. Had that which has taken place at Wittemberg taken place at Leipsic (the duke's residence), I would instantly have mounted my horse and gone thither, even though (let your Highness pardon the expression,) for nine days it should have done nothing but rain Duke Georges, and every one of them been nine times more furious than he is. What is he thinking of in attacking me? Does he take Christ, my Lord, for a man of straw?[2] The Lord be pleased to avert the dreadful judgment which is impending over him!

"It is necessary for your Highness to know that I am on my way to Wittemberg under a more powerful protection than that of an elector. I have no thought of soliciting the assistance of your Highness: so far from desiring your protection, I would rather give

---

[1] Furit Satanas; et fremunt vicini undique, nescio quot mortibus et infernis. (L. Ep. ii, p. 153.) Satan rages, and the neighbours mutter on every side, with I know not how many deaths and hells. [2] Er Hält meinen Herrn Christum für ein Mann aus Stroh geflochten. (Ibid. p. 139.)

you mine. If I knew that your Highness could or would protect me, I would not come to Wittemberg. No sword can give any aid to this cause. God alone must do all without human aid or co-operation. He who has most faith is the best protector. Now I observe that your Highness is still very weak in the faith.

"But since your Highness desires to know what to do, I will answer with all humility. Your electoral Highness has already done too much, and ought to do nothing at all. God does not wish and cannot tolerate either your cares and labours, or mine. Let your Highness, therefore, act accordingly.

"In regard to what concerns myself, your Highness must act as elector. You must allow the orders of his imperial Majesty to be executed in your towns and rural districts. You must not throw any difficulty in the way, should it be wished to apprehend or slay me;[1] for none must oppose the powers that be save He who established them.

"Let your Highness then leave the gates open, and respect safe-conducts, should my enemies themselves, or their envoys, enter the states of your Highness in search of me. In this way you will avoid all embarrassment and danger.

"I have written this letter in haste that you may not be disconcerted on learning my arrival. He with whom I have to deal is a different person from Duke George. He knows me well, and I know something of him.

"Borne, the Conductor Hotel, Ash Wednesday, 1522.

"Your Electoral Highness's most humble Servant,

"MARTIN LUTHER."

Thus Luther was drawing near to Wittemberg. He wrote to the prince, but not to apologise. Immovable confidence filled his heart. He saw the hand of God in the cause, and this sufficed him. Never, perhaps, was the heroism of faith more conspicuously displayed. One of the editions of Luther's works has on the margin these words, "This is a marvellous production of the third and last Elias."[1]

On Friday, the 7th March, Luther again entered Wittemberg, having been five days in coming from Eisenach. Professors, students, citizens, all gave full utterance to their joy. They had recovered the pilot who alone could bring off the ship from the shallows on which it had been cast.

The elector, who was with his court at Lockau, was much affected on reading Luther's letter. He felt desirous to defend him before the Diet, and wrote to Schurff, "Let him send me a letter explaining his motives for returning to Wittemberg, and let him say

---

[1] Und ja nicht wehren .... so sie mich fahen oder tödten will. (L. Ep. ii, p. 140.)
" Der wahre, dritte und letzte Elias . . . . (L. Op. (L.) xviii, p. 271.)

also in it that he returned without my permission." Luther agreed to do so.

"I am ready," wrote he to the prince, "to endure the displeasure of your Highness and the anger of the whole world. Are not the inhabitants of Wittemberg my brood? Has not God entrusted them to me? And am not I bound to expose myself to death for them? I fear, moreover, the breaking out in Germany of some great revolution by which God will punish our country. Let your Highness be well assured that the decision in heaven has been very different from that at Nuremberg."[1] This letter was written the very day of Luther's arrival.

The next day being the eve of the first Sunday of Lent, Luther repaired to the house of Jerôme Schurff, where Melancthon, Jonas, Amsdorff, and Augustin Schurff were met. Luther eagerly asked them many questions, and they were informing him of all that had taken place, when it was announced that two foreign students wished to speak to Doctor Jerôme. On appearing in the midst of this meeting of doctors, the two youths of St. Gall were at first abashed, but they soon recovered on perceiving among them the knight of the Black Bear, who immediately went up to them, accosted them as old acquaintances, smiled to them, and pointing with his finger to one of the doctors, said, "That is Philip Melancthon of whom I spoke to you." In honour of the meeting at Jena, the two Swiss spent the whole day with the doctors of Wittemberg.

One great thought occupied the Reformer, and made him forget the joy he felt at being again in the midst of his friends. No doubt the theatre on which he now appeared was obscure: it was in a small town of Saxony that he was going to raise his voice, and yet his undertaking had all the importance of an event which was to influence the destinies of the world. Many nations and many ages were to feel its effects. The point to be determined was, whether this doctrine which he had drawn from the word of God, and which was destined to exert so powerful an influence on the future progress of humanity, would be stronger than the principles of destruction which threatened its existence—whether it was possible to reform without destroying, and to pave the way for further progress, without destroying that already made. To silence fanatics in the first heat of enthusiasm, to master a whole multitude broken loose, to calm them down, and bring them back to order, peace, and truth; to break the force of this impetuous torrent which was threatening to throw down the rising edifice of the Reformation, and scatter its wrecks around;—such was the work for which

---

[1] L. Ep. ii, p. 143. Luther had to change this passage in his letter at the request of the Elector.

Luther had returned to Wittemberg. But would his influence be sufficient? This events only could determine.

The soul of the Reformer shuddered at the thought of the combat which awaited him. He stood up like a lion goaded on to battle, and shaking his bushy mane, " Now is the time," said he, " to trample Satan under foot, and combat the angel of darkness. If our adversaries retire not of their own accord, Christ will constrain them. We are the masters of life and death, we who believe in the Master of life and death."[1]

But at the same time, the impetuous Reformer, as if subdued by a higher power, refused to make use of the anathemas and thunders of the Word, and became a humble pastor, a meek shepherd of souls. "It is by the Word," said he, " that we must fight, by the Word overturn and destroy what has been established by violence. I am unwilling to employ force against the superstitious or the unbelieving. Let him who believes approach; let him who believes not stand aloof. None ought to be constrained. Liberty is of the essence of faith."[2]

The next day was Sabbath, and on that day, in the Church, in the pulpit, the people were again to behold the teacher whom for nearly a year the Wartburg had concealed from every eye. The news spread in Wittemberg—Luther is returned—Luther is going to preach. These news passing from mouth to mouth were in themselves a powerful diversion to the notions by which the people had been led astray. The hero of Worms is going again to appear Crowds press forward from all directions, and on Sabbath morning the church was filled with an attentive and excited audience.

Luther divines the feeling of his hearers: he mounts the pulpit, and there stands in presence of the flock whom he was wont to lead like one gentle sheep, but who had now broken loose and assumed the appearance of an untamed bull. His discourse is simple, yet dignified, replete at once with force and mildness. He might have been described as a tender parent just returned to his children, enquiring how they have behaved, and telling them kindly of what he had heard respecting them. He candidly acknowledges the progress which they had made in the faith. Having thus prepared and gained their minds, he continues in the following terms:—

"But there must be more than faith: there must be charity. When a man with a sword in his hand is by himself, it is of no consequence whether or not he keeps it in the scabbard, but if he is in the midst of a crowd, he must act in such a manner as not to hurt any one.

---

[1] Domini enim sumus vitæ et mortis. (L. Ep. ii, p. 150.) [2] Non enim ad fidem et ad ea quæ fidei sunt, ullus cogendus est. (Ibid., p. 151.) For no man must be driven by compulsion to faith and the things thereto appertaining.

"How does a mother do with her child? At first she gives it milk, and thereafter the most easily digested food. Were she to begin by giving it flesh and wine, what would the result be? . . .

"So ought we to do with our brethren. Have you had enough of the breast, my friend? very well; allow your brother to have it as long as you have had it yourself.

"Behold the sun. . . . There are two things he gives us—light and heat. There is no king so powerful as to be able to interrupt his rays: they come to us in a straight line; but the heat radiates and transfuses itself in all directions. Thus faith ought to be like light, straight and inflexible; but charity should, like heat, radiate in all directions, and bend to meet all the wants of our brethren."

Luther having thus prepared his hearers, comes to still closer quarters.

"The abolition of the mass, you say, is conformable to Scripture. Agreed. But what order, what decorum have you observed? You ought to have presented fervent prayers to the Lord: you ought to have applied to constituted authority, which, in that case, might have been able to perceive that the work was of God. . ."

Thus spake Luther. The bold man who had at Worms withstood the princes of the earth, produced a powerful impression by these words of wisdom and peace. Carlstadt and the prophets of Zwickau, who for some weeks had been so high and mighty, and who had agitated and lorded it over Wittemberg, became dwarfs when placed beside the prisoner of the Wartburg.

"The mass," he continues, " is a bad thing: God is inimical to it: it must be abolished, and I could wish that over the whole world it were supplanted by the supper of the Gospel. But let nobody be driven from it by violence. The affair must be committed to God. His Word must act, not we. And why? you will say. Because I do not hold the hearts of men in my hand as the potter does the clay. We have a right to speak, but not to act. Let us preach—the rest belongs to God. If I employ force, what shall I obtain? Grimace, appearances, apishness, human ordinances, hypocrisy . . . . But there will be no sincerity of heart, no faith, no charity. Any work in which these three things are wanting wants every thing, and I would not give a pin for it.[1]

"The first thing to be gained from people is their heart, and for this it is necessary to preach the gospel. Then the Word will descend on one heart to-day, and on another to-morrow, and operate in such a way that each will withdraw from the mass, and abandon it. God does more by his mere Word than you and I, and

---

[1] Ich wollte nicht einen Birnstiel drauf geben. (L. Op. L. xviii, p. 255.)

all the world could do by uniting our utmost strength. God takes possession of the heart, and when the heart is taken every thing is taken.

"I do not say this in order to re-establish the mass. Since it is down, let it, in God's name, so remain. But was the matter gone about as it ought to have been? Paul, having one day arrived at Athens, a great city, found altars erected to false gods. He went from one to another, viewed them all, and touched none. But he quietly repaired to the market-place, and declared to the people that all their Gods were only idols. His words took possession of their hearts, and the idols fell without being touched by Paul.

"I wish to speak, to preach, to write, but I wish not to constrain any one, for faith is a voluntary matter. See what I have done! I have withstood the pope, indulgences, and the papists, but without tumult and violence. I have put forward the Word of God— have preached—have written, but this is all I have done. And while I was asleep, or seated in a friendly way at table with Amsdorff and Melancthon, conversing with them over a pot of Wittemberg beer, the Word which I had preached overthrew the papacy, assailing it more effectually than was ever done by prince or emperor. I have done nothing: the Word alone has done all. Had I chosen to appeal to force, perhaps Germany might have been bathed in blood. But what would have been the consequence? Ruin and desolation to soul and body. I therefore remained quiet, and allowed the Word itself to have free course in the world. Do you know what the Devil thinks when he sees recourse had to force in order to spread the gospel among men? Seated, with his arms across, behind the flames of hell, Satan, with malignant leer, and frightful smile, says—'Ah, how sagely these fools are playing my game.' But when he sees the Word running and wrestling alone on the field of battle, then it is he feels uneasy, and his knees tremble : he mutters, and swoons with terror."

Luther again appeared in the pulpit on Tuesday: his powerful eloquence again resounded in the midst of a deeply impressed audience. He preached successively on Wednesday, Thursday, Friday, Saturday, and Sabbath. He passed in review the destruction of images, the distinction of meats, the observances at the supper, the restoration of the cup, and the abolition of confession. He showed that those points were still more indifferent than the mass, and that the authors of the disorders, which had taken place at Wittemberg, had grossly abused their liberty. He gave utterance alternately to accents of Christian charity and to bursts of holy indignation.

In particular, he inveighed forcibly against those who communicated thoughtlessly at the Lord's Supper. "What makes the Christian," said he, "is not the external eating, but the internal and spiritual eating which is produced by faith, and without which, all forms whatsoever are only show and vain grimace. Now this faith consists in firmly believing that Jesus Christ is the Son of God; that being ladened with our sins and iniquities, and having borne them upon the cross, he is himself the sole, the all-powerful expiation: that he is now continually in the presence of God, that he reconciles us with the Father, and has given us the sacrament of his body in order to confirm our faith in this ineffable mercy. If I believe these things, God is my defender: with him I defy sin, death, hell, devils—they cannot do me any harm, nor even ruffle a hair of my head. This spiritual bread is the consolation of the afflicted, the cure of the sick, the life of the dying, the food of the hungry, and the treasure of the poor. He, then, who is not sorry for his sins, ought not to come to this altar: what would he do there? Ah! let our conscience accuse us, let our hearts be torn at the thought of our faults, and we will not approach the holy sacrament with so much rashness."

Crowds ceased not to fill the temple: numbers even flocked from the neighbouring towns to hear the new Elias. Capito, among others, came and spent two days at Wittemberg, and heard two of the doctor's sermons. Never had Luther and the chaplain of cardinal Albert been so much of one mind. Melancthon, the magistrates, the professors, and all the people, were overjoyed.[1] Schurff, delighted at this issue of an affair which promised to be so serious, hastened to acquaint the Elector, to whom he wrote, Friday, 15th March, (the day on which Luther had delivered his sixth discourse.) "What joy the return of doctor Martin diffuses among us! His discourses, by the help of divine grace, are daily bringing back our poor erring souls into the way of truth. It is clear as the sun that the Spirit of God is in him, and that by his special appointment he has returned to Wittemberg."[2]

In fact these discourses are models of popular eloquence, though not of the sort which aroused men's minds in the days of Demosthenes or even Savonarola. The task which the orator of Wittemberg had to perform was more difficult. It is easier to rouse a wild beast than to calm its fury. The thing required was to appease a fanatical multitude; to tame passions which had been let loose and this Luther did. In his eight discourses the Reformer did not allow a single painful allusion to escape, a single word calculated to offend the authors of the disturbances. But the more

[1] Grosse Freude und Frohlocken unter Gelehrten und Ungelehrten. (L. Op. xviii. p. 286.) [2] Aus sonderlicher Schickung des Allmachtigen .... (Ibid.)

moderate, the stronger he was ; the greater the delicacy towards those who had gone astray, the more he avenged insulted truth. How could the people of Wittemberg resist his powerful eloquence? The discourses which recommend moderation are usually attributed to moderation, policy, or fear. Here there was nothing of the kind. Luther appeared before the people of Wittemberg braving the excommunication of the pope, and the proscription of the emperor. He returned, though forbidden by the Elector, who declared his inability to defend him. Even at Worms, Luther had not shown more courage. He was confronting the most threatening dangers, and accordingly his voice was not disregarded. This man who braved the scaffold was entitled to exhort others to submission. He may boldly preach obedience to God, who, in doing so, exposes himself to every kind of persecution from man. At Luther's preaching, objections vanished, tumult was appeased, sedition ceased its clamour, and the citizens of Wittemberg returned to their quiet homes.

Gabriel Didymus, an Augustin monk, and the one who had been most enthusiastic, had not lost a word spoken by the Reformer. "Dont you think Luther an admirable teacher?" asked a hearer, under deep emotion. "Ah!" replied Gabriel, "methinks I hear the voice not of a man, but an angel."[1] Shortly after, he openly acknowledged his error. "He is become another man," said Luther.[2]

The same effect was not at first produced on Carlstadt. Despising study, and affectedly visiting the workshops of mechanics, that he might there get a knowledge of the Scriptures, he felt hurt, when he saw his work crumbling to pieces before the appearance of Luther.[3] In his eyes this was equivalent to an arrest laid on the Reformation itself. Accordingly he had always a depressed, gloomy, and discontented look. He, however, sacrificed his self-love to peace, suppressed his vindictive feelings, was reconciled, apparently at least, with his colleague, and shortly after resumed his course at the University.[4]

The principal prophets happened not to be at Wittemberg when Luther arrived. Nicholas Storck had been scouring the country, and Mark Stubner had quitted the hospitable roof of Melancthon. It may be their prophetical spirit had vanished and they had neither "*voice*" nor "*answer*,"[5] from the moment they learned that this new Elias was bending his steps towards this new

---

[1] Imo, inquit, angeli, non hominis vocem mihi audisse videor. (Camerarius, p. 12.)
[2] In alium virum mutatus est. (L. Ep, ii, p. 156.) [3] Ego Carlstadium offendi, quod ordinationes suas cessavi. (L. Ep. ii p. 177.) I offended Carlstadt, because I put a stop to his arrangements. [4] Philippi et Carlstadii lectiones, ut sunt optimæ . . . (Ibid. p. 284.) The lectures of Philip and Carlstadt, as they are most excellent. [5] 1 Kings, xviii, 29.

Carmel. The old schoolmaster Cellarius had been left alone. Meanwhile, Stubner having been informed that the sheep of his flock were dispersed, returned in all haste. Those who had remained faithful to the "heavenly prophecy" gathered round their master, relating Luther's discourses to him, and asking with uneasiness what they were to think.[1] Stubner exhorted them to remain firm in their faith. "Let him show himself," exclaimed Cellarius, "let him grant us a conference, let him allow us to explain our doctrine, and we shall see...."

Luther had little inclination to meet with these men; he knew that there was in them a violent, impatient, haughty spirit, which could not endure warnings, however charitably given, and who claimed submission to their every word as a sovereign authority.[2] Such are the enthusiasts of all times. Still, as an interview was asked, the doctor could not refuse it. Besides, it might be useful to the simple ones of the flock to unmask the imposture of the prophets. The conference took place. Stubner spoke first, and explained how he proposed to renew the Church and change the world. Luther listened with great calmness.[3] "Nothing that you have said," replied he, at length, gravely, "rests on the Holy Scriptures. It is all fable." At these words Cellarius loses all self-possession; he raises his voice, gesticulates like a madman, stamps and strikes the table that was before him;[4] gets into a passion, and exclaims that it is an insult to presume to speak thus to a man of God. Then Luther resumes, "St. Paul declares that the proofs of his apostleship were manifested by miracles: prove yours by miracles." "We shall," replied the prophets.[5] "The God whom I worship," replied Luther, "will keep a bridle hand on your gods." Stubner, who had remained more calm, fixing his eyes on the Reformer, said to him with an air of inspiration, "Martin Luther, I am going to declare to you what is now passing in your soul. You are beginning to think that my doctrine is true." Luther, after a few moments' silence, replied. "The Lord rebuke thee, Satan." At these words all the prophets are transported. "The Spirit! the Spirit!" they exclaim. Luther, with that cool disdain, and that cutting, yet familiar language, which was one of his characteristics, says, "I care not a fig for your *spirit*."[6] The clamour is redoubled. Cellarius was especially

---

[1] Rursum ad ipsum confluere . . . (Camerar. p. 52.) Again flocked to him.
[2] Vehementer superbus et impatiens . . . credi vult plena auctoritate, ad primam vocem . . . (L. Epp. ii, p. 179.) Excessively proud and impatient . . . he insists on being believed implicitly on his first word. [3] Audivit Lutherus placide. (Camer. p. 52.) [4] Cum et solum pedibus et propositam mensulam manibus feriret. (Ibid.) Both struck the ground with his feet, and the little table before him with his hands. [5] Quid pollicentes de mirabilibus affectionibus. (Ibid. p. 53.) Making some promise of miraculous affections. [6] Ihren Geist haue er über die Schnauze. (L. Op. Altenburg Augs. iii, p. 137.)

violent. He raged, roared, and foamed.¹ Not a word more could be heard. At length the prophets withdrew, and the same day quitted Wittemberg.

Thus Luther had accomplished the work for which he had left his retreat. He had withstood fanaticism, and chased from the bosom of the renovated church the enthusiasm and disorder which were trying to invade it. If with one hand the Reformation overthrew the musty decretals of Rome, with the other it repelled the pretensions of the mystics, and secured the living and immutable Word of God in possession of the territory which it had conquered. The character of the Reformation was thus well established. It behoved constantly to move between these two extremes, equally distant from the convulsive throes of fanatics and the lifeless state of the papacy.

A population aroused, misled, and broken loose from all restraint, is appeased, becomes calm and submissive, and the most perfect tranquillity is restored to a city which, a few days before, was like a raging sea.

Complete liberty was moreover established at Wittemberg. Luther continued to reside in the convent, and to wear the monastic dress; but every one was free to do otherwise. Communicants, in taking the supper, might content themselves with a general, or ask a particular absolution. One established principle was to reject nothing but what was opposed to a clear and formal declaration of the Holy Scriptures.² This was not indifference. On the contrary, religion was thus brought back to what constitutes its essence. Religious sentiment was drawn away from accessory forms when it had been well nigh lost, and again placed on its true basis. Thus the Reformation was saved, and doctrine could continue to be developed in the Church in accordance with charity and truth.

CHAPTER IX.

Translation of the New Testament—Faith and Scripture—Opposition—Importance of Luther's Publication—Need of a Systematic Exposition—Melancthon's *Common Places*—Original Sin—Salvation—Free-will—Effect of the Common places.

No sooner was the calm re-established than the Reformer turned towards his dear Melancthon, and asks his assistance in putting the finishing hand to the version of the New Testament,

---

¹ Spumabat et fremebat et furebat. (L. Epp. ii, p. 179.) ² Ganz klare und gründliche Schrift.

which he had brought from the Wartburg.[1] Melancthon, as early as 1519, had laid down the grand principle, that the fathers ought to be explained according to Scripture, and not Scripture according to the fathers. Continuing thoroughly to investigate the writings of the New Testament, he felt at once enraptured with their simplicity, and struck with their profundity. "Here only," was the open declaration of one so familiar with all the philosophers of antiquity—"Here only is found the true food of the soul." Hence he gladly responded to Luther's invitation, and thereafter the two friends spent many long hours together, in studying and translating the inspired Word. Often did they interrupt their laborious researches to give vent to their admiration. "Reason thinks," said Luther, "Oh, if I could only once hear God; to hear Him I would run to the end of the world . . . . Listen, then, O man, my brother! . . . . God, the creator of heaven and earth is speaking to you. . . ."

The printing of the New Testament was begun and carried on with unexampled zeal.[2] It seemed as if the workmen themselves felt the importance of the work which they were preparing. Three presses were employed, and ten thousand sheets were printed daily.[3]

At length, on the 21st September, appeared the complete edition of three thousand copies, in two volumes, folio, with this simple title: *The New Testament — German — Wittemberg.* It bore no human name. Every German could thenceforth procure the Word of God for a moderate sum.[4]

The new translation, written in the very spirit of the sacred books, in a language still recent, and displaying its many beauties for the first time, seized, enraptured, and deeply impressed the humblest of the people, as well as the most elevated classes. It was a national work; it was the people's book: it was more, it was truly the book of God. Even enemies could not withhold their approbation of this admirable work, while some indiscreet friends of the Reformation, struck with the beauty of the work, imagined that they beheld in it a second inspiration. This translation did more to propagate Christian piety than all the other writings of Luther. The work of the sixteenth century was thus placed on a basis which could not be shaken. The Bible given to the people brought back the human mind which for ages had been wandering in the tortuous labyrinth of scholastics, to the divine source of salvation. Accordingly the success of the work was prodigious. In a short

---

[1] Verum omnia nunc elimare coepimus Philippus et ego. (L. Ep. ii, 176.) But Philip and I now began to revise the whole. [2] Ingenti labore et studio. (Ibid., p. 236.) With immense labour and study. [3] Singulis diebus decies millia chartarum sub tribus prelis. (Ibid.) [4] A florin and a half, about half-a-crown sterling.

time all the copies were disposed of. A second edition appeared in December, and, in 1533, seventeen editions of Luther's New Testament had been printed at Wittemberg; thirteen at Augsburg; twelve at Bale; one at Erfurth; one at Grimma; one at Leipsic; thirteen at Strasburg.[1] . . . . Such were the mighty engines which lifted and transformed the Church and the world.

The first edition of the New Testament was still at press when Luther engaged in the translation of the Old Testament. This work, begun in 1522, was prosecuted without interruption. It was published in parts as it was finished, in order more rapidly to satisfy the impatience which was manifested in all quarters, and make it more easy for the poor to purchase it.

From Scripture and faith, two sources, which, in substance, are only one, evangelical life flowed, and is still diffused in the world. These two principles combated two fundamental errors; faith was opposed to the Pelagian tendency of Catholicism; Scripture, to the tradition and authority of Rome. Scripture led to faith and faith led back to Scripture. "Man cannot do any meritorious work: the free grace of God, which he receives by faith in Christ, alone saves him." Such was the doctrine proclaimed in Christendom; and the tendency of this doctrine was to urge Christians to the study of Scripture. In fact, if faith in Christ is every thing in Christianity—if the practices and ordinances of the Church are nothing—what we ought to adhere to is not the word of the Church but the word of Jesus Christ. The tie which unites to Christ will become all in all to the believer. What cares he for the external tie which unites him to an external Church enslaved to human opinions? . . . . Thus, as the doctrine of the Bible had urged Luther's contemporaries towards Jesus Christ, so the love which they had for Jesus Christ in its turn urged them towards the Bible. They returned to Scripture, not as is imagined in our day, from a philosophical principle, from a feeling of doubt or a longing for investigation, but because they found in it the word of Him whom they loved. "You have preached Christ to us," said they to the Reformer, "enable us now to hear his own voice." And they eagerly laid hold of the sheets which were delivered to them as they would a letter come from heaven.

But if the Bible was thus joyfully received by those who loved Christ, it was repulsed with hatred by those who preferred the traditions and practices of men. Violent persecution awaited this work of the Reformer. On hearing of Luther's publication, Rome trembled. The pen which transcribed the sacred oracles was the realisation of that which the Elector Frederick had seen in his

[1] Gesch. d. deutsch. Bibel Uebersetz.

dream, and which, reaching as far as the seven hills, had caused the tiara of the papacy to totter. The monk in his cell and the prince on his throne sent forth a cry of rage. Ignorant priests shuddered at the thought that every citizen, every peasant even, would now be in a condition to debate with them on sacred subjects. The King of England denounced the work to the Elector Frederick, and Duke George of Saxony. But, previous to this, as early as November, the duke had enjoined all his subjects to deliver every copy of Luther's New Testament into the hands of the magistrates. Bavaria, Brandenburg, Austria, all the states devoted to Rome, issued similar decrees. In some towns a sacrilegious pile was erected, and the books were burnt in the market-place.[1] Thus, in the sixteenth century, Rome renewed the attempts by which Paganism had tried to destroy the religion of Jesus Christ at the moment when the empire was escaping from priests and their idols. But who can arrest the triumphant progress of the gospel? "Even since my prohibition," wrote Duke George, "several thousand copies have been sold and read in my States."

God, in diffusing his Word, made use of the very hands which were endeavouring to destroy it. The Catholic theologians, seeing it impossible to suppress the Reformer's work, published the New Testament in a translation of their own. It was Luther's translation, with occasional corrections by the editors. No objection was made to the reading of it. Rome knew not as yet that, wherever the Word of God is established, her power is in danger. Joachim of Brandenburg gave full permission to his subjects to read any translation of the Bible, Latin or German, provided it came not from Wittemberg. The inhabitants of Germany, those of Brandenburg in particular, thus made a rapid advance in the knowledge of the truth.

The publication of the New Testament constitutes an important epoch in the Reformation. If the marriage of Feldkirchen was the first step in passing from doctrine to practice, if the abolition of monastic vows was the second, if the establishment of the Lord's Supper was the third, the publication of the New Testament was perhaps the most important of all. It effected a complete change in society—not only in the presbytery of the priest, the cell of the monk, and the service of the Church, but also in the mansions of the great, and the dwellings both of the citizens in towns, and of the rural population. When the Bible began to be read in the households of Christendom, Christendom was changed. There were thenceforth new customs, new manners, new conversations, a new life. With the publication of the New Testament the Re-

[1] Qui et alicubi in unum congesti rogum publicum combusti sunt.

formation came forth from the school and the Church, and took possession of the firesides of the people.

The effect produced was immense. The Christianity of the primitive Church, brought forth by the publication of the Holy Scriptures from the oblivion into which it had fallen for ages, was thus presented to the eyes of the nation, and this fact is sufficient to justify the attacks which had been made upon Rome. The humblest individuals, provided they knew the German alphabet, women, and mechanics, (this is the account given by a contemporary, a great enemy of the Reformation,) read the New Testament with avidity.[1] Carrying it about with them, they soon knew it by heart, while its pages gave full demonstration of the perfect accordance between the Reformation of Luther and the Revelation of God.

Still it was only by piecemeal that the doctrine of the Bible and of the Reformation had till then been established. Some one truth had been established in this writing, and some one error attacked in that. The remains of the ancient edifice and the materials of the new lay scattered in confusion over a large space of ground; but the new edifice itself was still wanting. The publication of the New Testament was fitted to supply this want. The Reformation, on receiving this work, could say,—There is my system! But as every person is ready to maintain that the system he holds is that of the Bible, the Reformation behoved to give a systematic form to what she had found in Scripture: This Melancthon did in her name.

He had advanced with cautious but sure steps in his theological career, and had always boldly published the results of his enquiries. So early as 1520, he had declared that in several of the seven sacraments he saw only an imitation of Jewish ceremonies; and, in the infallibility of the pope, only an arrogant pretence, equally at variance with Scripture and common sense. "To combat these dogmas," said he, "we have need of more than one Hercules."[2] Thus Melancthon had arrived at the same point with Luther, though by a calmer and more scientific path. The moment had arrived when it behoved him in his turn to make a confession of his faith.

In 1521, during Luther's captivity, his celebrated work '*On the Common Places of Theology*,' had presented Christian Europe with a body of doctrine solidly based, and admirably proportioned. A simple and majestic system was exhibited to the astonished view

---

[1] Ut sutores, mulieres, et quilibet idiotæ . . . avidissime legerent. (Cochlæus, p. 50.) So that shoe-makers, women, and the most illiterate read with the greatest avidity.

[2] Adversus ouas non uno nobis, ut ita dicam, Hercule opus est. (Corp. Ref. i, p. 137.)

of the new generation. The translation of the New Testament vindicated the Reformation to the common people: the *Common Places* of Melancthon vindicated it to the learned.

The Christian Church was fifteen centuries old, and no similar work had yet appeared. Abandoning the ordinary methods of scholastic theology, Luther's friend, at length presented Christendom with a theological system derived solely from Scripture, and exhibiting a spirit of life and intellect, a force of truth and simplicity of expression in striking contrast with the subtle and pedantic systems of the schools. The most philosophical minds and the strictest theologians alike agreed in admiring it.

Erasmus described the work as a host set in admirable array against the pharisaical tyranny of false teachers;[1] and, while declaring that he did not agree with the author on all points, he added, that, though he had always loved him, he never loved him so much as after reading this work. "So true is it," says Calvin, at a later period, in introducing the work to France, "that, in treating Christian doctrine, the greatest simplicity is the greatest virtue."[2]

But none was so much overjoyed as Luther. This work was, through life, the object of his admiration. Those isolated sounds which, in the deep emotion of his soul, his quivering hand had drawn from the harp of the prophets and apostles, were here arranged in enrapturing harmony. Those scattered stones, which he had laboriously quarried out of the Sacred volume, were now formed into a majestic building. Hence he invariably recommended the reading of this work to the youths who came to prosecute their studies at Wittemberg, saying to them, "If you would be theologians, read Melancthon."[3]

According to Melancthon, a deep conviction of the misery to which man has been reduced by sin, is the basis on which the structure of Christian theology must be reared. This incalculable calamity is the primary fact, the generating idea in theological science, the characteristic which distinguishes it from all sciences which have reason only for their instrument.

The Christian theologian, probing to the very bottom of man's heart, explained its laws and mysterious attractions, as the philosopher of a later period explained the laws and attractions of bodies. "Original sin," said he, "is an inclination born with us, a kind of

---

[1] Video dogmatum aciem pulchre instructam adversus tyrannidem pharisaicam. (Er. Ep. p. 949.) I see an array of doctrine admirably drawn up against pharisaical tyranny. [2] La Somme de Théologie, par Philippe Melancthon. (Genève, 1521. Jehan Calvin aux lecteurs.) [3] He elsewhere terms it "Librum invictum non solum immortalitate sed et canone ecclesiastico dignum." (De servo arbitrio.) An unanswerable work; worthy not only of immortality, but of the Sacred canon.

impulse which is pleasing to us, a kind of force which draws us into sin, and which has been transmitted by Adam to all his posterity. As there is in fire a native force which carries it upward, as there is in the magnet a natural power to attract steel, so there is in man a primary force disposing him to evil. I acknowledge that Socrates, Xenocrates, and Zeno, displayed constancy, temperance, and chastity: these shadows of virtue existed in impure minds, they proceeded from the love of self, and hence they must be regarded not as genuine virtues, but as vices."[1] These words may seem harsh; but they are so only when we misapprehend Melancthon's meaning. None was more disposed than he to recognise in the heathen virtues deserving of human esteem; but he laid down this great truth, that the sovereign law given by God to all his creatures is, to love him above all things. Now if man, in doing what God commands, does it, not from love to God, but from love to self, will God approve of his presuming to prefer himself to his infinite majesty, and will there be nothing vicious in an act containing indirect rebellion against his supremacy?

The theologian of Wittemberg afterwards shows how man is saved from this wretchedness. "The apostle," says he, "calls you to contemplate the Son of God on the right hand of his Father, as a powerful Mediator who intercedes for us; and he asks you to be assured that your sins are forgiven, and that you are accounted righteous, and received by the Father for the sake of his Son, offered as a victim on the cross."[2]

What makes this first edition of the *Common Places* particularly remarkable, is the manner in which the theologian of Germany speaks of free will. He perceives, perhaps, still more clearly than Luther had done, being more of a theologian than he, that this doctrine could not be separated from that which constituted the essence of the Reformation. The justification of man, before God, proceeds only from faith: this is the first point. This faith is produced in man's heart only by the grace of God: this is the second point. Melancthon is well aware that, by conceding to man any natural ability to believe, the great doctrine of grace established in the first point, will be destroyed in the second. He had too much discrimination and knowledge of the Scriptures to be mistaken in so weighty a matter. But he went too far. Instead of confining himself within the limits of the religious question, he takes up the metaphysical question, maintaining a fatalism

---

[1] *Loci communes theologici.* Basil, 1521, p. 35. This edition is very rare. For latter revisions, see the edition of Erlangen, 1828, formed in that of Bale, 1561.

[2] Vult te intueri Filium Dei sedentem ad dextram Patris, mediatorem interpellatem, pro nobis. (Ibid.) He wishes them to contemplate the Son of God sitting the right hand of the Father as a Mediator interceding for us.

which might cause God to be regarded as the author of evil, and which, consequently, has no foundation in Scripture. "All that happens," said he, "happening necessarily according to divine predestination, it is evident that our will has no liberty."[1]

But the object which Melancthon had especially in view, was to present theology as a system of godliness. The schoolmen had frittered doctrine away until they deprived it of life. The Reformer's task, therefore, was to bring it back to life. In subsequent editions, Melancthon saw the necessity of giving a clear exposition of doctrine.[2] But the case was somewhat different in 1521. "To know Christ," said he, "is to know his benefits.. Paul, in his Epistle to the Romans, when wishing to give a summary of Christian doctrine, does not philosophise on the mystery of the Trinity, on the mode of the incarnation, on creation, action, and passion, etc. Of what, then, does he speak? Of the law— of sin—of grace. On these the knowledge of Christ depends."[3]

The publication of this system of doctrine was of inestimable service to the cause of the gospel. Calumny was refuted, and prejudice subdued. In churches, courts, and universities, Melancthon was admired for his genius, and loved for the beauties of his character. Even those who did not know the author were won to his creed by his work. Several had been repulsed by the harshness and occasional violence of Luther's language; but here was a man who, with great elegance of style, exquisite taste, admirable clearness, and the most exact method, expounded the powerful truths which had suddenly burst forth and shaken the world. The work was in general request, was read with avidity, and studied with ardour. So much meekness and modesty won all hearts. So much nobleness and force subdued them; while the upper classes of society, till then undecided, were gained by a wisdom which expressed itself in such beautiful language.

On the other hand, the enemies of the truth, whom Luther's formidable blows had not struck down, remained for some time mute and disconcerted after the appearance of Melancthon's Treatise. It told them that there was another man as worthy of their hatred as Luther. "Alas!" they exclaimed, "unhappy Germany! to what extremities must this new birth reduce you?"[4]

From 1521 to 1595, seventy-seven editions of the *Common*

[1] Quando quidem omnia quæ eveniunt, necessario eveniunt juxta divinam prædestinationem, nulla est voluntatis nostræ libertas. (Loci comm. theol. Bale, 1521, p. 35.)
[2] See in the edition of 1561, reprinted in 1829, pages 14 to 44, the chapters entitled:— De tribus personis ;—De divinitate Filii ;—De duabus naturis in Christo ;—Testimonia quod Filius sit persona ;—Testimonia refutantia Arianos ;—De discernendis proprietatibus humanæ et divinæ naturæ Christi ;—De Spiritu sancto, etc. etc.
[3] Hoc est Christum cognoscere, beneficia ejus cognoscere, etc. (ibid.) [4] Heu! infelicem hoc novo partu Germaniam! . . . Cochl.)

Places appeared, without counting translations After the Bible, it is, perhaps, the book which contributed most powerfully to the establishment of evangelical doctrine.

CHAPTER X.

Opposition—Henry VIII.—Wolsey—The Queen—Fisher—Thomas More—Luther's Books burnt—Henry attacks Luther—Presentation to the Pope—Effect on Luther—Force and violence—His book—Reply of the Bishop of Rochester—Reply by More—Step by the King.

While the "grammarian," Melancthon, was by his mild accents giving such effectual aid to Luther, men in power, hostile to the Reformer, were turning with violence against him. Escaped from the Wartburg, he had again appeared on the stage of the world, and at the news his old enemies had resumed all their rage.

Luther had been three months and a half at Wittemberg, when rumour, with all its exaggerations, brought him the news that one of the greatest kings of Christendom had risen up against him. The head of the house of the Tudors, a prince, uniting in his person the houses both of York and Lancaster, and on whose head, after torrents of blood had been shed, the red rose and the white rose were at length combined,—Henry VIII, the powerful king of England, who aspired to re-establish the ancient influence of his crown on the continent, and especially in France, had just composed a book against the poor monk of Wittemberg. In a letter to Lange, 26th June, 1522, Luther writes, "A great boast is made of a little book by the king of England." [1]

Henry VIII was then thirty-one years of age: "he was tall, strong-built, and proportioned, and had an air of authority and empire;" [2] his features expressing the vigour of his intellect. Of a vehement temper, determined to make every thing bend to the violence of his passions, and thirsting for glory, he at first concealed his faults under a kind of boisterousness common to youth, and was surrounded by flatterers who encouraged them. He often repaired with his band of favourites to the house of his chaplain, Thomas Wolsey, son of a butcher of Ipswich. This man, gifted with great abilities, of an excessive ambition, and an arro-

---

[1] Jactant libellum regis Angliæ; sed leum illum suspicor sub pelle tectum. (L. Ep. ii, p. 213.) They boast of a little book by the king of England, but I suspect a *lion* (play upon the name Lee, Henry's chaplain) hid under his skin. [2] Collier's Eccl. Hist. of Great Britain, fol. ii, p. 1.

gance which knew no bounds, being patronised by the bishop of Winchester, chancellor of the kingdom, had rapidly advanced in the favour of his master, whom he attracted to his house by the seduction of pleasures and irregularities, in which the young prince would not have ventured to indulge in his own palace. Such is the account given by Polydore Virgil, at that time the pope's sub-collector in England.[1] At these licentious meetings the chaplain outstripped the young courtiers who accompanied Henry VIII. He was seen forgetting the gravity of a minister of the altar, singing, dancing, laughing, frolicking, using obscene language, and fencing.[2] In this way he soon obtained the first place in the king's council, and governing the kingdom with absolute sway, was courted by all the princes of Christendom.

Henry, living in a round of balls, festivities, and jousts, foolishly squandered the treasures which had been slowly amassed by the avarice of his father. Magnificent tournaments succeeded each other without interruption. The king, who, in manly beauty, surpassed all the combatants,[3] invariably took the lead. If, for an instant, the contest appeared doubtful, the dexterity and strength of the prince, or the adroit policy of those opposed to him, assured him the victory, and the arena resounded with shouts of applause. The vanity of the young prince was inflated by these easy triumphs; and there was no species of success to which he did not think himself entitled to aspire. The queen was occasionally present among the spectators. Her grave figure, her downcast look, her sedate and melancholy air, contrasted with the boisterous sounds of these festivities. Henry VIII, shortly after his accession to the throne, had, for reasons of state, married Catherine of Arragon, who was five years older than himself, the widow of his brother, Arthur, and aunt to Charles V. While her husband was giving himself up to pleasure, the virtuous Catherine, with a piety truly Spanish, rose at midnight to take silent part in the prayers of the monks.[4] She threw herself upon her knees, without cushion or carpet. At five o'clock in the morning, after a short repose, she was again up: she was clad in the habit of St.

---

[1] Domi suæ voluptatum omnium sacrarium fecit, quo regem frequenter ducebat (Polyd. Virgilius, Angl. Hist. Bale, 1570, fol. p. 635.) He made his house the abode of voluptuousness, and often led the king thither. Polydore Virgil had apparently suffered from Wolsey's pride, and been hence disposed to exaggerate the misdeeds of this minister. [2] Cum illis adolescentibus una psallebat, saltabat, sermones leporis plenos habebat, ridebat, jocabatur. (Ibid.) [3] Eximia corporis forma præditus, in qua etiam regiæ majestatis augusta quædam species elucebat. (Sanderus de Schismate Anglicano, p. 4.) The work of Sanders, papal nuncio in Ireland, must be read with caution; for false and calumnious assertions are not wanting in it, as has been observed, even by Cardinal Quirini and the Roman Catholic Dr. Lingard. (See Hist. o. England, by latter, t. vi, p. 173.) [4] Surgebat media nocte ut nocturnis religiosorum precibus interesset. (Sander. p. 5.)

Francis, for she had entered the tertiary order of this saint; then, hastily covering it with royal vestments,[1] she repaired to the church at six, to the holy offices.

Two beings, living in two such different worlds, could not remain long united.

Romish piety, however, had other representatives besides Catherine, at the court of Henry VIII. John Fisher, Bishop of Rochester, on the borders of seventy, equally distinguished by his learning and the purity of his morals, was the object of general veneration. He had been the oldest counsellor of Henry VII, and the Duchess of Richmond, the grandmother of Henry VIII, when on her death-bed, had sent for Fisher and recommended to his care the youth and inexperience of her grandson. Amidst his irregularities the king long venerated the bishop as a father.

A man much younger than Fisher, a layman and lawyer, had begun to attract general attention by his genius and the nobleness of his character. He was named Thomas More, and was the son of a judge of the King's Bench. Poor, austere, indefatigable in exertion, he had endeavoured at twenty to extinguish the passions of youth, by wearing a hair shirt and subjecting himself to discipline. One day, when attending mass, being sent for by the king, he replied, that the service of God must take precedence of that of his majesty. Wolsey brought him under the notice of Henry VIII, who employed him on different embassies, and vowed to have a great affection for him. He often sent for him and conversed with him about the planets, Wolsey, and theology.

In fact, the king himself was no stranger to the Romish doctrines. It would even appear that, if Arthur had lived, Henry would have been destined to the archiepiscopal see of Canterbury. Thomas Aquinas, St. Bonaventura;[2] tournays, festivals; Elizabeth Blunt, and other mistresses besides, all mingled in the thoughts and actions of this prince, who caused masses of his own composition to be chanted in his chapel.

As soon as Henry VIII heard of Luther, his wrath was kindled against him; and scarcely was the decree of the Diet of Worms known in England, when he ordered the papal bull to be executed against the Reformer's books.[3] On the 12th May, 1521, Thomas Wolsey, who, to the office of Chancellor of England, united those of Cardinal and Roman legate, repaired to St. Paul's in solemn procession. This man, whose pride knew no bounds, thought him-

---

[1] Sub regio vesti u *Divi Francisci* habitu utebatur. (Sander., p. 5.)
[2] Legebat studiose libros divi Thomæ Aquinatis. (Polyd. Virgil, p. 634.) He studiously read the books of Thomas Aquinas. [3] Primum libros Lutheranos, quorum magens jam numerus pervenerat in manus suorum Anglorum, comburendos curavit. (Ibid. 664.) His first care was to burn Luther's books, a great number of which were in the hands of his subjects.

self the equal of kings. His chair was of gold, his bed of gold, and cloth of gold covered the table at which he dined.[1] On this occasion he displayed great pomp. The haughty prelate walked, surrounded by his household, consisting of eight hundred individuals, among whom were barons, knights, and cadets of the most distinguished families, who hoped by serving him to obtain public appointments. Gold and silk were not only conspicuous on his dress, (he was the first ecclesiastic who had ventured to clothe so sumptuously,[2]) but also on the trappings and harness of his horses. Before him a priest of a stately figure carried a rod, surrounded by a crucifix; behind him another, no less stately, carried the archiepiscopal cross of York: a nobleman walking at his side carried his cardinal's hat.[3] He was attended by nobles, prelates, ambassadors of the pope and the emperor, and these were followed by a long train of mules, carrying trunks with the richest and most splendid coverings. At London, amidst this magnificent procession, the writings of the poor monk of Wittemberg were carried to the flames. On arriving at the cathedral, the proud priest made even his cardinal's hat be placed upon the altar. The virtuous Bishop of Rochester took his station at the foot of the cross, and there, in an animated tone, inveighed against heresy. The impious writings of the heresiarch were then brought forward and devoutly burned in presence of an immense crowd. Such was the first news which England received of the Reformation.

Henry did not choose to stop here. This prince, whose sword was ever raised against his enemies, his wives, and his favourites, in a letter to the Elector Palatine thus expresses himself, "It is the devil who, by Luther as his organ, has kindled this immense conflagration. If Luther will not be converted, let the flames consume him and his writings."[4]

Even this was not enough. Henry, convinced that the progress of heresy was owing to the ignorance of the German princes, thought that the moment was come for displaying all his learning. The conquests of his battle-axe allowed him not to doubt of the conquests reserved for his pen. But another passion still—one which is always strong in little minds—vanity, spurred on the king. He felt humbled at having no title to oppose those of "Catholic" and "Most Christian," borne by the kings of Spain and France, and he was long a suppliant at the Romish court for a similar distinction. What better fitted to procure such a title than an attack upon

[1] Ut sella aurea, ut pulvino aureo, ut velo aureo ad mensam. (Ibid.)
[2] Primus episcoporum et cardinalium, vestitum exteriorem sericum sibi induit. (Ibid. p. 633.) [3] Galerum cardinalium, ordinis insignem, sublime a ministro præferebat... super altare collocabat. (Ibid. p. 645.) The cardinal's hat, the badge of his rank, was carried aloft by a servant... and placed on the altar.
[4] Knapp's Nachlese, ii, p. 458.

heresy? Henry, therefore, threw aside the royal purple, and descended from his lofty throne into the arena of theologians. He made a compilation from Thomas Aquinas, Peter Lombard, Alexander Hales, and Bonaventure, and the world beheld the publication of the *Defence of the Seven Sacraments against Martin Luther, by the most invincible King of England, France, and Ireland, Henry, Eighth of the name.*

"I will throw myself before the Church," said the King of England in this writing, "I will receive in my breast the poisoned darts of the enemy who is assailing her.[1] To this the present state of affairs calls me. Every servant of Jesus Christ, whatever be his age, rank, or sex, must bestir himself against the common enemy of Christendom.[2]

"Let us arm ourselves with double armour—with heavenly weapons, that by the arms of truth we may vanquish him who combats with the arms of error. But let us also arm ourselves with terrestrial armour, in order that, if he proves obstinate in his wickedness, the hand of the executioner may constrain him to silence; and he may thus, for once at least, be useful to the world by his exemplary punishment."[3]

Henry VIII could not conceal the contempt which he felt for his able opponent. "This man," said the crowned theologian, "seems as if he were in labour: he makes incredible efforts, but only brings forth wind.[4] Pluck off the dress of arrogant expression in which his absurdities are clothed, just as an ape is clothed in purple, and what will remain? . . . . Miserable, empty sophistry!"

The king defends, in succession, the mass, penance, confirmation, orders, and extreme unction. He spares no insulting epithets, calling his opponent by turns an infernal wolf, a venomous viper, a limb of the devil. Even Luther's honesty is assailed. Henry VIII crushes the mendicant monk with his royal anger, and, in the words of a historian, "writes as 'twere with his sceptre."[5]

Still, however, it must be admitted, the work was not bad for the author and his age. The style is not without vigour. But the public could not content themselves with merely doing it justice. A burst of applause received the theological treatise of the powerful king of England. "The most learned work that ever the sun saw,"[6] exclaimed some. "It deserves," rejoined others, "to be compared with the works of St. Augustin. He is a Constantine,

---

[1] Meque adversus venenata jacula hostis eam oppugnantis objicerem (*Assertio septem sacramentorum adv. M. Lutherum*, in prologo.) [2] Omnis Christi servus, omnis ætas, omnis sexus, omnis ordo consurgat. (Ibid.) [3] Et qui nocuit verbo malitiæ, supplicii prosit exemplo. (Ibid.) [4] Mirum est quanto nixu parturiens, quam nihil peperit, nisi merum ventum. (Ibid.) [5] Collier. Eccl. Hist. Gr. Br., p. 17. [6] Burnet, Hist. of the Ref. of England, i, p 30.

a Charlemagne." "He is more," exclaimed a third party, "he is a second Solomon!"

These exclamations were soon heard beyond the limits of England. Henry desired the Dean of Windsor, John Clarke, his ambassador to the pope, to deliver his book to the sovereign pontiff. Leo X received the ambassador in full consistory. Clarke, in presenting the royal work, said, "The king, my master, assures you that, after refuting the errors of Luther with his pen, he is ready to combat his adherents with the sword." Leo X, deeply gratified with this promise, replied that the book of the king of England could only have been composed with the aid of the Holy Spirit, and named Henry "*Defender of the Faith*," a title which the kings of England still bear.

The reception given to the king's work at Rome contributed greatly to its circulation. In a few months several thousands of copies issued from different presses.[1] "The whole Christian world," says Cochlœus, "was filled with admiration and joy."[2]

These extravagant praises increased the vanity of the Chief of the Tudors. He was brought to fancy he had written with some degree of inspiration.[3] Afterwards he would not submit to the least contradiction. To him the papacy was no longer at Rome but at Greenwich, and infallibility rested on his own head. At a later period this contributed greatly to the Reformation of England.

Luther read Henry's book with mingled disdain, impatience, and indignation. The falsehood and insults which it contained, but especially the air of contempt and pity affected by the king, irritated the doctor of Wittemberg in the highest degree. The thought that the pope had crowned the writing, and that the enemies of the Gospel were everywhere trampling on the Reformation and the Reformer, as already overthrown and vanquished, increased his indignation. Besides, what occasion had he for delicacy? Was he not fighting for a king greater than all the kings of the earth? Evangelical mildness seemed to him out of season: eye for eye, tooth for tooth. He kept no measure. Pursued, goaded, tracked, and wounded, the raging lion turned round and prepared to tear his enemy. The Elector, Spalatin, Melancthon, and Bugenhagen, tried in vain to appease him. They would have prevented him from replying, but he was not to be stopped. "I will not deal mildly with the King of England;" said he, "it is in vain, (I know it is,) to humble myself, to yield, beseech, and try the ways of peace. I will at length show myself more terrible than the ferocious beasts who are constantly butting me with their horns. I will

[1] Intra paucos menses, liber ejus a multis chalcographis in multa millia multiplicatus. (Cochlœus, p. 44.) [2] Ut totum orbem christianum et gaudio et admiratione repleverit. (Ibid.) [3] Burnet's Preface.

let them feel mine: I will preach and irritate Satan until he wears himself out, and falls down exhausted."[1] If this heretic retracts not, says the new Thomas, Henry VIII, he must be burnt. Such are the weapons now employed against me: first, the fury of stupid asses and Thomastical swine, and then the fire.[2] Very well! Let these swine come forward, if they dare, and burn me! Here I am, waiting for them. My wish is, that my ashes, thrown after my death into a thousand seas, may arise, pursue, and engulph this abominable crew. Living, I will be the enemy of the papacy: burnt, I will be its destruction! Go, swine of St. Thomas, do what seemeth to you good. You shall ever find Luther as a bear in your way, and a lion in your path. He will thunder upon you from all quarters, and leave you no peace until he has brayed your brains of iron, and ground to powder your foreheads of brass."

At the outset Luther upbraids Henry VIII with having based his doctrines only on the decrees and sentences of men. "For me," says he, "I cease not to cry, the Gospel! the Gospel!—Christ! Christ! while my opponents cease not to reply—Customs! Customs!—Ordinances! Ordinances!—Fathers! Fathers! "*Let your faith*," says St. Paul, "*stand not in the wisdom of men, but in the power of God.*" And the apostle, by this thunderbolt from heaven, overthrows and scatters, like the dust before the wind, all the silly crotchets of this Henry. In confusion and consternation the Thomists, the papists, and the Henrys fell to the ground, before the thunder of these words."[3]

He afterwards refutes the king's production in detail, overthrowing his arguments, one by one, with clearness, ability, and a thorough knowledge of the Holy Scriptures and the history of the Church, but also with a confidence, disdain, and occasionally a violence at which we must not be surprised.

On arriving at the conclusion, Luther again expresses indignation at his opponent for drawing arguments only from the fathers: this was the essence of the whole controversy. "To all the sayings of fathers, men, angels, devils," says he, "I oppose not the antiquity of custom, not the multitude, but the Word of the Eternal Majesty, the Gospel, which they themselves are constrained to approve. By it I hold; on it I rest; in it I glory, triumph, and exult over papists, Thomists, Henrys, and all the hellish stye.[4] The King

---

[1] Mea in ipsos exercebo cornua, irriturus Satanam, donec effusis viribus et conatibus corruat in se ipso. (L. Ep. ii, p. 236.) [2] Ignis et furor insulsissimorum asinorum et Thomisticorum porcorum. (Contra Henricum Regem. Op. (L.) ii, p. 331.) This tract occasionally reminds us of the great agitator of Ireland, only there is more strength and mildness in the orator of the sixteenth than in that of the nineteenth century. (See the British Critic, Nov. 1835, Art. Reign of O'Connell.) "Soaped swine of civilised society," etc., p. 30. [3] Confusi et prostrati jacent a facie verborum istius tonitrui. (Contra Henricum regem. Op. (L.) ii, p. 336.
[4] Hic sto, hic sedeo, hic maneo, hic glorior, hic triumpho, hic insulto papistis ..

of Heaven is with me, and therefore I fear nothing even should a thousand Augustins, a thousand Cyprians, and a thousand churches, of which Henry is the defender, rise up against me. It is a small matter for me to despise and lash an earthly king who himself has not feared, in his writing, to blaspheme the King of Heaven and profane his holiness by the most audacious falsehood.[2]

"Papists," exclaims he, in concluding, "will you not desist from your vain pursuits? Do as you please: the result, however, must be, that before the Gospel which I, Martin Luther, have preached, popes, bishops, priests, monks, princes, devils, death, sin, and whatever is not Jesus Christ, or in Jesus Christ, shall fall and perish."[3]

Thus spoke the poor monk. His violence, certainly, cannot be excused, if it is judged by the rule to which he himself appeals, viz., the Word of God. We cannot even justify it by alleging either the coarseness of the age—for Melancthon was able to discover his courtesy in his writings—or the energy of his disposition, for, if this energy had some effect on his language, passion had still more. The best course, therefore, is not to attempt to defend it. However, to be just, let it be observed, that in the sixteenth century this violence did not seem so strange as it appears in the present day. The learned were then one of the existing powers as well as princes. Henry had attacked Luther by becoming an author. Luther replied conformably to the law received in the Republic of Letters, viz., that the thing to be considered is the truth of what is said, and not the quality of him who says it. Let us also add, that when this very king turned against the pope, the insults which he received from the Romish writers, and the pope himself, far exceeded anything that had been said by Luther.

Besides, if Luther called doctor Eck an ass, and Henry VIII a hog, he indignantly rejected the intervention of the secular arm, whereas Dr. Eck wrote a dissertation to prove that heretics ought to be burned: and Henry erected scaffolds agreeably to the precepts of the doctor of Ingolstadt.

A deep sensation was produced at the king's court. Surrey, Wolsey, and the tribe of courtiers broke off the pomps and festivities of Greenwich, to vent their indignation in contumely and sarcasm. The venerable bishop of Rochester, who had been delighted when he saw the young prince, who had been early committed to his charge, breaking a lance for the Church, was deeply wounded by the monk's attack, and immediately replied to it. His words are very characteristic of his time and his Church.

(Contra Henricum regem. Op. (L.) ii, p. 342.) Here I stand, here I sit, here I remain, here I glory, here I triumph, here I trample on the papists.
[1] Nec magnum si ego regem terræ contemno. (Ibid., p. 344, verso.) [2] L. Op Leipz. xviii, p. 209.

"Catch for us the small foxes that spoil the vines, says Christ in the Song of Songs. This shows," says Fisher, "that we must lay hands on heretics before they grow up. Now Luther has become a great fox,—a fox so old, and cunning, and malicious, that it is very difficult to catch him. What do I say? a fox! .... he is a mad dog, a ravening wolf, a cruel bear, or rather all these animals at once ; for the monster has several beasts in his bosom."[1]

Thomas More also descended into the arena to encounter the monk of Wittemberg. Although a layman, he pushed his zeal against the Reformation the length of fanaticism, if he did not push it the length of blood. When young noblemen undertake the defence of the papacy, their violence often outstrips that of ecclesiastics themselves. "Reverend brother, father, drunkard, deserter of the Augustin order, mi shapen bacchanalian as to both kinds of law, untaught teacher of sacred theology."[2] Such are the terms addressed to the Reformer by one of the most illustrious men of his time. Then explaining the mode in which Luther has composed his book against Henry, he says, "He called together his companions, and asked each to go his way, and rummage for buffoonery and insult. One went to waggoners and boatmen, another to baths and gambling houses, a third to barbers' shops and taverns, a fourth to mills and brothels. Every thing they heard most insolent, filthy, and infamous, they noted down, and bringing it back, threw it into that impure sink called the mind of Luther." "If he retracts his lies and calumnies," he continues, "if he lays aside his folly and fury, if he again swallows his abominations,[3] he will find some one to debate gravely with him. But if he continues as he has begun, jesting, raging, playing the mountebank, slandering, vomiting nothing but filth,[4] .... then let others do as they will; for us, we prefer leaving the little friar alone with his fury and his filth."[5] Thomas More had better have reserved his own. Luther had never stooped so low in his style. He made no reply.

This production increased Henry's attachment to More. He once paid him a visit in his modest dwelling at Chelsea. After dinner, the king walked with him in his garden, with his arm resting on the shoulder of his favourite, while Lady More and her children, concealed behind the lattice, could not withdraw their astonished eyes. After one of these walks, More, who knew Henry's character,

[1] Canem dixissem rabidum, imo lupum rapacissimum, aut sævissimam quamdam ursam. (Cochlœus, p. 60.) [2] Reverendus frater, pater, potator, Lutherus. (Ibid., p. 61.) [3] Si .... suas resorbeat et sua relinquat stercora. (Ibid., p. 62.) [4] Sentinas, cloacas, latrinas .... stercora. (Ibid., p. 63.) [5] Cum suis .... et stercoribus .... relinquere. (Ibid., p. 62.) Cochlœus quotes these passages exultingly, as being, to his taste, the finest in Sir Thomas More's production. M. Nisard, on the contrary, in his work on More, whose apology he makes with so much warmth and learning, admits "that the filth inspired by the passion of the Catholic is such as to render translation impossible." (Revue des deux Mondes, v, p. 592.)

said to his wife, "If my head could gain him a single castle in France, he would never hesitate."

The king, thus defended by the Bishop of Rochester and his future chancellor, had no occasion to resume his pen. Confounded at seeing himself treated in the face of Europe as a mere author, Henry abandoned the dangerous position he had taken up, and throwing away his theological pen, had recourse to the more efficacious methods of diplomacy.

An ambassador set off from the court at Greenwich with a letter from the king to the Elector and the Dukes of Saxony. Henry thus expressed himself: "Luther, the true dragon fallen from heaven, is pouring out his venomous floods on the earth. He is stirring up revolt in the Church of Jesus Christ, abolishing the laws, insulting the powers, exciting laymen against priests, laymen and priests against the pope, and subjects against kings, his only wish being to see Christians fighting together and destroying each other, and the enemies of our faith grinning with delight over the scene of carnage.[1]

"What is this doctrine which he terms evangelical but the doctrine of Wickliffe? Now, most honoured uncles, I know what your ancestors did to destroy it. They pursued it in Bohemia as if it had been a wild beast, and causing it to fall into a trap, there enclosed and barricaded it. You will not allow it to escape by your negligence, steal into Saxony, and take possession of all Germany, sending forth from its fuming nostrils the fire of hell, and spreading far and wide the conflagration which your country so often desired to extinguish in its blood.[2]

"Wherefore, most excellent friends, I feel myself called to exhort you, and even to implore you by all that is most sacred, speedily to strangle the cursed sect of Luther. Put no one to death if it can possibly be avoided; but if heretical obstinacy continues, shed blood without fear in order that this abominable sect may cease from under heaven."[3]

The Elector and his brother referred the king to the future Council. Thus Henry was far from succeeding in his object. "So great a man mingling in the dispute," says Paul Sarpi, "served to excite more curiosity and procure universal favour for Luther, as usually happens in combats and tournays, where the spectators always incline to the weakest party, and take pleasure in giving a higher place to his humble exploits.

[1] So ergiest er, gleich wie eine Schlang vom Himmel geworfen. (L. Op. xviii, p. 212.) The original is in Latin—Velut a cœlo dejectus serpens, virus effundit in terras.
[2] Und durch sein schädlich Anblasen das höllische Feuer aussprühe. (Ibid., p. 213.)
[3] Oder aber auch mit Blut vergiessen. (Ibid.) [4] History of the Council of Trent, pp. 15, 16.

CHAP. XI

General Movement—The Monks—How the Reformation is Accomplished—Ordinary Believers—The Old and the New Teachers—Printing and Literature—Booksellers and Hawkers.

In fact, an immense movement was taking place. The Reformation which, after the Diet of Worms was supposed to be shut up with its first teacher within the narrow chamber of a strong castle, burst forth, spreading throughout the empire, and even throughout Christendom. The two parties, till then confounded, began to stand apart from each other, and the partisans of a monk who had nothing on his side but his eloquence, fearlessly took up their position confronting the servants of Charles V, and Leo X. Luther had just quitted the walls of the Wartburg, the pope had excommunicated all who had adhered to him, the imperial diet had condemned his doctrine, princes were hastening to crush it in the greater part of the Germanic States, the ministers of Rome were tearing it to pieces before the people by their violent invectives, the other states of Christendom were calling upon Germany to sacrifice an enemy, whose attacks they dreaded even at a distance; and yet this new and not numerous party, without organisation, without connecting ties, with nothing, in short, to concentrate the common strength, had already, by the energy of their faith and the rapidity of their conquests, spread terror over the vast, ancient, and mighty domain of Rome. Every where, as in the first breathings of Spring, the seed was seen bursting forth from the ground without effort, and, as it were, spontaneously. Every day gave evidence of new progress. Individuals, villages, burghs, whole towns, united in the new confession of the name of Jesus Christ. There was stern resistance and dreadful persecution; but the mysterious power which urged forward the people was irresistible, and the persecuted hastening on and advancing, amid exile, imprisonment, and scaffolds, were every where succeeding against the persecutors.

The monastic orders, which Rome had stretched over Christendom, like a net destined to take souls and hold them captive, were the first to break these bonds, and rapidly propagate the new doctrine throughout the Western Church. The Augustins of Saxony had advanced with Luther, having, like him, that intimate experience of the divine Word which gives an interest in God himself, and so dispenses with Rome and her arrogant pretensions. But in the other convents of the order, evangelical light had also arisen. Sometimes it was old men who, like Staupitz, had preserved the sound doctrines of truth in the bosom of ill-used Christendom, and were now asking God to let them depart in peace because their eyes had seen his salvation. At other times, it was young men who, with all the eagerness of early life, had received the lessons of Luther. At Nuremberg, Osnabruck, Dettingen, Ratisbon, Hesse, Wurtemberg, Strasburg, Antwerp, the Augustin convents turned towards Christ, and by their courage provoked the wrath of Rome.

But the movement was not confined to the Augustins. They were imitated in the monasteries of the other orders by bold individuals, who, in spite of the clamour of such monks as were unwilling to abandon their carnal observances, in spite of wrath, contempt, and sentences of condemnation, in spite of discipline and cloistral prisons, fearlessly raised their voice for this holy and precious truth, which, after so many painful searches, so many distressing doubts, so many internal struggles, they had found at last. In the greater part of the cloisters, the most spiritually minded, the most pious and best informed of the inmates declared in favour of Reform. In the Franciscan convent at Ulm, Eberlin and Kettenbach attacked the servile works of monachism, and the superstitious practices of the Church, with an eloquence which might have carried a nation, calling, in one breath, for the suppression of the abodes of monks and the abodes of debauchery. Stephen Kemp, another Franciscan, standing alone, preached the gospel at Hamburg, and with undaunted breast, withstood the hatred, envy, menaces, snares, and attacks of priests, irritated when they saw the people forsaking their altars and crowding with enthusiasm to his sermons.[1]

Often even the heads of convents were the first to move in the direction of Reform. At Halberstadt, Neuenwerk, Halle, and Sagan, the priors set their monks the example, or at least declared that if any monk felt his conscience burdened by monastic vows, so far from detaining him in the convent, they would take him on their shoulders to carry him out.[2]

In fact, throughout Germany, monks were seen depositing their frocks and cowls at the door of their monastery. Some were expelled by the violence of the friars or abbots; others of a mild and pacific character could not endure the disputes which were perpetually springing up, the insult, clamour, and hatred which pursued them even in their sleep. The majority were convinced that the monastic life was opposed to the will of God and the Christian life. Some had arrived gradually at this conviction, and others

---

[1] Der ubrigen Prediger Feindschafft, Neid, Nachstellungen, Pratlcken und Schrecken. (Seckendorff, p. 457.) [2] Ibid., p. 811. Stentzel. Script. Rer. Siles, i, p. 457

all at once while reading some passage of the Bible. Idleness, coarseness, ignorance, and meanness, the essential characteristics of the mendicant orders, produced ineffable disgust in men of an exalted spirit, who felt it impossible any longer to endure the company of their vulgar associates. A Franciscan begging his round presented himself one day, with his box in his hand, at a smithy in Nuremberg, "Why," said the smith to him, "do you not rather gain your bread by working with your own hands? At these words the sturdy monk threw away his dress, and seizing the hammer with a vigorous hand, made it fall with force on the anvil. The useless mendicant had become an honest mechanic. His box and frock were sent back to the monastery.[1]

Nor were monks the only persons who ranged themselves under the standard of the gospel; priests in still greater numbers preached the new doctrine. But it did not even need preachers to diffuse it: it often acted on the minds of men, and awoke them from their deep sleep before any one had addressed them.

In towns, burghs, and even villages, Luther's writings were read in the evening at the fireside, or in the house of the schoolmaster. Some of the inhabitants were struck by this reading; they applied to the Bible to clear up their doubts, and were astonished when they saw the strange contrast between their Christianity and the Christianity of the Bible. Hesitating for a time between Rome and the Holy Scriptures, they took refuge in that living word which shed a sudden and delightful light on their souls. Meanwhile, some evangelical preacher appeared, perhaps a priest, perhaps a monk. He spoke with eloquence and conviction;[2] he declared that Christ had satisfied fully for the sins of the people, proving from Scripture the vanity of human works and penances. A formidable opposition burst forth. The clergy and frequently the magistrates used every effort to bring back those souls which they would have destroyed; but there was in the new preaching an accordance with Scripture, and a hidden energy which won men's hearts, subduing the most rebellious. At the risk of their goods, or, if need were, at the risk of their lives, they embraced the cause of the gospel, and abandoned the barren, fanatical orators of the papacy.[3] Sometimes the people irritated at being so long imposed upon compelled the priests to withdraw, but more frequently the priests, abandoned by their flocks, without tithes, without offerings, went off in sadness, of their own accord, to go and seek a living else-

---

[1] Ranke Deutsche Geschichte, ii, p. 70. [2] Eaque omnia prompte, alacriter, eloquenter (Cochlœus. p. 52.) [3] Populo odibiles catholici concionatores. (Ibid.) The catholic preachers were odious to the people.

where.[1] And while the props of the ancient hierarchy withdrew sullen and downcast, sometimes taking leave of their old flocks in words of malediction, the people overjoyed at having found truth and liberty, gathered round the new preachers with acclamation, and eager to hear the word, carried them, as it were, in triumph into the church and the pulpit.[2]

A powerful doctrine which came from God was then renovating society. The people or their leaders frequently wrote for some man of known faith to come and enlighten them, and he, for the love of the gospel, forthwith abandoned all—family, friends, and country.[3] Persecution often forced the friends of the Reformation to quit their homes. Arriving in some place where it was not yet known, finding some house which offered an asylum to poor travellers, they spoke of the gospel, read some pages of it to the attentive burghers, and obtained leave, perhaps at the request of their new friends, to preach one sermon in the church. Then a vast conflagration burst forth in the town, and the utmost efforts were unable to extinguish it.[4] If permission to preach in the church was denied, they preached elsewhere. Every place became a church. At Husum in Holstein, Herman Tast, who was on his way from Wittemberg, and against whom the parish clergy had shut the church, preached to an immense crowd in the burying-ground, under the shade of two large trees, not far from the spot where, seven centuries before, Anschar had proclaimed the gospel to the pagans. At Arnstadt, the Augustin, Gaspard Güttel, preached in the market place. At Dantzig, the gospel was preached on a hill in the neighbourhood of the town. At Gosslar, a student of Wittemberg preached the new doctrine in a grove of linden trees, a circumstance which procured for the evangelical Christians the name of *Linden Brothers.*

While the priests were exhibiting in the eyes of the people a sordid avidity, the new preachers thus addressed them—"We received it freely, and we give it to you freely."[5] An idea often proclaimed from the pulpit by the new preachers, viz., that Rome had, of old, sent the Germans a corrupted gospel, and that Germany was now, for the first time, hearing the Word of Jesus Christ in its divine and primitive beauty, produced a profound impression.[1] The great idea of the equality of all men, and of an

[1] Ad extremam redacti inopiam, aliunde sibi victum quærere cogerentur. (Cochlœus, p. 53.) Being reduced to extreme want they were obliged to seek their living elsewhere. [2] Triumphantibus novis prædicatoribus, qui sequacem populum verbo novi Evangelii sui ducebant. (Ibid.) To the exultation of the new preachers who drew the people after them by the preaching of the new gospel. [3] Multi, omissa re domestica, in speciem veri Evangelii, parentes et amicos relinquebant. (Ibid.) Many abandoning their domestic affairs for a show of the true gospel forsook their parents and friends. [4] Ubi vero aliquos nacti fuissent amicos in ea civitate. (Ibid., p. 54.) When they had found some friends in that city. [5] Mira eis erat liberalitas. (Ibid., p. 53.) Their liberality was wonderful.

universal brotherhood in Jesus Christ, enraptured those who had long been weighed down under the yoke of feudalism and the papacy of the middle ages.[2]

Often unlettered Christians, with the New Testament in their hands, offered to defend the Reformed doctrine. The Catholics, adhering to Rome, withdrew in alarm; for the business of studying the Holy Scriptures was committed to priests and monks only. These accordingly saw themselves obliged to come forward. A discussion commenced, but the priests and monks, overwhelmed by laymen with quotations from the Holy Scriptures, soon knew not what to oppose to them.[3] . . . . "Unfortunately," says Cochlœus, "Luther had persuaded his followers that faith was to be given only to the oracle of the sacred books." A shout arose in the assembly, and proclaimed the shameful ignorance of these old theologians, who, till then, had passed with their party for men of learning.[4]

The humblest individuals, even the weaker sex, with the help of the Word, persuaded and gained converts. Extraordinary acts are done in extraordinary times. At Ingolstadt, under the very eyes of Doctor Eck, a young weaver read the writings of Luther to the assembled multitude. In the same place, the university having resolved to force a retractation from a pupil of Melancthon, a female, named Argula of Staufen, undertook his defence, and challenged the professors to a public disputation. Women and children, artisans and soldiers, were more learned in the Bible than teachers in schools, and priests at altars.

Christendom was divided into two camps, whose appearance presented a striking contrast. Confronting the old supporters of the hierarchy, who had neglected the acquisition of languages and the cultivation of letters (this is the account given by one of themselves), stood a generous youth, accustomed to study, deeply read in the Scriptures, and familiar with the masterpieces of antiquity.[5] Gifted with a ready understanding, an elevated mind, and an intrepid heart, these youths soon acquired such knowledge, that for a long time none could compete with them. Their superiority to their contemporaries consisted, not merely in their living faith, but also in an elegance of style, a savour of antiquity, a true philosophy, a knowledge of the world, completely unknown to the

---

[1] Eam usque diem nunquam germane prædicatam. (Coch. p. 53.) That till that day it never had been preached in Germany. [2] Omnes æquales et fratres in Christo. (Ibid.) [3] A laicis Lutheranis, plures scripturæ locos, quam a monachis et presbyteris. (Ibid. p. 54.) More passages of Scripture were quoted by Lutheran laics than by monks and presbyters. [4] Reputabantur Catholici ab illis ignari Scripturarum. (Ibid.) The Catholics were reported by them to be ignorant of the Scriptures. [5] Totam vero juventutem, eloquentiæ litteris, linguarumque studio deditam . . . . in partem suam traxit. (Ibid.) All the youth devoted to eloquence, literature, and the study of languages, he drew over to his party.

theologians, *veteris farinæ*, (of the old stock) as Cochlœus himself designates them. Accordingly, when these young defenders of the Reformation happened to come in contact, at some public meeting, with the Roman doctors, they attacked them with so much ease and confidence, that the illiterate doctors hesitated, became confused, and fell, deservedly, into universal contempt.

The ancient edifice gave way under the weight of superstition and ignorance, and the new edifice was reared up on the basis of faith and knowledge. New elements were introduced into common life. Lethargy and stupidity were every where succeeded by a spirit of inquiry and thirst for instruction. An active, enlightened, and living faith took the place of superstitious observances and ascetic contemplation. Devout works succeeded devotee practices and penances. The pulpit was preferred to the ceremonies of the altar, and the ancient and sovereign authority of the Word of God was again established in the Church.

Printing, that mighty engine which the fifteenth century had invented, seconded all these efforts, and by means of its powerful projectiles, was continually making breaches in the walls of the enemy.

In Germany an immense impulse was given to popular literature. Up to 1517, only thirty-five publications had appeared; but the number increased with astonishing rapidity after the publication of Luther's theses. In 1518, we find seventy-one different works; in 1519, a hundred and eleven; in 1520, two hundred and eight; in 1521, two hundred and eleven; in 1522, three hundred and forty-seven; in 1523, four hundred and ninety-eight. . . And where were all these published? Almost invariably at Wittemberg. And who was their author? Most frequently, Luther. In 1522, two hundred and thirty writings of the Reformer appeared; and, in the following year, one hundred and eighty-three. This same year, the whole of the Catholic publications amounted only to twenty.[1] The literature of Germany was thus formed at the same time as its religion, amidst contention; and already gave promise of being learned, profound, bold, and active, as it has since appeared. The national mind was thus displayed, for the first time, in an unsophisticated form, and at the very moment of its birth was baptised with the fire of Christian enthusiasm.

What Luther and his friends composed, others disseminated. Monks, convinced of the unlawfulness of monastic ties, desirous to substitute a life of activity for long idleness, but too ignorant to be themselves preachers of the Word, traversed the provinces, and

[1] Panzer's Annalen der Deutsch. Litt.—Ranke's Deutsch Gesch. ii, p. 79.

visited the hamlets and huts, selling the works of Luther and his friends. Germany was soon covered with these bold *colporteurs*.[1] Printers and booksellers eagerly received all the writings in defence of the Reformation, but declined those of the opposite party, which were usually a mere compound of ignorance and barbarism.[2] When any one of them ventured to sell a book in favour of the papacy, and to expose it at fairs, at Frankfort, or elsewhere, dealers, purchasers, or literary men, assailed him with a shower of derision and sarcasm.[3] In vain had the emperor and the princes issued severe edicts against the writings of the Reformers. Whenever an inquisitorial visit was to be made, the merchants, who had secret notice of it, concealed the books which were proscribed; and the people, always eager for what is sought to be kept from them, afterwards got possession of these writings, and read them more greedily than before. These things were not confined to Germany. Luther's writings were translated into French, Spanish, English, and Italian, and disseminated among these nations.

CHAP. XII.

Luther at Zwickau—The Castle of Freyberg—Worms—Frankfort—Universal movement—Wittemberg, the centre of the Reformation—Luther's sentiments.

If the humblest individuals inflicted such heavy blows on Rome, what must it have been, when the monk of Wittemberg made his own voice be heard? Shortly after the defeat of the new prophets, Luther, dressed as a layman, crossed the territory of Duke George in a car. His frock was concealed, and his appearance was that of an ordinary citizen of the country. Had he been recognised, or had he fallen into the hands of the angry duke, perhaps it would have been all over with him. He was going to preach at Zwickau, the cradle of the new prophets. No sooner was this known at Schneeberg, Annaberg, and the neighbourhood, than crowds began to flock to it. Fourteen thousand persons arrived in the town, and as there was no church capable of containing such a multitude, Luther got up on the balcony of the town-house, and preached to an audience of twenty-five thousand, who covered the public square,

---

[1] Apostatarum, monasteriis relictis, infinitus jam erat numerus, in speciem bibliopolarum. (Cochlœus, p. 54.) An infinite number of apostates who had left their monasteries, now appeared in the form of booksellers.   [2] Catholicorum, velut indocta et veteris barbariei trivialia scripta, contemnebant. (Ibid.) They despised the writings of the Catholics as unlearned, or filled with the trifles of ancient barbarism.
[3] In publicis mercatibus Francofordiæ et alibi, vexabantur ac ridebantur. (Ibid.)

some of them seated on a heap of building materials, which happened to have been laid down.[1] The servant of Christ was speaking with fervour on the election of grace, when suddenly some cries were heard from the middle of the audience. An old woman, with haggard looks, was stretching out her bony arms from the top of the stone on which she stood, and seemed desirous, by her earnest gesture, to keep back the crowd, who were going to throw themselves at the feet of Jesus Christ. Her wild cries interrupted the preacher. Seckendorff says, "It was the devil in the shape of an old woman, trying to excite a disturbance."[2] But it was in vain: the voice of the Reformer having silenced the evil spirit, thousands of hearers were seized with a feeling of enthusiasm, exchanging looks, and shaking hands with each other. The monks, struck dumb, could not quell the storm, and shortly saw themselves obliged to quit Zwickau.

Duke Henry, the brother of Duke George, was residing in the castle of Freyberg. He was married to a princess of Mecklenburg, who, the year before, had given him a son, named Maurice. To a love of the table and pleasure, Henry joined the bluntness and rudeness of a soldier. He was, moreover, pious, after the fashion of the times, and had made one pilgrimage to the Holy Land, and another to St. James of Compostella. "At Compostella," he was wont to say, "I placed a hundred gold florins on the altar of the saint, saying to him, O! St. James, it was to please you I came hither; I make you a present of this money: but if those rogues (the priests) take it from you, I cannot help it: look then to yourself."[1]

A Franciscan and a Dominican, disciples of Luther, had for some time been preaching the gospel at Freyberg. The duchess, whose piety had inspired her with a horror at heresy, listened to their discourses, wondering how that sweet doctrine of a Saviour could be the doctrine which she had been made to dread so much. Her eyes were gradually opened, and she found peace in Jesus Christ. No sooner did it reach the ears of Duke George, that the gospel was preached at Freyberg, than he prayed his brother to set his face against these novelties. Chancellor Strehlin and the canons seconded him with their fanaticism. There was a great explosion at the court of Freyberg. Duke Henry harshly reprimanded and upbraided the pious duchess, who, on more than one occasion, shed tears over the cradle of her child. Her prayers and gentleness gradually won the duke's heart; the harshness of his nature was

[1] Von dem Rathhaus unter einem Zulauf von 25,000 Menschen. (Seck., p. 539.)
[2] Der Teufel indem er sich in Gestalt eines altes Weibes .... (Ibid.) [3] Lasst dir's die Buben nehmen .... (Ibid., p. 430)

softened; and complete harmony was established between the spouses, who could now pray together beside their son. A great destiny was reserved for this child; from this cradle, over which a Christian mother had so often poured forth her griefs, God was one day to bring forth the defender of the Reformation.

The inhabitants of Worms had been deeply moved by Luther's intrepidity. The magistrates durst not contravene the imperial decree, and all the churches were shut; but in an open space, covered with an immense assemblage, a preacher from a pulpit of rude construction preached the gospel with power. If the authorities made their appearance, the crowd dispersed in a moment, secretly carrying off the pulpit; but, when the storm blew over, it was immediately erected in some more distant spot, whither the crowd again flocked to hear the Word of Christ. This temporary pulpit was daily carried from place to place, and served to confirm the people in the impression which they had received from the grand scene at the Diet.[1]

In one of the free towns of the empire, Frankfort on the Maine, the greatest agitation prevailed. Ibach, a courageous evangelist, was there preaching salvation by Jesus Christ. The clergy, of whom Cochlœus, so well known by his writings and his hatred, was one, enraged at this audacious colleague, denounced him to the Archbishop of Mentz. The council, though timid, tried to defend him, but in vain: he was deposed by the clergy and banished. Rome triumphed, and all seemed lost. The faithful in humble life thought themselves for ever deprived of the Word. But at the moment when the citizens seemed disposed to yield to those tyrannical priests, several of the nobility declared in favour of the gospel. Max of Molnheim, Harmuth of Cronberg, George of Stockheim, Emerick of Reiffenstein, whose estates were in the neighbourhood of Frankfort, wrote to the council, "We are constrained to oppose these wolves." In an address to the clergy, they say, "Embrace the evangelical doctrine, recal Ibach, or we will withhold our tithes . . ."

The people who relished the Reformed doctrine were emboldened by this language of the nobles; and, one day, when Peter Mayer, the priest most opposed to the Reformation and the persecutor of Ibach, was going to preach against the heretics, a great tumult suddenly arose. Mayer took fright, and rushed out of the church. This commotion decided the Council, who issued an order enjoining all preachers simply to preach the Word of God, or quit the town.

The light which had radiated from Wittemberg as its centre, was thus diffused over the whole empire. In the west,—the dis-

[1] So Hessen sie eine Canzel machen, die man von einem Ort zum andern . . . . Seck., p. 436.

tricts of Berg, Cleves, Lippstadt, Munster, Wesel, Miltenberg, Mentz, Deux-Ponts, and Strasburgh, heard the gospel. In the south,—Hof, Schlesstadt, Bamberg, Esslingen, Hall in Suabia, Heilbronn, Augsburg, Ulm, and may other places hailed it with joy. In the east,—the duchy of Liegnitz, Prussia, and Pomerania opened their gates to it. In the north,—Brunswick, Halberstadt, Gosslar, Zell, Friesland, Bremen, Hamburgh, Holstein, and even Denmark and other neighbouring countries were moved at the sound of the new doctrine.

The Elector had declared that he would give the bishops full liberty to preach in his States, but that he would not deliver any person up to them. Accordingly the evangelical preachers, persecuted in other countries, soon began to take refuge in Saxony. Ibach of Frankfort, Eberlin of Ulm, Kauxdorf of Magdeburg, Valentine Musteus, whom the canons of Halberstadt had horribly mutilated,[1] and other faithful ministers from all parts of Germany, flocked to Wittemberg as the only asylum in which they could feel secure. There, by intercourse with the Reformers, they had their own faith strengthened, and communicated the results of their experience and of the light which they had received; just as the water of rivers is brought back by the clouds from the boundless ocean, to feed the glaciers from which it formerly flowed into the plain.

The work, which was in course of development at Wittemberg thus composed of many different elements, was constantly becoming more and more the work of the nation—of Europe—of Christendom. This school, founded by Frederick, and animated by Luther, was the centre of the vast revolution which was renewing the Church, and imprinted on it a real and living unity, far superior to the apparent unity of Rome. The Bible reigned at Wittemberg, and its oracles were every where heard. This university, the most recent of all, had acquired, in Christendom, the rank and influence which had hitherto belonged to the ancient university of Paris. The crowds who flocked to it from every part of Europe, told the wants of the Church and the nations, and, on quitting its walls, now become sacred in their eyes, carried back to the Church and to the people the word of grace, destined to cure and save the nations.

Luther, at the sight of this success, felt his courage strengthened. He saw a feeble enterprise, begun amid numerous fears and agonies, changing the face of the Christian world, and he was astonished.

---

[1] Aliquot ministri canonicorum capiunt D. Valentinum Mustæum et vinctum manibus pedibusque, injecto in ejus os freno, deferunt per trabes in inferiores cœnobii partes, ibique in cella cerevisiaria eum castrant. (Hamelmann. Hist. renati Evangelii, p. 880.) Some servants of the canons lay hold of Valentine Musteus, and, after tying his hands and feet, and gagging him, carry him on a barrow to the lower vaults of the monastery, and there, in a cell, mutilated him.

He had foreseen nothing of the kind when he first rose up against Tezel. Prostrating himself before the God whom he adored, he acknowledged that this work was His work, and he triumphed in the conviction of having gained a victory which could not again be wrested from him. "Our enemies threaten us with death," said he to the Chevalier Harmuth of Cronberg, "had they as much wisdom as they have folly, it would, on the contrary, be life that they would threaten us with. It is not mere jest or insult to threaten Christ and Christians with death, in other words, those who are the masters and the conquerors of death.[1] It is as if I were to try to frighten a man by saddling his steed and helping him to mount it. Do they not know, then, that Christ is risen from the dead? As to them, he is still lying in the sepulchre. Where do I say? In hell. But we, we know that he lives!" He was indignant at the idea of being regarded as the author of a work, in the minutest details of which, he recognised the hand of God. "Several," said he, "believe on my account; but those only are in the truth who would remain faithful, though they were to believe (which God forbid) that I had denied Jesus Christ. The true disciples believe not in Luther, but in Jesus Christ. For my own part, I care not for Luther.[2] Be he saint, or be he rogue, what is it to me? It is not him I preach, it is Christ. If the devil can take him, let him take him. But let Christ remain with us, and we shall remain also."

In fact it were vain to attempt to explain this movement by natural means. The literati, it is true, whetted their pens, and threw sharp darts at the monks and the pope: the cry of freedom, which Germany had so often raised against the tyranny of the Italians, again resounded in castles and provinces: the people rejoiced when they heard the notes of the "nightingale of Wittemberg," a pressage of the spring which was every where beginning to bud.[3] But the movement which was then taking place was not similar to that which a longing for earthly freedom produces. Those who say that the Reformation was produced by offering the property of convents to princes, marriage to priests, and liberty to the people, strangely misapprehend its nature. No doubt, a useful employment of the funds which had till then fostered the idleness of monks, no doubt marriage and liberty, both of them gifts from God, might favour the development of the Reformation, but the moving force was not there. An internal revolution was then produced in the depths of the human heart. The Christian people again learned to love, forgive, pray, suffer, and even die for

---

[1] Herren und Seigmänner des Todes. (L. Ep. ii, p. 164.) [2] Ich kenne auch selbst nicht den Luther. (Ibid., p. 168.) [3] *Wittemberger Nachtigal*, a collection of poetry by Hans Sachs, 1523.

a truth which promised repose only in heaven. The Church was transformed. Christianity burst the swathes which had so long enwrapt it, and again returned full of life to a world which had forgotten its ancient power. The hand which made the world was again at work upon it, and the gospel re-appearing amidst the nations, pursued its course in spite of the powerful and reiterated efforts of kings and priests, in the same way as the ocean, when the hand of God presses on its waves, rises calmly and majestically along the shore, while no human power is capable of arresting its progress.

BOOK TENTH.

CHAP. I.

AGITATION, REVERSES, AND PROGRESS.

(1522-1526.)

Political element—Want of Enthusiasm at Rome—Siege of Pampeluna—Courage of Inigo—Transformation—Luther and Loyola—Visions—The two principles.

The Reformation, which at first had existed only in the heart of some pious individuals, had entered the worship and life of the Church. It was natural for it to take a new step—to penetrate into civil relations and the movements of nations. Its progress was invariable from within to without. We shall now see this great revolution taking its place in the political world.

For nearly eight centuries Europe formed a vast sacerdotal state. Emperors and kings were under the patronage of popes. Though there had been in France and especially in Germany energetic resistance to audacious claims, Rome had finally succeeded, and princes had been seen acting as the docile executioners of her horrible judgments, fighting in order to secure her empire against private Christians subject to their sway, and on her account profusely shedding the blood of their people.

No assault could be made on this vast ecclesiastical state, of which the pope was the head, without powerfully affecting political relations.

At this time two great ideas agitated Germany: on the one hand, a renovation of faith was desired; on the other, a national government, in which the Germanic states should be represented, and a counterpoise thereby formed to the power of the emperors.[1]

The Elector Frederick had insisted on this at the election which had given a successor to Maximilian, and young Charles had acceded to it. A national government, consisting of the emperor

---

[1] Pfeffel. Droit Publ. de l'All., 590.—Robertson's Charles V, iii, 114.—Ranke, Deutsche Gesch.

and the representatives of the electors, and circles had in consequence been formed.

Thus Luther reformed the Church, and Frederick of Saxony reformed the state.

But while in correspondence to the religious reform, important political modifications were introduced by the heads of the nation, there was a danger that "the commonalty" might also begin to move, and, by religious and political excesses, compromise both reformations.

This violent and fanatical intrusion of the populace and certain of their leaders, which seems inevitable whenever society is shaken and transformed, failed not to be manifested in Germany at the time of which we now treat.

There were other causes besides which gave rise to these agitations.

The emperor and the pope had leagued against the Reformation, which seemed destined to fall under the blows of such mighty adversaries. Policy, interest, and ambition, prompted Charles V and Leo X to attempt its destruction. But these are poor champions against the truth. Devotedness to a cause, which is regarded as sacred, can only be overcome by counter devotedness. Now Rome, docile to the impulse of Leo X, was enthusiastic for a sonnet or a melody, but insensible to the religion of Jesus Christ. Even when visited with some less frivolous thought, instead of purifying herself and returning to the Christianity of the Apostles, she became engrossed with alliances, wars, conquests, treaties, under which she might save her provinces, while with cool disdain she left the Reformation to revive religious enthusiasm, and move forward in triumph to still nobler conquests. The enemy, whose destruction had been vowed in the cathedral of Worms, presented himself, full of courage and might: the struggle behoved to be keen; blood must flow.

Meanwhile, some of the most pressing dangers with which the Reformation was threatened seemed to diminish. One day, before the publication of the edict of Worms, young Charles, when standing at a window with his confessor, had said, putting his right hand upon his heart, "I swear that I will cause the first person, who, after the publication of my edict, will declare himself a Lutheran, to be hung at this window."[1] But ere long his zeal had become greatly cooled. His project of re-establishing the ancient glory of the holy empire had been received with coldness.[2] Dissatisfied with

---

[1] Sancte juro. . . . eum ex hac fenestra meo jussu suspensum iri. (Pallavicini, i, p. 130.) [2] Essendo tornato dalla Dieta che sua Maestà havera fatta in Wormatia escluso d'ogni conclusion buona d'ajuti e di favori che si fussi proposto d'ottenere in essa. (Instruttione al Card. Farnese. M.S. in the Bibl. Corsini, published by Ranké.)

Germany, he quitted the banks of the Rhine, proceeded to the Low Countries, and took advantage of the period of his residence there to give the monks some gratifications, which he found himself unable to grant them within the empire. Luther's works were burnt at Ghent by the hands of the executioner with all possible solemnity. More than fifty thousand spectators were present at this auto-da-fe, and the emperor himself countenanced it with an approving smile.[1] He next proceeded to Spain, when wars and troubles compelled him, for some time at least, to let Germany alone. Since the power which he claims in the empire is refused, let others pursue the heretic of Wittemberg. He is engrossed by graver cares.

In fact, Francis I, impatient to come to blows with his rival, had thrown down the gauntlet. Under the pretext of reinstating the children of John of Albert, king of Navarre, in their patrimony, he had begun a long and bloody struggle, which was to last as long as his life, by sending into that kingdom, under the command of Lesparre, an army, whose rapid conquests were not arrested till they arrived before the fortress of Pampeluna.

On these strong fortifications an enthusiasm was to be kindled, which should one day oppose the enthusiasm of the Reformer, and breathe into the papacy a new spirit of energy, devotedness, and power. Pampeluna was to be the cradle of the rival of the monk of Wittemberg.

The chivalric spirit which had so long animated the Christian world now existed only in Spain. The wars against the Moors scarcely ended in the Peninsula and still constantly renewed in Africa, distant and adventurous expeditions in foreign lands, kept alive in the Castilian youth that enthusiastic and spirited valour of which Amadis had been the *beau ideal*.

Among the defenders of Pampeluna was a young gentleman named Don Inigo Lopez of Recalde, the cadet of a family of thirteen children. Brought up at the court of Ferdinand the Catholic, Recalde, richly endowed with personal graces,[2] skilful in the use of the sword and the lance, was ardent in the pursuit of chivalric renown. To deck himself in glittering armour, to mount a noble steed,[3] to expose himself to the brilliant dangers of a tournay, to run hazardous adventures, to take part in the impassioned debates of factions,[4] and display as much devotion to St. Peter as to his mistress—such was the life of this young knight. The governor

---

[1] Ipso Cæsare, ore subridenti, spectaculo plausit. (Pallavicini, i, p. 130.)
[2] Cum esset en corporis ornatu elegantissimus. (Maffei, Vita Loyolæ, 1586, p. 3.)
[3] Equorumque et armorum usu præcelleret. (Ibid.)   [4] Partim in factionum rixarumque periculis, partim in amatoria vesania . . . tempus consumeret. (Ibid.) Spent his time partly in the perils of brawls and factions, and partly in amours.

of Navarre having gone into Spain to ask assistance, had left Pampeluna in the charge of Inigo and a few nobles. The latter, seeing the superiority of the French troops, resolved to withdraw. Inigo conjured them to make head against Lesparre. Finding that their purpose could not be shaken, he turned upon them with looks of indignation, accused them of cowardice and perfidy, and then threw himself single handed into the fortress, determined to defend it at the cost of his life.[1]

The French, who had met with an enthusiastic reception in Pampeluna, having summoned the governor of the citadel to capitulate, "Let us," said the fiery Inigo to his companions, " bear any thing sooner than surrender."[2] The French began to batter the walls with their powerful engines, and soon after attempted an assault. The Spaniards, animated by the courage and words of Inigo, repulsed the assailants with their arrows, swords, and halberts. Inigo fought at their head. Standing on the wall with blazing eye, the young knight brandishing his sword, dealt blows on the enemy. All at once a bullet struck the wall at the place where he was defending; a shivered stone severely wounded the knight in his right leg, and the shot, in rebounding, broke his left. Inigo fell insensible.[3] The garrison immediately surrendered, and the French, filled with admiration at the courage of their young opponent, caused him to be carried in a litter to his friends and parents in the Castle of Loyola. In this seignorial mansion, from which he afterwards took his name, Inigo was born, eight years after Luther, of one of the most distinguished families in the kingdom.

A painful operation had become necessary. Amidst the most acute sufferings, Inigo clenched his hands, but did not utter a single cry.[4]

Constrained to a painful repose, he behoved somehow to employ his lively fancy. In the absence of romances of chivalry, which he had hitherto been accustomed to devour, he was furnished with the Life of Christ, and the Flowers of the Saints. This reading, in his solitary and sickly condition, produced an extraordinary impression on his mind. He thought he saw the noisy life of tournaments and battles, which till then had completely engrossed his youth, withdrawn, effaced, and extinguished, and, at the same time, a more glorious career opened on his astonished sight. The humble actions of the saints and their heroic sufferings suddenly appeared to him more deserving of praise than all the feats

---

[1] Ardentibus oculis, detestatus ignaviam perfidiamque, spectantibus omnibus, in arcem solus introit. (Maffei, Vita Loyolæ, 1586, p. 6.) [2] Tam acri ac vehementi oratione commilitonibus dissuasit. (Ibid.) [3] Ut e vestigio seminanimis alienata mente corruerit. (Ibid.) [4] Nullum aliud indicium dedit doloris, nisi ut coactus in pugnum digitos valde constringeret. (Ibid.)

of chivalry. Stretched on his feverish bed, he gave himself up to the most contradictory thoughts. The world which he was abandoning, and the other whose holy macerations he was welcoming, appeared to him at the same moment, the one with its pleasures, the other with its severities. These two worlds carried on a fierce combat in his soul. "What," said he, "if I were to do what St. Francis or St. Dominic have done?"[1] Then the image of the mistress to whom he had devoted his heart presenting itself to his imagination, he exclaimed with natural vanity, "She is not a countess, she is not a duchess; but she is more."[2] But these thoughts left a feeling of bitterness and weariness, whereas his plan of imitating the saints filled him with peace and joy.

From that time his choice was fixed. When scarcely recovered, he resolved to bid adieu to the world. After having, like Luther, partaken of an entertainment with his companions in arms, he set out alone,[3] in the greatest secrecy, for the solitary abodes which the hermits of St. Benedict had hewn out in the rock in the mountains of Montserrat. Urged on, not by a conviction of his sins or the need of divine grace, but by a longing to become the "knight of Mary," and gain renown by mortifications and pious works, like all the army of the saints, he confessed during three days, gave his rich clothing to a beggar, put on sackcloth, and girded himself with a cord.[4] Then calling to mind the celebrated vigil of Amadis of Gaul, he hung up his sword before an image of Mary, and passed the night watching in his new and strange costume. Sometimes on his knees, sometimes standing, but always in prayer, and with the pilgrim's staff in his hand, he employed himself in all the devout exercises which Amadis of Gaul had of old performed. "Thus," observes the jesuit, Maffei, one of the biographers of the saint, "while Satan was arming Martin Luther against all laws, human and divine, and while this infamous heresiarch was appearing at Worms, and there declaring impious war on the apostolic see, Christ, in the exercise of his divine providence, was raising up this new champion, and binding him—him, and at a later period, all his followers, —to the service of the Roman pontiff, opposing him to the licentiousness and fury of heretical perverseness."[5]

Loyola, still lame in one leg, dragged along through winding and desert paths to Manresa, and there entered a convent of

---

[1] Quid si ego hoc agerem quod fecit b. Franciscus, quid si hoc quod b. Dominicus? (Acta Sanct., vii, p. 634.) [2] Non era condessa, ni duquessa, ma era su estado mas alto .... (Ibid.) [3] Ibi duce amicisque ita salutatis, ut arcana consiliorum suorum quam accuratissime tegeret. (Maf., p. 16.) Then having saluted his commander and friends so as most carefully to hide his secret plans. [4] Pretiosa vestimenta quibus erat ornatus, pannoso cuidam largitus, sacco sese alacer induit ac fune præcinxit. (Ibid., p. 20.) [5] Furori ac libidini hæreticæ pravitatis opponeret. (Ibid., p. 21.)

Dominicans, that he might devote himself, in this obscure spot, to the severest penances. Like Luther, he daily begged his bread from door to door.[1] He remained seven hours on his knees, and flagellated himself thrice every day ; at midnight he was again at prayer. He allowed his hair and nails to grow, and it would have been impossible to recognise the young and brilliant knight of Pampeluna in the pale wan monk of Manresa.

Meanwhile, the moment had arrived, when the religious ideas which had hitherto been to Inigo merely a sport of chivalry, were to reveal themselves to him with greater seriousness, and make him feel a power of which he was still ignorant. Suddenly, without any presentiment of what was to happen, the joy which he had hitherto experienced disappeared.[2] In vain did he apply to prayer and the singing of hymns—he could find no rest.[3] His imagination had ceased to surround him with amiable illusions: he was left alone with his conscience. He could not comprehend a state which was so novel to him; and he asked, in alarm, whether God, for whom he had made so many sacrifices, was still angry with him. Night and day terrors agitated his soul: he shed bitter tears, and with loud cries called for the peace which he had lost . . . . but all in vain.[4] He then resumed the long confession which he had made at Montserrat. "It may be," thought he, " I have forgotten something." But the confession only increased his agony, by reminding him of all his faults. He wandered gloomy and depressed : his conscience cried aloud, that during his whole life he had done nothing but heaped sin upon sin; and the unhappy man, overwhelmed with terror, made the cloister echo with his groans.

Strange thoughts then found admission into his heart. Experiencing no comfort in confession and the various ordinances of the Church,[5] he began, like Luther, to doubt their efficacy. But, instead of turning aside from human works and applying to the all-sufficient work of Christ, he asked if he ought not again to pursue worldly glory. His soul darted impetuously towards the world from which he had fled;[6] but he immediately drew back in alarm.

Was there, then, some difference between the monk of Manresa

---

[1] Victum ostiatim precibus infimis emendicare quotidie. (Maf. p. 23.) [2] Tunc subito nulla præcedente significatione prorsus exui nudarique se omni gaudio sentiret. (Ibid. p. 27. Then, suddenly, without any previous warning, he felt himself divested of all joy. [3] Nec jam in precibus, neque in psalmis, . . . ullam inveniret delectationem aut requiem. (Ibid.) Nor could he now find any delight, or rest in prayers or psalms. [4] Vanis agitari terroribus, dies noctesque fletibus jungere (Ibid. p. 28.) He was agitated by vain terrors, weeping night and day. [5] Ut nulla jam res mitigare dolorem posse videretur. (Ibid. p. 29.) That now nothing seemed able to mitigate his pain. [6] Et sæculi commodis repetendis magis quodam impetu cogitaveri*. (Ib'd. p. 30.)

and the monk of Erfurth? In secondary features, doubtless, there was, but the state of their souls was the same. Both had a deep conviction of the magnitude of their sins. Both sought reconciliation with God, and wished to have the assurance of it in their hearts. Had a Staupitz, with the Bible in his hand, presented himself at the convent of Manresa, Inigo might, perhaps, have become the Luther of the Peninsula. These two great men of the sixteenth century—these two founders of the two spiritual powers, which, for three hundred years, have been warring with each other, were at this time brethren; and, perhaps, had they met, Luther and Loyola would have fallen into each other's arms, and mingled their tears and their vows.

But these two monks were, from this moment, to follow very different paths.

Inigo, instead of perceiving that his remorse was sent to urge him to the foot of the cross, persuaded himself that these internal upbraidings came not from God, but from the devil; and adopted the resolution of thinking no more of his sins, of effacing them, and consigning them to eternal oblivion.[1] Luther turned toward Christ, Loyola only fell back upon himself.

Inigo was shortly after confirmed in the conclusion at which he had arrived, by visions. His own resolutions had been substituted for the grace of Christ, and his own imagination for the Word of Christ. The voice of God, in his conscience, he had regarded as the voice of a demon; and, accordingly, his future history exhibits him as given up to the inspirations of the spirit of darkness.

One day Loyola met an old woman, just as Luther, in the time of his agony, had been visited by an old man. But the Spanish female, instead of telling the penitent of Manresa of the remission of sins, foretold him of apparitions of Jesus. Such was the Christianity to which Loyola, like the prophets of Zwickau, had recourse. Inigo did not seek the truth in the Holy Scriptures, but in their stead imagined immediate communications from the kingdom of spirits. His life soon consisted only of extacies and contemplations.

One day, while going to the church of St. Paul, which is situated outside the town, plunged in meditation, he followed the banks of the Llobregat. At last he sat down. His eyes were fixed on the river, which was slowly rolling its deep waters at his feet, and he became completely absorbed in meditation. Suddenly he was seized with extacy: he saw, with his eyes, what men scarcely

---

[1] Sine ulla dubitatione constituit præteritæ vitæ labes perpetua oblivione conterere. (Maf. p. 31.) He unhesitatingly resolved to bury the pollutions of his past life in perpetual oblivion.

comprehend, after much reading, watching, and labour.[1] He rose up, stood on the brink of the river, and seemed to himself to become a new man: he afterwards put himself upon his knees before a cross, which happened to be in the neighbourhood, disposed to sacrifice his life in the cause, the mysteries of which had just been revealed to him.

From that time his visions became more frequent. One day, while seated on the stair of St. Dominic, at Manresa, he was singing hymns to the Holy Virgin. Suddenly his soul was seized with extacy; he remained motionless, absorbed in contemplation; the mystery of the Holy Trinity was revealed to his eyes under magnificent symbols.[2] He shed tears, sobbed aloud; and during the whole day ceased not to speak of the ineffable vision.

These numerous apparitions had dissipated all his doubts. Unlike Luther, he believed, not because the things of faith were written in the Word of God, but in consequence of the visions which he had seen. "Even though there had been no Bible," say his apologists, "even had these mysteries never been revealed in Scripture,[3] he would have believed them, for God had been unveiled to him."[4] Luther, on receiving his degree of doctor, had taken an oath to the Holy Scriptures, and the authority of the Word of God, the only infallible authority, had become the fundamental principle of the Reformation. Loyola took his oath to dreams and visions; and fantastical apparitions became the principle of his life and of his faith.

The residence of Luther in the convent of Erfurth, and that of Loyola in the convent of Manresa, explain to us respectively the Reformation and the modern papacy. We shall not follow the monk who was to re-animate the exhausted powers of Rome to Jerusalem, whither he repaired on quitting the cloister. We shall meet with him again in the course of this history.

CHAP. II.

Victory of the Pope—Death of Leo X—Oratory of Divine Love—Adrian VI—Sch of Reform—Opposition.

While these things were passing in Spain, Rome herself seemed to assume a more serious character. The great patron of music,

---

[1] Quæ vix demum solent homines intelligentia comprehendere. (Maf. p. 32.)
[2] En figuras de tres teclas.   [3] Quod etsi nulla scriptura, mysteria illa fidei doceret. (Acta Sancta.) For, were there no scripture, he would teach these mysteries of faith.   [4] Quæ Deo sibi aperiente cognoverat. (Maf. p. 34.)

hunting, and festivity disappeared from the pontifical throne to give place to a grave and pious monk.

Leo X had felt great delight on hearing of the edict of Worms, and the captivity of Luther, and forthwith, as a token of his victory, had caused the effigy and writings of the Reformer to be given to the flames.[1] This was the second or third time that the papacy had enjoyed this pleasure. At this time, Leo, wishing to testify his gratitude to Charles V, united his army to that of the emperor. The French were obliged to quit Parma, Placenza, and Milan, which latter town was entered by a cousin of the pope, Cardinal Giulio de Medici. The pope was thus mounting to the pinnacle of power.

This was at the beginning of the winter of 1521. Leo X was accustomed to pass the autumn in the country, and at this time left Rome without his surplice, and, what, says his master of the ceremonies, was still more scandalous, in boots. He had hawking at Viterbo, and stag-hunting at Corneto, enjoyed the sport of fishing in the lake of Bolsena, and then went to pass some time in the midst of festivities at Malliana, his favourite residence. Musicians, improvisatori, all artists whose talents could enliven this delicious villa surrounded the sovereign pontiff. He was here at the time when news reached him of the taking of Milan. The whole villa was immediately astir. The courtiers and officials could not restrain their joy. The Swiss fired *feux de joie*, and Leo, in transport, walked up and down his room the whole night, often looking out of his window at the rejoicings of the Swiss and the people. He returned to Rome, fatigued, but intoxicated with delight. Scarcely had he returned to the Vatican when he was suddenly taken ill. "Pray for me," said he to his servants. He had not even time to receive the holy sacrament, and died in the vigour of life (forty-seven), in the hour of triumph, and amid the noise of festivity.

The people, while accompanying the hearse of the sovereign pontiff, gave utterance to invectives. They could not forgive his having died without the sacraments, and left debts consequent on his great expenditure. "Thou didst rise to the pontificate as a fox," said the Romans, "there thou playedst the lion, and now thou art gone like a dog."

Such was the mourning with which Rome honoured the pope who excommunicated the Reformation, and whose name serves to mark one of the great epochs in history.

---

[1] Comburi jussit alteram vultus in ejus statua, alteram animi ejus in libris. (Pallavicini, i, p. 128.) He caused two images to be burned, the one of his person in his effigy, the other of his mind in his books.

Meanwhile a feeble re-action against the spirit of Leo and Rome had already begun in Rome herself. Some pious individuals had there founded an oratory for their common edification,[1] near the place where tradition bears that the meetings of the primitive Christians were held. Contarini, who had heard Luther at Worms, took the lead among these priests. In this way a species of Reformation began at Rome almost at the same time as at Wittemberg. It has been truly said that wherever there are germs of piety, there are also germs of reform. But these good intentions were soon to be dissipated.

At other times the choice of a successor to Leo X would have fallen on a Gregory VII, or an Innocent III, if they could have been found, but the interest of the empire now took precedence of that of the Church, and Charles V behoved to have a pope who was devoted to himself. The Cardinal de Medici, afterwards pope under the name of Clement VII, seeing that he could not yet obtain the tiara, exclaimed, " Take the Cardinal of Tortosa, who is old and universally regarded as a saint." This prelate, born at Utrecht, of burgher parentage, was, in fact, elected, and reigned under the name of Adrian VI. He had formerly been a professor at Louvain, and afterwards became preceptor to Charles, by whose influence, as emperor, he was, in 1517, invested with the Roman purple. The Cardinal de Vio seconded the proposal. " Adrian," said he, " had, through the doctors of Louvain, a great share in Luther's condemnation."[2] The cardinals, worn out and off their guard, appointed this stranger; but shortly on recovering themselves, " they were," says a chronicler, " as it were dead with amazement." The idea that the rigid Netherlander would not accept the tiara, at first, somewhat solaced them; but this was of short duration. Pasquin caricatured the pontiff elect under the figure of a schoolmaster, and the cardinals under that of boys whom he was chastising. The populace were so enraged that the members of the conclave were happy to escape without being thrown into the river.[3] In Holland, on the contrary, there were great rejoicings at having given a pope to the Church. "Utrecht planted—Louvain watered—the emperor has given the increase," was displayed on tapestry hung in front of the houses. Some one wrote beneath, " And God did nothing at all in the matter!"

Notwithstanding the dissatisfaction originally expressed by the people of Rome, Adrian VI repaired thither in August, 1522, and

---

[1] Si unirono in un oratorio, chiamato del divino amore, circa sessanta di loro, (Caracciolo Vita da Paolo IV. MS., Ranke.) About sixty of them formed an oratory, named the Oratory of Divine Love. [2] Doctores Lovanienses accepisse consilium a tam conspicuo alumno. (Pallavicini, p. 136.) That the doctors of Louvain had been counselled by their distinguished alumnus. [3] Sleidan. Hist of the Ref., i, p. 121.

was well received. It was said, that he had more than five thousand benefices at his disposal, and every one counted on obtaining a share. For long the papal throne had not been occupied by such a pontiff. Just, active, learned, pious, simple, of irreproachable manners, he did not allow himself to be blinded either by favour or anger. He arrived at the Vatican with his old housekeeper, whom he charged to continue to provide for his modest wants in the magnificent palace which Leo had filled with luxury and dissipation. He had none of the tastes of his predecessor. When shown the magnificent statue of the Laocoon, which had been discovered a few years before, and purchased, for a large sum, by Julius II, he turned away coldly, saying, "these are pagan idols." "I would far rather," he wrote, "serve God as provost of Louvain, than as pope of Rome."

Adrian, struck with the danger with which the Reformation menaced the religion of the middle ages, and not, like the Italians, with those to which it exposed Rome and its hierarchy, was sincerely desirous to combat and arrest it; and it seemed to him that the best method of succeeding was, a reform of the Church produced by the Church herself. "The Church," said he, "is in need of a reform, but we must proceed in it step by step." "The opinion of the pope," says Luther, "is that between two steps there must be an interval of several ages." In fact, there were ages when the Church was moving towards a Reformation. It was no longer time to temporise, it was necessary to act.

Adrian, faithful to his plan, was engaged in clearing the city of the profane, of forgers, and usurers. The task was not easy; for they formed a considerable part of the population.

At first the Romans jeered at him, but shortly they hated him. Sacerdotal ascendancy, and the immense profits which it produced —the might of Rome—the sports, luxury, and festivities which abounded in it, would all be irrecoverably lost by a return to apostolic manners.

In particular, the restoration of discipline encountered energetic opposition. "To succeed in it," said the grand penitentiary, (a cardinal,) "it would first be necessary to bring back Christian fervour. The cure is too much for the strength of the patient, and will be his death. Have a care that, in trying to preserve Germany, you do not lose Italy."[1] In fact, Adrian had soon much more to dread from Romanism than from Lutheranism.

Attempts were made to bring him back to the path which he was desirous to quit. The old and wily Cardinal Soderino de Volterra, an intimate friend of Alexander VI, Julius II, and

[1] Sarpi Hist. of the Coun. of Trent, p. 29.

Leo X,[1] often expressed himself to honest Adrian in terms fitted to acquaint him with the part, to him so novel, which he was called to perform. "The heretics," said he to him one day, "have at all times spoken of the corrupt manners of the court of Rome; notwithstanding, the popes have never changed them." On another occasion he said, "Hitherto it has not been by reforms that heresies have been extinguished, but by crusades." "Ah," replied the pontiff, with a deep sigh, "how unfortunate the condition of the popes, since they have not even the liberty of doing good."[2]

CHAP. III

Diet of Nuremberg—Invasion of Selyman—The Nuncio demands the Death of Luther—The Preachers of Nuremberg—Promise of Reform—National Grievances—Decree of the Diet—Thundering Letter of the Pope—Luther's Advice.

On the 23rd March, 1522, before Adrian's arrival at Rome, the Diet had assembled at Nuremberg. Previous to this, the Bishops of Mersburg and Misnia had asked permission from the Elector of Saxony to make a visitation of the convents and churches in his states. Frederick, thinking that the truth should be strong enough to resist error, had given a favourable answer. The visitation took place. The bishops and their doctors preached fiercely against reform. They exhorted, threatened, supplicated: but their arguments seemed without force, and, when wishing to recur to more efficacious weapons, they asked the secular arm to execute their decrees, the Elector's ministers replied, that the affair required to be examined by the Bible, and that the Elector could not, at his advanced age, sit down to the study of theology. These efforts of the bishops did not bring back a single soul to the fold of Rome; and Luther who, a short time after, travelled over these countries and made his powerful eloquence be heard, effaced any feeble impressions which they had produced.

There was reason to fear that Archduke Ferdinand, the emperor's brother, would do what Frederick had refused. This young prince, who presided at part of the sittings of the Diet, gradually assuming more resolution, might, in his zeal, rashly draw the sword which his more prudent and politic brother wisely left in its sheath. In fact, Ferdinand had commenced a cruel persecution of the partisans of the Reformation in his hereditary states of Austria. But for the deliverance of reviving Christianity, God repeatedly employed the same instrument which he had used in destroying corrupted

[1] Per lunga esperienza delle cose del mundo, molto prudente e accorto. (Nardi. Hist. Fior., lib. 7.) [2] Sarpi, p. 21.

Christianity. The crescent appeared in the terrified provinces of Hungary. On the 9th of August, after a siege of six weeks, Belgrade, the bulwark of that kingdom and of the empire, yielded to the assaults of Solyman. The followers of Mahomet, after their evacuation of Spain, seemed desirous to re-enter Europe by the East. The Diet of Nuremberg forgot the monk of Worms to think only of the Luther of Constantinople. But Charles V kept both adversaries in his view. Writing the pope from Valladolid on the 31st October, he said, "It is necessary to arrest the Turks and punish the partisans of the poisonous doctrines of Luther with the sword."[1]

The storm which seemed to have turned away from the Reformation, and proceeded toward the East, gathered anew over the head of the Reformer. His return to Wittemberg, and the zeal which he then displayed, had awakened the old hatred. "Now that we know where to take him," said Duke George, "let the decree of Worms be carried into execution!" It was even confidently affirmed in Germany that both the emperor and Adrian would appear together at Nuremberg to advise this.[2] "Satan feels the wound which he has received," said Luther, "and, therefore, puts himself into all this rage. But Christ has already stretched forth his hand, and will trample him under his feet in spite of the gates of hell."[3]

In December, 1522, the Diet again assembled at Nuremberg. Every thing appeared to announce that, if Solyman was the great enemy who engrossed the attention of the Spring Session, Luther would be the engrossing one of the Winter Session. Adrian VI, being of German origin, flattered himself his countrymen would give him a more favourable reception than a pope of Italian origin could hope for.[4] He accordingly charged Chieregati, whom he had known in Spain, to repair to Nuremberg.

No sooner was the Diet met than several princes made violent speeches against Luther. The Cardinal Archbishop of Salzburg, who was in the full confidence of the emperor, was desirous that prompt and decisive measures should be taken before the arrival of the Elector of Saxony. The Elector Joachim of Brandenburg, always resolute in his course, and the Chancellor of Treves, were equally pressing for the execution of the edict of Worms. The other princes were in a great measure undecided and divided in opinion. The state of turmoil in which the Church was placed,

[1] Dass man die Nachfolger derselben vergiften Lehre, mit dem Schwert strafen mag. (L. Op. xvii, p. 321.) [2] Cum fama sit fortis et Cæsarem et Papam Nurnbergam conventuros. (L. Ep. ii. p. 214.) [3] Sed Christus qui cœpit conte et eum. (Ibid. [4] Quod ex ea regione venirent, unde nobis secundum carnem origo est (Papal Brief, (L.) Op. l. ii, p. 352.)

filled her most faithful servants with anguish. The Bishop of Strasburg broke out in full Diet with the exclamation, "I would give one of my ten fingers not to be a priest."[1]

Chieregati, in unison with the Archbishop of Salzburg, demanded the death of Luther. "It is necessary," said he, on the part of the pope, and with a papal brief in his hands, "it is necessary to amputate this gangrened limb from the body.[2] Your fathers at Constance put to death John Huss and Jerome of Prague; but they revive in Luther. Follow the glorious example of your ancestors, and, with the assistance of God and St. Peter, carry off a magnificent victory over the infernal dragon."

On hearing the brief of the pious and moderate Adrian, the most of the princes were seized with terror.[2] Several were beginning to have a better understanding of the arguments of Luther, and had hoped other things of the pope. So then, Rome, under an Adrian, refuses to acknowledge her faults: she is still preparing her thunder, and the Germanic provinces are to be covered with desolation and blood. While the princes kept a mournful silence, the prelates and the members of the Diet were in an uproar. "Let him be put to death,"[3] exclaimed they, within hearing of the envoy of Saxony, who was present at the sitting.

Very different expressions were heard in the churches of Nuremberg. Crowds flocked into the chapel of the Hospital and the churches of the Augustins, St. Sibbald and St. Laurence, to the preaching of the gospel. Andrew Osiander preached powerfully in the latter church. Several princes, and, in particular, Albert, Margrave of Brandenburg, who, in his quality of Grand Master of the Teutonic Order, took rank immediately after the archbishop, was a frequent attendant. Monks quitting the convents of the town, learned trades, in order to gain a livelihood by their own hands.

Chieregati could not tolerate this boldness. He demanded that the rebellious priests and monks should be cast into prison. The Diet, notwithstanding strong opposition from the envoys of the Elector of Saxony and the Margrave Casimir, resolved to order the apprehension of the monks, but agreed previously to communicate the nuncio's complaints to Osiander and his colleagues. A committee, with the fanatical Cardinal Salzburg for its president, was entrusted with the execution of it. The danger was imminent: the struggle was on the eve of commencing; and it was with the National Council that it was to commence.

However, the citizens prevented it. While the Diet was de-

---

[1] Er wollte einen Finger drum geben. (Seck., p. 568.) [2] Resecandos ut membra jam putrida a sano corpore. (Pallav., 1, 158.) [3] Einen grossen Schrecken eingejagt. (Seck., p. 552.) [4] Nicht anders geschrien denn: *Crucifige! Crucifige!* (L. Op. xviii, 367.)

liberating as to what should be done in regard to their ministers, the wn council was deliberating as to what should be done in regard to the resolution of the Diet. The decision was, that, if it was attempted, by the strong hand, to carry off the ministers of the town, they would with the strong hand set them at liberty. Such a resolution was significant. The Diet, in astonishment, intimated to the nuncio that it was contrary to law to apprehend the ministers of the free town of Nuremberg without having convicted them of heresy.

Chieregati was deeply moved at this new affront to the omnipotence of the pope. "Very well," said he proudly to Ferdinand, "do nothing but leave me to act. I will seize these heretical preachers in the pope's name."[1] No sooner had the Cardinal Archbishop of Mentz, and the Margrave Casimir been apprised of this strange resolution than they repaired in haste to the legate, and implored him to abandon it. The nuncio showed himself inflexible, declaring that within the bosom of Christendom the pope must be obeyed. The two princes took leave of the legate, saying, "If you persist in your design, we call upon you to give us intimation; for we will quit the town before you have proceeded to lay hands on these preachers."[2] The legate abandoned his project.

Having no longer any hope of succeeding in the way of authority, he resolved to have recourse to other expedients, and with this view communicated to the Diet the intentions and injunctions of the pontiff, which he had hitherto concealed.

But honest Adrian, who was a stranger to the world, by his very frankness injured the cause which he had so much at heart. "We know well," said he, in the resolutions transmitted to his legate, "that for several years many abuses and abominations have existed in the holy city.[3] The contagion has spread from the head into the members; it has descended from the popes to the other ecclesiastics. We desire the reformation of this Roman court whence proceed so many evils; the whole world desires it, and it was with a view to its accomplishment that we were resigned to mount the pontifical throne."

The partisans of Rome blushed for shame when they heard these strange words. Like Pallavicini, they thought the confession too frank.[4] On the contrary, the friends of the Reformation rejoiced

---

[1] Sese auctoritate pontifica curaturum ut isti caperentur. (Corp. Ref., i, p. 606.)
[2] Priusquam illi caperentur, se urbe cessuros esse. (Ibid.) [3] In eam sedem aliquot jam annos quædam vitia irrepsisse, abusus in rebus sacris, in legibus violationes, in cunctis denique perversionem. (Pallav., i, p. 160.) That for several years past certain vices had crept into that see—abuses in sacred matters, violations of law, and perversion in every thing. (See also Sarpi, p. 25. L. Op. xviii, p. 329, etc.)
[4] Liberioris tamen quam par erat, sinceritatis fuisse visum est, ea conventui patefacere. (Ibid., p. 162.)

on hearing Rome proclaiming her corruption. There was no longer any doubt that Luther was right since the pope himself declared it.

The reply of the Diet showed how much the authority of the sovereign pontiff had fallen in the empire. The spirit of Luther seemed to have passed into the hearts of the representatives of the nation. The moment was favourable. Adrian's ear was open; the emperor was absent; the Diet resolved to collect into one body all the grievances which Germany complained of against Rome, and despatch them to the pope.

The legate, alarmed at this determination, supplicated and menaced by turns, but in vain. The secular estates were decided and the ecclesiastical offered no opposition. Eighty-four grievances were specified. The abuses and stratagems of the Roman court in making extortions on Germany,—the scandals and profanations of the clergy,—the irregularities and simony of the ecclesiastical tribunals,—the encroachment on the secular power in enslaving consciences, were exposed with equal frankness and force. The states hinted that human traditions were the source of all this corruption. They concluded thus: "If these grievances are not redressed within a limited time, we will consider other means of escaping from all this oppression and suffering."[1] Chieregati, foreseeing the fearful detail into which the Diet would enter, quitted Nuremberg in haste, that he might not be the bearer of so disagreeable and insolent a message.

Still, was there not room to apprehend that the Diet might be willing to compensate for their boldness by sacrificing Luther? It was thought so at first; but a spirit of truth and justice had fallen on this assembly. They, like Luther, demanded that a free council should be convened in the empire, and added, that until it took place the pure gospel only should be preached, and nothing should be printed without the approbation of certain individuals of character and learning.[2] These resolutions enable us to apprehend the immense progress which the Reformation had made since the Diet of Worms; and yet the Saxon envoy, the Chevalier von Feilitsch protested solemnly against any censure which the Diet might pronounce, how moderate soever the terms might be. The decision of the Diet was regarded as a first victory gained by the Reformation, and was to be succeeded by others still more decisive. Even the Swiss, in their mountains, thrilled with joy. "The Roman pontiff is vanquished in Germany," said Zuinglius: "all that remains is to wrest his arms from him. This

---

[1] Wie sie solcher Beschwerung und Drangsaal entladen werden. (L. Op. xviii, p. 354.)
[2] Ut pie placideque purum Evangelium prædicaretur. (Pallav., i, p. 166.) That the pure gospel should be wisely and quietly preached. (See also Sleidan, i, p. 135.)

is the battle we have now to wage, and it will be the fiercest; but we have Christ as witness of the combat."[1] Luther declared aloud that God had inspired the edict of the princes.[2]

There was great wrath in the Vatican among the ministers of the papacy. What! it is not enough to have a pope who disappoints all the hopes of the Romans, and in whose palace there is neither music nor play; must secular princes, moreover, hold a language which Rome detests, and refuse the death of the heretic of Wittemberg!

Adrian himself was very indignant at the proceedings in Germany. It was on the Elector of Saxony he discharged his anger. Never, perhaps, did Rome sound an alarm more energetic, sincere, and even more impressive.

"We have waited long, perhaps too long," said the pious Adrian, in the brief which he addressed to the Elector, "we were desirous to see if God would not be pleased to visit your soul, and enable you at last to escape from the snares of Satan. But where we hoped to gather grapes, we have gathered only sour grapes. The spirit has blown in vain. Your iniquities have not melted away. Open your eyes then, and see the greatness of your fall!

"If the unity of the Church has been broken, if the simple have been turned aside from the faith which they had sucked at the breasts of their mother, if the churches are deserted, if the people are without priests, and the priests no longer receive the honour which is due to them, if Christians are without Christ—to whom do we owe it, if not to yourself?[3] . . . If Christian peace has fled the earth, if the world is full of discord, rebellion, robbery, assassination, conflagration, if the cry of war resounds from east to west, if a universal battle is preparing, you, still you are the cause!

"Do you not see that sacrilegious man (Luther), tearing to pieces the images of the saints, and even the sacred cross of Jesus Christ, with his guilty hands, and trampling them under his impure feet? . . . . Do you not see him, in his impious wrath, stirring up the laity to wash their hands in the blood of the priests, and throw down the churches of the Lord?

"What matters it, though the priests whom he attacks be bad priests? Has not the Lord said, '*Do what they say, and not what they do*,' thus pointing at the honour which is due to them, even when their conduct is culpable.[4]

[1] Victus est ac ferme profligatus e Germania romanus pontifex. (Zw. Ep. 313, 11th Oct., 1523.) The Roman pontiff was almost conquered and driven from Germany.
[2] Gott habe solches E. G. eingeben. (L. Op. xviii, 476.) [3] Dass die Kirchen ohne Volk sind, dass die Völker ohne Priester sind, dass die Priester ohne Ehre sind, und dass die Christen ohne Christo sind. (Ibid. p. 371.) [4] Wenn sie gleich eines verdammten Lebens sind. (Ibid. p. 379.)

"Rebellious apostate, he is not ashamed to defile the vessels consecrated to the Lord; he plucks from their sanctuaries the holy virgins consecrated to Christ, and gives them to the devil; he takes the priests of the Lord and gives them up to infamous prostitutes . . . . Frightful profanation, at which the pagans even would have been horrified, had they seen it in the pontiffs of their idols!"

"Of what punishment, of what suffering, think you, then, we shall deem you worthy? . . . . Take pity on yourself, take pity on your miserable Saxons; for if you are not speedily converted, God will cause his vengeance to descend upon you.

"In the name of God Almighty and of our Lord Jesus Christ, whose representative on the earth I am, I declare to you, that you will be punished in this world, and plunged into the eternal fire in that which is to come. Repent and be converted! . . . Two swords are suspended over your head, the sword of the empire, and the sword of the popedom. . . . ."

The pious Frederick trembled on reading this menacing brief. A short time before he had written to the Emperor to say, that old age and sickness rendered him incapable of occupying himself with these affairs; and the reply given to him was the most arrogant letter that ever a sovereign prince had received. Weakened by age, he cast his eyes on that sword which he had carried to the holy sepulchre in the days of his strength. He began to think it might be necessary to unsheath it in defence of the consciences of his subjects, and that already on the brink of the grave, he would not be able to go down to it in peace. He immediately wrote to Wittemberg for the advice of the fathers of the Reformation.

There, also, troubles and persecutions were foreseen. "What shall I say," exclaimed the mild Melancthon, "to what side shall I turn? We are overwhelmed with hatred, and the world is transported with rage against us."[1] Luther, Linck, Melancthon, Bugenhagen, and Amsdorff, consulted together, as to the answer to be returned to the Elector. They all proposed nearly the same answer. Their opinion is very striking.

"No prince," said they, "can undertake a war without the consent of the people from whose hands he received the government.[2] Now, the people have no wish to fight for the gospel, for they do not believe it. Let the princes, then, not take up arms; they are princes of the nations, in other words, of unbelievers." Thus it

---

[1] Quid dicam? quo me vertam? (Corp. Ref. i, p. 627.) [2] Principi nullum licet suscipere bellum, nisi consentiente populo, a quo accepit imperium. (Ibid. p. 601.)

was the impetuous Luther who asked sage Frederick to put up the sword into its sheath. He could not give a better answer to the charge brought against him by the pope, of stirring up the laity to wash their hands in the blood of the clergy. Few characters have been less understood than his. This opinion is dated the 8th February, 1523. Frederick restrained himself.

The wrath of the pope soon bore its proper fruits. The princes who had expounded their grievances against Rome, frightened at their boldness, sought to appease him by compliance. Several besides declared that victory must remain with the pontiff of Rome, as he appeared to be the stronger. "In our day," said Luther, "princes content themselves with saying, three times three make nine, or twice seven make fourteen: the account is correct,[1] the affair will succeed. Then our Lord God rises up and says—'For how much, then, do you count me? . . . For a cipher, perhaps?' Then he turns their calculations upside down, and their accounts prove erroneous."

CHAP. IV.

Persecution—Efforts of Duke George—The Convent of Antwerp—Miltenberg—The three Monks of Antwerp—The Scaffold—Martyrdom at Brussels.

The flame breathed forth by the humble and meek Adrian kindled the conflagration. His remonstrance caused an immense sensation throughout Christendom. Persecution, which had for some time been arrested, again commenced. Luther trembled for Germany, and strove to lay the storm. "If the princes," said he, "set themselves in opposition to the truth, the result will be a tumult, which will destroy princes, magistrates, priests, and people. I tremble at the thought of soon seeing all Germany swim in blood.[2] Let us interpose as a wall and preserve our people from the Lord's anger. The people are no longer what they have been hitherto.[3] The sword of civil war is suspended over the heads of kings. They wish to destroy Luther, but Luther wishes to save them. Christ lives and reigns: I shall live and reign with him."[4]

These words were without effect: Rome was hastening on towards scaffolds and blood. The Reformation, like Jesus Christ, had not come to bring peace, but a sword. For the purposes of God, persecution was necessary. As objects are hardened by fire,

---

[1] So kehrt er ihnen auch die Rechnung gar um. (L. Op. xxii, 1831.)
[2] Ut videar mihi videre Germaniam in sanguine natare. (L. Ep. ii, p. 156.)
[3] Cogitent populos non esse tales modo, quales hactenus fuerunt. (Ibid. p. 157.)
[4] Christus meus vivit et regnat, et ego vivam et regnabo. (Ibid p. 158.)

to protect them from the influence of the atmosphere, so a trial by fire was to secure evangelical truth against the influence of the world. But this fire did more: it served, as in the early days of Christianity, to kindle an universal enthusiasm for the cause so virulently persecuted. There is in man, when he begins to know the truth, a holy indignation against injustice and violence. An instinctive feeling, which comes from God, urges him to take part with the oppressed, and, at the same time, the constancy of martyrs raises and captivates him, and hurries him on towards the saving doctrine which gives so much courage and so much peace.

Duke George headed the persecution. But he deemed it a small matter to employ it in his own states. He wished, above all, to see its ravages in electoral Saxony—the focus of heresy—and he did every thing to shake the Elector Frederick, and Duke John. Writing them from Nuremberg, he says, "Merchants just come from Saxony relate, with regard to it, things which are strange and contrary to the honour of God and the saints: the sacrament of the supper is there received with the hand. The bread and wine are consecrated in the *vulgar tongue;* the blood of Christ is put in ordinary vessels; and, at Eulenberg, to insult the priest, a man even entered the church mounted on an ass! . . . . What is the consequence? The minerals with which God had enriched Saxony begin to be exhausted since the innovating preachings of Luther. Oh! would to God that those who boast of having raised up the gospel in the electorate had rather carried it to Constantinople. Luther has a soft and pleasant voice, but a venomous tail, which stings like that of the scorpion. Let us prepare for the battle. Let us throw these apostate monks and profane priests into chains and that without delay: for our remaining locks as well as beards grow white, and remind us that we have only a few days for action." [1]

Thus wrote Duke George to the Elector, who replied firmly and mildly, that whosoever should do a criminal act within his States should not escape condign punishment; but that matters of conscience must be left to God. [2]

George not being able to persuade Frederick, hastened, in his own neighbourhood, to give proof of his severity against the cause which he hated. He imprisoned the monks and priests who adhered to Luther. He ordered back the students belonging to his states who were studying at the universities tainted with the Reformation, and he ordered all New Testaments in the vulgar tongue to be delivered up to the magistrates. The same course was followed in Austria, Wurtemberg, and the Duchy of Brunswick.

[1] Wie ihre Bärt und Haare ausweisen. (Seck., p. 482.) [2] Müsse man solche Dinge Gott überlassen. (Ibid. 485.)

But it was in the Low Countries which were under the immediate authority of Charles V, that the persecution burst forth with greatest fury. The Augustin convent at Antwerp was full of monks who had received the truth of the gospel. Several of the friars had resided some time at Wittemberg, and from 1519 preached salvation by grace in their church, with great energy. The prior, James Probst, who was of a fiery temperament, and Melchior Mirisch, who was, on the other hand, distinguished for ability and prudence, were arrested and carried to Brussels, about the end of 1521. Probst, surprised and terrified, recanted. Melchior Mirisch found means of softening his judges, and escaped both condemnation and recantation.

These persecutions did not intimidate the monks who were left in the convent of Antwerp. They continued vigorously to preach the gospel. The people flocked to hear them, and the church of the Augustins proved too small, as that of Wittemberg had done. In October, 1522, the storm which was gathering over their heads burst: the convent was shut up, and the monks were imprisoned and condemned to death.[1] Some made their escape. Some females, forgetting the timidity of their sex, rescued one of them, Henry of Zuphten, from his executioners.[2] Three young monks, Henry Voes, John Esch, and Lambert Thorn, for some time eluded the search of the inquisitors. All the vessels of the convent were sold, the building was barricaded, and the holy sacrament removed from it as from a place become infamous. Margaret, the regent of the Low Countries, received it solemnly into the church of the holy Virgin.[3] Orders were given, that this heretical monastery should be razed to its foundations; and several citizens and females who had received the gospel with joy were cast into prison.[4]

Luther was much grieved on learning these tidings. "The cause which we defend," said he, "is no longer a simple game: it wishes blood: it demands life.[5]

The fates of Mirisch and Probst were to be very different. The prudent Mirisch soon became the docile servant of Rome, and the executioner of the imperial decrees against the adherents of the Reformation.[6] On the contrary, Probst, who had escaped from the inquisitors, bewailed his fault, withdrew his recantation, and, at Bruges in Flanders, boldly preached the doctrine which he had abjured. Arrested anew and imprisoned at Brussels, his death seemed inevitable.[7] A franciscan, moved with pity, aided his escape, and Probst "saved by a miracle of God," says Luther, arrived at

---

[1] Zum Tode verurtheilet. (Seck., p. 548.)   [2] Quomodo mulieres vi Henricum liberarint. (L. Ep. ii, p. 265.)   [3] Susceptum honorifice a domina Margareta. (Ibid.)   [4] Cives aliquos, et mulieres vexatæ et punitæ. (Ibid.)   [5] Et vitam exiget et sanguinem. (Ibid. p. 181.)   [6] Est executor Cæsaris contra nostros. (Ibid. p. 207.)   [7] Domo captum, exustum credimus. (Ibid. p. 214.)

Wittemberg, where his double deliverance filled the hearts of the friends of the Reformation with joy.[1]

The Romish priests were every where in arms. The town of Miltenberg on the Maine, belonging to the Elector-Archbishop of Mentz, was one of the Germanic cities which had received the Word of God with the greatest readiness. The inhabitants were strongly attached to their pastor, John Draco, one of the most enlightened men of his time. He was compelled to retire, but the Roman ecclesiastics quitted at the same time, dreading the popular vengeance. An evangelical deacon alone remained to administer spiritual consolation. At the same time troops from Mentz entered and spread over the town, uttering blasphemies, brandishing their swords, and giving themselves up to debauchery.[2]

Some evangelical Christians fell under their blows,[3] others were seized and thrown into dungeons, the Romish rites were again set up, the reading of the Bible was prohibited, and the inhabitants were forbidden to speak of the gospel, even in their most private intercourse. On the entry of the troops the deacon had taken refuge in the house of a poor widow. He was denounced to the rulers, who sent a soldier to seize him. The humble deacon hearing the soldier, who was seeking his life, advancing with hasty steps, quietly waited for him, and when the door was hastily opened he rose mildly to meet him, and embracing him cordially said, "I salute you, my brother; here I am, plunge your sword into my bosom."[4] The fierce soldier, astonished, let his sword fall from his hand, and would not allow any harm to be done to the pious evangelist.

Meanwhile the inquisition of the Low Countries, thirsting for blood, scoured the country, and searched every where for the young Augustins who had escaped from the persecution of Antwerp. Esch, Voes, and Lambert, were at last discovered, chained, and carried to Brussels. Egmondanus, Hochstratten, and some other inquisitors, summoned them before them. Hochstratten asked, "Do you retract your assertion that the priest has not power to pardon sins, and that pardon belongs to God only?" He next enumerated all the evangelical doctrines, and summoned them to abjure them. "We recant nothing," exclaimed Esch and Voes firmly; "we will not abjure the Word of God; we will sooner die for the faith!"

[1] Jacobus, Dei miraculo liberatus qui nunc agit nobiscum. (L. Ep. ii, p. 182.) This letter, which in Wette's collection bears the date of 14th April, must be posterior to June. For Luther, on the 27th June, says, that Probst has been taken a second time, and is to be burnt. It may be admitted that Probst was in Wittemberg between his two imprisonments, for Luther would not have said of a Christian who had saved himself by a recantation that he had been delivered by a miracle of God. Perhaps the date should be read, not 'in die S. Tiburtii,' but 'in die Turiafi,' which would bring it to 13th July, which seems to me the more probable date. [2] So sie doch schändlicher leben denn Huren und Buben. (Ibid., ii, p. 482.) [3] Schlug etliche todt (Seck., p. 604.) [4] Sey gegrüst, mein Bruder. (Scultet., ann. i, p. 173.)

Inquisitor.—" Do you confess that you have been led astray by Luther?"

The Young Augustins.—" Just as the apostles were led astray by Jesus Christ."

The Inquisitors.—" We pronounce you heretics, who deserve to be burnt alive; and we hand you over to the secular arm."

Lambert was silent: he was afraid of death: anguish and doubt agitated his soul. "I ask four days," said he, in a suppressed tone. He was taken back to prison. As soon as this period was expired, the sacerdotal consecration was formally withdrawn from Esch and Voes, who were handed over to the council of the Regent of the Low Countries. The council handed them over hand-cuffed to the executioner. Hochstratten, and three other inquisitors accompanied them even to the scaffold.[1]

When arrived near the scaffold, the young martyrs eyed it calmly; their constancy, their piety, their youth,[2] drew tears even from the inquisitors. When they were bound, the confessors approached: "We ask you once more, Will you receive the Christian faith?"

The Martyrs.—" We believe in the Christian Church; but not in your Church."

A half hour passed away: it was hoped that the prospect of so frightful a death would intimidate the youths. But, the only persons who were calm amidst the agitated crowd which covered the public square, they sung psalms, occasionally interrupting this employment to say boldly, "We wish to die for the name of Jesus Christ."

"Be converted, be converted," exclaimed the inquisitors, "or you will die in the name of the devil."—" No," replied the martyrs: "we will die as Christians for the truth of the gospel."

The pile was set on fire. While the flame ascended slowly, divine peace filled their hearts; and one of them even went so far as to say, "I feel as if reclining on a bed of roses."[3] The solemn hour had come: death was at hand: the two martyrs, with loud voice, exclaimed, " *O Domini Jesu, Fili David, miserere nostri!* " "Lord Jesus, Son of David, have mercy on us!" Then they began in a solemn voice to repeat the creed.[4] At length the flames reached them; but, before depriving them of life, burned the cords with which they were bound to the pile. One of them taking advantage of his liberty, threw himself on his knees, and thus worshipping his Master,[5] with clasped hands, exclaimed,—" Lord Jesus, Son

---

[1] Facta est hæc res Bruxellæ in publico foro, place at Brussels in the public market place. (Ibid.) Not yet thirty years of age. (Brandt, Hist. der Reformatie i, p. 79.) bolum fidei, says Erasmus. (Ep. i, p. 1278.) Knie gefallen. (J. Op. xviii, p. 481.)
(L. Ep. ii, p. 361.) The execution took
[2] Nondum triginta annorum.
[3] Dit schijnen mij als roosen te zijn.
[4] Admoto igni, canere cœperunt symbolum fidei.
[5] Da ist der eine im Feuer auf die

of David, have mercy on us!" The fire surrounded their bodies: they sung the *Te Deum laudamus.* Shortly after their voice was stifled by the flames, and all that remained of them was their ashes.

The execution had lasted four hours. It was on the 1st July, 1523, that the first martyrs of the Reformation thus gave their lives for the gospel.

All good men shuddered when they heard of it. The future excited great alarm. "Executions begin," said Erasmus.[1] "At length," exclaimed Luther, "Jesus Christ gathers some fruit from our doctrine. He forms new martyrs."

But the joy which Luther felt at the fidelity of these two Christian youths was damped by the thought of Lambert. He was the most learned of the three, and had taken the place of Probst, as preacher, at Antwerp. Agitated in his dungeon, and afraid of death, he was still more alarmed by his conscience, which reproached him with his cowardice, and urged him to confess the gospel. Shortly after having got the better of his fears, he boldly proclaimed the truth, and died like his brethren.[2]

A rich harvest was produced from the blood of these martyrs. Brussels turned towards the gospel.[3] "Wherever Aleander raises a scaffold," said Erasmus, "the effect is the same as if he sowed heretics."[4]

"Your bonds are my bonds," exclaimed Luther, "your dungeons my dungeons, and your scaffolds my scaffolds!"[5] We are all with you and the Lord is at our head." He then wrote a beautiful poem in celebration of the death of the young monks. In a short time the poem was sung in Germany and the Netherlands, in town and country, every where producing an enthusiastic feeling for the faith of the martyrs:—

> No! their ashes will not die;
> Abroad their holy dust will fly,
> And scatter'd o'er earth's farthest strand,
> Raise up for God a warlike band.
> Satan, by taking life away,
> May keep them silent for a day;
> But death has from him victory wrung,
> And Christ in every clime is sung.[6]

[1] Cœpta est carnificina. (Ep. p. 1429.) [2] Quarta post exustus est tertius frater Lambertus. (L. Ep. ii, p. 361.) [3] Ea mors multos fecit Lutheranos. (Er. Ep. p. 952.) That death made many Lutherans. Tum demum cœpit civitas favere Luthero. (Ibid., p. 1676.) Erasmus to Duke George. Ea civitas antea purissima. (Ibid., p. 1430.) [4] Ubicunque fumos excitavit nuntius, ibi diceres fuisse factam hæreseon sementem. Ibid.) [5] Vestra Vincula mea sunt, vestri carceres et ignes mei sunt. (L. Ep. ii, p. 464.)
[6] Die Asche will nicht lassen ab,
Sie stäubt in allen Landen,
Hie hilft kein Bach, Loch, noch Grab . . (L. Op. xviii, p. 484.

CHAP. V.

New Pope—The Legate Campeggio—Diet of Nuremberg—Demand of the Legate—Reply of the Diet—Project of a Secular Council—Alarm and efforts of the Pope—Bavaria—League of Ratisbon—Rigour and Reform—Political Schisms—Opposition—Intrigues of Rome—Edict of Bruges—Rupture.

Adrian would doubtless have persisted in violent courses. The inefficacy of his attempts to arrest the Reformation, his orthodoxy, his zeal, his rigour, his conscience even would have made him a cruel persecutor. Providence put it out of his power. On the 14th September, 1523, he died, and the Romans, delighted at their deliverance from this rigid stranger, decked the gate of his physician with flowers, placing over them the inscription—" To the saviour of his country."

Julius de Medici, cousin of Leo X, succeeded, under the name of Clement VII. From the day of his election, no more was heard of religious reform. The new pope, like many of his predecessors, thought only of upholding the privileges of the papacy, and employing them as the means of extending his power.

Wishing to repair the faults of Adrian, Clement sent to Nuremberg a legate of his own temper, one of the ablest prelates of his court, the Cardinal Campeggio, a man of great experience in business, and acquainted with almost all the princes of Germany. The legate, who had been received with great pomp in the towns of Italy, soon became aware of the change which had taken place in the empire. On entering Augsburg, wishing, according to custom, to give his benediction to the people, he was received with laughter. He held it as pronounced, and entered Nuremberg incognito, without repairing to the Church of St. Sebald, where the clergy were in attendance. No priests went before him in sacerdotal garments, no crucifix was carried before him in state.[1] One would have said it was an ordinary individual walking along the street. Every thing announced to the papacy that its reign was drawing to a close.

The Diet had again been opened at Nuremberg, in January, 1524. A storm threatened the national government, which had owed its existence to the firmness of Frederick. The Suabian league, the wealthiest towns of Germany, and, above all, Charles V, had vowed its destruction. It was accused of favouring the new heresy.

---

[1] Communi habitu, quod per sylvas et campos ierat, per mediam urbem . . . sine clero, sine prævia cruce. (Cochl., p. 92.)

Accordingly, it was resolved to renew the administration without retaining one of the old members. Frederick, in vexation, immediately quitted Nuremberg.

The festival of Easter being at hand, Osiander and the evangelical preachers redoubled their zeal. The former preached openly, that antichrist entered Rome the very day Constantine the Great quitted it to take up his residence at Constantinople. The consecration of branches, and several of the other ceremonies of the festival were omitted; four thousand persons received the Supper in both kinds, and the Queen of Denmark, the emperor's sister, received it publicly in the same form in the castle. " Ah!" exclaimed the Archduke Ferdinand in a transport of rage, "I wish you were not my sister." " The same womb carried us," replied the queen, " and I will sacrifice every thing to please you except the Word of God."[1]

Campeggio shuddered on beholding so much hardihood, but affecting to despise the laughter of the people, and the sermons of the preachers, trusting to the support of the emperor and the pope, he reminded the Diet of the edict of Worms, and demanded that the Reformation should be suppressed by force. At these words several of the princes and deputies expressed their indignation. " What," said they to Campeggio, " have become of the grievances presented to the pope by the Germanic nation?" The legate, in accordance with his instructions, assumed an air of simple astonishment. " Three copies of that production," said he, " reached Rome, but we had no official communication of it, and I could not believe that a document so unbecoming could have emanated from your lordships."

The Diet was indignant at this reply. If this is the way in which their representations are received by the pope, they, too, in their turn, will know how to receive those which he may be pleased to address to them. " The people," said several deputies, " are thirsting for the Word of God, and to force it from them, as ordered by the edict of Worms, were to cause torrents of blood to be shed."

The Diet immediately proceeded to prepare an answer to the pope. Not having power to abolish the edict of Worms, they appended a clause which virtually annulled it. " It is necessary," said they, " to conform to it *so far as possible*."[2] Several States had declared that it was impossible. At the same time evoking the importunate shade of the Councils of Constance and Basle, the

[1] Wolle sich des Wortes Gottes halten. (Seckend. p. 613.)
[2] Quantum eis possibile sit .. (Cochl., p. 84.)

Diet demanded that an universal Council of Christendom should be convened in Germany.

The friends of the Reformation did not stop here. What was to be expected from a council, which, perhaps, never would be called, and which, in all events, would be composed of bishops from all nations? Would Germany submit its anti-Roman feelings to prelates from Spain, France, England, and Italy? The national government having been overthrown, its place must be supplied by a national assembly to protect the interests of the people.

In vain did Hannaart, who had been sent from Spain by Charles V, and all the partisans of Rome and the empire, oppose this project. The majority of the Diet were inflexible. It was agreed that a Diet, a secular assembly, should meet at Spires in November, to regulate all religious questions, and that the States should direct their theologians forthwith to prepare a list of the controverted points, to be submitted to this august assembly.

The task was immediately commenced. Each province prepared its document. Never had Rome been threatened with a mightier explosion. Franconia, Brandenburg, Henneberg, Windsheim, Wertheim, Nuremberg, declared, in evangelical terms, against the seven sacraments, the abuses of the mass, the worship of saints, and the supremacy of the pope. "Here," said Luther, "is money of a good stamp." Not one of the questions generally agitated will be passed over in silence in this national council. The majority will obtain general measures. . . . . The unity of Germany, its independence, and Reformation will be secured.

At this news the pope could not restrain his anger. What! Is it dared to establish a secular tribunal to decide on religious matters, and that contrary to his authority?[1] If this monstrous resolution is executed, no doubt, Germany is saved, but Rome is destroyed! A consistory was assembled in all haste, and from the agitated state of the senators, it might have been supposed that the Germans were marching on the Capital. "The thing necessary," said Aleander, "is to pluck the electoral hat from the head of Frederick." "The kings of England and Spain," said another cardinal, "must threaten to break off all intercourse with the free towns." At last the congregation decided, that the only means of safety was to stir up heaven and earth, in order to prevent the meeting at Spires.

The pope immediately wrote the emperor. "If I am the first to face the storm, it is not because I am the only person threatened

[1] Pontifex ægerrime tulit . . . . intelligens novum de religione tribunal eo pacto excitari citra ipsius auctoritatem. (Pallav. j, p. 182.) The pontiff took it very ill . . . when he heard that, in that way, a new religious tribunal was erected without his authority.

by it, but because I sit at the helm. The rights of the empire are attacked even more than the dignity of the court of Rome."

While the pope sent this letter into Castille, he laboured to obtain allies in Germany. He had soon gained one of the most powerful houses of the empire, that of the Dukes of Bavaria. The edict of Worms had not been better observed there than elsewhere, and the evangelical doctrine had made great progress; but, about the end of 1521, the princes of the country having been shaken by Dr. Eck, the Chancellor of the University of Ingolstadt, had approximated to Rome, and issued an edict, by which they enjoined all their subjects to remain faithful to the religion of their fathers.[1]

The Bavarian bishops testified their alarm at the proposed encroachment of the secular power; and Eck set out to Rome to petition the pope to extend the influence of the princes. The pope granted every thing, and even bestowed on the dukes a fifth of the ecclesiastical revenues of their country.

Thus, at a time when the Reformation had not assumed any organised form, Roman Catholicism had recourse to powerful institutions for its support; and Catholic princes, sanctioned by the pope, laid hands on the revenues of the Church long before the Reformation ventured to touch them. What, then, must be thought of the charges which the Roman Catholics have so often made in this respect?

Clement VII could count upon the Dukes of Bavaria in quelling the formidable assembly of Spires. Shortly after, the Archduke Ferdinand, the Archbishop of Salzburg, and several other princes were also gained.

But this did not satisfy Campeggio. Germany must be divided into two camps. Germans must be set against Germans.

During his stay at Stuttgard, the legate, in concert with Ferdinand, had sketched the plan of a league against the Reformation. "There is every thing to be feared," said he, "from an assembly, where the popular voice will be heard. The Diet of Spires may destroy Rome and save Wittemberg. Let us close our ranks and arrange our order of battle."[2] Ratisbon was fixed on as the place of rendezvous.

Notwithstanding of the jealousy between the houses of Bavaria and Austria, Campeggio succeeded, in the end of June, 1524, in bringing about a meeting in this town, between the Dukes of Bavaria and the Archduke Ferdinand. The Archbishop of Salzburg, and the bishops of Trent and Ratisbon, joined them. The bishops

---

[1] Erstes baierisches Religions Mandat. (Winter, Gesch. der Evang. Lehre in Baiern, i, p. 310.) [2] Ibid., p. 156.

of Spires, Bamberg, Augsburg, Strasburg, Basle, Constance, Freisingen, Passau, and Brixen, were represented by deputies.

The legate opened the meeting, with an energetic picture of the dangers to which the Reformation exposed the princes and clergy. "Let us extirpate heresy, and save the Church," exclaimed he.

The conferences continued during fifteen days in the town-house of Ratisbon. A grand ball, which was kept up during a whole night, enlivened this first Catholic assembly, held by the papacy against the rising Reformation.[1] The measures intended to destroy the heretics were afterwards resolved.

The princes and bishops engaged to execute the edicts of Worms and Nuremberg—to allow no change in public worship—to give no toleration within their States to any married ecclesiastic—to recall all the students belonging to their States who might be at Wittemberg, and to employ all the means in their power for the extirpation of heresy. In regard to difficult passages of Scripture, preachers were enjoined to confine themselves to the interpretation given by the fathers of the Latin Church, viz., Ambrose, Jerome, Augustine, and Gregory. Not daring, in presence of the Reformation, to re-establish the authority of the schoolmen, they contented themselves with laying the first foundations of Roman orthodoxy.

On the other hand, not being able to shut their eyes to the scandals and corrupt manners of the priests,[2] they agreed on a scheme of reform, in which they agreed to pay regard to those German grievances in which the court of Rome were least concerned. Priests were forbidden to engage in trade, to haunt taverns, frequent dances, and engage over the bottle in discussing articles of faith.

Such was the result of the confederation of Ratisbon.[3] While taking up arms against the Reformation, Rome conceded somewhat to it. In these resolutions may be observed the first influence of the Reformation of the sixteenth century, in effecting an internal revival in catholicism. The gospel cannot display its power without compelling its opponents in some way to imitate it. Emser had opposed a translation of the Bible to the translation of Luther, and Eck *Common Places* to those of Melancthon;[4] and now Rome opposed to the Reformation those partial attempts at reform to which we owe modern catholicism. But all these acts of Rome were in reality only subtile expedients to escape from the danger which threatened her, branches plucked,

---

[1] Ranke. Deutsche Gesch. ii, p. 159. [2] Improbis clericorum abusibus et perditis moribus. (Cochl. p. 91.) The wicked abuses and abandoned morals of the clergy.
[3] Ut Lutheranae factioni efficacius resistere possint, ultronea confederatione sese constrixerunt. (Ibid.) That they might the more effectually resist the Lutheran faction, they voluntarily entered into a confederacy. [4] Enchiridion, seu Loci Communes contra Haereticos. 1525.

it is true, from the tree of the Reformation, but planted in a soil in which they could only die. Life was wanting, and always will be wanting, to similar attempts.

We are here presented with another fact. At Ratisbon the Roman party formed the first league which destroyed German unity. It was in the camp of the pope that the signal for battle was given. Ratisbon was the cradle of that schism—that political disruption of Germany, which still, in our day, so many Germans deplore. The national assembly of Spires might, by sanctioning and generalising the Reformation of the Church, have secured the unity of the empire. The separatist conventicle of Ratisbon rent the nation for ever into two parties.[1]

Meanwhile the projects of Campeggio did not at first succeed so well as had been imagined. Few princes responded to the call. The most decided opponents of Luther, Duke George of Saxony, the Elector Joachim of Brandenburg, the ecclesiastical electors, and the imperial towns took no part in it. The feeling was, that the pope's legate was forming in Germany a Roman party against the nation itself. The popular sympathies counterbalanced the religious antipathies, and the *Reformation of Ratisbon* soon became the object of popular derision. But the first step was taken: the example was given. It was thought that there would afterwards be little difficulty in strengthening and extending the Roman league. Those who still hesitated would find it impossible to avoid being hurried along by the progress of events. To the legate Campeggio belongs the honour of having discovered the mine which brought the Germanic liberties within a finger's breadth of destruction. Thenceforth Luther's cause ceased to be entirely of a religious nature; the dispute of the monk of Wittemberg held a place in the politics of Europe. Luther is going to be eclipsed, and Charles V, the pope, and the princes will be the principal characters on the theatre where the great drama of the sixteenth century is to be performed.

The assembly of Spires, however, was still in perspective: it might repair the mischief which Campeggio had done at Ratisbon. Rome, therefore, used every effort to prevent it. "What!" said the deputies of the pope, not only to Charles V, but to his ally Henry VIII and the princes of Christendom, "What! do those proud Germans pretend to decide questions of faith in a national assembly! Apparently, kings, the imperial majesty, all Christendom, the whole world will be obliged to stoop to their decrees."

The moment was well chosen for influencing the emperor. The war between this prince and Francis I was at its height. Pescara

[1] Ranke Deutsche Gesch. ii, p. 163.

and the Constable de Bourbon had quitted Italy in May, and, having entered France, laid siege to Marseilles. The pope, who did not regard this attack with a friendly eye, was able to make a powerful diversion in the rear of the imperial army. Charles, who must have been afraid to displease him, did not hesitate, but at once sacrificed the independence of the emperor for the favour of Rome and the success of his struggle with France.

On the 15th July, Charles, at Burgos in Castille, issued an edict in which, in an imperious and impassioned tone, he declared " that it belonged to the pope alone to assemble a council—to the emperor alone to ask it: that the meeting fixed to take place at Spires could not, and would not, be tolerated: that it was strange in the German nation to undertake a work which all the other nations of the world, even with the pope, would not be entitled to do; that the proper course was to hasten the execution of the decree of Worms against the new Mahomet."

Thus, from Spain and Italy proceeded the stroke which arrested the progress of the gospel in Germany. This did not satisfy Charles. In 1519 he had offered to Duke John, the Elector's brother, to marry his sister, the Archduchess Catherine, to John Frederick, the duke's son, and heir to the electorate. But was not this the house of Saxony which maintained the principles of religious and political independence in Saxony, and which Charles hated? He determined to break entirely with the troublesome and criminal representative of evangelical and national ideas, and gave his sister in marriage to John III, king of Portugal. Frederick who, in 1519, had been indifferent to the overtures of the king of Spain, was able, in 1524, to suppress the indignation he felt at the emperor's conduct, but Duke John keenly expressed what he felt at the blow thus inflicted.

Thus the two hostile camps which were long to rend the empire became more distinctly marked.

CHAP. VI.

Persecution—Gaspard Tauber—A Bookseller—Cruelties in Wurtemberg, Salzburg, Bavaria, Pomerania—Henry of Zuphten.

The Romish party did not stop here. The alliance of Ratisbon was not to be a mere form. It was necessary that it should be sealed with blood. Ferdinand and Campeggio went down the Danube together from Ratisbon to Vienna, and, during the voyage, gave to each other promises of cruelty. Persecution immediately commenced in the Austrian states.

A citizen of Venice, named Gaspard Tauber, had circulated the works of Luther, and had himself written against the invocation of saints, purgatory, and transubstantiation.[1] Being thrown into prison, he was summoned by the judges, as well theologians as lawyers, to retract his errors. It was thought that he was willing to do so, and every thing was prepared to give the people of Vienna the solemn spectacle. On the birth-day of Mary, two desks were erected in the cemetery of St. Stephen, the one for the leader of the choir, who was to chant in celebration of the heretic's repentance, and the other for Tauber himself. The form of recantation was put into his hand:[2] the people, the singers, and the priests were waiting in silence. Whether Tauber had not given any promise, or whether, at the moment of abjuration, his faith suddenly revived with new force, he exclaimed, "I am not convinced, and I appeal to the Holy Roman Empire." The ecclesiastics, the choir, and the people were amazed. But Tauber continued to demand death sooner than deny the gospel. He was beheaded, and his body was burnt.[3] His courage made a lasting impression on the citizens of Vienna.

At Bude, in Hungary, an evangelical bookseller, named John, had circulated the New Testament, and Luther's writings, throughout the country. He was tied to a stake, then all his books were gradually piled around him, and set on fire. John displayed unshaken courage, exclaiming, from the midst of the flames, that he was happy in suffering for the Lord.[4] "Blood succeeds blood," exclaimed Luther, on hearing of his death, "but this noble blood which Rome is pleased to shed, will at length suffocate the pope with all his kingdoms and all his kings."[5]

Fanaticism became more and more inflamed: evangelical ministers were driven from their churches; magistrates were banished: sometimes dreadful executions took place. In Wurtemberg an inquisitor named Reichler, caused the Lutherans, and especially their preachers, to be hung on trees. Barbarians were seen coolly nailing ministers to the stake by the tongue, so that the poor sufferers in struggling or tearing themselves from the

---

[1] Atque etiam proprios ipse tractatus perscripserim. (Coch. p. 92, verso.) I have also read tracts by himself. [2] See Coch., Ib. Cum igitur ego Casparus Tauber, etc. [3] Credo te vidisse Casparis Tauber historiam martyris novi Viennæ, quem cæsum capite scribunt et igne exustum pro verbo Dei. (Luther to Hausmann, 12 Nov. 1524, ii, p. 563.) I believe you have seen the account of Gaspard Tauber the new martyr, at Vienna, who is said to have been beheaded and burnt in the flames for the Word of God. [4] Idem accidit Budæ in Ungaria bibliopolæ cuidam Johanni, simul cum libris circa eum positis exusto, fortissimeque passo pro Domino. (Ibid.)
[5] Sanguis sanguinem tangit, qui suffocabit papam cum regibus et regnis suis (Ibid.)

wood to which they were fastened, to regain their liberty were horribly mutilated, and thus were made the instruments of depriving themselves of that gift of speech, which they had long employed in preaching the gospel.[1]

The same persecutions were carried on in the other States of the Catholic League. An evangelical minister of Salzburg was on the way to prison, where he would have ended his days. While the officers, who had him in charge, were drinking in an inn on the road, two peasants, moved with compassion, eluded their vigilance, and delivered the pastor. The wrath of the arch ishop was inflamed against the poor youths; and, without any legal process, he gave orders that they should be beheaded. They were led away secretly, at an early hour, beyond the town. When they arrived at the spot where they were to suffer, the executioner himself hesitated: "for," said he, "they have not been tried." "Do what I command you," sharply replied the commissary of the archbishop, "and leave the responsibility to the prince!" And the heads of the young deliverers immediately fell under the sword.[2]

Persecution raged especially in the States of the Dukes of Bavaria: the priests were deposed, and the nobles banished from their castles; informers were employed over the whole country; distrust and terror reigned in all hearts. A magistrate, named Bernard Fichtel, was journeying to Nuremberg on the affairs of the duke; on the highway he fell in with Francis Burkhard, professor at Ingolstadt, a friend of Dr. Eck. Burkhard accosted him, and they travelled on together. After supper, the professor began to speak of religion. Fichtel, being aware of his companion, reminded him that the new edict prohibited such conversation. "Between us," replied Burkhard, "there is no room for fear." Fichtel then said, "I do not believe that this edict can ever be executed," and expressed himself in an equivocal manner on the subject of purgatory. He added that it was a horrible thing to inflict death for religious opinions. At these words Burkhard could not restrain himself. "What more just," exclaimed he, "than to cut off the heads of all these villains of Lutherans!" He, however, parted with Fichtel on good terms, but hastened to inform upon him. Fichtel was cast into prison; and the poor man, who had never thought of becoming a martyr, and whose convictions were not deep, only escaped death by the disgrace of a recantation. There was now no safety any where: not even in the bosom of a friend.

But the death which Fichtel escaped, others met. In vain was

---

[1] Ranke Deutsche Gesch. ii, p. 174.   [2] Zauner, Salzburger Chronik, iv, p. 561.

it to preach the gospel only in secret.[1] The dukes persecuted it in the shade, in concealment, under the roofs of houses, in secret retreats, in the fields.

"The cross and persecution," said Luther, "reign in Bavaria: these ferocious beasts carry it with fury."[2]

Even the north of Germany was not sheltered from these cruelties. Bogislas, Duke of Pomerania, having died, his son, who had been brought up at the court of Duke George, persecuted the gospel; Suaren and Knipstraw were obliged to save themselves by flight.

But it was in Holstein that one of the strongest instances of fanaticism was given.

Henry of Zuphten, who had escaped, as we have seen, from the convent of Antwerp, was preaching the gospel at Bremen; Nicholas Boye, pastor at Mehldorf, in the Dittmarches, and several pious persons in that district having invited him to preach the gospel to them, he complied. Forthwith, the prior of the Dominican, and the vicar of the official of Hamburg, consulted together. "If he preaches, and the people listen to him," said they, "all is lost!" The prior, after a wakeful night, got up early in the morning, and proceeded to the wild and sterile moor, where the forty-eight regents of the country usually assembled. "The monk of Bremen is arrived," said he to them, "to ruin all the Dittmarches." These forty-eight simple and ignorant men, who were assured that they would acquire great renown by ridding the world of the heretical monk, resolved to put him to death without having either seen or heard him.

It was Saturday, and the prior wishing to prevent Henry from preaching on Sunday, arrived at midnight at the house of pastor Boye, with the letter of the forty-eight regents. "If it is God's will that I die in the Dittmarches," said Henry Zuphten, "heaven is as near there as any where else.[3] I shall preach."

He mounted the pulpit and preached powerfully. The hearers, touched and inflamed by his eloquence, had scarcely left the church when the prior put into their hands a letter from the forty-eight regents, forbidding them to allow the monk to preach. They immediately sent their representatives to the heath, and, after long debate, the Dittmarches agreed that, considering their complete ignorance of the matter, they would wait till Easter. But the enraged prior waited on some of the regents, and anew inflamed their zeal. "We will write him," said they. "Beware of doing

[1] Verbi non palam seminati. (L. Ep. ii. p. 559.) [2] In Bavaria multum regnat crux et persecutio . . . . (Ibid.) [3] Der Himmel wäre da so nahe als anderswo. L. Op. xix, 330.)

so," replied the prior; "if he begins to speak, nothing can be done to him. He must be seized during the night, and burnt before he can open his mouth."

It was so resolved. The day after the feast of the Conception, after it was night, the *Ave Maria* was tolled. At this signal, all the peasants of the neighbouring villages assembled, to the number of five hundred, and their leaders having caused five hogsheads of Hamburgh beer to be pierced, in this way inspired them with great courage. Midnight struck as they reached Mehldorf. The peasants were armed; the monks carried torches; the whole proceeded, without order, uttering furious cries. On arriving at the village, they kept a profound silence lest Henry should escape.

The doors of the curacy were suddenly burst open, and the drunken peasants rushed in, striking at every thing that came in their way. They threw down vases, kettles, goblets, clothes, snatched up whatever gold or silver they could find, and pouncing on the poor pastor, struck him, crying, "Kill him! kill him!" They then threw him into the mire. But Henry was their object. They pulled him from his bed, bound his hands behind his back, and dragged him after them. "What brought you here?" they asked. Henry having answered mildly, they exclaimed, "Away! away! if we listen to him we will become heretics like himself." He had been hurried naked over the ice and snow, his feet were bleeding, and he begged they would put him on horseback. "Good sooth," replied they in derision, "we are going to furnish heretics with horses! Get along!" And they continued to drag him till they reached the heath. A woman, who was at the door of her house, as the poor servant of God passed, began to cry. "Good woman," said Henry to her, "weep not for me." The bailie pronounced his condemnation. Then one of the furious men who had brought him, struck the servant of Jesus Christ over the head with a sword: another struck him with a club. Next a poor monk was brought to receive his confession. "Brother," said Henry to him, "did I ever do you any harm?" "No," replied the monk. "Then I have nothing to confess to you." The monk withdrew in confusion. Many ineffectual attempts were made to light the pile. In this way the martyr stood for two hours before these furious peasants—calm, and with his eyes raised towards heaven. As they were binding him to throw him on the pile, he began to make confession of his faith. "Burn first," said a peasant, striking him on the mouth with his fist, "and you will speak after." He was thrown down, but fell on the side of the pile. John Holme, seizing a club, struck him on the breast, and he lay stretched out dead on the burning faggots. "Such is the true history of the sufferings of the holy martyr, Henry of Zuph-ten."[1]

CHAP. VII.

Divisions—Lord's Supper—Two Extremes—Carlstadt—Luther—Mysticism of the Anabaptists—Carlstadt at Orlamund—Mission of Luther—Interview at dinner—Conference of Orlamund—Carlstadt banished.

The Reformation, while the Romish party were every where drawing the sword against it, was undergoing new developments. It is not at Zurich or Geneva, but at Wittemberg, the centre of the Lutheran revival, that we must trace the beginnings of that Reformed Church, of which Calvin has become the greatest doctor. These two great families slept in the same cradle. The union ought also to have crowned their age. But the question of the Supper having been once raised, Luther violently rejected the reformed element, and found himself and his Church in an exclusive Lutheranism. The chagrin which he felt at this rival doctrine deprived him somewhat of the good humour which was natural to him, and gave him a spirit of distrust, a habitual dissatisfaction and irritation, which he had not shown previously.

It was between two old friends—between the champions, who, at Leipsic, had fought together against Rome—between Carlstadt and Luther that this dispute arose. Their attachment to contrary doctrines proceeded, both in the one and in the other, from estimable feelings. In fact, there are two extremes in religion; the one consists in materialising, the other in spiritualising every thing. The former is the extreme of Rome—the latter that of the mystics. Religion, like man himself, consists of body and soul; the pure idealists, as well as the materialists, are equally wrong both in religion and in philosophy.

Such is the grand discussion which lies hid under the dispute as to the Supper. While, on a superficial glance, we see only a paltry quarrel about words, a more profound examination discovers in it one of the most important controversies which can occupy the human mind.

The Reformers thus form two great divisions; but each of them carries with it a portion of the truth. Luther, with his adherents, mean to combat an exaggerated spiritualism. Carlstadt, and the reformed, attack a hateful materialism. Each opposes the error

[1] Das ist die wahre Historie, etc. (L. Op. xix, p. 333.

which he deems most fatal, and, in opposing it, perhaps goes beyond the truth. But no matter; each of them is true in its general tendency, and though belonging to different armies, these two distinguished doctors are ranged under one common banner—that of Jesus Christ, who alone is the truth in its fullest extent.

Carlstadt thought that nothing could be more hurtful to true piety than confidence in external ceremonies, and in a certain magical influence in the sacraments. Rome had said, that external participation in the sacrament of the Supper was sufficient to save, and this principle had materialised religion. Carlstadt saw nothing better fitted to spiritualise it anew than to deny all bodily presence of Christ; and he taught that the sacred repast was merely a pledge to believers of their redemption.

On this subject Luther took quite an opposite direction. He had at the outset maintained the view which has just been indicated. In his writing on the mass, which appeared in 1520, he said, "I can every day enjoy the sacraments, if only I remember the word and promise of Christ, and with it nourish and strengthen my faith." Neither Carlstadt, Zuinglius, nor Calvin, has ever said any thing stronger. It even seems that, at this period, the idea often occurred to him, that a symbolical explanation of the Supper would be the most powerful weapon completely to overthrow the whole popish system; for in 1525 he says that, five years before, he had fought many hard battles in defence of this doctrine;[1] and that any one who could have proved to him that there was nothing but bread and wine in the Supper, would have done him an immense service.

But new circumstances occurred, which engaged him in an opposition, sometimes passionate, to these very views to which he had so nearly approximated. The fanaticism of the Anabaptists explain the direction which Luther then took. These enthusiasts were not satisfied with setting little value on what they called the external word, in other words, the Bible, and pretending to special revelations of the Holy Spirit; they also went the length of despising the sacrament of the Supper as something external, and to speak of internal communion as alone true. Thenceforth, in all the attempts which were made to explain the doctrine of the Supper in a symbolical manner, Luther saw nothing but the danger of shaking the authority of the Holy Scriptures, of substituting arbitrary allegories for their true meaning, of spiritualising every thing in religion, making it consist not in divine graces but in human impressions; and thus substituting for true Christianity a mysticism, a theosophy, a fanaticism, which would inevitably be-

[1] Ich habe wohl so harte Anfechtungen da erlitten. (L. Ep. p. 577.)

come its tomb. It must be acknowledged that, but for the powerful opposition of Luther, the mystical, enthusiastic, and subjective tendency, would then, in all probability, have made rapid progress, and trampled under foot all the blessings which the Reformation was destined to diffuse in the world.

Carlstadt, impatient at not being able freely to develope his faith at Wittemberg, urged by his conscience to combat a system, which, according to him, "lowered the death of Christ, and annihilated his righteousness," resolved "to make an outbreak for the love of poor deluded Christendom." He quitted Wittemberg in the beginning of 1524, without notice either to the university or the chapter, and repaired to the little town of Orlamund, whose church was under his superintendence. He caused the vicar to be deposed, and himself to be appointed pastor in his stead; and in spite of the chapter, the university, and the Elector, fixed himself in this new post.

Here he soon disseminated his doctrine. "It is impossible," said he, "to find in the real presence any advantage which does not flow from faith without it; it is therefore useless." In explaining the words of Christ in the institution of the supper, he had recourse to an interpretation which the Reformed Churches have not received. In the Leipsic discussion, Luther had explained the words, "*Thou art Peter, and on this rock I will build my Church*," by separating the two clauses, and applying the latter to the person of the Saviour. "In the same way," said Carlstadt, "*take, eat*, refers to the bread; but, *this is my body*, refers to Jesus Christ, who then showed himself, and intimated by the symbolical sign of the breaking of bread, that the body was soon to be destroyed."

Carlstadt did not stop here. No sooner had he broke loose from the tutelage of Luther, than he felt a revival of his zeal against images. His imprudent harangues, his enthusiastic expressions, must easily, in these times of fermentation, have inflamed men's minds. The people, thinking they heard a second Elijah, broke the idols of Baal. This zeal reached the surrounding villages. The Elector wished to interfere; but the peasants answered him, that it was necessary to obey God rather than man. The prince resolved to send Luther to Orlamund to establish peace. Luther saw in Carlstadt a man devoured by a love of renown,[1] a fanatic, who would allow himself to be carried the length of making war on Jesus Christ himself. Frederick might, perhaps, have made a wiser choice. Luther set out, and Carlstadt saw his troublesome rival once more disarranging his plans of reform, and arresting his course.

Huc pe pulit eum insana gloriæ et laudis libido. (L. Ep. ii, p. 551.) To this an insane thirst for praise and glory impelled him.

Jena is on the road to Orlamund. On arriving in this town, on the 23rd August, Luther mounted the pulpit at seven in the morning, and spoke for an hour and a half in presence of a numerous audience, against fanaticism, rebellion, the destruction of images, and contempt of the real presence, in particular, inveighing strongly against the innovations of Orlamund. He did not name Carlstadt, but every one could see that he had him in view.

Carlstadt, whether by chance or design, was at Jena, and among the number of Luther's hearers. He hesitated not to apply for an explanation of the discourse. Luther was at dinner with the prior of Wittemberg, the burgomaster, the clerk, and pastor of Jena, and several officers in the service of the emperor and the margrave, when a letter from Carlstadt was put into his hands, asking an interview; he handed it to those next him, and replied to the bearer, "If Doctor Carlstadt chooses to come to me, well; if he does not choose to do so, I will dispense with it." Carlstadt arrived. His arrival produced a strong sensation in the party. The greater part eager to see the two lions at close quarters, ceased dining and stared, while the more timid grew pale with fear.

Carlstadt, on the invitation of Luther, sat down opposite to him, and then said, "Doctor, in your sermon to-day you put me in the same class with those who preach rebellion and assassination. I say that charge is false."

Luther.—" I did not name you, but since you have felt hit, good and well."

After a moment of silence, Carlstadt resumed.

" I engage to prove, that, on the doctrine of the Sacrament, you have contradicted yourself, and that no man, since the days of the apostles, has taught it so purely as I have done."

Luther.—" Write—debate!"

Carlstadt.—"I challenge you to a public discussion at Wittemberg or Erfurth, if you procure me a safe-conduct."

Luther.—" Fear nothing doctor."

Carlstadt.—" You bind me hand and foot, and when you have put it out of my power to defend myself, you strike me."[1]

There was a pause. Luther resumed.

" Write against me, but publicly, not in secret."

Carlstadt.—" If I thought you were speaking in earnest I would do so."

Luther.—" Do it, and I'll give you a florin."

Carlstadt.—" Give it, I accept it."

At these words, Luther put his hand in his pocket and drew out a gold florin, and giving it to Carlstadt, said, " Take it, and attack me valiantly."

[1] Ihr bandet mir Hände et Füsse, darnach schlugt Ihr mich. (L. Op. xix, p. 150.)

Carlstadt, holding the gold florin in his hand, turned to the party, and said, "Dear friends, this is my arrhals, a pledge that I am authorised to write against Doctor Luther; I take you all to witness."

Then bending the florin that it might be known again, he put it into his purse, and shook hands with Luther. Luther drank his health, and Carlstadt returned it. "The more vigorous your attacks, the more agreeable they will be," resumed Luther.

"If I fail," replied Carlstadt, "it will be my own fault."

They again shook hands, and Carlstadt returned home.

Thus, says a biographer, in the same way as from a single spark often arises the conflagration of a whole forest, from a small beginning arose a great division in the Church.[1]

Luther proceeded to Orlamund, and arrived there ill prepared by the scene at Jena. He assembled the council and the church, and said, "Neither the Elector nor the university is willing to recognise Carlstadt as your pastor." "If Carlstadt is not our pastor," replied the treasurer of the Town Council, "St. Paul is a false teacher, and your books are lies, for we have chosen him."

As he said these words, Carlstadt entered. Some of the persons near Luther motioned to him to be seated, but Carlstadt, going straight up to Luther, said to him, "Dear doctor, allow me to give you welcome?

Luther.—"You are my enemy. You have my gold florin as a pledge."

Carlstadt.—"I mean to continue your enemy, so long as you continue the enemy of God and of his truth."

Luther.—"Begone; I cannot allow you to appear here."

Carlstadt.—"This is a public meeting. If your cause is just, why fear me?"

Luther (to his servant.)—"Make ready, make ready; I have nothing to do with Carlstadt, and since he will not leave, I start."[2]

At the same time Luther rose up. Then Carlstadt withdrew.

After a momentary pause, Luther resumed, "Prove by Scripture that it is right to destroy images."

A Counsellor.—"Doctor, you will grant that Moses knew the commandment of God," *(opening a Bible.)* "Very well; here are his words, 'Thou shalt not make unto thee any graven image, or any likeness.'"

Luther.—"This passage refers only to the images of idols. If I hang up a crucifix in my chamber without worshipping it, what harm can it do me?"

[1] Sicut una scintilla sæpe totam sylvam comburit. (M. Adam, Vit. Carlst. p. 83.) Our narrative is taken in great part from the Acts of Reinhard, pastor of Jena, an eye-witness, but friend of Carlstadt. Luther charges him with inaccuracy.
[2] Spann an, spann an. (L. Op. xix, p. 154.)

A Shoemaker.—" I have often taken off my hat to an image which happened to be in my room or on the road; this is an act of idolatry which robs God of the glory due to him alone."

Luther.—" It will be necessary then, because of abuse, to destroy females, and throw our wine into the street." [1]

Another Member of the Church.—" No: they are creatures of God, which we are not enjoined to destroy."

After the conference had lasted some time longer, Luther and his people got up into their carriage, astonished at what had passed, and without having succeeded in convincing the inhabitants, who also claimed for themselves the right of freely interpreting and expounding the Scriptures. There was great agitation in Orlamund; the people insulted Luther, some even cried to him, "Begone, in the devil's name. May you break your neck before you get out of our town." [2] Never yet had the Reformer been subjected to such humbling treatment.

He repaired to Kale, the pastor of which had also embraced the doctrines of Carlstadt. Here he resolved to preach. On entering the pulpit he found the remains of a crucifix in it. At first he was deeply moved; but immediately recovering himself, he gathered the fragments into a corner of the pulpit, and delivered a sermon which contained no allusion to the circumstance. "I wished, by contempt," said he afterwards, " to have my revenge of the devil."

The nearer the Elector approached his end, the more he seemed to fear that the Reformation was going too far. He gave orders that Carlstadt should be deprived of his situations, and that he should quit not only Orlamund, but the electoral States. In vain did the church of this town interpose in his behalf; in vain did they ask that he should be allowed to reside among them as a citizen, and give an occasional sermon; in vain did they represent that they valued the truth of God more than the whole world, and even than a thousand worlds, had God created a thousand.[3] Frederick was inflexible; he even went the length of refusing the money necessary for his journey. Luther was no party to this harshness of the prince; it was foreign to his nature, and this he showed at an after period. But Carlstadt regarded him as the author of his misfortune, and filled Germany with his complaints and lamentations. He wrote a farewell letter to his friends of Orlamund. This letter, for the reading of which the bells were rung, and which was heard by the assembled Church amidst tears,[4] was signed,

---

[1] So muss du des Missbrauchs halber auch. (L. Op. xix. p. 155.) [2] Two of the most distinguished historians at present possessed by Germany, add, that the people of Orlamund threw stones and dirt at Luther; but Luther says the very contrary:—" Dass ich nit mit Steinen und Dreck ausgeworffen ward." (L. Ep. ii, p. 579.) [3] Höher als tausend Welten. (Seck., p. 628.) [4] Quæ Publice vocatis per campanas lectæ sunt omnibus simul flentibus. (L. Ep. ii, p. 558.)

"Andrew Bodenstein, banished by Luther without having been either heard or convicted by him."

It is painful to see this bitter quarrel between two who had formerly been friends, and were both excellent men. A feeling of sadness was experienced by all the disciples of the Reformation. What was to become of it, now that its most illustrious defenders had come to blows? Luther saw these fears, and tried to calm them. "Let us fight," said he, "as fighting for another. The cause is God's, the management God's, the glory God's.[1] He will fight and conquer without us. Let that which must fall, fall. Let that which is to stand, stand. It is not our own cause that is in question, nor is it our own glory that we seek."

Carlstadt retired to Strasburg, where he published several productions. "He was thoroughly acquainted," says Dr. Scheur, "with Latin, Greek, and Hebrew;" Luther acknowledged the superiority of his erudition. Of an elevated spirit, he sacrificed his reputation, his rank, his country, his bread even, to his convictions. At a later period he retired to Switzerland. It was there he ought to have broached his doctrines; his independence required the free atmosphere in which an Œcolampadius and a Zuinglius breathed. His doctrine soon attracted almost as much attention as Luther's Theses had obtained. Switzerland seemed to be gained, and with it Bucer and Capito.

Luther's indignation being now at its height, he published one of the most powerful, but also one of the most violent, of his controversial writings, viz.: his book "*Against the Heavenly Prophets.*"

Thus the Reformation, attacked by the pope, attacked by the emperor, attacked by the princes, began also to tear itself to pieces. It appeared on the point of sinking under so many disasters, and certainly must have sunk if it had only been a work of man. But, when on the point of sinking, it arose with new energy.

CHAPTER VIII.

Progress—Resistance to the Leaguers—Meeting between Philip of Hesse and Melancthon—The Landgrave gained over to the Gospel—The Palatinate, Luneburg, Holstein—The Grand Master at Wittemberg.

The Catholic League of Ratisbon and the persecutions which followed it, produced a powerful re-action in the population of Ger-

[1] Causa Dei est, cura Dei est, opus Dei est, victoria Dei est, gloria Dei est. (L. Ep. ii. p. 556.)

many. The Germans were not disposed to allow themselves to be deprived of that word of God which had at length been restored to them. To the orders of Charles V, to the bulls of the pope, to the menaces and scaffolds of Ferdinand, and the other Catholic princes, their reply was, "We shall keep it."

Scarcely had the leaguers left Ratisbon, when the deputies of the towns, whose bishops had taken part in this alliance, feeling surprised and indignant, met at Spires, and resolved that their preachers should, in spite of the bishops, preach the gospel—and the gospel alone—conformably to the doctrine of tne prophets and apostles. They next proposed to present a firm and unanimous remonstrance, to the National Assembly.

It is true, the imperial letter, dated from Burgos, arrived, and disturbed their thoughts. Nevertheless, towards the end of the year, the deputies of these towns, and several of the nobles, met at Ulm, and took an oath of mutual defence, in the event of attack. Thus, to the camp formed by Austria, Bavaria, and the bishops, the free towns immediately opposed another; which raised the standard of the gospel and national freedom.

While the free towns thus took the advanced posts of the Reformation, several princes were gained to the cause. Early in June, 1524, Melancthon was returning on horseback from a visit to his mother, accompanied by Camerarius and some other friends, when, near Frankfort, he fell in with a brilliant train. It was Philip of Hesse, who, three years before, had visited Luther at Worms, and who was now on his way to the games of Heidelberg, which were to be attended by all the princes of Germany.

Thus Providence brought Philip successively into contact with the two Reformers. It was known that the distinguished doctor had gone on a visit to his native district, and one of the landgrave's knights said to him, "I believe it is Melancthon." The young prince immediately put spurs to his horse, and coming up to the doctor, said to him, "Are you Philip?" "I am," replied the scholar, somewhat intimidated, and preparing respectfully to dismount.[1] "Stay," said the prince, " turn round and come and spend the night with me, there are some subjects on which I wish to have a conversation with you; fear nothing." "What could I fear from such a prince as you?" replied the doctor. "Ah! Ah!" said the landgrave laughing, "were I to take you away and give you up to Campeggio, he would not be sorry, I believe." The two Philips rode along side of each other. The prince put questions, and Melancthon answered. The landgrave was delighted with the clear and striking views presented to him. Melancthon at last

[1] Honoris causa de equo descensurus. (Camer., p. 94.)

begging he might be allowed to continue his journey, Philip of Hesse had difficulty in parting with him. "On one condition," said he, "and it is, that, on your return, you will write carefully on the subjects which we have been discussing, and send me the production."[1] Melancthon promised. "Go, then," said Philip, "and pass freely through my states."

Melancthon drew up, with his usual talent, "*An Abridgement of the Revived Doctrine of Christianity.*"[2] This concise and powerful production made a decisive impression on the landgrave, who, shortly after his return from the Heidelberg games, without actually joining the free towns, issued an ordinance, in which, opposing the league of Ratisbon, he commanded that the gospel should be preached in all its purity. He himself embraced it with the energy of his character. "Sooner," exclaimed he, "abandon my body, and my life, my states, and my subjects, than the Word of God." A monk, the friar minor Ferber, perceiving the prince's leaning to the Reformation, wrote him a letter, reproaching him with his conduct, and conjuring him to remain faithful to Rome. "I resolve," replied Philip, "to remain faithful to the ancient doctrine, but such as is contained in Scripture." Then he proved, with great force, that man is justified only by faith. The monk, astonished, held his peace.[3] The landgrave was called "Melancthon's Scholar."[4]

Other princes took a similar direction. The Elector Palatine, refused to lend himself to any persecution. The Duke of Luneburg, nephew to the Elector of Saxony, began to reform his states, and the King of Denmark ordered, that in Schleswig and Holstein, every man should be free to worship God according to his conscience.

The Reformation made a still more important conquest. A prince, the important effects of whose conversion began at this time to turn away from Rome. One day, towards the end of June, shortly after Melancthon's return to Wittemberg, Luther's chamber was entered by the grand master of the Teutonic Order, Albert, Margrave of Brandenburg. The chief of the chevalier monks of Germany, who was then in possession of Prussia, had gone to the Diet of Nuremberg to invoke the aid of the empire against Poland. He returned with a contrite heart. On the one hand, the sermons of Osiander and the reading of the gospel had convinced him that his condition of monk was contrary to the Word of God; on the other, the breaking up of the national government had taken away

---

[1] Ut de quæstionibus quas audisset moveri aliquid diligenter conscriptum curaret. (Camer. p. 94.) [2] Epitome renovatæ ecclesiasticæ doctrinæ. [3] Seckend. p. 738.
[4] Princeps ille discipulus Philippi fuit a quibusdam appellatus. (Camer. p. 95.)

all hope of the assistance which he had gone to claim. What then will he do? .... The Saxon Counsellor Planitz, with whom he quitted Nuremberg, asked him to visit the Reformer. "What think you of the rule of my order?" asked the disturbed and agitated prince at Luther. Luther hesitated not: he saw that a conduct conformable to the gospel could alone save Prussia also. "Implore," said he to the grand master, "implore the help of God; reject the absurd and incongruous rule of your order; put an end to this abominable and truly hermaphrodite supremacy, which is neither religious nor secular.[1] Shun false and seek true chastity —marry, and in place of this nameless monster found a lawful empire."[2] These words pointed out distinctly to the soul of the grand master a situation of which he had till then only had an imperfect glimpse. A smile lighted up his features, but he had too much prudence to declare himself; he held his peace.[3] Melancthon, who was present, spoke in similar terms as Luther, and the prince departed for his states, leaving the Reformers in the belief that the seed which they had sown in his heart would one day bear fruit.

Thus Charles V and the pope had opposed the national assembly of Spires, from a fear that the Word of God might gain all who attended it; but the Word of God could not be bound. It was prohibited to be preached in one of the halls of a town in the Low Palatinate. Well! it had its revenge by diffusing itself throughout all the provinces. It aroused the people, enlightened princes, and, throughout the empire, displayed that divine power of which neither bulls nor ordinances could ever deprive it.

CHAPTER IX.

Reformers—The Church of All Saints—Fall of the Mass—Literature—Christian Schools—Science offered to the Laity—Arts—Moral Religion, Esthetical Religion—Music—Poetry—Painting.

While the people and their rulers were thus pressing toward the light the Reformers were striving to produce a general revival, to penetrate the whole mass with the principles of Christianity. The form of worship first engaged their attention. The time fixed by the Reformer on his return from the Wartburg had arrived.

---

[1] Ut loco illius abominabilis principatus, qui hermaphrodita quidam. (L. Ep. ii, p 527.) [2] Ut contempta ista stulta confusaque regula, uxorem duceret. (Ibid.) [3] Ille tum arrisit, sed nihil respondit. (Ibid.)

"Now," said he, "that men's hearts have been strengthened by divine grace, the scandals which polluted the Lord's kindgom must be made to disappear, and something must be attempted in the name of Jesus." He demanded that the communion should be dispensed in both kinds, that every thing should be retrenched from the Supper which tended to convert it into a sacrifice,[1] that Christian assemblies should never meet without hearing the Word preached,[2] that the faithful, or at least priests and students, should meet every morning at four or five o'clock to read the Old, and every evening, at five or six, to read the New Testament,—that on Sunday, the whole Church should assemble, morning and after-noon, and that the leading object in worship should be the preaching of the Word.[3]

In particular, the church of All Saints, at Wittemberg, aroused his indignation. There 9,901 masses were annually celebrated, and 35,570 pounds of wax burnt. So says Seckendorf. Luther called it a "sacrilegious Tophet." "There are," said he, "only three or four lazy bellies who still worship this shameful Mammon, and did I not restrain the people, this house of all Saints, or rather all devils, would long ago have made a noise in the world, the like of which was never heard."

The struggle commenced around this church. It was like one of those ancient sanctuaries of Paganism in Egypt, Gaul, and Germany, which behoved to fall, in order that Christianity might be established.

Luther, desiring that the mass should be abolished in this cathedral, on the 1st March, 1523, addressed a first petition on the subject to the chapter; and, on the 11th July, addressed a second.[4] The canons, in reply, urged the orders of the Elector, "What have we to do here," replied Luther, "with orders from the prince? He is a secular prince. His business is with the sword, and not with the ministry of the gospel." Luther here clearly draws the distinction between the Church and the State. "There is only one sacrifice," says he again, "which wipes away sins, Christ, who once offered himself, and we have faith in him, not by works or by sacrifices, but solely by faith in the Word of God."

The Elector, who felt his end drawing near, was repugnant to new reforms. But new urgency was joined to that of Luther. Jonas, provost of the cathedral, thus addressed the Elector:—"It is time to act. A manifestation of the gospel, so bright as that we

---

[1] Weise christliche Messe zu halten. (L. Op. L. xxii, p. 232.) [2] Die christliche Gemeine nimmer zoll zusammen kommen, es werde denn daselbst Gottes Wort geprediget. (Ibid. p. 226.) [3] DassWort im Schwange gehe. (Ibid. p. 227.)
[4] L. Ep. ii, p. 308, and 354.

now have, usually lasts no longer than a ray of the sun. Let us, therefore, make haste."[1]

This letter of Jonas not having changed the Elector's views, Luther lost patience. He thought the moment to give the fatal blow had arrived, and addressed a threatening letter to the chapter. "I beg you amicably, and solicit you seriously, to put an end to all this sectarian worship. If you refuse, you shall, by God's help, receive the recompense which you deserve. I say this for your guidance; and I demand a distinct and immediate answer—yes, or no—before next Sunday, that I may know how to act. God grant you grace to follow his light.

MARTIN LUTHER,
"Thursday, 8th Dec., 1524."   "Preacher at Wittemberg."[2]

At the same time the rector, two burgomasters, and ten counsellors, repaired to the dean, and solicited him, in the name of the university, the council, and the community of Wittemberg, " to abolish the great and horrible impiety committed against the divine majesty in the mass."

The chapter was obliged to surrender. It declared that, enlightened by the Holy Word of God,[3] it acknowledged the abuses to which its attention had been directed, and published a new order of service, which began to be observed on Christmas, 1524.

Thus fell the mass in this famous sanctuary, where it had so long withstood the reiterated assaults of the Reformers. The Elector Frederick, suffering under an attack of the gout, and drawing near his end, was not able, notwithstanding all his efforts, to prevent this great act of reformation. He saw the divine will in it, and yielded. The fall of the Roman observances in the church of All Saints, hastened their end in many of the churches of Christendom. There was every where the same resistance, but there was also the same victory. In vain did priests, and in many places even princes, attempt to throw obstacles in the way; they failed.

But it was not worship merely that the Reformation had to change. She, at an early period, placed the school by the side of the Church; and these two great institutions, mighty in regenerating nations, were equally revived by her. The Reformation, when she first appeared in the world, was intimately allied with literature; and this alliance she forgot not in the day of her triumph.

Christianity is not a mere development of Judaism. It does not try, as the papacy would fain do, to confine men again in the swaddling bands of external ordinances and human doctrines. Christianity is a new creation; it seizes man within, and trans-

---

[1] Corp. Reformat. i, p. 636.   [2] L. Ep. ii, p. 565.   [3] Durch das Licht des heiliger Gottlichlen Wortes . . . (L. Op. xviii, p. 502.)

forms him in his inmost heart; so that he no longer has any need of rules from other men. Through the help of God, he can of himself and by himself, discern what is true, and do what is good.[1]

To conduct human nature to this state of independence which Christ has purchased for it, and deliver it from the nonage in which Rome had so long kept it, the Reformation behoved to developc the whole man, renewing his heart and his will by the Word of God, and enlightening his understanding by the study of sacred and profane literature.

Luther understood this. He felt that, in order to secure the Reformation, it was necessary to work upon youth, to improve schools, and propagate in Christendom the knowledge necessary to a profound study of the Holy Scriptures. Accordingly, this was one of the objects of his life. He felt this, particularly at the period which we have now reached, and applied to the counsellors of all the towns of Germany for the foundation of Christian schools. "Dear Sirs," said he to them, " so much money is annually expended on muskets, roads, and embankments, why should not a little be spent in giving poor youth one or two schoolmasters? God is knocking at our door; happy are we if we open to him. The divine Word now abounds. O! dear Germans, buy, buy, while the market is before your houses. The Word of God and its grace are like a wave which ebbs and goes away. It was with the Jews, but it has passed; and they no longer have it. Paul brought it to Greece, but it passed away; and Greece now belongs to the Turk. It came to Rome and Latium, but thence too it has passed; and Rome now has the pope.[2] Do not suppose you are to have this word for ever. The contempt shown for it will chase it away. Wherefore, let him who would have it seize it, and keep it.

"Give attention to children," continues he, still addressing magistrates, " for many parents are like ostriches; they grow callous towards their young, and contented with having laid the egg, give themselves no farther trouble. The prosperity of a town consists, not merely in collecting great treasures, building strong walls, and erecting fine houses, and possessing brilliant armies. If fools come and pounce upon it, its misfortunes will then only be the greater. The true good of a town, its safety and strength, is to have a great number of learned, serious, honest, and well-educated citizens. And whose fault is it, that at present the number of these is so small, if it is not yours, O, magistrates! who have allowed youth to grow up like grass in the forest?"

Luther particularly insists on the study of literature and languages. "What use is there, it is asked, in learning Greek

[1] Hebrews, viii, 5, 11.   [2] Aber hin ist hin; sie haben nun den Papst. (L. Op. W. x, p. 535.)

and Hebrew? We can read the Bible in German." "Without languages," replies he, "we should not have received the gospel.... Languages are the sheath which contains the sword of the Spirit;[1] they are the casket which contains the jewels, the vessel which contains the liquor; and as the gospel expresses it, they are the baskets in which are preserved the bread and fishes to feed the people. If we abandon languages, the result will be, that we shall not only lose the gospel, but also become unable to speak and write in Latin or in German. So soon as the cultivation of them ceases, the gospel is in decay, and ready to fall under the power of the pope. But now that languages are again in honour, they diffuse so much light, that the whole world is astonished; and every one must confess that our gospel is almost as pure as that of the Apostles themselves. The holy fathers, in ancient times, were often mistaken, because they did not know languages; in our days, some, as the Vaudois of Piedmont, do not think languages useful; but though their doctrine is good, they often want the true meaning of the sacred text, they find themselves unarmed against error, and I much fear their faith will not remain pure.[2] Had not languages made me sure of the meaning of the Word, I might have been a pious monk, and have peaceably preached the truth in the obscurity of a cloister; but I should have allowed the pope, sophists, and their antichristian empire to stand."[3]

Luther does not confine himself to the education of ecclesiastics; he is desirous that knowledge should no longer be monopolised by the Church; he proposes to give a share of it to the laity, who, till now, had been disinherited. He proposes that libraries should be established, and that they should not be confined to a collection of the editions of the schoolmen and fathers of the Church, but should also contain the works of orators and poets, even though they should be pagans, as well as works on the fine arts, law, medicine, and history. "These writings serve," says he, "to explain the works and miracles of God."

This work of Luther is one of the most important which the Reformation has produced. It takes science out of the hands of the priests, who had monopolised it, like those of Egypt in ancient times, and restores it to all. From the impulse thus given by the Reformation, have proceeded the greatest developments of modern times. Those laymen, literary and learned, who now assail the Reformation, forget that they themselves are its work, and that without it they should still be placed, like ignorant children, under

---

[1] Die Sprachen sind die Scheide, darinnen dies Messer des Geistes stecket. (L. Op. W. x, p.535.) [2] Es sey oder werde nicht lauter bleiben. (Ibid.) [3] Ich hatte wohl auch können fromm seyn und in der Stille recht predigen. (Ibid.)

the rod of the clergy. The Reformation discerned the intimate union subsisting between all the sciences; she was aware that, as all science comes from God, so it leads back to God. Her wish was that all should learn, and that they should learn all. "Those who despise profane literature," said Melancthon, "have no higher respect for sacred theology. Their contempt is only a pretext by which they try to hide their sloth."[1]

The Reformation was not contented with giving a strong impulse to literature, she also gave a new impulse to the arts. Protestantism is often charged with being inimical to the arts, and many Protestants readily admit the charge. We will not enquire whether or not the Reformation ought to prevail; we will content ourselves with observing, that impartial history does not confirm the fact on which this accusation rests. Let Roman Catholicism plume itself on being more favourable to the arts than Protestantism—all very well. Paganism was still more favourable to them; and Protestantism places her fame on a different ground. There are religions in which the esthetical tendencies of man occupy a more important place than his moral nature. Christian sentiment is expressed, not by the productions of the fine arts, but by the actings of Christian life. Every sect that abandons the moral tendency of Christianity, thereby loses even its right to the Christian name. Rome has not abandoned this essential characteristic, but Protestantism preserves it in much greater purity. Its glory consists in the thorough investigation of whatever belongs to the moral being, and in judging of religious acts, not from their external beauty and the manner in which they strike the imagination, but according to their internal worth and the relation which they bear to the conscience; so that, if the papacy is above all, as a distinguished writer has proved,[2] an esthetical religion, Protestantism is, above all, a moral religion.

Still, although the Reformation addressed man primarily as a moral being, it addressed the whole man. We have just seen how it spoke to his understanding, and what it did for literature: it spoke also to his sensibility, his imagination, and contributed to the development of the arts. The Church was no longer composed merely of priests and monks; it was the assembly of the faithful. All were to take part in worship; and the hymns of the clergy were to be succeeded by those of the people. Accordingly, in translating the Psalms, Luther's object was to adapt them to the singing of the church. In this way a taste for music was diffused over the whole country.

[1] Hunc titulum ignaviæ suæ prætextunt. (Corp. Ref. i, p. 613.) [2] Chateaubriand, Genie du Christianisme.

"After theology," said Luther, "it is to music I give the first place and the highest honour.[1] A schoolmaster," he again said, "must be able to sing; without it I will not even look at him."

One day, when some fine pieces were sung to him, he rapturously exclaimed, "If our Lord God has conferred such admirable gifts on this earth, which is only an obscure recess, what will it be in the eternal life, in a state of perfection!" . . . From the days of Luther the people sung; the Bible inspired their hymns; and the impulse given at the period of the Reformation, at a later period, produced those magnificent oratorios which seem to be the complete perfection of the art.

The same impulse was given to poetry. It was impossible, in celebrating the praises of God, to be confined to mere translations of the ancient hymns. Luther's own soul, and that of several of his contemporaries, raised by faith to the sublimest thoughts, and excited to enthusiasm by the battles and perils which incessantly threatened the rising Church; inspired, in short, by the practical genius of the Old and the faith of the New Testament, soon gave utterance to their feelings in religious poems, in which poetry and music united and blended their holiest inspirations. Thus the sixteenth century beheld the revival of that divine poetry, which, from the very first, had solaced the sufferings of the martyrs. We have already seen how, in 1523, Luther employed it in celebrating the martyrs of Brussels: other sons of the Reformation followed in his steps. Hymns were multiplied, and spreading rapidly among the people, contributed powerfully to awaken them from their slumbers. It was in this same year that Hans Sach sung *The Nightingale of Wittemberg*. The doctrine which, for four centuries had reigned in the Church, he regards as the moonlight, during which men wandered in the desert. The nightingale now announces the sun, and singing to the light of day, rises above the clouds of the morning.

While lyric poetry thus arose from the highest inspirations of the Reformation, satire and the drama, under the pen of Hutten, Mürner, and Manuel attacked the most crying abuses.

It is to the Reformation that the great poets of England, Germany, and perhaps France, owe their lofty flight.

Of all the arts, painting is the one on which the Reformation had the least influence. Nevertheless it was renewed, and in a manner sanctified, by the universal movement which then agitated all the powers of the human mind. The great master of this period, Lucas Cranach, fixed his residence at Wittemberg, where he lived on intimate terms with Luther, and became the painter of the

---

[1] Ich gebe nach der Theologie, der Musica den nähesten Locum und höchste Ehre (L. Op. W. xxii, p. 2253.)

Reformation. We have seen how he represented the contrasts between Christ and antichrist (the pope), and thus gained a place among the most powerful instruments of the revolution which was transforming the nations. As soon as he had acquired new convictions, he consecrated his chaste pencil to drawings in harmony with Christian belief, and shed on groups of children, blessed by the Saviour, the grace with which he had previously adorned legendary saints, male and female. Albert Durer was also won by the preaching of the Word, and his genius took a new flight. His master-pieces date from this period. From the features with which, from that period, he painted the Evangelists and Apostles, we see that the Bible was restored to the people, and that from it the painter drew a depth, a force, a life, and grandeur, which he never could have found in himself.[1]

Still, however, it must be acknowledged, painting is the art whose religious influence is most liable to strong and well-founded objections. Poetry and music came from heaven, and will again be found in heaven; but painting is constantly seen united to grave immoralities or fatal errors. After studying history, or seeing Italy, we are made aware that humanity has little to expect from that art. But whatever may be thought of this exception which we have thought it our duty to make, our general remark holds true.

The Reformation of Germany, while making its first address to the moral nature of man, has given to the arts an impulse which they could not have received from Roman Catholicism.

Thus, there was a universal progress in literature and the arts, in spirituality of worship, in the souls of nations and their rulers. But this magnificent harmony, which the gospel every where produced in the days of its revival, was about to be disturbed. The song of the Nightingale of Wittemberg was to be interrupted by the hissing of the storm and the roaring of the lions. A cloud, in one moment, spread over Germany, and a lovely day was succeeded by a dismal night.

CHAP. X.

Political ferment—Luther against Revolution—Thomas Munzer—Agitation—The Black Forest—The Twelve Articles—Luther's Advice—Helfenstein—Advance of the peasants—Advance of the imperial army—Defeat of the peasants—Cruelty of the princes.

A political fermentation, one very different from that which the gospel produces, had long been working in the empire. Borne down

[1] Ranke, Deutsche Geschichte, ii. p. 85.

by civil and ecclesiastical oppression, bound in several countries to the baronial lands, and sold along with them, the people threatened to rise in fury, and burst their chains. This agitation had been manifested long before the Reformation by several symptoms, and thenceforth religion had been blended with political elements. It was impossible, in the 16th century, to separate these two principles so intimately associated in the life of nations. In Holland, at the end of the previous century, the peasantry had risen up, placing on their colours, as a kind of armorial bearings, bread and cheese, the two great blessings of these poor people. "The shoe alliance" had shown itself in the neighbourhood of Spires, in 1503 In 1513, it had been renewed at Brisgau, and been encouraged by priests. In 1514, Wurtemburg had witnessed "the league of poor Conrad," the object of which was to maintain, by revolt, "the rights of God." In 1515, Carinthia and Hungary had been the theatre of dreadful commotions. These seditions had been suppressed by torrents of blood; but no redress had been given to the people. A political reform was, therefore, no less necessary than a religious reform. The people were entitled to it; but it must be confessed they were not ripe for enjoying it.

Since the Reformation had commenced these popular agitations had been renewed; the minds of men had been absorbed by other thoughts. Luther, whose piercing eye discerned the condition of his countrymen, had, even from the height of the Wartburg, addressed grave exhortations for the purpose of keeping down agitation.

"Revolt," he had said, "does not produce the amelioration which is desired, and God condemns it. What is revolt but taking vengeance into our own hands? The devil is labouring to excite those who embrace the gospel to revolt in order to bring it into reproach, but those who have perfectly understood my doctrine do not revolt." [1]

Every thing gave reason to fear that the popular indignation could not be much longer restrained. The government which Frederick of Saxony had had so much difficulty in forming, and which possessed the confidence of the nation, was dissolved. The emperor, whose energy might, perhaps, have supplied the want of this national administration, was absent; the princes, whose union had always constituted the strength of Germany, were divided; and the new declaration of Charles V against Luther, in taking away all hope of future harmony, deprived the Reformer of a portion of the moral authority, by which, in 1522, he had succeeded

[1] Luther's treue Ermahnung an alle Christen sich vor Aufruhr und Empörung zu hüten. (L. Op. xviii, p. 288.)

in calming the storm. The principal embankments which had hitherto confined the torrent were broken down, and nothing could restrain its fury.

The religious movement did not produce the political agitation, but in several places it allowed itself to be borne along by its tumultuous waves. Perhaps even more should be conceded; it is, perhaps, necessary to admit that the movement given to the people by the Reformation gave new force to the discontent which was prevailing in the nation. The violence of Luther's writings, the intrepidity of his actions and his words, the harsh truths which he told, not only to the pope and the prelates, but also to princes themselves, must have contributed to inflame minds already in a state of effervescence. Accordingly Erasmus did not omit to tell him, "We are now gathering the fruits that you have sown."[1] Moreover, the gladsome truths of the gospel now at length brought fully to light, stirred all hearts, and filled them with hope and expectation. But many unregenerate souls remained unprepared by Christian repentance, faith, and freedom. They wished indeed to reject the yoke of the pope, but they wished not to accept the yoke of Christ. Accordingly, when princes devoted to Rome, sought, in their wrath, to stifle the Reformation, though true Christians knew how to bear these cruel persecutions with patience, the multitude fumed and broke out. Seeing their wishes pent in in one direction, they procured an outlet for them in another. "Why," said they, "when the Church calls all men to a noble freedom, why should slavery be perpetuated in the state? Why, when the gospel speaks only of meekness, should government reign only by force?" Unhappily at the time when religious reform was received with equal joy by princes and people, political reform, on the contrary, was opposed by the most powerful portion of the nation; while the former had the gospel for its rule and support, the latter had no other principles than violence and despotism. Accordingly, while the one kept within the limits of truth, the other, like an impetuous torrent, quickly overlept these, and also those of justice. But to attempt not to see an indirect influence of the Reformation in the disturbances which broke out in the empire, were, in my opinion, to give proof of partiality. By means of religious discussions a fire had been kindled in Germany, and it was impossible that some sparks should not fly off from it, of a nature fitted to inflame the passions of the people.

The pretensions of some fanatics to heavenly inspiration, augmented the evil. While the Reformation had constantly appealed from the pretended authority of the Church to the real authority of

[1] Habemus fructum tui spiritus. (Erasm. Hyperasp. b. 1.)

Scripture, these enthusiasts rejected not only the authority of the Church, but also that of Scripture. They spoke only of an internal word, of a revelation of God within, and overlooking the natural corruption of their heart, they gave themselves up to all the intoxication of spiritual pride, and imagined themselves to be saints.

"To them," says Luther, "the Holy Scripture was only a dead letter, and all began to cry *Spirit! Spirit!* But, assuredly, I will not follow where their spirit leads them. May God, in his mercy, preserve me from a Church where there are none but saints.[1] I wish to remain where the humble, feeble, and sickly are—who know and feel their sin, and who, without ceasing, sigh and cry to God from the bottom of their heart to obtain his consolation and assistance." These words of Luther are profound, and mark the change which was taking place in his views as to the nature of the Church. They show, at the same time, how much the religious principles of the revolters were opposed to the Reformation.

The most remarkable of these enthusiasts was Thomas Munzer. He was not without talents, had read the Bible, was zealous, and might have been able to do good, if he had known how to collect his agitated thoughts, and find peace of heart. But not knowing himself, and being void of true humility, he was possessed with a desire to reform the world, and, like all enthusiasts, forgot that reform ought to begin at himself. Mystical treatises which he had read in his youth had given a false direction to his mind. He first appeared at Zwickau, quitted Wittemberg after Luther's return, discontented with the inferior part he was playing there, and became pastor of the small town of Alstädt in Thuringia. Here he could not long remain quiet. He accused the Reformers of founding, by their attachment to the letter, a new papism, and of founding churches which were not pure and holy.

" Luther," said he, " has delivered consciences from the yoke of the pope; but he has left them in a carnal freedom, and has not carried them forward in spirit toward God."[2]

He thought himself called by God to remedy this great evil. According to him the revelations of the *Spirit* were the means by which his reform was to be accomplished. " He who possesses this Spirit," said he, " has true faith, even though he should never in his life see the Holy Scriptures. Pagans and Turks are more proper to receive it than many Christians who call us enthusiasts." When he thus spoke he had Luther in his eye. " In order to receive this Spirit," added he, "it is necessary to mortify the body,

---

[1] Der barmherzige Gott berhü'e mich ja für der Christlichen Kirche, daren eitel heilige sind. (On John, i, 2. L. Op. (W.) vii, p. 1469.) [2] Führete sie nicht weiter in G....... (L. Op. xix, p. 294.)

wear shabby clothes, let the beard grow, have a gloomy air, keep silence,[1] frequent retired spots, and beg God to give us a sign of his favour. Then God will come and speak with us as he once did with Abraham, Isaac, and Jacob. Did He not do so, it would not be worth men's while to pay any attention to him.[2] I have received a commission from God to assemble his elect in a holy and eternal alliance."

The agitation and ferment working in men's minds, were only too favourable to the propagation of their enthusiastic ideas. Man loves the marvellous, and every thing that flatters his pride. Münzer, having drawn a portion of his flock into his views, abolished church music, and all ceremonies. He maintained, that, to obey princes, " devoid of reason," was to serve God and Mammon. Then, marching at the head of his parishioners to a chapel near Alstadt, and which was resorted to by pilgrims from all quarters, he threw it down. Obliged, after this exploit, to flee the country, he wandered up and down in Germany, and went as far as Switzerland, carrying with him, and communicating to all who would listen to him, the plan of a universal revolution. He every where found men's minds prepared; he threw gunpowder on burning coals, and a violent explosion was the immediate result.

Luther, who had repelled the warlike enterprises of Sickingen,[3] could not allow himself to be carried away by the tumultuous movements of the peasantry. Happily, for social order, the gospel had him in charge; for what might have happened had he given his vast influence to their camp? .... He always firmly maintained the distinction between spiritual and secular; he ceased not to repeat, that what Christ emancipated by his Word was immortal souls, and, while with one hand he attacked the authority of the Church, he with the other equally maintained the power of princes. "A Christian," said he, "must endure death a hundred times sooner than give the least countenance to the revolt of the peasants." In a letter to the Elector, he says, "What particularly delights me is, that these enthusiasts make a boast to every one who listens to them, that they are not of us. They say it is the Spirit that prompts them. But I reply,—It is a bad spirit that bears no other fruit than the pillaging of convents and churches: the greatest robbers' on the face of the earth can do as much."

At the same time Luther, who wished others to have the same liberty that he desired for himself, dissuaded the prince from rigorous measures. "Let them preach as they will, and against

---

[1] Saur sehen, den Bart nicht abschneiden. (L. Op. xix, p. 294.) [2] Munzer's expression is low and profane:—Er wollt in Gott scheissen wenn er niebt mit ihm redet, wie mit Abraham. (His. Munzer by Melancthon.—Ibid., p. 295. [3] First Volume, Book I.

whomsoever they see it good ; for it is necessary that the Word of God itself should lead the van and give them battle. If theirs is the true Spirit, he will not fear our severities: if ours is the true, he will not fear their violence. Let us leave the spirits to struggle and fight with each other.[1] Some perhaps will be seduced, as there is no battle without wounds ; but he who fights faithfully will be crowned. Nevertheless, if they will take the sword, your highness must forbid it, and order them to quit the country."

The revolt broke out in the districts of the Black Forest, and the sources of the Danube, which had so often been agitated by popular commotions. On the 19th July, 1524, some Thurgovian peasants rose up against the Abbot of Reichenau, who refused to give them an evangelical preacher. Thousands were soon assembled around the little town of Tengen, for the rescue of an ecclesiastic who was kept prisoner. The revolt spread with inconceivable rapidity from Suabia, as far as the countries of the Rhine, Franconia, Thuringia, and Saxony. All these countries had risen in January, 1525.

Towards the end of this month, the peasants published a declaration in twelve articles, in which they demanded liberty to choose their own pastors, the abolition of small tithes and villanage, the taxes on heritage, liberty of hunting, fishing, and cutting wood. Each demand was supported by a quotation from Scripture. "If we are mistaken," said they in conclusion, "Luther can put us right by Scripture."

The opinions of the Wittemberg theologians were asked. Luther and Melancthon gave theirs—each separately. They are very characteristic. Melancthon, who regarded every kind of disturbance as a great crime, oversteps his usual gentleness, and cannot give strong enough expression to his indignation. The peasants are criminals, against whom he invokes all laws, human and divine. If friendly conference proves ineffectual, the magistrates must pursue them as robbers and assassins. "However," he adds, (and it was indeed necessary that some one trait should remind us of Melancthon) let there be pity shown to orphans in inflicting the punishment of death."

Luther's opinion of the revolt was the same as Melancthon's ; but he had a heart which beat at the wretchedness of the people. He, on this occasion, showed a lofty impartiality, and told the truth frankly to both parties. He first addressed the princes, and more especially the bishops :

"You," said he to them, " are the cause of the revolt. Your invectives against the gospel, your culpable oppression of the little ones of the Church, have brought the people to despair. It is not

---

[1] Man lasse die Geister auf platzen und treffen. (L. Ep. ii. p. 547.)

the peasants, dear lords, who rise up against you; it is God himself who wishes to oppose your fury.[1] The peasants are only the instruments whom he is employing to humble you. Think not to escape the punishment which he is preparing for you. Even should you succeed in destroying all these peasants, God would of the very stones raise up new ones to chastise your pride. If I wished revenge, I would laugh in my sleeve—look on while the peasants act—or even stimulate their rage; but God forbid! . . . . Dear lords, for the love of God, lay aside your indignation, treat the poor people with discretion as you would persons drunk and bewildered. Suppress these commotions by gentleness, lest a conflagration break forth, and set all Germany in a blaze. Among their twelve articles are some which are just and equitable."

This exordium was fitted to gain the confidence of the peasants, and make them listen patiently to the truths which he had to tell them. He represented to them that a great part of their demands were doubtless well founded; but that to revolt was to act like pagans—that the duty of Christians was patience, and not war—and that, if they continued to rise in the name of the gospel, against the gospel itself, he would regard them as more dangerous enemies than the pope. "The pope and the emperor," continued he, "have united against me; but the more the pope and the emperor have stormed, the greater the progress which the gospel has made . . . . Why so? Because I have never drawn the sword, nor called for vengeance—because I have not had recourse either to tumult or revolt. I have committed all to God, and awaited his strong hand. It is neither with the sword nor the musket that Christians fight, but with suffering and the cross. Christ, their captain, did not handle the sword: he hung upon the tree."

But in vain did Luther give utterance to these most Christian expressions. The people were too much excited by the fanatical discourses of the leaders of the revolt to lend their ear as formerly to the Reformer. "He is playing the hypocrite," they said: "he is flattering the princes. He has waged war with the pope, and yet he would have us to submit to our oppressors!"

The revolt, instead of being calmed, became more formidable. At Weinsberg, Count Louis of Helfenstein, and seventy men under his command, were condemned to death. A party of peasants held their pikes before them in close phalanx; others chased and drove back the count and his soldiers on this bristling forest.[2] The wife of the unhappy Helfenstein, a natural daughter of the Emperor Maxi-

---

[1] Gott ists selber der sebtz sich wider euch. (L. Op. xix, p. 254.)
[2] Und jechten ein Grassen durch die Spiesse. (Malthesius, p. 46.)

milian, with an infant of two years old in her arms, fell on her knees, and, with loud cries, implored the life of her husband, and endeavoured to stop the murderous band; a young boy, who had been in the service of the count, and had joined the rebels, capered near him, playing the dead march on a fife, as if the victims had been dancing to it. All perished: the child was wounded in its mother's arms, and she herself was thrown on a dung cart, and so taken to Heilbronn.

On hearing of these cruelties, a cry of horror was heard among the friends of the Reformation, and a fearful struggle took place in Luther's feeling heart. On the one hand the peasants, deriding his representations, pretended to revelations from heaven, made an impious use of the threatenings of the Old Testament, proclaimed the equality of ranks, and a community of goods, defended their cause with fire and sword, and had recourse to barbarous executions. On the other hand, the enemies of the Reformation asked the Reformer with a malignant smile, if he did not know that it was easier to kindle a fire than to extinguish it? Indignant at their excesses—alarmed at the thought that they might arrest the progress of the gospel—Luther no longer hesitated; all delicacy was at an end; he broke loose against the rebels with all the force of his character, and, perhaps, exceeded the just limits within which he ought to have confined himself.

"The peasants," said he, "commit these horrible sins towards God and towards men, and, by so doing, deserve the death both of the body and the soul. First, they revolt against the magistrates to whom they have sworn fidelity. Next, they rob and pillage convents and castles. Last of all, they cloak their crimes with the mantle of the gospel. If you do not put a mad dog to death you will perish yourself, and the whole country with you. He who is slain in fighting for magistrates will be a true martyr, if he has fought with a good conscience. Luther afterwards gives an energetic picture of the culpable violence of the peasantry in compelling simple and peaceful men to enter their alliance, and so drag them into the same condemnation. He then adds, " Wherefore, dear lords, aid, save, deliver, have pity on these poor people. Strike, stab, and kill who can . . . . If you die you cannot have a happier end, for you die in the service of God, and to save your neighbour from hell."[1]

Neither gentleness nor force could arrest the popular torrent. It was no longer for divine service that the church bell sounded; whenever its grave and solemn sounds were heard rising from the

---

[1] Deinen Nehesten zu retten aus der Holle. (L. Op. xix, p. 266.)

plains, it was the tocsin, and all rushed to arms. The people of the Black Forest had mustered around John Muller of Bulgenbach. Of an imposing appearance, clothed in a red mantle, and with a red bonnet on his head, this leader paraded proudly from village to village, followed by his peasants. Behind him on a car, adorned with ribbons and branches of trees, waved the three-coloured flag, black, red, and white, the signal of revolt. A herald, decked in the same colours, read the twelve articles, and called on the people to join the movement. Whoever refused was excluded from the community.

This procession, which was at first peaceable, soon became more restless. "The barons," they exclaimed, "must be forced to join the alliance." And, to bring them to this, they pillaged their granaries, emptied their wine cellars, fished the baronial ponds, laid the castles of those nobles who resisted them in ruins, and burned convents. Resistance inflamed the rage of these rude men. Equality no longer satisfied them: they would have blood; and vowed that every man who wore a spur should bite the dust.

On the approach of the peasants, the towns, unable to resist, opened their gates and joined the rebels. In every place they entered, pictures were torn, and crucifixes broken to pieces. Armed females ran up and down the streets threatening the monks When defeated in one place, they again mustered in another, and defied the most formidable armies and bodies of troops. A committee of peasants was established at Heilbronn. The Counts of Lowenstein being captured, were clothed in a white frock, with a white baton in their hands, and made to swear to the twelve articles. Brother George, and you brother Albert, said a tinker to the Counts of Hohenloe, who had repaired to the camp, "Swear to conduct us as brethren; for you also are now peasants: you are no longer lords." The equality of ranks, that dream of all democrats, was established in aristocratic Germany.

A great number of nobles, some from fear and others from ambition, now joined the revolters. The famous Götz of Berlichingen, when he saw his people refuse to obey him, wished to fly to the Elector of Saxony; but his wife, who was in childbed, in order to keep him near her concealed the Elector's reply. Götz, almost hemmed in, was obliged to place himself at the head of the rebellious host. On the 7th May, the peasants entered Wurtzburg, and were received by the citizens with acclamation. The troops of the princes and knights of Suabia, who had assembled in this town, evacuated it, and retired in haste to the citadel, the last rampart of the nobility.

But the movement had already extended to other parts of Germany. Spires, the Palatinate, Alsace, and Hesse, acknowledged the twelve articles, and the peasants threatened Bavaria, Westphalia, the Tyrol, Saxony, and Lorraine. The Margrave of Baden, having refused the articles, was obliged to flee. The coadjutor of Fuldah acceded to them, laughing. The small towns said that they had no lances to oppose to the revolters. Mentz, Treves, and Frankfort, obtained the liberties which they claimed.

An immense revolution is taking place throughout the empire. The ecclesiastical and secular taxes which oppress the peasants, must be suppressed, the property of the clergy will be secularised to compensate the princes, and provide for the wants of the empire; imposts must be abolished, with the exception of a tribute, which will be paid every ten years; the governing power, recognised by the New Testament, will alone subsist; all other princes will cease to reign; sixty-four free tribunals will be established, and men of all classes will have seats in them; all states will return to their primitive destination; ecclesiastics will, henceforth, only be pastors of churches; princes and knights will only be defenders of the weak; unity of weights and measures will be introduced; and only one species of money will be coined throughout the empire.

Meanwhile, the princes had recovered from their first stupor, and George of Truchsess, general-in-chief of the imperial army, was advancing from the direction of the Lake of Constance. He defeated the peasants on the 2nd of May, at Beblingen, marched on the town of Weinsberg, where the unfortunate Helfenstein had perished, and burnt and razed it, ordering the ruins to be kept up as an eternal memorial of the treachery of the inhabitants. At Fürfeld, he joined the Elector Palatine and the Elector of Treves, and they all advanced in a body towards Franconia.

Frauenburg, the citadel of Wurtzburg, still held out for the princes, and the grand army of the peasants continued under its walls. On learning the approach of Truchsess, they determined on the assault, and on the 15th of May, at nine in the evening, the trumpets sounded, the three-coloured flag was unfurled, and the peasants rushed to the attack, uttering fearful cries. Sebastian of Rotenhan, one of the warmest friends of the Reformation, had the command of the castle. He had placed the defence on a formidable footing, and when he exhorted the soldiers courageously to repel the assault, all had sworn to do so, by raising three of their fingers to heaven. The most dreadful combat then took place. The energy and despair of the peasants was answered by the fortress with petards, showers of sulphur and boiling pitch, and discharges of artillery. The peasants thus struck by invisible enemies, were for a moment surprised, but their fury soon increased. Night advanced, and the struggle was prolonged. The fortress, lighted up by thousands of battle fires, seemed, amid the darkness, like a proud giant, vomiting flames, and single-handed amidst the cannons' roar struggling for the safety of the empire, against the ferocious valour of savage hordes. Two hours after midnight the peasants, having failed in all their efforts, at last withdrew.

They proposed to negotiate either with the garrison or with Truchsess, who was advancing at the head of his army. But this was to abandon their position. Violence and victory alone could save them. After some irresolution, they determined to set out and meet the imperial army; but the artillery and the cavalry made frightful ravages in their ranks. At Königshofen and next at Engelstadt these poor creatures were completely defeated. The princes, nobles, and bishops, abusing their victory, displayed unheard-of cruelty. The prisoners were hung up along the roads. The bishop of Wurtzburg, who had fled, returned, and going over his whole diocese with executioners, watered it at once with the blood of rebels, and the blood of the peaceable friends of the Word of God. Götz of Berlichingen was condemned to perpetual imprisonment. The Margrave Casimir, of Anspach, put out the eyes of eighty-five peasants, who had sworn that they would never again look upon this prince, and cast upon the world this band of blind men, who went up and down holding each other by the hand, feeling their way, stumbling and begging their bread. The wretched boy, who had played the death march of Helfenstein, was chained to a stake, a fire was kindled around him, and the knights stood by laughing at his horrible contortions.

The ritual was every where established in its ancient form. The most flourishing and populous countries of the empire now presented to the traveller only heaps of carcases and smoking ruins. Fifty thousand men had perished, and the people almost every where lost the little freedom which they had hitherto enjoyed. Such was, in the south of Germany, the fearful end of this revolt.

CHAPTER XI.

Munzer at Mulhausen—Appeal to the People—March of the Princes—End of the Revolt—Influence of the Reformers—Sufferings—Change.

But the evil was not confined to the south and west of Germany. Münzer, after traversing part of Switzerland, Alsace, and Suabia, had again directed his steps towards Saxony. Some citizens of Mulhausen invited him into their town, and appointed him their pastor. The town council having resisted, Münzer deposed it, and named another, composed of his friends, with himself at their head. Entertaining the utmost contempt for the Christ, "sweet as honey whom Luther preached," he determined to have recourse to the most energetic measures. "It is necessary," said he, "to make all the nations of Canaan perish by the sword, as Joshua did." He established a community of goods, and pillaged the convents.[1] Luther, 11th April, 1525, wrote to Amsdorff, "Münzer is King and Emperor of Mulhausen, and no longer merely its pastor." The poor no longer worked; if any one needed cloth or corn, he went and asked it of some rich neighbour; if refused, the poor man seized it; if the rich man resisted, he was hung. Mulhausen being an independent town, Münzer was able to exercise his power without opposition almost for a year. The revolt of the south of Germany led him to believe that it was time to extend his new kingdom. He caused cannon of large calibre to be cast in the Franciscan convent, and endeavoured to make a rise among the peasants and the miners of Mansfeld. "How long will you still sleep?" said he to them in a fanatical proclamation, "rise and fight for the Lord! It is time. France, Germany, and Italy are on the march. On! on! on! Dran! dran! dran! Pay no regard to the distress of the ungodly. They will beseech you like children, but remain pitiless. Dran! dran! dran! The fire burns. Let your sword be always reeking with blood.[2] Dran! dran! dran! Work while it is day." The letter was signed, "Münzer, servant of God against the ungodly."

The country people, eager for plunder, flocked to his banners. Every where, in the districts of Mansfeld, Stolberg, Schwarzberg, in Hesse, the Duchy of Brunswick, the peasants rose. The convents of Michelstein, Ilsenburg, Walkenried, Rossleben, and many others near the Hartz, or in the plains of Thuringia, were completely pillaged. At Reinhardsbrunn, which Luther had visited, the tombs of the ancient landgraves were profaned, and the library destroyed.

Terror spread far and wide. At Wittemberg even some uneasiness was felt. These teachers who had not feared either the emperor or the pope, saw themselves obliged to tremble before a mad man. They were constantly looking out for the news, and counted every step of the revolters. "We are here," said Melancthon, "in great danger. If Münzer succeeds it is all over with us, at least if Christ do not save us. Münzer advances with a cruelty

---

[1] Omnia simul communia. (L. Op. xix, p. 292.)
nicht kalt werden von Blut. (Ibid., p. 289.)
[2] Lasset euer Schwerdt

worse than that of the Scythians,[1] and it is impossible to mouth the atrocious menaces which he throws out."

The pious Elector had long hesitated as to the course he ought to pursue. Münzer had exhorted him, him and all princes to be converted, " because," as he said, " their hour was come ;" and he had signed his letters, " Münzer, armed with the sword of Gideon." Frederick had been desirous to bring back these bewildered men by gentleness. When dangerously ill, he had written on the 14th April, to his brother John,—" Perhaps these poor people have had more than one ground for revolt. Ah, the poor are oppressed in many ways by their temporal and spiritual lords." And when he was reminded of the humiliation, revolutions, and dangers to which he was exposed if he did not powerfully suppress the rebellion, he replied, " Hitherto I have been a powerful Elector, having horses and carriages in abundance ; if it is now the Lord's will to take them from me, I will walk on foot." [2]

The first of the princes who had recourse to arms was the young landgrave, Philip of Hesse. His knights and soldiers vowed to live and die with him. After pacifying his own States, he directed his course towards Saxony. Duke John, the Elector's brother, Duke George of Saxony, and Duke Henry of Brunswick, advanced in the other direction, and united their forces with those of Hesse The peasants frightened at the sight of this army, took refuge on a hill, where, without discipline, without armour, and the greater part without courage, they made a rampart of their waggons. Münzer did not even know how to prepare powder for his immense cannon. No assistance appeared. The army hemmed in the rebels who began to despond. The princes taking pity on them offered conditions, which they seemed disposed to accept, when Münzer betook himself to the most powerful instrument which enthusiasm can bring into play. " To-day," said he, " we shall see the arm of the Lord, and all our enemies will be destroyed." At that moment a rainbow appeared, and Münzer took advantage of it. " Fear not," said he to the burghers and peasants, " I will receive all the bullets which will be shot at you in my sleeve." [3] At the same time he ordered a young gentleman, Maternus of Gcholfen, an envoy of the princes, to be cruelly murdered, that he might in this way deprive the rebels of all hope of pardon.

The landgrave having assembled his troops, said to them, " I know well that we princes are often in fault, for we are men ; but it is God's pleasure that princes be honoured. Let us save our

---
[1] Moncerus plus quam Scythiam crudelitatem præ se fert. (Corp. Ref., i, p. 741.)
[2] So wolle er hinkünftig zu fuss gehen. (Seck., p. 685.) [3] Ihr sollt sehen dass ich alle Büchsensteine in Ermel fassen will. (L. Op. xix, 297.)

wives and our children from the fury of these murderers. The Lord will give us the victory; for he has said, "*He who resists the power resists the ordinance of God.*" Philip then gave the signal for attack. This was on the 15th May, 1525. The army moved forward; but the crowd of peasants remained immovable, singing the hymn, "Come Holy Spirit," and waiting till heaven should declare in their favour. The artillery soon broke the main body, carrying death and consternation into the midst of them. Their fanaticism and courage at once forsook them—they were seized with a panic, and fled in disorder. Five thousand perished in the flight. After the battle, the princes and their victorious troops entered Frankenhausen. A soldier having gone up to the loft of the house where he was quartered, found a man in bed.[1] "Who are you?" said he to him. "Are you a rebel?" Then having discovered a portfolio, he took it, and found letters in it addressed to Thomas Münzer. "Are you Thomas," said the trooper. The sick man, in consternation, said, "No." But the soldier using dreadful threats, Münzer, (for it was indeed he) confessed who he was. "You are my prisoner," said the soldier. Being taken before Duke George and the landgrave, Münzer ended by saying that he had done right in trying to chastise the princes since they opposed the gospel. "Wretch," said they to him, "think of all those whose destruction you have caused." But he replied with a smile, in the midst of his anguish, "They would have it so." He received the sacrament under one kind, and was beheaded along with Pfeiffer his lieutenant. Mulhausen was taken, and the peasants were loaded with chains.

A noble having observed in the crowd of prisoners a peasant of good appearance, approached him, and said, "Well, my lad, which government pleases you best—that of peasants or that of princes?" The poor man replied with a sigh, "Ah, my lord, there is no knife whose blade cuts so keenly as the tyranny of one peasant over another." [2]

The remains of the revolt were extinguished in blood. Duke George, in particular, displayed great severity. In the States of the Elector there was neither punishment nor execution.[3] The Word of God, preached in all its purity, had shown its efficacy in restraining the tumultuous passions of the people.

In fact, Luther had never ceased to combat the rebellion, which he regarded as the forerunner of the universal judgment. He had spared nothing—instruction, entreaty, not even irony. At the end of

---

[1] So findet er einen am Bett. [2] Kein Messer Scherpfer schirrt denn wenn ein Baur des andern Herr wird. (Mathesius, p. 48.) [3] Hic nulla carnificina, nullum supplicium.

the articles prepared by the rebels at Erfurth, he had added as a supplementary article: "*Item*, the following article has been omitted: Henceforth the honourable council shall have no power; it shall have nought to do but sit like an idol or a log; the community will chew all its meat for it, and the council will govern bound hand and foot. Henceforth the waggon will go before the horses, the horses hold the reins, and all go on admirably, conformably to the fine project which these articles expound."

Luther did not content himself with writing. While the tumult was at its height, he left Wittemberg, and travelled over several of the districts where the greatest agitation reigned. He preached and laboured to soften down men's spirits, and his hand, which God rendered powerful, directed, calmed, and brought back to their old channel, those furious torrents which had burst their banks.

The teachers of the Reformation every where exerted the same influence. At Halle, Brentz, by the promises of the divine Word, raised the drooping spirits of the burghers, so that four thousand peasants had fled before six hundred citizens.[1] At Ichterhausen, a multitude of peasants having assembled with the intention of demolishing several castles, and putting the noble proprietors to death, Frederick Myconius went to them alone, and such was the power of his eloquence that their design was immediately abandoned.[2]

Such was the part acted by the Reformers and the Reformation in the midst of the revolt. They combated it with all their might by the sword of the Word, and energetically maintained the principles which alone are capable, at all times, of preserving order and obedience among the nations. Accordingly, Luther maintained that if the power of sound doctrine had not arrested the fury of the people, the revolt would have caused much greater ravages, and completely overthrown both Church and State. There is every reason to believe that this dismal foreboding would have been realised.

If the Reformers thus combated sedition, it was not without receiving severe shocks from it. The moral agony which Luther had first felt in the cell at Erfurth was perhaps at its greatest height after the revolt of the peasants. A great transformation among mankind is not produced without suffering on the part of those who are the instruments of it. To complete the work of Christianity, the agony of the cross was necessary; but He who hung

---

[1] Eorum animos fractos et perturbatos verbo Dei erexit. (M. Adam, Vit. Brentii, p. 441.) [2] Agmen rusticorum qui convenerant ad demoliendas arces unica oratione sic compescuit. (Ibid., p. 178.)

upon the cross addresses each of his disciples in the words, "*Are ye able to be baptised with the baptism that I am baptised with?*"

On the part of the princes it was incessantly repeated that Luther and his doctrine were the cause of the revolt, and however absurd this idea was, the Reformer could not see it so generally received without a feeling of deep grief. On the part of the people, Münzer and all the leaders of the sedition represented Luther as a vile hypocrite, a flatterer of the great;[1] and these calumnies were readily credited. The violent terms in which Luther denounced the rebels had offended even moderate men. The friends of Rome triumphed;[2] all were against him, and the wrath of his age lay as a burden upon him. But what tore his soul most of all was to see the work of heaven thus dragged through the mire, and placed in the same rank with the most fanatical projects. He here recognised his Gethsemane; he saw the bitter cup which was presented to him, and anticipating universal desertion, exclaimed, "*Omnes vos scandalum patiemini in ista nocte.*"[3]

Still amidst all this bitterness of feeling he preserved his faith. "He," said he, "who enabled me to trample the enemy under foot when he rose up against me like a cruel dragon or a raging lion, will not permit this enemy to crush me now that he appears with the perfidious aspect of the serpent.[4] I behold these misfortunes, and I lament them. I have often asked myself if it would not be better to allow the papacy quietly to take its own course, rather than see so many disturbances and divisions break out in the world. But no! Far better rescue some from the devil's throat than leave them all under his murderous fangs."[5]

It was at this period that a revolution in Luther's mind which had begun in the Wartburg was completed. The internal life no longer sufficed him; the Church and her institutions assumed a high importance in his eyes. The boldness with which he had demolished, stopped at the sight of more radical demolition; he felt that it was necessary to preserve, guide, build up, and from amidst the bloody ruins with which the wars of the peasants covered Germany, the edifice of the New Church began slowly to arise.

These disturbances left a deep and lasting emotion. The population was struck with terror. The masses who had sought in the Reformation only political liberty, withdrew

---

[1] Quod adulator principum vocer. (L. Ep. ii, p. 671.) [2] Gaudent papistæ de dissidio nostro. (Ibid., p. 612.) The papists rejoice at our [3] "All ye shall be offended because of me this night." Matt. xxvi, 31. (Ibid. p. 671.) [4] Qui cum toties hactenus sub pedibus meis calcavit et contrivit leonem et draconem, non sinet etiam basiliscum super me calcare. (Ibid.) He who has hitherto so often bruised and trampled the lion and the dragon under my feet, will not allow the adder to trample upon me. [5] Es ist besser einige aus dem Rachen des Teufels herausreissen. (L. Op. ii, ed. ix, p. 961.)

spontaneously when they saw that spiritual liberty alone was offered them. The opposition of Luther to the peasants was equivalent to a renunciation of the ephemeral favour of the people. An apparent calm was soon established, and the turmoil of enthusiasm and sedition,[1] was, throughout Germany, succeeded by a silence which terror inspired.

Thus the popular passions, the revolutionary cause, the prosecution of a radical equality failed in the empire, but the Reformation did not fail. These two movements, which many confound, are clearly distinguished by their different results. Revolt came from beneath, the Reformation from above. A few cavalry and cannon were sufficient to suppress the former, but the latter ceased not to rise, strengthen, and increase in spite of the incessantly renewed attacks of the empire and the Church.

CHAP. XII.

Two Issues—Death of Frederick—The Prince and the Reformer—Catholic Alliance—Projects of Charles—Dangers.

Still, however, the cause of the Reformation seemed at first doomed to perish in the abyss which engulphed the popular liberties. A sad event which now occurred seemed destined to hasten its end. At the moment when the princes were marching against Münzer, ten days before his defeat, the old Elector of Saxony,—he whom God had raised up to defend the Reformation against attacks from without,—was descending into the tomb.

His strength was daily decaying, and the horrors with which the war of the peasants was accompanied, were breaking his compassionate heart. "Ah!" exclaimed he, with a deep sigh; "if it were God's will, I would gladly die. No longer do I behold on the earth either love or truth, or faith, or any thing that is good."[2]

Turning his eyes from the combats with which Germany was resounding, the pious prince calmly prepared for his departure, in his castle of Lochau. On the 4th May, he sent for his chaplain, the faithful Spalatin. "You do well," said he to him, gently, as he entered, "to come and see me; for the sick should be visited." Then ordering his couch to be wheeled towards the table, near which Spalatin was seated, he ordered all his attendants to retire,

[1] Ea res—Incussit, vulgo terrorem . . : ut nihil usquam moveatur. (Corp. Ref. 2.752
[2] Noch etwas gutes mehr in der Welt. (Seck., p. 702.)

and affectionately taking hold of Spalatin's hand, spoke to him of Luther, the peasants, and his approaching departure. At eight in the evening Spalatin returned, when the prince opened his whole heart to him, and confessed his sins, in the presence of God. The next day (5th May), he received the communion in both kinds. He had no member of his family near him—his brother and nephew having set out with the army; but, his domestics were around him, according to the ancient custom of those times. With eyes fixed on the venerable prince, who had been so kind a master, they were all melted in tears.[1] "My little children," said he, with a gentle voice, "if I have offended any one of you, let me have pardon for the love of God; for we princes often give pain to inferiors, and that is wrong." Thus Frederick verified the words of the apostle—"Let the rich rejoice, in that he is made low; because as the flower of the grass he shall pass away."[2]

Spalatin, who did not again leave him, warmly set before him the rich promises of the gospel; and the pious Elector, in its powerful consolations, enjoyed ineffable peace. The evangelical doctrine was no longer viewed by him as the sword which attacks error, pursues it wherever it is found, and after a vigorous struggle, finally overcomes it; it distilled in his heart like the rain and the dew, filling it with hope and joy. The present world was forgotten, and Frederick saw only God and eternity.

Feeling death rapidly approaching, he destroyed the testament which he had written several years before, and in which he recommended his soul to the "Mother of God," and dictated another, in which he cast himself upon the sacred merits of Jesus Christ alone "for the forgiveness of his sins;" and declared his firm conviction that "he was ransomed by the precious blood of his beloved Saviour."[3] After this he said, "I can do no more;" and at five in the evening gently fell asleep. "He was a child of peace," exclaimed his physician, "and he has departed in peace." "O, death!" said Luther, "how bitter to those whom thou leavest in life."[4]

Luther, who was then in Thuringia, trying to calm it, had never seen the Elector but at a distance, at Worms, standing beside Charles V. But these two men had met in soul, the first moment the Reformation appeared. Frederick longed for nationality and independence—as Luther longed for truth and Reformation. No doubt, the Reformation was, first of all, a spiritual work; but it was perhaps necessary, to its first success, that it should link itself to some national interest. Accordingly, no sooner had Luther made a

[1] Das alle Umstehende zum weinen bewegt. (Seck. p. 702.) [2] James, i, 10.
[3] Durch das theure Blut meines allerliebsten Heylandes erlöset. (Ibid. p. 703.)
[4] O mors amara! (L. Ep. ii, p. 659.)

stand against indulgences, than the alliance between the prince and the monk was tacitly concluded—an alliance purely moral, without contract, without writing, without words even, and in which the strong gave no other aid to the weak than to allow him to act. But now that the vigorous oak, under whose shelter the Reformation had gradually grown up was hewn down—now that the enemies of the gospel were every where displaying new hatred and strength, while its partisans were obliged to hide themselves or be silent, nothing seemed able to defend it against the sword of its furious persecutors.

The confederates at Ratisbon who had vanquished the peasants in the south and west of the empire, every where struck at the Reformation, as well as the revolt. At Wurtzburg and Bamberg, several of the most peaceable citizens, some even who had opposed the peasants, were put to death. "No matter," it was openly said, "they were adherents of the gospel." This was enough to make them lose their heads.[1]

Duke George hoped to make the landgrave and Duke John share in his love and his hatred. "See," said he to them, after the defeat of the peasants, and showing them the field of battle, "see the mischiefs engendered by Luther." John and Philip seemed to give some hope of adopting his views. "Duke George," said the Reformer, "imagines he is to triumph now that Frederick is dead; but Christ reigns in the midst of his enemies: in vain do they gnash their teeth; their desire will perish."[2]

George lost no time in forming a confederation, similar to that of Ratisbon, in the north of Germany. The Electors of Mentz and Brandenburg—Dukes Henry and Eric of Brunswick, and Duke George, met at Dessau, and there, in July, concluded a Roman alliance.[3] George urged the new Elector, and the landgrave, his son-in-law, to give in their adherence to it. Then, as if to announce what were to be its results, he beheaded two citizens of Leipsic, in whose house some of the Reformer's writings had been found.

At the same time a letter of Charles V, dated Toledo, arrived in Germany, appointing a new diet to be held at Augsburg. Charles wished to give a new constitution to the empire, that would enable him to dispose, at pleasure, of the forces of Germany. The religious divisions furnished him with the means. He had only to let loose the Catholics on the evangelicals. When they had mutually enfeebled each other, he would obtain an easy triumph over

---

[1] Ranke Deutsche Gesch. ii, p. 226. se omnia posse. (L. Ep. iii, p. 22.) turos sese esse omnia . . . (Ibid.)
[2] Dux Georgius, mortuo Frederico, putat
[3] Habito conciliabulo conjuraverunt restituros sese esse omnia . . . (Ibid.) Having held a meeting, bound to restore all things.

both. Down with the Lutherans! was the emperor's watchword.[1]

Thus, there was a kind of universal league against the Reformation. Never had the soul of Luther been so oppressed with fears. The remains of Munzer's sect had sworn that they would have his life, and his only protector was no more. Duke George, he was informed, intended to apprehend him even in Wittemberg.[2] The princes, who might have been able to defend him, hung down their heads, and seemed to have forsaken the gospel. The university, already thinned by disturbances, was, it was said, to be suppressed by the new Elector. Charles, victorious at Pavia, was assembling a new diet, with the view of giving the finishing blow to the Reformation. What dangers, then, must he not have foreseen . . . . That anguish, those inward sufferings which had often wrung cries from Luther, tore his soul. How shall he resist so many enemies? Amidst these agitations, in presence of these many perils, beside the corpse of Frederick almost before it was cold, and the dead bodies of the peasants who strewed the plains of Germany—who would have thought it—Luther married!

CHAP. XIII.

The Nuns of Nimptsch—Luther's Feelings—End of the Convent—Luther's Marriage—Domestic Happiness.

In the monastery of Nimptsch, near Grimma, there were, in 1523, nine nuns, who diligently read the Word of God, and had perceived the contrast between the Christian life and the life of the cloister. Their names were—Magdalene Staupitz, Eliza Canitz, Ave Grossn, Ave and Margaret Schoufeld, Laneta Golis, Margaret and Catherine Zeschau, and Catherine Bora. The first proceeding of these young persons, after they had withdrawn from the superstitions of the monastery, was to write their parents. "The salvation of our souls," they said, "does not allow us to continue any longer to live in a cloister."[3] The parents, fearing the trouble which such a resolution might give them, harshly repulsed the desire of their daughters. The poor nuns knew not what to do. How were they to leave the monastery? They trembled at the thought of so desperate a step. At last, the disgust which the papal worship produced, carried the day. They promised not to quit each other, but to repair, in a body, to some respectable place,

---

[1] Sleidan, Hist. of the Ref. i, p. 214.   [2] Kelt Luther's Leben, p. 160.   [3] Der Seelen Seligkeit halber. (L. Ep. ii, p. 325.)

decently, and in order.[1] Leonard Koppe and Wolff Tomitzch, two worthy and pious citizens of Torgau, offered their assistance.[2] They accepted it, as sent by God himself, and left the convent of Nimptsch without meeting with any opposition, as if the hand of the Lord had opened the gates for them.[3] Koppe and Tomitzch received them in their car; and, on the 7th April, 1523, the nine nuns, astonished at their own hardihood, stopped, with emotion, before the gate of the old Augustin convent, where Luther was residing.

"It is not I who have done it," said Luther on receiving them; " but would to God I could thus save all captive consciences, and empty all cloisters."[4] Several persons made an offer to the doctor to receive the nuns into their houses, and Catherine Bora was taken into the family of the burgomaster of Wittemberg.

If, at that time, Luther had any thought of preparing for some solemn event, it was to mount the scaffold—not approach the hymeneal altar. Many months later, his answer to those, who spoke to him of marriage was, " God can change my heart as he pleases; but now, at least, I have no thought whatever of taking a wife; not that I do not feel some inclination for the married state: I am neither wood nor stone; but I am in daily expectation of the death and punishment due to a heretic."[5]

Still every thing in the Church continued to advance. The monastic life, an invention of man, was every where succeeded by the habits of domestic life. On Sunday, 9th October, Luther having risen as usual, laid aside his Augustin frock, put on the dress of a secular priest, and then made his appearance in the church, where the change produced the greatest joy. Christendom, which had renewed its youth, gave a glad welcome to all which announced that old things were passed away.

Shortly after the last monk quitted the convent, but Luther still remained; his steps alone were heard in its long passages, and he sat alone in silence in the refectory, which was wont to echo with the tattle of the monks. An eloquent solitude! one which attested the triumphs of the Word of God! The convent had ceased to exist. Towards the end of 1524, Luther sent the keys of the monastery to the Elector, stating that he would see where God might be pleased to give him food.[6] The Elector gave the convent to the university, and asked Luther to continue to reside

---

[1] Mit aller Zucht und Ehre an redliche Stätte und Orte kommen. (L. Ep. ii, p. 323.).
[2] Per honestos cives, Torgavienses adductæ. (Ibid. p. 319.) [3] Mirabiliter evaserunt. (Ibid.) They made a miraculous escape. [4] Und alle Klöster ledig machen. (Ibid. p. 322.) [5] Cum expectem quotidie mortem et meritum hæretici supplicium. (Ibid. p. 570, 30th November, 1524.) [6] Muss und will ich sehen wo mich Gott ernähret. (Ibid. p. 582.)

in it. The abode of the monks was soon to become the hearth of a Christian family.

Luther, whose heart was so well fitted to relish the sweets of domestic life, honoured and loved the married state; it is even probable that he had an attachment for Catherine Bora. For a long time his scruples, and the thought of the calumnies to which the step might give rise, had prevented him from thinking of her; and he had made an offer of poor Catherine, first to Baumgartner of Nuremberg,[1] and then to Doctor Glatz of Nuremberg. But when he saw Baumgartner refuse Catherine, and Glatz refused by her, he asked himself more seriously, if he should not form the connection in his own person.

His old father, who had been so much grieved at his embracing the ecclesiastical state, urged him to marry.[2] But there was one idea which perpetually presented itself to Luther's conscience with new energy; marriage is a divine—celibacy a human institution. He had a horror at every thing that came from Rome. "I wish," said he, to his friends, "to preserve no part of my papistical life."[3] He prayed night and day, beseeching the Lord to deliver him from his uncertainty. At length all scruples were dissipated by one consideration. To all the motives of convenience and personal feeling which led him to apply to himself the words, "*It is not good that man should be alone,*"[4] was added a motive of a still higher nature and greater power. He saw, that if he was called to marriage as a man, he was still more called to it as a Reformer. This decided him.

"If this monk marries," said his friend, lawyer Schurff, "he will make the world and the devil burst with laughter, and destroy the work which he has begun."[5] This saying made a very different impression on Luther from what might have been supposed. To defy the world, the devil, and his enemies, and, by an action, fitted, as was thought, to destroy the work of the Reformation, to prevent the success of it from being in any way ascribed to him, was the very thing which he desired. Hence, boldly lifting his head, he replied "Very well, I shall do it. I shall play this trick to the world and the devil—I will give this joy to my father, I will marry Catherine." By marrying, Luther broke still more completely with the institutions of the papacy. He confirmed the doctrine which he had preached by his example, and encouraged the timid entirely to renounce their errors.[6] At this time,

---

[1] Si vis lætam tuam Boram tenere. (L. Ep. ii, p. 563.) [2] Aus Begehren meines lieben Vaters. (Ibid. iii, p. 2.) [3] Ibid. p. 1. [4] Genesis, ii, 18. [5] Risuros mundum universum et diabolum ipsum. (M. Ad. Vit. Luth. p. 130.) [6] Ut confirmem facta quæ docui, tam multos invenio pusillanimes in tanta luce Evangelii. (L. Ep. iii. p. 13.) That I may, by act, confirm what I have taught, so many do I find pusillanimous in this great light of the gospel.

Rome was, apparently, here and there regaining part of the territory which she had lost: she was, perhaps, beginning to cherish a hope of victory; and lo, a mighty explosion carries surprise and terror into her ranks, and makes her more fully aware of the courage of the enemy, whom she thought she had tamed. "I wish," said Luther, "to bear testimony to the gospel, not only by my words, but also by my works. In the face of my enemies, who already triumph, and sing jubilee, I mean to marry a nun, in order that they may understand and know that they have not vanquished me.[1] I do not marry in the hope of living long with my wife; but seeing people and princes letting loose their fury against me, foreseeing that my end is near, and that after my death they will trample my doctrine under foot. I mean to leave, for the edification of the weak, a striking confirmation of what I have taught here below."[2]

On the 11th June, 1525, Luther repaired to the house of his friend and colleague, Amsdorff. He asked for Pomeranus, whom he distinguished by the name of "the Pastor," to bless his union. The celebrated painter, Lucas Cranach, and Doctor John Apelles, acted as witnesses. Melancthon was not present.

Luther's marriage made a noise throughout Christendom. He was assailed from all quarters with accusations and calumnies. "It is incest!" exclaimed Henry VIII. "A monk marrying a vestal!" said some.[3] "Antichrist must be born of this union," said others; for there is a prophecy that he is to spring from a monk and a nun." On this Erasmus observed, with a sarcastic smile, "If the prophecy be true, how many thousands of Antichrists must the world already contain!"[4] But while Luther was thus assailed, several wise and moderate men within the pale of the Romish Church took up his defence. "Luther," said Erasmus, "has married a member of the illustrious house of Bora, but without dowry."[5] A still more venerable testimony was given to him. The teacher of Germany, Philip Melancthon, whom this bold step had at first amazed, said, in that solemn tone, to which even his enemies listened with respect,—"If it is pretended that there is any thing unbecoming in the marriage of Luther, it is a lie and a calumny.[6] I think he must have done violence to his own feelings

---

[1] Nonna ducta uxore in despectum triumphantium et clamantium, Io! Io! hostium. (L. Ep. iii, p 21.) [2] Non duxi uxorem ut diu viverem, sed quod nunc propiorem finem meum suspicarer. (Ibid. p. 32.) I have not married for long life, but because I suspect my end is drawi. g near. [3] Monachus cum vestali copulareter. (M. Ad. Vit. Luth. p. 131.) [4] Quot Antichristorum millia jam olim hab t mundus. (Er. Ep. p. 789.) [5] Erasmus adds :—"Partu maturo sponsæ vanus erat rumor. (Ibid. pp. 780, 789.) There was a foolish rumour that his wife was about to have a child. [6] Ὅτι ψεῦδος τοῦτο καὶ διαβολή ἐστι. (Corp. Ref. i, p. 753, ad Cam.)

in marrying. Married life is a humble, but it is also a holy state—if there is such a state in the world—and the Scriptures uniformly represent it as honourable in the sight of God."

Luther was at first moved on seeing so much contempt and wrath poured out upon him. Melancthon redoubled his friendship and regard,[1] and the Reformer was soon able to see in the opposition of men only a sign of the approbation of God. "Did I not offend the world," said he, "I should have reason to tremble, lest what I have done should not be agreeable to God."[2]

There was an interval of eight years between Luther's attack on indulgences, and his marriage with Catherine Bora. It would thus be difficult, though it is still attempted, to attribute his zeal against the abuses of the Church to an impatient desire of marrying. He was at this time forty-two years of age, and Catherine Bora had been two years at Wittemberg.

Luther was happy in his marriage. "The greatest gift of God," said he, "is a pious amiable spouse, who fears God, loves her house, and with whom one can live in peace and perfect confidence." Some months after his marriage, he announced to one of his friends that Catherine had hopes of becoming a mother.[3] A son was born about a year after the marriage.[4] The sweets of domestic life soon dissipated the clouds which the anger of his enemies had at first raised around him. His Ketha, (Kate,) as he called her, showed the greatest affection for him—comforted him, when he was depressed, by quoting passages of the Bible to him, relieved him from all the cares of ordinary life, sat beside him during his hours of leisure, embroidered the portrait of her husband, reminded him of the friends to whom he had forgotten to write, and often amused him by her simple-hearted questions. There appears to have been a certain degree of pride in her temper: hence Luther sometimes called her "Sir Kate." He one day said in jest, that, if he were still unmarried, he would hew an obedient wife for himself out of stone, for such an one no where existed in reality. His letters fully expressed his fondness for Catherine. He called her "his dear and affectionate wife,"—"his dear and amiable Kate." Luther's humour was more sportive in Catherine's society; and this happy turn of mind continued with him ever after, even amidst the greatest dangers.

The almost universal corruption of the clergy had brought the priesthood into the greatest contempt, and though there were some

---

[1] Πασα σπουδὴ καὶ εὔνοια. (Corp. Ref., i, p. 753, ad Cam.) [2] He adds Offenditur etiam in carne ipsius divinitatis et creatoris. (L. Ep. iii, p. 32)
[3] 21st October, 1525. Catena mea simulat vel vere implet illud Genes. iii. Tu dolore gravida eris. (Ibid., p. 35) [4] Mir meine liebe Kethe einen Hansen Luther wracht hat gestern um zwei. (8th June, 1526. Ibid. p. 119.)

true servants of God, their isolated virtues could do away with it. Domestic peace, conjugal fidelity, the surest foundations of earthly happiness, were continually disturbed in town and country by the licentiousness of monks and priests. None were secure against their attempts at seduction. They took advantage of the free access which they had into the bosom of families, and sometimes also of the intimate intercourse furnished by the confessional, to instil a deadly poison into their penitents, and so gratify their vicious propensities. The Reformation, by abolishing the celibacy of priests, re-established the sacredness of the marriage tie. The marriage of ecclesiastics put an end to an immense number of secret crimes. The Reformers became models to their flocks in the most intimate and important relation of life, and the people were not slow in expressing their joy at again seeing the ministers of religion become husbands and fathers.

CHAP. XIV.

The Landgrave—The Elector—Prussia—Reformation—Secularisation—The Archbishop of Mentz—Conference of Friedewalt—Diet—Alliance of Torgau—Resistance of the Reformers—Alliance of Magdeburg—The Catholics redouble their efforts—Marriage of the Emperor—Threatening Letters—The two Parties.

Luther's marriage at first seemed to add to the embarrassment of the Reformation, which was still suffering from the shock which it had received from the revolt of the peasants. The sword of the emperor and the princes had always been drawn against it, and its friends, the landgrave and the new Elector, seemed discouraged and afraid to speak out.

However, this state of things was not of long duration. The young landgrave soon stood up boldly. Ardent and courageous, like Luther, he had been won by the charms of the Reformer's character. He threw himself into the cause of the Reformation with the eagerness of youth, and at the same time studied it with the gravity of a maturer intellect.

In Saxony, the place of Frederick had not been supplied either in regard to wisdom or influence; but his brother, the Elector John, instead of the passive part of protection, interfered more directly, and with more courage in religious affairs. When quitting Weimar on the 16th August, 1525, he intimated to the assembled priests, " I desire that in future you preach the pure Word of God, without any human addition." Some old ecclesiastics, who did not know how to obey, replied with great simplicity, "We are not forbidden, however, to say mass for the dead, nor to bless water and salt."—"Every thing," resumed the Elector, "ceremonies as well as preaching, ought to be regulated by the Word of God."

The young landgrave shortly after formed the strange project of converting his father-in-law, Duke George. Sometimes he proved the sufficiency of Scripture, sometimes attacked the mass, the papacy, and vows. Letter succeeded letter, and all the declarations of the Word of God were alternately opposed to the faith of the old duke.[1]

These efforts did not prove useless. The son of Duke George was gained to the Reformation. But Philip failed with his father-in-law. "In one hundred years," said the latter, "it will be seen who is in the right."—"Sad words," said the Elector of Saxony. "What kind of faith is it that stands in need of such a trial?"[2] "Poor duke .... He will wait long. God, I fear, has hardened him as he did Pharaoh."

In Philip the evangelical party found a bold and intelligent leader, capable of withstanding the formidable attacks which their enemies were preparing. But is there not reason to regret that the head of the Reformation was, from this moment, a man of war, instead of being a mere disciple of the Word of God? The human element was enlarged, and the spiritual element diminished. This was detrimental. For every work ought to be developed according to its own nature, and that of the Reformation was essentially spiritual.

God was multiplying its supports. A powerful state on the frontiers of Germany, Prussia, gladly arrayed itself under the gospel standard. The chivalric and religious spirit which had founded the Teutonic order had gradually died away with the times which gave it birth. The knights, now seeking only their private interest, had produced dissatisfaction among the people subject to them. Poland had profited by this in 1466 to obtain from the order a recognition of her sovereignty. The people, the knights, the grand master, the Polish government, were so many opposite powers, which were continually jostling each other, and rendered the prosperity of the country impossible.

Then came the Reformation, and in it was recognised the only means of deliverance to this unhappy people. Brismann, Speratus, Poliander, (Dr. Eck's secretary at the Leipsic discussion,) and others preached the gospel in Prussia.

One day a mendicant, from the countries subject to the Teutonic knights, arrived at Wittemberg, and, halting before Luther's door, with solemn voice sang Poliander's beautiful hymn,—

---

[1] Rommels Urkundenbuch, i, p. 2. [2] Was das für ein Glaube sey, der eine solche Erfahrung erfordert. (Seckend. p. 739.)

"To us at length salvation comes."[1] The Reformer, who had never heard the hymn, listened with astonishment and rapture. The foreign accent of the singer increased his joy. "Again! again!" exclaimed he, when the mendicant had finished. He then asked him where he got the hymn, and his tears began to fall when he learned that from the shores of the Baltic a cry of deliverance was resounding even in Wittemberg. Then clasping his hands, he thanked God.[2]

In fact, salvation was there.

"Take pity on our misery," said the people of Prussia to the grand master, "and give us preachers who proclaim the pure gospel of Jesus Christ." Albert at first gave no answer, but he entered into conference with Sigismund, King of Poland, his uncle and sovereign lord, who acknowledged him as hereditary Duke of Prussia.[3] The new prince entered his capital of Konigsberg amid the ringing of bells, and the acclamations of the people; all the houses were splendidly decorated, and the streets strewed with flowers. "There is only one order, said Albert, and that is Christendom." The monastic orders disappeared, and the divine order was re-established.

The bishops gave up their secular rights to the new duke; the convents were turned into hospitals; the gospel was preached even in the humblest village, and, in the following year, Albert married Dorothea, daughter of the King of Denmark, whose "faith in the one only Saviour" was immoveable.

The pope called upon the Emperor to exercise severity against this "apostate" monk, and Charles put Albert under the ban.

Another prince, of the family of Brandenburg, Albert, Archbishop of Mentz, was then on the point of following the example of his cousin. The war of the peasants threatened the ecclesiastical states in particular; the Elector, Luther, all Germany believed that they were on the eve of a great revolution. The archbishop thinking that the only means of saving his principality was secretly to secularise it, asked Luther to prepare the people for this bold step.[4] This Luther did by a letter which he prepared for them, and intended to publish. "God," said he, "has laid a heavy hand on the clergy: they must fall: nothing can save them."[5] But the war of the peasants having terminated much more speedily than had been imagined, the cardinal kept his temporal possessions; his fears were dissipated, and he renounced the project of secularisation.

---
[1] Es ist das Heyl uns kommen her.
[2] Dankte Gott mit Freuden. (Seck. p. 668.)   [3] Sleidan, Hist. of the Ref. p. 220.
[4] Seckend. p. 712.   [5] Er muss herunter. (L. Ep. ii, p. 674.)

While John of Saxony, Philip of Hesse, and Albert of Prussia openly professed the Reformation, and thus the place of prudent Frederick was supplied by three princes of resolution and courage, the holy work made progress in the Church and among the nations. Luther solicited the Elector to establish the evangelical ministry throughout the States instead of the priesthood of Rome, and to appoint a general visitation of the churches.[1] About the same time episcopal powers began to be exercised, and ministers to be consecrated. "The pope, the bishops, the monks, and the priests, need not make a noise. We are the Church. There is no other Church than the assembly of those who have the Word of God, and are purified by it."

All this could not be said and done without producing a powerful re-action. Rome had thought the Reformation extinguished in the blood of the rebellious peasants, but every where its flames re-appeared brighter and fiercer. She resolved to make a new effort. The pope and the emperor wrote threatening letters, the one from Rome, the other from Spain. The imperial government prepared to replace matters on the ancient footing, and it was seriously proposed entirely to crush the Reformation at the approaching Diet.

The electoral prince of Saxony and the landgrave, alarmed, met on the 7th November, at the castle of Friedewalt, and agreed that their deputies at the Diet should act on a common understanding. Thus, in the forest of Sullingen were formed the first elements of an evangelical alliance opposed to the leagues of Ratisbon and Dessau.

The Diet was opened, on the 11th December, at Augsburg. The evangelical princes did not attend in person. The deputies of Saxony and Hesse spoke out boldly at the outset. "The revolt of the peasants," said they, " was occasioned by imprudent severity. Neither by fire nor sword can the truth of God be plucked out of men's hearts. If you resolve on employing violence against the Reformation, the result will be more dreadful evils than those which you have just with difficulty escaped."

It was felt that the resolution which should be taken could not fail to be of immense importance. Every one was desirous to put off the decisive moment in order to gain additional strength. It was, therefore, resolved to meet again at Spires in May following. The rescript of Nuremberg was meantime to continue in force. "Then," said they, " we will thoroughly decide the points of holy faith, righteousness, and peace."

The landgrave prosecuted his design. In the end of February,

---

[1] L. Ep. iii, 28, 38, 51, etc.   [2] Dass Kirche sey allein diejenige, so Gottes Wort haben und damit gereiniget werden. (Corp. Ref. i, p. 766.)

1526, he had a conference with the Elector at Gotha. The two princes agreed that if they were attacked on account of the Word of God, they would unite their whole forces to resist their adversaries. This alliance was ratified at Torgau. It was to have important results.

The landgrave did not think the alliance of Torgau sufficient. Convinced that Charles V was seeking to form a league "against Christ and his holy Word," he wrote letter after letter to the Elector representing the necessity of uniting with other states. "For myself," said he, "I would die, and be chased from my throne, sooner than abjure the Word of God."[1]

At the electoral court there was great uncertainty. In fact, there was a serious obstacle to the union of the evangelical princes. This obstacle was in Luther and Melancthon. Luther wished that the evangelical doctrine should be defended by God alone. He thought that the less men interfered with it, the more manifest the interposition of God would appear. All the measures proposed to be taken seemed to him attributable to cowardly timidity and culpable distrust. Melancthon feared that the alliance of the evangelical princes was the very thing to bring on the war which it was wished to avoid.

The landgrave did not allow himself to be arrested by these considerations, and endeavoured to induce the states around him to join the alliance, but his efforts were not crowned with success. Frankfort refused to become a party to it. The Elector of Treves withdrew his opposition, and accepted of a pension from the emperor. The Elector Palatine himself, whose evangelical leanings were well known, rejected the propositions of Philip.

The landgrave thus failed in the direction of the Rhine, but the Elector, notwithstanding of the advice of the theologians of the Reformation, entered into negotiation with the princes who had at all times rallied round the throne of Saxony. On the 12th June, the Elector and his son, the Dukes Philip, Ernest, Otho, and Francis of Brunswick and Luneburg, Duke Henry of Mecklenburg, Prince Wolf of Anhalt, Counts Albert and Gebhard of Mansfeld, met at Magdeburg, and there, under the precedency of the Elector, formed an alliance similar to that of Torgau.

"God Almighty," said these princes, "having in his ineffable mercy caused his holy and eternal Word, the food of our souls and our greatest treasure here below, to appear again amongst men; and powerful manœuvres having been employed on the part of the clergy and their adherents, to annihilate and extirpate it, we being firmly assured that He who has sent it to glorify his name upon

[1] Seck. p. 763.

the earth, is able also to maintain it, engage to preserve this holy Word to our people, and for this end to employ our goods, our lives, our states, our subjects, all that we possess—confiding not in our armies, but solely in the omnipotence of the Lord, whose instruments we desire to be."[1] So spoke the princes.

The town of Magdeburg was two days after received into the alliance, and the new Duke of Prussia, Albert, Duke of Brandenburg, gave in his adherence to it in a special form.

The evangelical alliance was formed, but the dangers which it was intended to avert became every day more alarming. The priests and princes friendly to Rome had seen this Reformation which they thought completely strangled, suddenly rise up before them in a formidable shape. The partisans of the Reformation were already almost as powerful as those of the pope. If they have the majority in the Diet, it is easy to divine what the ecclesiastical states have to expect. Now then or never! The question is no longer merely the refutation of a heresy; a powerful party must be combated. Other victories than those of Dr. Eck must now save Christendom.

Decisive measures had already been taken. The metropolitan chapter of the primary church of Mentz had convened a meeting of all its suffragans, and decided on sending a deputation to the emperor and the pope, to ask them to save the Church.

At the same time Duke George of Saxony, Duke Henry of Brunswick, and the Cardinal-Elector Albert, had met at Halle, and had also resolved to address Charles V. "The detestable doctrine of Luther," said they, "makes rapid progress. Every day attempts are made to gain even us, and when gentle means fail, attempts are made to compel us by stirring up our subjects. We invoke the assistance of the emperor."[2] Accordingly, after the conference, Brunswick himself set out for Spain to decide Charles.

He could not have arrived at a more favourable moment. The emperor had just concluded with Francis the famous treaty of Madrid; and as he seemed to have nothing to fear in that quarter, his eyes were now turned wholly to Germany. Francis I had offered to pay half the expenses of the war, whether against the heretics or against the Turks.

The emperor was at Seville, on the eve of marriage with a princess of Portugal, and the banks of the Guadalquiver were re-echoing with the sound of festivities. A brilliant nobility, and immense crowds of people thronged the ancient capital of the Moors. Under the arches of the magnificent cathedral was displayed all the

---

[1] Allein auf Gott den Allmächtigen, als dessen Werkzeuge sie handeln. (Hortleber Ursache des deutschen Krieges, i. p. 1490.) [2] Schmidt, Deutsche Gesch, viii, p. 202.

pomp of the Church. A papal legate officiated, and never, even in the days of the Arabs, had Andalusia seen a more splendid and imposing ceremony.

This was the time when Henry of Brunswick arrived from Germany, and besought Charles V to save the Church and the empire, which were now attacked by the monk of Wittemberg. His request was immediately taken into consideration, and the emperor determined on decisive measures.

On the 25th March, 1526, he wrote to several of the princes and towns which adhered to Rome, and at the same time gave the Duke of Brunswick a special commission, to say to them, that with deep grief he had learned that the continual progress of Luther's heresy was threatening to fill Germany with sacrilege, devastation, and blood—that, on the other hand, he had extreme pleasure in seeing the fidelity of the great majority of the States—that, neglecting every other affair, he was going to quit Spain and repair to Rome to make arrangements with the pope, and thenceforth return to Germany, to combat the detestable pest of Wittemberg; that as to themselves they ought to adhere stedfastly to their faith; and if the Lutherans sought to draw them into error by stratagem or force, they should enter into close union with each other, and resist boldly; that he would shortly arrive and support them with all his authority.[1]

On the return of Brunswick to Germany, the Catholic party were overjoyed, and proudly lifted their heads. The Dukes of Brunswick, and Pomerania, Albert of Mecklenburg, John of Juliers, George of Saxony, the Dukes of Bavaria, and all the ecclesiastical princes thought themselves sure of victory after they read the threatening letters of the conqueror of Francis I. They would repair to the approaching Diet, they would humble the heretical princes, and, if they did not otherwise submit, would compel them by the sword. Duke George is confidently affirmed to have said, "I may be Elector of Saxony whenever I please;"[2] an expression to which it was afterwards attempted to give a different turn. One day the duke's chancellor said at Torgau with an air of triumph,[2] "Luther's cause cannot hold out long, it had better be looked to."

Luther, in fact, did look to it, but not in the sense thus implied: he attentively followed the designs of the enemies of the Word of God, and thought, as well as Melancthon, that he would soon see thousands of swords drawn against the gospel. But he sought his strength in a higher source than man. "Satan," wrote he to Fre-

[1] Archives of Weimar.   [2] Ranke, Deutsch Gesch. ii, p. 349. Rommel Urkunden p. 22.

derick Myconius, " is giving full vent to his fury; wicked pontiffs are conspiring and threatening us with war. Exhort the people to fight valiantly before the throne of God by faith and prayer, so that our enemies, being overcome by the Spirit of God, may be compelled to make peace. The first want, the first work is prayer; let the people know that they are now exposed to the edge of the sword and the fury of the devil, and let them pray."[1]

Thus, every preparation was made for a decisive combat. The Reformation had on its side the prayers of Christians, the sympathies of the people, and the rising influence of mind which no power could arrest. The papacy had in its favour the ancient order of things, the power of ancient custom, the zeal and hatred of formidable princes, and the power of that great emperor whose dominion extended over two worlds, and who had just given so rude a check to the glory of Francis I.

Such was the posture of affairs at the opening of the Diet at Spires. At present we return to Switzerland.

[1] Ut in mediis gladiis et furoribus Satanæ posito et periclitanti. (L. Ep. iii, p. 100.

BOOK ELEVENTH.

DIVISION, SWITZERLAND, GERMANY.

1523—1527.

CHAP. I.

Unity in Diversity—Primitive Faith and Liberty—Formation of Roman Unity—
A Monk and Leo Juda—Theses of Zuinglius—The discussion of January.

WE are going to see the diversities, or, as they have been called, the *variations* of the Reformation. These form one of its most essential features.

Unity in diversity, and diversity in unity, is the law of nature, and also the law of the Church.

Truth is like the light of the sun. The light, as it descends from heaven, is always one and the same, and yet it assumes different colours on the earth, according to the objects on which it falls. In the same manner, expressions, which differ somewhat from each other, may sometimes express the same Christian idea, contemplated under different points of view.

How dull should creation be, were this immense variety of forms and colours which constitute its riches, replaced by an absolute uniformity! In like manner, how desolate the appearance, if all created beings formed only a single magnificent unity.

Divine unity has its rights; human diversity has its rights also. It is not necessary in religion to annihilate either God or man. If you have no unity, your religion is not of God; if you have no diversity, it is not of man. Now, it ought to be of both. Would you erase from the creation one of the laws which God has imposed upon it, viz., that of an immense diversity? "*Even things without life,*" says St. Paul, "*whether pipe or harp, except they give a distinction in the sounds, how shall it be known what is piped or harped?*" 1 Cor. xiv, 7. But if there is in religious things a diversity, caused by the difference of individuality, and which, consequently, must exist even in heaven, a diversity there is which has been caused by the fall of man, and is a serious calamity.

There are two tendencies which equally lead to error. The former exaggerates the diversity, and the latter the unity. The doctrines essential to salvation form the boundary between these two directions. To exact more than these doctrines is to infringe on the diversity—to exact less is to infringe on the unity.

The latter excess is that of rash and rebellious spirits, who turn away from Jesus Christ to form human systems and doctrines.

The former exists in various exclusive sects, and, in particular, in that of Rome.

The Church should reject error. Did she not do so Christianity could not be maintained. But, were we to push this idea to an extreme, the result would be, that the Church would require to oppose the smallest deviation, and involve herself in disputes about words. Faith would be swaddled, and Christian sentiment brought into bondage. Such was not the condition of the Church in the days of true Catholicism—I mean the first centuries. It rejected the sectaries who assailed the fundamental truths of the gospel; but these truths admitted, it left faith at full liberty. Rome soon abandoned these wise limits, and in proportion as a domination and doctrine of man was formed in the Church there arose also a unity of man.

A human system being once invented, its rigour increased from age to age. Christian liberty, which had been respected by the catholicism of the first ages, was first limited, then chained, then stifled. Conviction, which, according to the laws of human nature and the Word of God, ought to be formed freely in the heart and the understanding of man, was imposed externally as fully formed and symmetrically arranged by his masters. Reflection, will, sentiment, all the faculties of the human mind, which, in due subordination to the Word and the Spirit of God, ought to labour and produce freely, were abridged in their liberty, and compelled to expand in forms previously determined. The spirit of man became like a mirror, on which foreign objects are represented, but which possesses nothing of its own. Doubtless there still were souls taught directly by God. But the great majority of Christians had thenceforth only the convictions of others: a faith properly belonging to the individual became a rarity. The Reformation alone restored this treasure to the Church.

Still there was for sometime a space, within which the human mind was allowed to range, certain opinions which it might admit or reject at pleasure. But, as a besieging army, always drawing closer and closer around the town, does not allow the garrison to stir beyond the precincts of the walls, and at length obliges it to surrender, in the same way was the hierarchy seen, in every age, and almost every year, abridging the space which it had granted provisionally to the human mind, until, at length, the space was entirely encroached upon, and ceased to exist. Everything that was to be believed, loved, or done, was regulated and fixed in the bureaus of the Roman chancery. The faithful were relieved from the trouble of examining, thinking, and wrestling; they had only to repeat the formula which they had been taught.

From that time, if there appeared in the bosom of Roman catholicism any man who inherited the catholicism of the apostolic times, that man, incapable of expanding within the limits to which he had been confined, behoved to overleap them, and show anew to the astonished world the lofty flight of the Christian who acknowledges no law save that of God.

The Reformation, then, in restoring liberty to the Church, behoved to restore to her her original diversity, and people her with families, united by the great features of resemblance which they derive from their common head, but differing in secondary features and bespeaking the inherent varieties of human nature. It were, perhaps, to be desired that this diversity could subsist in the universal Church without producing sects. Still, it ought to be remembered, that sects are only the expression of this diversity.

Switzerland and Germany, which, till now, had been developed independently of each other, came into contact at the period, the history of which we are now to trace, and exemplified this diversity which was to become one of the characteristic features of Protestantism. We shall see men perfectly agreed on all the great points of faith, differing, however, on secondary questions. No doubt, passion mingled in these discussions; but while deploring this sad mixture, Protestantism, far from disguising the diversity, acknowledges and proclaims it. The path by which she leads to unity is long and difficult, but her unity is real.

Zuinglius was making progress in the Christian life. While the gospel had delivered Luther from the profound melancholy to which he had formerly abandoned himself in the convent of Erfurth, and given him a serenity which often assumed the form of joyfulness, and of which the Reformer thenceforth gave numerous proofs, even in face of the greatest dangers, Christianity had had quite a contrary effect on the joyous child of the mountains of Tockenburg. Withdrawing Zuinglius from his volatile and worldly life, it impressed a gravity on his character that was not natural to it. This serious turn was very necessary. We have seen how, towards the end of 1522, numerous enemies seemed to rise up against the Reform.

ation.[1] Zuinglius was every where loaded with invectives, and disputes often took place, even in churches.

Leo Juda, small in stature,[2] says a biographer, but full of charity for the poor, and of zeal against false teachers, had arrived at Zurich towards the end of 1522, to discharge the office of pastor of the church of St. Peter, having been succeeded at Einsidlen by Oswald Myconius.[3] He was a valuable acquisition to Zuinglius and the Reformation.

One day, shortly after his arrival, he heard an Augustin monk, in the church to which he had been called to be pastor, vehemently preaching, that man is able of himself to satisfy the justice of God. "Reverend father prior," exclaimed Leo, "listen for an instant, and you, dear citizens, keep quiet; I will speak as becomes a Christian." He then proved to the people the unsoundness of the doctrine which they had just heard.[4] There was great agitation in the church, and several forthwith angrily assailed the "little priest," who had come from Einsidlen. Zuinglius appeared before the great council; desiring to give an account of his doctrine in presence of the deputies of the bishop, and the council in their desire to see an end put to these dissensions, summoned a conference for the 29th January, 1523. The news quickly spread over Switzerland. "There is going to be a *diet* of vagabonds at Zurich," said the adversaries spitefully—"all the footpads will be there."

Zuinglius, preparatory to the contest, published sixty-seven theses. Openly in the eyes of all Switzerland, the mountaineer of Tockenburg boldly attacked the pope.

"All," said he, "who maintain that the gospel is nothing without the confirmation of the Church, blaspheme God.

"The only way of salvation to all men who have been, are, or are to be, is Jesus Christ.

"All Christians are the brethren of Christ, and brethren of each other, and they have no fathers on the earth; thus, orders, sects, and parties fall.

"No constraint should be laid on those who do not acknowledge their error, provided they do not, by seditious conduct, disturb the peace."

Such were some of the theses of Zuinglius.

On the morning of Thursday the 29th of January, more than six hundred persons met in the hall of the great council at Zurich.

---

[1] Vol. II, Book viii. [2] Er war ein kurzer Mann. (Füsslin Beytrüge, iv, p. 44.) [3] Ut post abitum Leonis, monachis aliquid legam. (Zw. Ep. p. 253.) That after Leo's departure I may read to the monks. [4] J. J. Hottinger, Helv. Kirch. Gesch. iii, p. 105.

Citizens and strangers, learned men, persons of distinction, and ecclesiastics, had responded to the call of the council. "What," it was asked, "is to be the result of all this?"[1] Nobody dared to answer; but the attention, excitement, and agitation of the assembly, showed plainly that great things were expected.

Burgomaster Roust, who had fought at Marignan, presided. The chevalier, James of Anwyl, grand master of the episcopal court of Constance, Faber the vicar-general, and several doctors, represented the bishop. Schaffhausen had sent Doctor Sebastian Hofmeister; he was the only deputy from the cantons so long as the Reformation was in its infancy in Switzerland. On a table in the middle of the hall was the Bible, and beside it stood a teacher. This was Zuinglius. "I am agitated and tormented on all sides," he had said; "but still I remain firm, leaning not on my own strength, but on the rock, which is Christ, through whose aid I can do all things."[2]

Zuinglius arose. "I have preached," said he, "that salvation is found only in Jesus Christ; and for this I am stigmatised throughout Switzerland as a heretic, a seducer, a rebel. . . . . Now then, in the name of God, here I am to answer."[3] . . . .

All eyes now turned towards Faber, who rose and replied, "I was not sent here to debate, but only to listen." The assembly, in surprise, began to laugh. "The Diet of Nuremberg," continued Faber, "has promised a council in a year; we should wait for it."

"What!" said Zuinglius, "is not this great and learned assembly as good as a council?" Then addressing the counsellors, he said, "Gracious lords, defend the Word of God."

Profound silence followed this appeal; after some time it was broken by the burgomaster. "If any one has any thing to say," said he, "let him do so." There was again silence. Zuinglius then said, "I implore all my accusers (and I know there are several of them here) to come forward, and for the love of truth, show wherein I deserve blame." Nobody said a word. Zuinglius renewed his demand a second and third time: it was in vain. Faber being close pressed, for a moment forgot the reserve which he had imposed on himself, to declare that the pastor of Filispach, who was detained in prison, had been convinced by him of his error; but he immediately became reserved as before. In vain was he urged to explain the reasons by which he had convinced the pastor. He was obstinately silent. The spectators, becoming impatient at

[1] Ein grosses Verwunderen, was doch uss der Sach werden wollte. (Bullinger, Chron. i, p. 97.)   [2] Immotus tamen maneo, non meis nervis nixus, sed petra Christo, in quo omnia possum. (Zw. Ep. p. 261.)   [3] Nun wohlan in dem Namen Gottes, hie bin ich. (Bullinger, Chron. p. 98.)

the silence of the Roman doctors, a voice was heard from the bottom of the hall, exclaiming, "Where are now those valiant men,[1] who speak so loud in the streets? Ho! come forward, here is your man!" Nobody presented himself. Then the burgomaster said, with a smile, "It seems, that the famous sword which smote the pastor of Filispach is not to come out of its scabbard to-day." So saying, he adjourned the meeting.

In the afternoon, when the assembly again met, the council declared, that Master Ulric Zuinglius, not having been censured by any one, should continue to preach the Holy Gospel, and that all the other priests of the canton should teach only what they could establish by the Holy Scriptures.

"God be praised," exclaimed Zuinglius, "who is pleased that his Holy Word should reign in heaven and on the earth." Faber could not now restrain his indignation. "The theses of Master Ulric," said he, "are contrary to the honour of the Church and the doctrine of Christ, and I will prove it." "Do so," exclaimed Zuinglius. But Faber refused to do it any where but at Paris, Cologne, or Friburg. "I won't have any other judge than the gospel," said Zuinglius; "sooner will the earth open than you succeed in shaking a single word contained in it."[2] "The gospel," said Faber, "always the gospel! .... We could live holily in peace and charity even though there were no gospel."[3]

At these words the audience rose up in indignation, and the discussion closed.

CHAP. II.

Caresses of the Pope—Progress of the Reformation—The image of Stadelhofen—Sacrilege—The Ornaments of the Saints.

The Reformation, having gained the day, was now to hasten its conquests. After this conflict of Zurich, where the ablest champions of the papacy had remained mute, who would have the courage to oppose the new doctrine? Meanwhile, other weapons were tried. The firmness of Zuinglius, and his republican leanings, misled his enemies, and hence special methods were employed for the purpose of overcoming him. While Rome was pursuing Luther

---

[1] The monks. Wo sind nun die grossen Hansen .... (Zw. Op. i, p. 124.)
[2] Ee müss das Erdrych brechen. (Zw. Op. i, p. 148.) [3] Man möcht dennocht früntlich, fridlich und tugendlich läben, wenn glich kein Evangelium were. (Bull. Chron. p. 107. Zw. Op. i, p. 152.)

with her anathemas, she endeavoured to gain the Reformer of Zurich by gentle methods. Scarcely had the discussion closed, when Zuinglius was visited by the son of burgomaster Roust, the captain of the pope's guards, accompanied by the legate Einsius, who had in charge for him a pontifical brief, in which Adrian VI called Zuinglius his well-beloved son, and acquainted him with "his very particular regard." [1] At the same time, the pope made Zink be pressed to gain Zuinglius. "What, then, does the pope commission you to offer?" asked Oswald Myconius. "Every thing," replied Zink, "except the pontifical see." [2]

There was no mitre and crozier, no cardinal's hat that the pope would not have given to gain the Reformer of Zurich. But in regard to him Rome was under strange illusions. All her offers were unavailing. The Romish Church had a more inveterate enemy in Zuinglius than in Luther. He cared less than Luther did for the ideas and rites of former ages. To provoke his attack upon any custom innocent in itself, it was enough that it was attached to some abuse. The Word of God, he thought, was alone entitled to stand.

But if Rome so little understood what was taking place in Christendom, she had counsellors who tried to correct her mistake.

Faber, irritated at seeing the pope thus humbling himself before his adversary, hastened to enlighten him. A courtier, who had always a smile upon his lips and honied words in his mouth, Faber was, by his own account, the friend of every body, even of those whom he was accusing of heresy. But his hatred was mortal. Hence, the Reformer, playing on the word Faber said, "The vicar of Constance is a fabricator . . . . of lies. Let him openly proceed to arms, and see how Christ defends us." [3]

These words were not a vain bravado; for while the pope was speaking to Zuinglius of his eminent virtues, and of the particular confidence which he had in him, the enemies of the Reformer were multiplying in Switzerland. Veteran soldiers, leading families, and mountain shepherds, were uniting in their hatred against this doctrine, which was at variance with their tastes. At Lucerne a pompous spectacle was announced under the name of *The Passion of Zuinglius*. A dwarf, meant to represent the Reformer, was dragged to execution, crying, that they were going to put the heretic to death. Laying hold of some Zurichers who were at Lucerne, they obliged them to be spectators of this ridiculous exhi-

[1] Cum de tua egregia virtute specialiter nobis sit cognitum. (Zw. Ep. p. 266.)
[2] Serio respondit: Omnia certe præter sedem papalem. (Vit. Zwingli per Osw Myc.)
[3] Prodeant volo, palamque arma capiant . . . . (Zw. Ep. p. 292.)

bition. "They will not disturb my peace," said Zuinglius. "Christ will never be wanting to his people."[1] The Diet itself resounded with menaces against him. "Dear confederates," said counsellor Mullinen to the cantons, "oppose the Lutheran cause in time. . . . . . . At Zurich a man is no longer a master in his own house."

This agitation of the adversary announced what was taking place in Zurich still better than any proclamations could have done. In fact, the victory was yielding its proper fruit ; the conquerors gradually took possession of the country, and the gospel daily made new progress. Twenty-four canons, and a great number of chaplains, came, of their own accord to the council, to demand a reform of their statutes. It was resolved to supply the place of these idle priests by pious and learned men, commissioned to give the youth of Zurich a Christian and liberal education, and to establish, instead of their Latin vespers and masses, a daily exposition of a chapter of the Bible according to the Hebrew and Greek text, first for the learned, and then immediately after for the people.

All armies unfortunately contain blundering recruits, who detach themselves from the main body, and prematurely attack some point which ought for the time to have been left untouched. A young priest, named Louis Ketzer, having published in Germany a treatise, entitled "*The Judgment of God against Images*," a strong impression was produced, and images became the constant dislike of a portion of the population. When a man allows his attention to be engrossed by secondary matters, it is always to the detriment of more essential matters. A crucifix carefully sculptured and richly adorned had been placed on the outside of one of the gates of the town, at the place called Stadelhofen. The most ardent partisans of the Reformation shocked at the superstition to which this image gave occasion, were unable to pass it without expressing their indignation. A citizen named Claud Hottinger, " a worthy man," says Bullinger, "and well read in the Scriptures," having met the miller of Stadelhofen, to whom the crucifix belonged, asked when he meant to pull down his idols. "Nobody obliges you to worship them," replied the miller. "But do you not know," resumed Hottinger, "that the Word of God forbids us to have graven images?" "Very well," replied the miller, " if you are authorised to pull them down, I abandon them to you." Hottinger thought himself entitled to act, and shortly after, about the end of September, he set forth from the town with a number of citizens. On arriving at the crucifix, they quietly dug all around it until the

---

[1] Christum suis nunquam defuturum. (Zw. Ep. p. 278.)

image yielded to their efforts, and fell to the ground with a loud noise.

This bold action spread general alarm; one would have said that with the crucifix of Stadelhofen, religion itself had been overthrown. "These men are blasphemers! They are worthy of death!" exclaimed the friends of Rome. The council caused the iconoclast burghers to be apprehended.

"No;" said Zuinglius and his colleagues from the pulpit, "Hottinger and his friends are not guilty before God or worthy of death.[1] But they may be punished for having acted with violence, and without the authority of the magistrates."[2]

Meanwhile similar acts were repeated. One day a vicar, of the church of St. Peter, seeing a number of poor people before the church without food and clothing, said to one of his colleagues, turning towards some of the pompously decked images, "I would willingly strip these wooden idols in order to clothe these poor members of Jesus Christ." A few days after, at three in the morning, the saints, and all their ornaments, disappeared. The council ordered the vicar to be imprisoned, though he declared that he was not the guilty party. "What!" said the people, "was it bits of wood our Saviour ordered us to clothe? Is it on account of these images he will say to us, '*I was naked, and ye clothed me?*'" Thus, the Reformation, when discountenanced, became only the more powerful. The more it was curbed the more violently it sprang forward, threatening to bear down its opposition.

CHAP. III.

The October Discussion—Zuinglius on the Church—The Church—First Outline of Presbyterianism—Discussion on the Mass—Enthusiasts—A Voice of Wisdom—Victory—A characteristic of the Swiss Reformation—Moderation—Oswald Myconius at Zurich—The Revival of Letters—Thomas Plater of the Valois.

Even these excesses were to prove salutary. A new combat was necessary in order to secure new triumphs; for it is equally true in mental as in worldly affairs—that there is no conquest without a struggle. Since the soldiers of Rome remained motionless, the combat was to be provoked by rash sons of the Reformation. In fact, the magistrates were uncertain and at a loss how to act. They felt that their conscience required to be enlightened; and,

---

[1] An exposition of the same principles may be seen in the speeches of Messieurs De Broglie and Royer-Collard, in the famous debates on the law of sacrilege.
[2] Dorum habend ir unser Herren kein rächt zuinen sy zu töden. (Bull. Chr., p. 127.)

with this view, they resolved to institute a second public discussion in German, when the question of images should be tried by Scripture.

The Bishops of Coire, Constance, and Bale, the university of Bale, and the twelve cantons, were in consequence invited to send deputies to Zurich. The bishops refused the invitation. Remembering the sad figure their deputies had made at the previous discussion, they had no wish to renew these humiliating scenes. Let the evangelicals dispute if they will; but leave them to do it by themselves. The first time we were silent—the second we wont even appear. Rome, perhaps, imagined that there would be no combat from want of combatants. The bishops were not singular in refusing to come. The men of Underwalden replied that they had no learned men among them, but merely honest and pious priests, who explained the gospel as their fathers had done, and therefore they would not send any deputy to Zuinglius, "and the like of him;" but that, if they had him in their clutches, they would handle him in a way which would leave him no desire to repeat the same faults.[1] Schaffhausen and St. Gall alone sent representatives.

On Monday, 26th October, after sermon, an assembly of more than nine hundred persons, consisting of members of the Grand Council, and three hundred and fifty priests, filled the large hall of the town-house. Zuinglius and Leo Juda were seated at a table on which lay the Old and New Testament in the original tongues. Zuinglius first spoke, and, demolishing the authority of the hierarchy and its councils with a vigorous arm, established the rights of every Christian church, and claimed the liberty of the primitive ages—of those times when the Church had neither oecumenical nor provincial councils. "The Church universal," said he, "is diffused over the whole world, wherever there is faith in Jesus Christ, in the Indies as well as at Zurich. . . . . And, as to particular churches, we have them at Berne, at Schaffhausen—here also. But the popes, their cardinals, and their councils, are neither the Church universal nor the Church particular.[2] This assembly which I now address," he continued energetically, "is the church of Zurich; it desires to hear the Word of God, and it is entitled to enjoin whatever it deems conformable to the Holy Scriptures."

Thus Zuinglius leant upon the Church—but the true Church; not on priests only, but on the congregation of Christians—on the people. All that Scripture says of the Church in general, he applied to particular churches. He did not think that a church

---

[1] So wollten wir Ihm den Lohn geben, dass er's nimmer mehr thäte. (Simmler Samml., M S., ix.) [2] Der Päbste, Cardinäle und Bischöffe Concilia sind nicht die Christliche Kirche. (Füssl. Beytr., iii, p. 20.)

listening with docility to the Word of God, could be deceived. The Church he regarded as politically and ecclesiastically represented by the Great Council.[1] He at first discussed each question in the pulpit, and then, after men's minds were convinced of the truth, he laid the matter before the Great Council, who, being agreed with the ministers of the Church, adopted the decisions which she approved.[2]

In the absence of deputies from the bishop, the defence of the pope was undertaken by the old canon, Conrad Hoffman, who had been the means of calling Zuinglius to Zurich. He maintained that the Church, the flock, "the third estate," had no right to discuss such matters. "I was thirteen years at Heidelberg," said he, "I lived with a great scholar, called Doctor Joss, a worthy pious man, with whom, for a long time, I ate and drank, and lived on familiar terms; but he always said that it was unbefitting to discuss such subjects. You see well!" Every body was ready to laugh; but the burgomaster stopped the explosion. "Thus, then," continued Hoffman, "let us wait for a council. For the time being, I have no wish to discuss, but to submit to the bishop, even were he a rogue!"

"Wait for a council!" replied Zuinglius. "And who will attend a council? The pope and lazy ignorant bishops, who will do nothing of their own accord. No: that is not the Church! Höng and Küssnacht (two Zurich villages) are much more certainly a Church than all the bishops and popes put together!"

Thus Zuinglius claimed the restoration of the rights of the Christian people, whom Rome had disinherited of their privileges. The assembly before which he spoke was not, in his view, the Church of Zurich, but it was its primary representative. We have here the germs of the Presbyterian system. Zuinglius withdrew Zurich from the jurisdiction of the bishopric of Constance, detached it from the Latin hierarchy, and on the idea of the flock, of the Christian assembly, founded a new ecclesiastical constitution, to which other countries were at a later period to adhere.

The discussion was continued. Several priests having risen to defend images, but without appealing to the Holy Scriptures, Zuinglius and the other reformers employed the Scriptures in refuting them. "If no one rises," said one of the presidents, "to give Bible arguments in favour of images, we shall call upon some of their

---

[1] Diacosion Senatus summa est potestas Ecclesiæ vice. (Zw. Op. iii, p. 339.)

[2] Ante omnia multitudinem de quæstione probe docere ita factum est, ut quidquid diacosii cum verbi ministris ordinarent, jamdudum in animis fidelium ordinatum esset. (Ibid.) By thoroughly instructing the people, first of all in the question, the result was, that, whatever the council of two hundred, with the ministers of the Word enjoined, was already enjoined in the minds of the faithful.

defenders by name." Nobody coming forward, he called upon the curate of Wadischwyl. " He is asleep," cried one of the audience. The curate of Horgen was then called upon. " He sent me in his stead," replied his vicar; " but I dont wish to answer for him." The Word of God gave evident tokens of its power in the midst of this assembly. The friends of the Reformation were full of power, liberty and joy ; their opponents appeared speechless, uneasy, desponding. In succession were called the curates of Laufen, Glattfelden, Wetzikon, the rector and curate of Pfäffikon, the dean of Elgg, the curate of Bäretschwyl, the Dominican and Cordelier friars, who were known every where to preach up images, the Virgin, saints, and the mass, but all answered that they could not say any thing in their favour, and that, in future, they would apply to the study of the truth. " Hitherto," said one of them, " I have believed the ancient ; now I mean to believe the new doctors." " It is not us that you ought to believe," exclaimed Zuinglius, " it is the Word of God. The Scriptures alone never deceive." The meeting was protracted, and night drew on. President Hofmeister of Schaffhausen, rose and said, "Blessed be the Almighty and Eternal God who giveth us the victory in all things." He then exhorted the counsellors of Zurich to abolish images.

The meeting was again held Tuesday, under the presidency of Vadian, for the discussion of the doctrine of the mass. " Brethren in Christ," said Zuinglius, " far be it from us to think that there is any deception or falsehood in the blood of Christ.[1] Our only object is to show that the mass is not a sacrifice which one man can present to God for another man, unless, indeed, it can be shown that a man can eat and drink for his friend." Vadian having asked on two several occasions if any of those present were ready to defend the doctrine which was impugned, by Scripture, and nobody having answered, the canons of Zurich, the chaplains, and several other ecclesiastics, declared that they agreed with Zuinglius.

But no sooner had the Reformers thus vanquished the partisans of the ancient doctrines, than they were compelled to struggle against those impatient men who demand sudden and violent innovations, instead of wise and gradual reforms. The unhappy Conrad Grebel rose and said, "It is not enough to have discussed the mass— it is necessary to abolish its abuses."—"The council," replied Zuinglius, will issue a decree on this subject." Then Simon Stumpf exclaimed, " The Spirit of God has already decided ! why then remit it to the council for decision?"[2]

Commander Schmidt of Kussnacht rose up gravely and uttered

[1] Dass einigerley Betrug oder Falsch syg in dem reinen Blut und Fleisch Christi
[2] Der Geist Gottes urtheilet. (Ibid., i, p. 529.)

words full of wisdom. "Let us teach Christians," said he, "to receive Christ into their hearts.[1] Till this hour you have all gone after idols. Those of the plain have run to the mountains, and those of the mountains have run to the plain; the French to Germany, and the Germans to France. Now you know where you ought to go. God has united all things in Christ. Noble men of Zurich run to the true source; let Jesus Christ again enter on your territory, and resume his ancient empire."

This address made a deep impression, and none having appeared to contradict it, Zuinglius, under deep emotion, rose and said, "Gracious lords, God is with us! . . . He will defend his cause. Now, then, . . . in the name of God, . . . forward! . . ." Here he was so deeply agitated that he was obliged to stop. He wept and many wept with him.[2]

Thus terminated the discussion. The presidents rose; the burgomaster thanked them, and then this old warrior, addressing the council, said gravely, with the voice which had so often been heard on the battle-field. "Now, then, let us take into our hands the sword of the Word of God, . . . and may God prosper his own work."

This discussion of October, 1523, had been decisive. The greater part of the priests who had been present at it, returned full of zeal to different parts of the canton, and the effect of these days was felt all over Switzerland. The church of Zurich, which had always been, to a certain degree, independent of the bishopric of Constance, was now fully emancipated. Instead of resting through the bishop on the pope, it henceforth rested through the people on the Word of God. Zurich resumed the rights of which Rome had robbed it. The town and the country rivalled each other in the interest they felt for the work of the Reformation, and the Great Council only followed the movement of the people. On important occasions the town and villages intimated what their views were. Luther had restored the Bible to the Christian people. Zuinglius went farther, and restored their rights. This is a characteristic feature of the Reformation in Switzerland. It confided the maintenance of sound doctrine under God to the people, and recent events have shown that the people are better custodiers of this deposit than priests and pontiffs.

Zuinglius did not allow himself to be inflated by victory. On the contrary, the Reformation was proceeded with, by his desire, with great moderation. When the council asked his advice, he said,

[1] Wie sie Christum in ihren Herzen sollind bilden und machen (Zw. Op. i, p. 534.)
[2] Dass er sich selbst mit vil andren bewegt zu weinen. (Ibid., p. 537.)

"God knows my heart; he knows that I am disposed to build up and not to pull down. I know timid souls who require to be gently dealt with; let the mass then be for some time longer read in all the churches on Sunday, and let care be taken not to insult those who celebrate it."[1]

The council issued a decree to this effect. Hottinger and Hochrutiner, one of his friends, were banished from the canton for two years, and forbidden to return without permission.

At Zurich, the Reformation followed a wise and Christian course. Exalting this city higher and higher, it made it glorious in the eyes of all the friends of the Word of God. Accordingly, those in Switzerland who had hailed the new day which was rising on the Church, felt powerfully attracted toward Zurich. Oswald Myconius, driven from Lucerne, had remained for six months in the valley of Einsidlen, when one day as he was returning from a journey to Glaris,[2] worn out with heat and fatigue, he was met by his son, young Felix, who came running to tell him that he was called to Zurich to direct one of the schools. Oswald, unable to credit the good news, was suspended between hope and fear.[3] "I am yours," he at last wrote to Zuinglius. Geroldsek parted with him with regret, while sad thoughts filled his mind. "Ah!" said he to him; "all who profess Christ go away to Zurich; I fear that we shall one day all perish together,"[4]—a mournful presentiment which the death of Gerlodsek and so many other friends of the gospel was to realise too truly on the plains of Cappel.

Myconius at last found a safe port in Zurich. His predecessor, who from his stature, had been nick-named at Paris, "the great devil," had neglected his duties; Oswald devoted all his powers and all his heart to the fulfilment of them. He explained the Latin and Greek classics, and taught rhetoric and logic, while the youth of the town listened to him with joy.[5] Myconius was to be to the young what Zuinglius was to adults.

Myconius was first alarmed at the advanced scholars he was to have; but he gradually resumed courage, and had, ere long, distinguished among his pupils a youth of twenty-four, whose look bespoke a love of study. He was named Thomas Plater, and was originally from the Valais. In the beautiful valley where the torrent of the Viege after escaping from the ocean of glaciers and snow which surround Mount Rosa, rolls its turbulent waters between St. Nicholas and Stalden, on the mountain which rises on the right of the river, still stands the village of Grächen. It was the birth-

Ohne dass jemand sich unterstehe die Messpriester zu beschimpfen. (Wirtz, H. K. G. v. p. 208.) [2] Insper..to nuntio excepit me filius redeuntem ex Glareana. (Zw. Ep. p. 82?) [3] Inter spem et metum. (Ibid.) [4] Ac deinde omnes simul perиbd.. p. 323.) [5] Juventus illum lubens audit. (Ibid. p. 264.)

place of Plater. From the vicinity of these colossal Alps was to come forth one of the most original characters who figured in the grand drama of the 16th century. Placed at the age of nine with a curate, a relation, the little peasant, when beaten, as he often was, cried, to use his own words, like a hare when it is put to death. One of his cousins took him with him to visit the German schools. He was already more than twenty years of age, and, while running from school to school, could scarcely read.[1] Having arrived at Zurich, he firmly resolved to attend to his education; and having made a bench for himself in a corner of Myconius' school, said to himself, "There you will learn or die." The light of the gospel penetrated his heart. One morning, feeling very cold, and having nothing to heat the school stove, which it was his office to keep going, he said to himself, "You have no wood, and so many idols in the church." Though Zuinglius was to preach, and the bells had begun to ring, nobody was present. Plater silently entered the church, and carrying off a St. John that stood upon an altar, put it in the stove, saying, "Down with you, for you must pass through it." Doubtless, neither Myconius or Zuinglius would have approved the act.

In truth, unbelief and superstition, required to be combated with better weapons. Zuinglius and his colleagues had given the right hand of fellowship to Myconius, who daily expounded the New Testament in the church of Notre Dame to a large and attentive audience.[2] A public discussion, which took place on the 13th and 14th of January, 1524, had given a new blow to Rome. In vain had canon Koch exclaimed, "The popes, the cardinals, the bishops, and the councils, these are my church! . . . "

Every thing was advancing in Zurich; men's minds were enlightened, their hearts were fixed, the Reformation was established. Zurich was a fortress gained by the new doctrine, and from its walls that doctrine was to spread over the whole confederation.

CHAPTER IV.

Diet of Lucerne—Hottinger Arrested—His Death—Deputation of the Diet to Zurich—Abolition of Processions—Abolition of Images—The two Reformations—Appeal to the People.

The enemy was aware of this, and saw the necessity of resolving to strike a decisive blow. He had long enough been mute. The strong men of Switzerland, the cuirassed and steel-clad warriors at last re-

[1] See his autobiography.   [2] Weise Füsslin Beyt. iv, p. 66.

solved to rise; and they had never risen without reddening the battle-field with blood.

The Diet had met at Lucerne. The priests laboured to stir up the first council of the nation in their favour. Friburg and the Waldstetten showed themselves their ready instruments; Berne, Basle, Solenre, Glaris, Appenzel were undecided. Schaffhausen almost declared for the gospel, but Zurich alone stood up boldly as its defender. The partisans of Rome urged the Diet to yield to their demands and prejudices. "Let all be prohibited," said they, "to preach, or announce any thing new or Lutheran, secretly or publicly; and to speak or dispute on these topics in taverns and over their cups."[1] Such was the ecclesiastical law which the confederation was asked to establish.

Nineteen articles to this effect were drawn up, and being approved on the 26th January, 1523, by all the states except Zurich, were sent to all the bailies, with orders to see that they were strictly observed. "This," says Bullinger, "caused great joy among the priests, and great grief among the faithful." Persecution, being thus regularly organised by the superior authority of the confederation, now began.

One of the first who received the orders of the Diet was Henry Flackenstein of Lucerne, bailie of Baden, within whose jurisdiction Hottinger had retired on his banishment from Zurich, after throwing down the crucifix of Stadelhofen. Here he had not kept a watch upon his tongue, but one day at table in the Angel Inn, at Zurzach, had said that the priests were bad expounders of the Holy Scriptures, and that it was necessary to confide entirely to God alone.[2] The inn-keeper, who was constantly going and coming, bringing in bread and wine, became a listener to language which seemed to him very strange. Another day, Hottinger had been to see one of his friends, John Schutz of Schneyssingen. After they had dined together, Schutz asked, "What then is this new faith which the priests of Zurich are preaching." "They preach," replied Hottinger, "that Christ was once sacrificed for all Christians, that by this single sacrifice he has purified and ransomed them from all their sins, and they show, by the Holy Scriptures, that the mass is a lie."

Hottinger had afterwards quitted Switzerland, (this took place in February, 1523,) and gone on business across the Rhine to Waldshut. Measures were taken to make sure of him, and towards the end of February, the poor Zuricher, who suspected nothing, having again crossed the Rhine, no sooner reached Coblentz, a village on the left bank of the river, than he was arrested. He

[1] Es soll nieman in den Wirtzhüseren oder sunst hinter dem Wyn von Lutherischen oder nuwen Sachen uzid reden. (Bull. Chron. p. 144.) [2] Wie wir unser pitt Hoffnung und Trost allein uf Gott. (Ibid., p. 146.)

was taken to Klingenau. As he confessed his faith frankly, Flackenstein became irritated, and said, "I will take you where you will find your answer."

In fact, the bailie took him successively before the judges of Klingenau, before the superior tribunal of Baden, and at length, as none would declare him guilty, he took him before the Diet assembled at Lucerne. He was determined to find judges who would condemn him.

The Diet lost no time, and condemned Hottinger to be beheaded. On learning his sentence, he gave thanks to Jesus Christ. "Very good, very good," said James Troger, one of the judges, "we are not here to listen to sermons. You will babble some other time." "His head must first be taken off," said bailie Amort of Lucerne laughing, " but if it comes on again, we will all embrace his creed." "May God forgive those who condemn me," said the prisoner. Then a monk having put a crucifix to his lips, he pushed it away saying, "It is in the heart that we ought to receive Christ."

When he was led away to execution, several in the crowd could not refrain from tears. "I am going to eternal happiness," said he, turning towards them. On reaching the place of execution, he raised his eyes to heaven, and said, "I commit my soul into thy hands, O my Redeemer." Next moment his head rolled on the scaffold.

No sooner had Hottinger's blood been shed than the enemies of the Reformation took advantage of it still more to inflame the rage of the confederates. In Zurich itself must the evil be suppressed. The dreadful example which had just been given must have filled Zuinglius and his partisans with terror. One vigorous effort more and Hottinger's death will be followed by that of the Reformation. . . . The Diet immediately resolved that a deputation should be sent to Zurich, to ask the council and citizens to abjure their faith.

On the 21st of March, the deputation was received. "Ancient Christian unity," said the deputies, "is broken; the evil extends; already have the clergy of the four Waldstettes declared, that if aid is not given to them, they will be obliged to desist from their functions. Confederates of Zurich, join your efforts to ours; strangle this new faith;[1] depose Zuinglius and his disciples; then let us all unite in applying a remedy to the encroachments of the popes and their courtiers."

Thus spoke the enemy. What, then, were the men of Zurich to do? Would their hearts fail them, and their courage melt away with the blood of their fellow-citizen?

[1] Zurich selbigen ausreuten und untertrucken helfe. (Hott Helv. K. G. iii, p. 170.)

Zurich did not long leave her friends and enemies in uncertainty. The council answered calmly and nobly, that they could not make any concession when the Word of God was involved, and afterwards proceeded to reply in terms still more eloquent.

It had been customary, from the year 1351, that, on Whitsunday Monday, a numerous procession, in which every pilgrim bore a cross, should repair to Einsidlen to worship the Virgin. Great irregularities were committed during this festival,[1] which was established in memory of the battle of Tatwyll. The procession was to take place on the 7th May. On the application of the three pastors the council abolished it, and all the other processions were successively reformed.

Nor did they stop here. Relics, the source of many superstitions, were honourably buried.[2] Thereafter, on the demand of the three pastors, the council issued a decree purporting that, as God alone was to be honoured, images should be removed from all the churches of the canton, and their ornaments employed in relieving the poor. Twelve counsellors, (one from each tribe,) the three pastors, the architect of the town, blacksmiths, locksmiths, carpenters, and masons, repaired to the different churches, and, locking the doors behind them,[3] took down the crosses, picked away the figures in fresco, whitened the walls, and carried off the images, to the great joy of the faithful, who, said Bullinger, "saw in this act a brilliant homage rendered to God." In some country churches, the ornaments were burned to the honour and glory of God. Organs, which were frequently played in connection with divers superstitions, were abolished, and baptism was administered after a new formula, from which every thing not Scriptural was excluded.

Burgomaster Roust, and his colleague, gladly hailed the triumphs of the Reformation with their last look. They had lived long enough, and they died at the very time of this great revival.

The Swiss Reformation presents itself under an aspect very different from that of the German Reformation. Luther had set his face against the excesses of those who broke down the images in the churches of Wittemberg; but images fell in the presence of Zuinglius in the churches of Zurich. This difference is explained by the peculiarities of the two Reformers. Luther wished to retain in the Church every thing that was not directly contrary to Scripture, whereas Zuinglius wished to abolish every thing that could not be proved by Scripture. The German Reformer wished to remain united to the Church of former ages, and was satisfied with purging

---

[1] Uff einen creitzgang sieben unehelicher kinden überkommen wurdend. (Bullinger, Chr. p. 160. [2] Und es eerlich bestattet hat. (Ibid., p. 161.) [3] Habend die nach inen zu beschlossen

it of every thing that was opposed to the Word of God. The Zurich Reformer passed by all these ages, returned to apostolic times, and subjecting the Church to a complete transformation, laboured to re-establish it in its primitive form.

The Reformation of Zuinglius was therefore the more complete. The work which Providence had committed to Luther—the re-establishment of justification by faith—was doubtless the great work of the Reformation; but this work once finished, there remained others which, though perhaps secondary, were still important. This was, more especially, the work of Zuinglius.

In fact, two great tasks were given to the Reformers. Christian Catholicism, which was born amid Jewish pharisaism and Greek heathenism, had gradually yielded to the influence of these two religions, and thereby been transformed into Roman Catholicism. Now the Reformation, in as much as it had been called to purify the Church, was bound to emancipate it equally from the heathen and from the Jewish element.

The Jewish element existed especially in that department of Christian doctrine which bears reference to man. Catholicism had received from Judaism the pharisaical ideas of self-righteousness, and salvation by human powers, or works.

The heathen element existed especially in that department of Christian doctrine which relates to God. In Catholicism, the idea of an infinite God, whose all-sufficient power acts every where, and without ceasing, had been adulterated by heathenism. In its place the reign of symbols, images, and ceremonies, had been introduced into the Church, and the saints had become the demi-gods of the papacy.

Luther's Reformation was directed essentially against the Jewish element. This was the element with which he had to struggle, when an audacious monk was sent by the pope, to vend the salvation of souls for ready cash.

The Reformation of Zuinglius was specially directed against the Heathen element. This element he had encountered when in the Church of Our Lady of Einsidlen, as of old in the temple of Diana of Ephesus, a crowd who had flocked from all quarters, stupidly prostrated themselves before an idol decked in gold.

The Reformer of Germany proclaimed the great doctrine of justification by faith, and thereby gave a death-blow to the pharisaical righteousness of Rome. No doubt the Reformer of Switzerland did so also; the inability of man to save himself forms the basis of the work of all reformers. But Zuinglius did more. He proved the supreme, universal, exclusive existence and agency of God, and thus gave a mortal thrust to the pagan worship of Rome.

Roman Catholicism had exalted man and dishonoured God. Luther humbled man: Zuinglius exalted God.

These two tasks, which were theirs specially, but not exclusively, were both completed. That of Luther laid the foundation of the building: that of Zuinglius put on the cope-stone.

It was reserved for a still greater genius on the banks of the lake of Geneva, to impress both characters at once on the Reformation.[1]

But while Zuinglius was thus advancing with rapid strides at the head of the confederation, the temper of the cantons was always becoming more hostile. The Zurich government felt the necessity of being able to fall back on the people. The people, i. e., the assembly of the faithful, was, moreover, according to the principles of Zuinglius, the highest power on earth to which an appeal could be made. The council resolved to sound them, and ordered the bailies to put the question to all the communes, whether they were willing to endure every thing for the sake of Jesus Christ, "who," said the council, "gave for us sinners his life and blood."[2] The whole canton had taken a deep interest in the progress of the Reformation in the town, and in many places the houses of the peasantry had become Christian schools, in which the Holy Scriptures were read.

The proclamation of the council, which was read in all the districts, was received with enthusiasm. "Let our rulers," replied they, "adhere boldly to the Word of God. we will help them to maintain it;[3] and if any annoyance is given them, we will bring assistance to our brave fellow-citizens." The peasantry of Zurich showed then, as they have shown since, that the strength of the Church is in the Christian people.

But the people were not alone. The man whom God had placed at their head, responded nobly to their appeal. Zuinglius, as it were, multiplied himself for the service of God. All who, in the Helvetic cantons, endured any persecution for the gospel, applied to him.[4] The responsibilty of affairs, the care of the Church, anxious interest in the struggle carried on in all the Swiss vallies, formed the burdens of the Zurich evangelist.[5] At Wittemberg, news of his courage were received with joy. Luther and Zuinglius were two great luminaries placed in upper and lower Germany, and the doctrine of salvation, so powerfully preached by them, spread over the extensive regions, which descend from the heights of the Alps to the shores of the Baltic and the Northern Ocean.

[1] Litterarischer Anzeiger, 1840, No. 27. [2] Der sin rosenfarw blüt alein fur uns arme sünder vergossen hat. (Bull. Chr. p. 180.) [3] Meine Herrn sollten auch nur dapfer bey dem Gottsworte verbleiben. (Fussl. Beytr., iv, p. 107, where the replies of all the districts are given.) [4] Scribunt ex Helvetiis ferme omnes qu propter Christum premuntur. (Zw. Ep. p. 318.) [5] Negotiorum strepitus ej ecclesiarum curæ ita me undique quatiunt. (Ibid.) The noise of business, and the care of the churches so harass me on every side.

CHAP. V.

New Opposition—Œxlin carried off—The Family of the Wirths—The mob at the Convent of Ittingen—The Diet of Zug—The Wirths seized and given up to the Diet—Condemnation.

The Word of God could not thus triumphantly spread over extensive districts without arousing the indignation of the pope in his palace, the curates in their presbyteries, and the Swiss magistrates in their councils. Their terror increased every day. The people were consulted; the christian people again became of some weight in the Christian Church, and their faith and their sympathies were appealed to instead of the decrees of the Roman chancery . . . . This formidable attack required a still more formidable resistance. On the 18th April, the pope addressed a brief to the confederates, and the Diet assembled at Zug in the month of July, yielding to the pressing exhortations of the pontiff, sent a deputation to Zurich, Schaffhausen and Appenzel, to declare to these States its firm determination to destroy the new doctrine, and prosecute its adherents, in their goods, their honours, and even their lives. This warning was not heard in Zurich without emotion; but it was firmly answered, that, in matters of faith, obedience could only be given to the Word of God. On hearing this reply, Lucerne, Schwitz, Uri, Underwalden, Friburg, and Zug, gave loud utterance to their rage, and forgetting the reputation and strength which the accession of Zurich had of old given to the rising confederation, forgetting the precedence which had already been conceded to it, the simple and solemn oaths which had been taken to it, and the many common victories and reverses, these states declared that they would not sit in Diet with Zurich. Thus, in Switzerland, as in Germany, the partisans of Rome were the first to violate federal unity. But menaces and ruptures of alliance, were not sufficient. The fanaticism of the cantons demanded blood, and it was soon seen with what weapons the papacy sought to combat the Word of God.

A friend of Zuinglius, the excellent Œxlin,[1] was pastor at Berg, near Stein, on the Rhine. The bailie, Amberg, who had appeared to listen gladly to the gospel,[2] wishing to obtain this bailiwick, had promised the leading men in Schwitz to destroy the new faith. Œxlin, though he was not subject to his jurisdiction was the first on whom his severity was to be exercised.

On the night of 7th July, 1524, a knock was heard towards

[1] See Vol. ii, p. 387.   [2] Der war anfangs dem Evangelio günstig. (Bull, Chr., p.

midnight at the pastor's door. On being opened, the bailie's soldiers seized him, and carried him off prisoner, notwithstanding of his cries. Œxlin, on his part, thinking they were going to assassinate him, cried murder; the inhabitants got up in alarm, and the whole village was soon in a frightful tumult, the noise of which reached as far as Stein. The sentinel on guard at the castle of Hohenklingen fired the alarm cannon, the tocsin sounded, and the inhabitants of Stein, Stammheim, and the adjacent places, were all, in a few moments, in motion, inquiring, amid the darkness, as to what had happened in the district.

At Stammheim lived vice-bailie Wirth, whose two sons, Adrian and John, young priests full of piety and courage, earnestly preached the gospel. John, especially, in the fulness of faith, was ready to give his life to his Saviour. It was a patriarchal family. Anna, the mother, who had given the bailie a numerous family, and had brought them up in the fear of the Lord, was revered for her virtues over the whole district. On hearing of the tumult of Berg, the father and the two eldest sons came out of the house. The father's indignation was roused when he saw that the bailie of Frauenfeld had exercised his authority in an illegal manner. The sons were grieved to learn that their brother, their friend, he whose good example they loved to follow, was carried off as a criminal. Each of them seized a halbert, and, in spite of the fears of an affectionate wife and mother, the father and the two sons joined the band of the citizens of Stein, determined to deliver their pastor. Unhappily a crowd of those nondescript individuals who always spring up whenever there is any disturbance, were also astir. They set off in pursuit of the bailie's officers, who, hearing the tocsin and sounds of alarm, made all speed, and dragging along their victim, soon placed the Thur between themselves and their pursuers.

The people of Stein and Stammheim reached the river side, but having no means of crossing, stopped, and resolved to send a deputation to Frauenfeld. "Ah!" said bailie Wirth, "the pastor of Stein is so dear to us that I would willingly give up every thing for him, my goods, my liberty, and even my life."[1] The mob finding themselves near the convent of the Cordeliers of Ittingen, who were supposed to stimulate the tyranny of the bailie Amberg, entered, and got possession of the refectory. These miserable beings soon became intoxicated, and scenes of disorder ensued. Wirth implored them, but in vain, to quit the convent;[2] he even exposed himself to be maltreated by them. His son Adrian remained outside the cloister. John entered it, but distressed at what he saw

[1] Sunder die kuttlen im Buch fur Im wagan. (Bull. Chr., p. 193.) [2] Und budt sy um Gottes willen uss dem Kloster zu gand. (Ibid., p. 183.)

he immediately came out again.[1] The intoxicated peasants began to break into the wine cellars and stores, to break the furniture to pieces, and burn the books.

News of these disorders having reached Zurich, deputies from the council hastened to the spot, and ordered those who had come out of the canton to return to their homes. The order was obeyed. But a crowd of Thurgovians, attracted by the tumult, installed themselves in the convent, and there made good cheer. Suddenly, no one knew how, a fire broke out, and the convent was reduced to ashes.

Five days after, the deputies of the cantons met at Zug. Cries of revenge and death were heard in the assembly. "Let us march," said they, "with banners unfurled, on Stein and Stammheim, and smite their inhabitants with the sword." The vice-bailie and his two sons, on account of their faith, had long been the objects of special hatred. "If any one is guilty," said the deputy of Zurich, "let him be punished; but be it according to the laws of justice, and not by violence." Vadian, deputy of St. Gall, supported this view. Then the envoy, John Hug of Lucerne, unable to restrain himself, exclaimed, with dreadful oaths,[1] "The heretic, Zuinglius, is the father of all these revolts, and you, doctor of St. Gall, you favour his infamous cause, you aid him in securing its triumphs. . . . . You ought not to sit longer among us." The deputy of Zug endeavoured to restore peace, but in vain, Vadian retired; and, as some of the populace had designs upon his life, he secretly left the town, and arrived, by a devious course, at the convent of Cappel.

Zurich, determined to suppress all disorder, resolved, in the meantime, to apprehend those who had roused the anger of the confederates. Wirth and his sons were living peaceably at Stammheim. "Never will the enemies of God be able to overcome his friends," said Adrian Wirth from the pulpit. The father received information of the fate which awaited him, and was urged to fly with his sons. "No," said he: "trusting in God, I mean to wait for the officers." And, when the soldiers made their appearance at his house, he said, "My lords of Zurich might have spared themselves all this trouble; they had only to send a child for me, and I would have obeyed."[2] The three Wirths were led away to the prison of Zurich. Rutiman, bailie of Nussbaum, shared their fate. They were closely examined, but nothing was discovered in their conduct to criminate them.

As soon as the deputies had learned the imprisonment of these

[1] Dan es Im leid was. (Ibid., p. 195.) [2] Mit fluchen und wüten. (Bull. Chr., p. 181.)
[3] Dann hättind sy mir ein kind geschickt. (Ibid., p. 186.)

four citizens, they demanded that they should be sent to Baden, and gave orders, in the event of a refusal, to march upon Zurich and carry them off. "To Zurich," replied the deputies of this state, "it belongs to ascertain whether these men are guilty or not; and we have found no fault in them." Then the deputies of the cantons exclaimed, "Will you deliver them to us? Answer yes or no; and not one word more." Two of the deputies of Zurich took horse, and rode off at full speed to their constituents.

On their arrival all the town was in great agitation. If the prisoners were refused, the confederates would come and seek them with arms in their hands; and, if they were delivered, it was the same thing as giving them up to death. Opinions were divided. Zuinglius was decidedly for refusing. "Zurich," said he, "must remain faithful to its constitutions." At last it was thought that a middle course had been found. "We will remit the prisoners to you," said they to the diet, "but on condition that you will only examine them as to the affair of Ittingen, and not as to their faith." The Diet acceded to the terms; and on the Friday before St. Bartholomew's day (August, 1524,) the three Wirths and their friend, accompanied by four counsellors of state, left Zurich.

There was general lamentation. It was foreseen what fate awaited these two old men and these two youths. Nothing but sobbing was heard as they passed along. "Alas!" exclaims a contemporary, "what a mournful procession."[1] The churches were crowded. "God," exclaimed Zuinglius, "God will punish us. Ah! let us, at least, implore him to impart his grace to these poor prisoners, and strengthen their faith.[2]

On Friday evening the accused arrived at Baden, where an immense crowd was waiting for them. They were first taken to an inn and then to prison. They had difficulty in moving forward, the people pressed so close upon them to see them. The father, who walked in front, turned towards his sons, and mildly said to them, "See, my dear children, we are, as the apostle says, as it were appointed to death: for we are made a spectacle to the world, and to angels, and to men." 1 Cor. iv, 9. Then perceiving in the crowd his mortal enemy, bailie Amberg, the cause of all his misfortunes, he went up and offered him his hand, but the bailie turned away. Clasping his hand in his, he calmly said, "God lives in heaven, and knows all things."

The inquest commenced on the following day. Bailie Wirth was first brought in. He was put to the torture without regard to his character or his age; but he persisted in declaring that he was

---

[1] O weh! was elender Fahrt war das! (Bern. Weyss. Fussl. Beyt. iv, p. 56.)
[2] Sy troste und in warem glouben starckte. (Bull. Chr. p. 188.)

innocent of the pillaging and burning of Ittingen. He was then charged with destroying an image of St. Anne. .... Nothing could be proved against the other prisoners, except that Adrian Wirth was married, and preached after the manner of Zuinglius and Luther; and that John Wirth had given the sacrament to a sick person, without bell and taper.[1]

But the more their innocence was proved, the more the rage of their adversaries increased. From morning till noon the old man was kept under the torture. His tears could not soften his judges. John Wirth was still more cruelly tortured. "Tell us," he was asked in the midst of his agony, "tell us where you got your heretical faith? Was it from Zuinglius, or some other person?" And, as he exclaimed, "O merciful and eternal God, come to my aid and support me!" "Ah, well!" said one of the deputies to him, "where is now thy Christ?" When Adrian appeared, Sebastian of Stein, deputy of Berne, said to him, "Young man, tell us the truth; for if you refuse to tell it, I swear to you, by my knighthood, which I acquired in the very place where God suffered martyrdom, that we will open all the veins of your body in succession." Then the young man was attached to a cord, and as they swung him in the air, "My little master," said Stein, with a diabolical smile, "here is our marriage present,"[2] alluding to the marriage of the Lord's young servant.

The process being concluded, the deputies returned to their cantons to make their report, and did not return till four weeks after. The bailie's wife, the mother of the two young priests, repaired to Baden, with an infant in her arms, to intercede with the judges. John Escher of Zurich, accompanied her as advocate. Perceiving among the judges the landamman of Zug, Jerome Stocker, who had two different times been bailie of Frauenfeld. "Landamman," said he to him, "you know bailie Wirth: you know that he has all his life been an honest man." "You say true, my dear Escher," replied Stocker, "he never harmed any one; fellow citizens and strangers were always kindly received at his table; his house resembled a convent, an inn, an hospital.[3] Hence, if he had robbed or murdered, I would do everything in my power to obtain his pardon. But since he has burned St. Anne, the grandmother of Christ, he must die!" .... "God have mercy on us," exclaimed Escher.

The gates were shut. This was on the 28th September, and the deputies of Berne, Lucerne, Uri, Schwitz, Underwald, Zug, Glaris,

---

[1] On Kerzen, schellen und anders so bisshar geüpt ist. (Bull. Chr. p. 196.)
[2] Alls man inn am folter seyl uffzog, sagt der zum Stein: Herrli, das ist die gaab die wir üch zu üwer Hussfrowen schänckend. (Ibid., p. 190.) [3] Sin huss ist allwey gsin wie ein Kloster wirtshuss und pitall. (Ibid., p. 198.)

Friburg, and Soleure, having proceeded to judgment with closed doors, according to custom, pronounced sentence of death on bailie Wirth, his son John, who was strongest in the faith, and appeared to have carried the others along with him, and bailie Rutiman. Adrian, the second son, was granted to his mother's tears.

The officers proceeded to the tower to fetch the prisoners. "My son," said the father to Adrian, "do not avenge our death, although we have not deserved to suffer. . . . ." Adrian's tears fell fast. "My brother," said John to him, "the cross of Jesus Christ must always follow his word." [1]

After the judgment was read, these three Christians were taken back to prison; John Wirth walked in front, the two vice-bailies next, and a vicar followed. As they passed the castle bridge, where was a chapel consecrated to St. Joseph, "Prostrate yourselves, and invoke the saints," said the priest to the two old men. John Wirth, who was in advance, turned back on hearing these words, and cried out, "Father, remain firm. You know there is only one mediator between God and man, the man Christ Jesus." "Certainly, my son," replied the old man, "and with the help of his grace I will remain faithful unto the end." All three now began to repeat the Lord's Prayer, "Our Father which art in heaven." Then they passed the bridge.

They were afterwards led to the scaffold. John Wirth, whose heart was filled with the tenderest anxiety for his father, took farewell of him. "My dearly beloved father," said he to him, "henceforth you are no longer my father, and I am no longer your son; but we are brethren in Christ our Lord, for whose name I am to suffer death.[2] To-day, dearly beloved brother, if it pleases God, we shall go to him who is the father of us all. Fear nothing."— "Amen!" replied the old man, "and may God Almighty bless you, my beloved son, and my brother in Christ!"

Thus, on the threshold of eternity, this father and son took leave of each other, hailing the new mansions where they were going to be united by everlasting ties. The greater part of those around them were weeping bitterly.[3] Bailie Rutiman prayed in silence.

The three having knelt down, "in the name of Christ," were beheaded.

The multitude, on seeing the marks of the torture upon their bodies, gave loud utterance to their grief. The two bailies left twenty-two children, and forty-five grandchildren. Anne had to pay twelve

---

[1] Doch allwäg das crütz darby. (Bull. Chr. p. 198.) [2] Furohin bist du nitt me min Vatter und ich din sun, sondern wir sind brüdern in Christo. (Ibid., p. 104.) [3] Des gnadens weyneten vil Lüthen herzlich. (Ibid.)

gold crowns to the executioner, who deprived her husband and son of life.

Thus blood, pure blood had flowed. Switzerland and the Reformation were baptised with the blood of martyrs. The great enemy of the gospel had done his work; but in doing it his power was broken. The death of the Wirths was to hasten the triumphs of the Reformation.

CHAPTER VI.

Abolition of the Mass—Zuinglius' dream—Celebration of the Lord's Supper—Brotherly Charity—Original Sin—The Oligarchs against the Reformation—Divers Attacks.

It was not thought desirable to proceed to the abolition of the mass in Zurich, immediately after that of images; but now the moment seemed arrived.

Not only was evangelical light diffused among the people; but, moreover, the blows which the enemy struck, called upon the friends of the gospel to reply to them by striking demonstrations of their immoveable fidelity. Every time that Rome erects a scaffold, and cuts off heads, the Reformation will hold up the Word of the Lord, and cut off abuses. When Hottinger was executed, Zurich abolished images; now that the heads of the Wirths have rolled on the scaffold, Zurich will reply by the abolition of the mass. The more Rome increases her cruelties, the more will the Reformation see her power increase.

On the 11th April, 1525, the three pastors of Zurich presented themselves, with Megander and Oswald Myconius, before the great council, and petitioned for the re-establishment of the Lord's Supper. Their speech was grave;[1] all minds were solemnised; every one felt the importance of the resolution which the council was called to take. The mass, that mystery which, for more than three centuries, was the soul of the religious service of the Latin Church, behoved to be abolished; the corporal presence of Christ behoved to be declared an illusion, and the illusion itself made palpable to the people. To resolve on this required courage, and there were men in the council who shuddered at the very idea of it. Joachim Am-Grüt, under-secretary of State, terrified at the bold demand of the pastors, opposed it with all his might. "These words—*This is my body*," said he, "irresistibly prove

[1] Und vermanten die ernstlich. (Bull. Chr. p 263.)

that the bread is the body of Christ himself." Zuinglius observed, that in the Greek language ἐστι (is) is the only word to express *signifies;* and he quoted several instances in which this word is employed in a figurative sense. The great council being convinced, hesitated not; the evangelical doctrines had penetrated all hearts. Besides, now that the Church was separated from Rome, there was some satisfaction in making it as much so as possible, and in placing a deep gulf between her and the Reformation. The council accordingly ordered the abolition of the mass, and decreed that, next day, Holy Thursday, the Lord's Supper should be celebrated in accordance with apostolic usage.

Zuinglius was eagerly occupied with these thoughts; and, at night, after he closed his eyes, he continued searching out arguments to oppose his adversaries. The subject which had occupied him so much during the day, again presented itself in sleep. He dreamt that he was disputing with Am-Grüt, and could not answer his leading objection. Suddenly a person appeared, and said "Why do you not quote Exodus, xii, 11. '*Ye shall eat it in haste; it is the Lord's passover.*"' Zuinglius awoke, leapt out of bed, took up the Septuagint translation, and found in it the very word ἐστι (is) whose meaning here, by the confession of all, can only be *signifies.*

Here, then, we have in the very institution of the passover under the Old Testament, the meaning for which Zuinglius contends. How then, is it possible to avoid the conclusion that the two passages are parallel?

The next day Zuinglius selected this passage for his text, and spoke so forcibly, that he removed all doubts.

This circumstance, which is so naturally explained, and the expression used by Zuinglius, when he said, that he did not remember the appearance of the person whom he saw in his dream,[1] have given rise to the charge that the Reformer learned his doctrine from the devil.

Altars had disappeared; and their places were supplied by single tables, on which stood the bread and wine of the eucharist, while an attentive congregation thronged around. There was something solemn in the numbers. On Holy Thursday, the young; on Friday (Passion day), adults; and on Easter, the old, successively celebrated the Lord's death.[2]

The deacons read the passages of Scripture which refer to the sacrament, the pastors addressed an earnest exhortation to the flock, urging all those who, by continuing in sin, would defile the

---

[1] Ater fuerit an albus nihil memini, somnium enim narro. Whether he was black or white, I remember not; it was a dream. [2] Fusslin Beytr. i7, p. 64.

body of the Lord Jesus to abstain from this sacred supper. The people knelt; the bread was handed round on large platters or wooden plates, and each person broke a portion; the wine was dispensed in wooden cups—this being thought to approach nearest to the first institution. Surprise and joy filled all hearts.

Thus the Reformation was effected in Zurich. The simple celebration of the Lord's death seemed to have again infused into the Church the love of God, and the love of the brethren. The words of Jesus Christ were again spirit and life. While the different orders and different parties of the Church of Rome had never ceased to dispute with each other, the first effect of the gospel, on again entering the Church, was to establish charity among the brethren. The love of the primitive ages was restored to Christendom. Enemies were seen renouncing old and inveterate hatred, and embracing each other, after having eaten together of the bread of the eucharist. Zuinglius, delighted at these touching manifestations, thanked God that the Lord's Supper was again performing those miracles of love which the sacrifice of the mass had long ceased to produce.[1]

"Peace dwells in our city," exclaimed he; "among us no pretence, no dissension, no envy, no quarrel. Whence can such agreement come but from the Lord; and because the doctrine which we preach disposes us to innocence and peace?[2]

There were now charity and unity, but not uniformity. Zuinglius, in his "Commentary on True and False Religion," which he dedicated to Francis I, in March, 1525, the year of the battle of Pavia[3] had presented some truths, in the manner best fitted to gain a reception from human reason, in this following the example of several of the most distinguished scholastic theologians. Thus he had applied the term *disease* to original corruption, and restricted that of *sin* to the actual transgression of the law.[4] But these statements, though they called forth some remonstrances, did not interrupt brotherly love; for Zuinglius, while persisting in calling original sin a disease, added, that, in consequence of it, all men were undone, and that the only remedy was in Jesus Christ.[5] There was therefore no Pelagian error here.

[1] Mit grossem verwundern viler Lüthen und noch mit vil grössern fröuden deo glöubigen. (Bull. Chr. p. 264.) [2] Expositio fidei. (Zw. Op. ii, p. 241.) [3] Ut tranquillitatis et innocentiæ studiosos reddat. (Z. Ep. p. 390.) [4] De Vera et Falsa Religione Commentarius. (Zw. Op. iii, p. 145-325.) [5] Peccatum ergo *morbus* est cognatus nobis, quo fugimus aspera et gravia, sectamur jucunda et volup. tuosa : secundo loco accipitur peccatum pro eo quod contra legem fit. (Ibid., p. 204.) First, then, sin is a disease natural to us, by which we shun what is rough and grievous, pursue what is pleasing and voluptuous : in the second place, sin is taken for that which is done contrary to law. [6] Originali morbo perdimur omnes; remedio vero quod contra ipsum invenit Deus, incolumitati restituimur. (De Pecc. Origin. Decl ad Urb. Rhegium. (Ibid., Op. iii, p. 632.) We are all lost by original disease, but restored to safety by the remedy which God has provided against it.

But while the celebration of the Supper in Zurich was accompanied with a return to Christian brotherhood, Zuinglius and his friends had so much more to endure externally, from the irritation of adversaries. Zuinglius was not only a Christian leader; he was also a true patriot; and we know with what zeal he combated enlistment, pensions, and foreign alliances. He was convinced that these influences from abroad destroyed piety, blinded reason, and sowed discord. But his loud protestations must have hurt the progress of the Reformation. In almost all the cantons, the leaders who received foreign pensions, and the officers who led the Helvetic youth to battle, formed powerful factions, formidable oligarchies which attacked the Reformation, not so much from any view to the Church, as on account of the prejudicial effect it threatened to have to their interests and honours. They had already gained the day at Schwitz. This canton, in which Zuinglius, Leo Juda, and Myconius had taught, and which might have been expected to follow in the wake of Zurich, was again all at once opened to mercenary enlistments, and shut against the Reformation.

At Zurich even, some wretches, stirred up by foreign intrigues, attacked Zuinglius in the middle of the night, threw stones at his house, broke his windows, and with loud cries called him "the red Uli, the vulture of Glaris;" so that Zuinglius was awoke, and ran for his sword.[4] This circumstance is characteristic of the man.

But these isolated attacks could not paralyse the movement which was carrying forward Zurich, and beginning to shake Switzerland. They were only like stones thrown in to arrest a torrent. The waters, rising on every side, threatened to break down the strongest obstacles.

The Bernese having declared to the Zurichers that several states had refused to sit with them in diet in future. "Very well," replied those of Zurich, calmly raising their hands to heaven, as the men of Rutli in former days, "we have a firm assurance that God the Father, Son, and Holy Spirit, in whose name the Confederation was formed, will not forsake us, but will, at last, in mercy, give us a seat beside His Sovereign Majesty."[2] With such a faith the Reformation had nothing to fear. But will it gain similar victories in the other states of the Confederation? Will not Zurich be left alone in favour of the Word? Will Berne, Basle, and other cantons besides, remain subject to the power of Rome? We shall now see. Let as turn then towards Berne, and study the progress of the Reformation in the most influential state of the Confederation.

[1] Interea surgere Zuinglius ad ensem suum. (Zw. Op. iii, p. 411.)   [2] Bey ihm zuletzt sitzen. (Kirchhofer. Ref. v. Bern. p. 55.)

CHAPTER VII.

Berne—The Provost of Watteville—First Successes of the Reformation—Haller at the Convent—Accusation and Deliverance—The Monastery of Königsfeld—Margaret of Watteville to Zuinglius—The Convent open—Two opposite Champions—Clara May and the Provost of Watteville.

No where was the struggle to be keener than at Berne, where the gospel had at once powerful friends and formidable foes. At the head of the friends of the Reformation stood banneret John Weingarten, Bartholomew May, member of the little council, his sons, Wolfgang and Claudius, his grandchildren, James and Benedict, and, above all, the family of Watteville. The avoyer James Watteville, who had, from 1512, filled the first place in the republic, had early read the writings of Luther and Zuinglius, and had often conversed on the gospel with John Haller, pastor at Alsentingen, whom he had protected against his persecutors.

His son, Nicholas, aged thirty-one, had been for two years provost of the church of Berne; and, as such, in virtue of papal ordinances, enjoyed great privileges. Hence, Berthold Haller called him "our bishop."[1]

The prelates and the pope were exceedingly desirous to bind him to the interests of Rome,[2] and every thing might have been expected to estrange him from the knowledge of the gospel; but the agency of God was more powerful than the flattery of man. Watteville was converted from darkness to the pure light of the gospel, says Zuinglius.[3] The friend of Berthold Haller, he read all the letters which the latter received from Zuinglius, and could not sufficiently express his admiration.[4]

The interest of the two Wattevilles who were at the head, the one of the State, the other of the Church, might have been expected to carry the republic. But the opposite party was not less powerful.

Among its leaders were observed the schultheiss of Erlach, banneret Willading, and several patricians, whose interests were the same as those of the convents placed under their administration. Behind these influential individuals were an ignorant and corrupt clergy, who called the evangelical doctrine "an invention of hell".

---

[1] Episcopus noster *Vadivillius*. (Zw. Ep. p. 285.) [2] Tantum favoris et amicitiæ quæ tibi cum tanto summorum pontificum et potentissimorum episcoporum cœtu hactenus intercessit. (Zw. Op. i, old Latin Ed. p. 305.) You have had so much favour and friendship, from your intercourse hitherto, with so many pontiffs and powerful bishops. [3] Ex obscuris ignorantiæ tenebris in amœnam Evangelii lucem productum. (Ibid.) [4] Epistolas tuæ et eruditionis et humanitatis testes locupletissimas. . . . . (Zw. Ep. p. 287.) Your letters very complete evidence both of your learning and accomplishments.

In the month of July, counsellor Mullinen said in full assembly, "Dear confederates, take care that the Reformation do not gain upon us. In Zurich, people are not safe in their houses; they require soldiers to defend them." In consequence, application was made to John Heim, the lecturer of the Dominicans at Mentz, who came to Berne, and began to inveigh, from the pulpit, with all the eloquence of St. Thomas, against the Reformation.[1]

Thus the two parties were arrayed against each other, the struggle seemed inevitable, and even the result not doubtful. In fact, a common faith united a portion of the people to the most distinguished families of the state. Berthold Haller, full of confidence in the future, exclaimed, "Provided God's anger is not turned against us, it is impossible that the Word of God can be banished from this town, for the Bernese are hungering for it." [2]

Shortly after, two acts of the government seemed to throw the balance in the favour of the Reformation. The Bishop of Lausanne having announced an episcopal visitation, the council caused the provost Watteville intimate to him that the would have to dispense with it.[3] And, at the same time, the councils of Berne issued an ordinance, which, while it apparently made some concession to the enemies of the Reformation, consecrated its principles. They decreed that the Holy Gospel, and the doctrine of God, as it could be proved from the books of the Old and New Testament, should be preached freely and openly, and that nothing should be said of any doctrine, dispute or writing, proceeding from Luther or other teachers.[4] The surprise of the adversaries of the Reformation was great when they saw the evangelical ministers loudly appealing to this ordinance. This decree, which was the basis of all which followed, was the legal commencement of the Reformation in Berne. There was thenceforward more decision in the movement of this state, and Zuinglius, whose eye was attentive to all that took place in Switzerland, could write to the provost Watteville, "All Christians rejoice because of this faith which the pious town of Berne has just received."[5] "The cause is that of Christ," exclaimed the friends of the gospel;[6] and they devoted themselves to it with still greater courage.

The enemies of the Reformation, alarmed at these first advantages, formed their phalanx, and resolved to strike a blow which would ensure the victory. They conceived the project of disen-

[1] Suo Thomistico Marte omnia invertere. (Zw. Ep. p. 287.) To overturn every thing by his Thomistical prowess. [2] Famem verbi Bernates habent. (Ibid., p. 295.)
[3] Ut nec oppidum, nec pagos Bernatum visitare prætendat omnino. (Ibid.) That he should not propose at all to visit either the town or country of the Bernese.
[4] Alcin das heilig Evangelium und die leer Gottes frey, offentlich und unverborgen. (Bull. Chr. p. 111.) [5] Alle Christen sich allenthalben fröuwend des Glaubens . . . (Zw. Op. i, p. 426.) [6] Christi negotium agitur. (Zw. Ep. 9th May, 1523.)

cumbering themselves of those ministers whose audacious eloquence subverted the most ancient customs. A favourable opportunity soon occurred. There was in Berne, at the place now occupied by the hospital of the Isle, a convent of nuns of St. Dominic, dedicated to St. Michael. The day of this archangel (29th September) was a great festival in the monastery. This year it was attended by several ecclesiastics, among others, by Wittembach of Bienne, Sebastian Meyer, and Berthold Haller. Having entered into conversation with the nuns, among whom was Clara, daughter of Claudius May, one of the props of the Reformation, Haller said to her, in presence of her grandmother, "The merits of the monastic state are imaginary, whereas marriage is an honourable state, having been instituted by God himself." Some nuns, to whom Clara related the conversation of Berthold, raised cries of terror. It was soon circulated in the town; "Haller maintains that all nuns are children of the devil." . . . The opportunity sought by the enemies of the Reformation had arrived; they appeared before the lesser council, and referred to an ancient ordinance, which bore that any person carrying off a nun from the monastery should lose his head, but asked, "for a mitigation of the sentence," and that it should be considered sufficient without hearing the three ministers to banish them for life. The lesser council acceded to the petition, and the matter was speedily carried before the great council.

Thus Berne was on the eve of being deprived of her Reformers. The intrigues of the papal party had prevailed. But Rome, though she triumphed when she addressed the oligarchs, was beaten before the people and their representatives. No sooner had the names of Haller, Meyer, and Wittembach, the men whom all Switzerland venerated, been pronounced in the great council, than a powerful opposition was manifested to the lesser council and the clergy. "We cannot," exclaimed Tillman, "condemn the accused without hearing them. Their testimony is surely as good as that of some women." The ministers were then called. It was felt difficult to dispose of the affair. At length John of Weingarten said, "Let us give credit to both parties." It was so decided. The ministers were discharged, with a request, however, to meddle only with the pulpit and not with the cloister. But the pulpit was sufficient for them. The efforts of the enemy had redounded to their disgrace. The Reformation had gained a great victory. Accordingly, one of the patricians exclaimed, "Now that everything is said, Luther's affair must go forward."[1]

[1] Es ist nun gethan. Deu Lutherische Handel muss vorgehen. (Anshelm. Wirtz. K. G. V. p. 290.)

It did, in fact, go forward, and even in places where it might have been least expected. At Königsfeld, near the castle of Hapsburg, stood a monastery adorned with all the monastic magnificence of the middle ages, and containing the ashes of several members of the illustrious house which has given so many emperors to Germany. Here the greatest families of Switzerland and Suabia made their daughters take the veil. Not far from this spot, on 1st May, 1308, the Emperor Albert had fallen under the dagger of his nephew, John of Suabia, and the beautiful painted window of the church of Königsfeld represented the fearful punishments which had been inflicted on the relations and vassals of the guilty parties. Catherine of Waldburg-Truchsess, abbess of the convent, at the period of the Reformation, counted among her nuns Beatrice of Landenberg, sister of the Bishop of Constance, Agnes of Mullinen, Catherine of Bonnstetten, and Margaret of Watteville, the provost's sister. The liberty which this convent enjoyed, and which, at a former period had led to criminal irregularities, allowed the introduction of the Holy Scriptures, and the writings of Luther and Zuinglius. In a short time matters assumed an entirely new appearance. Near the cell to which Queen Agnes, the daughter of Albert, retired, besprinkled with blood, as it had been "Maydew," and where, spinning wool or working embroidery to ornament the church, she had mingled acts of devotion and thoughts of vengeance, Margaret Watteville had only thoughts of peace; read the Scriptures, and mingled salutary ingredients to compose an excellent electuary. Then, composing herself in her cell, the young nun ventured on the bold step of writing to the teacher of Switzerland. Her letter shows better than any observations could do, the Christian spirit which animated those pious females, who have been, and still, even in our day, are so much calumniated.

"Grace and peace through the Lord Jesus Christ, be ever given and multiplied to you, by God our Heavenly Father," said the nun of Königsfeld to Zuinglius. "Very learned, reverend, and dear Sir, I beseech you not to be offended with the letter which I write to you. The love which is in Christ urges me to do it, especially since I have learned that the doctrine of salvation grows from day to day by your preaching of the Word of God. Wherefore, I offer up thanks to God Almighty for enlightening us anew, and sending us, by his Holy Spirit, so many heralds of his Holy Word; at the same time, I earnestly beseech Him to clothe you with His might, you and all those who proclaim His glad tidings, that arming you against all the enemies of the truth, He may make His Divine Word grow in every heart. Very learned Sir, I venture to send you this small token of my affection. Deign not to despise it.

It is the gift of Christian charity. If this electuary does you good, and you have any wish for more, let me know; it would give me great delight to do something that might be agreeable to you. I am not alone in this. The feeling is common to all who love the gospel in our convent of Königsfeld. They present their salutations in Jesus Christ to your reverence, and we all together, without ceasing, recommend you to His mighty protection.[1]

"Saturday before Lætare, 1523."

Such was the pious letter of the nun of Königsfeld to the teacher of Switzerland.

A convent, into which gospel light had thus penetrated, could not long continue the practices of monastic life. Margaret Watteville, and her sisters, persuaded that they could serve God better in their families than in the cloister, asked leave to quit it. The council of Berne, in alarm, first tried to bring the nuns to reason; the provincial and the abbess had recourse by turns to threats and promises. But the sisters, Margaret, Agnes, Catherine, and their friends were immoveable. Next the rules of the convent were relaxed. The nuns were exempted from fasts and matins, and their income was increased; but they replied to the council, "It is not liberty of the flesh we ask, but liberty of the spirit. We, your poor and innocent prisoners, ask you to have pity on us." "*Our* prisoners, *our* prisoners," exclaimed banneret Krauchthaler, "I wont have them to be my prisoners." This, from one of the firmest supporters of convents, decided the council. The convent was thrown open, and shortly after, Catherine Bonnstetten married William Diesbach.

Still Berne, instead of frankly arraying itself on the side of the Reformers, kept a certain middle course, and endeavoured, as it were, to hold the balance between the two parties. A circumstance caused it to lay aside this equivocal procedure. Sebastian Meyer, lecturer to the Franciscans, published a recantation of Roman errors, which produced a great sensation. Pourtraying the life of convents, he said, "Their inmates live more impurely, fall more frequently, rise more tardily, walk more uncertainly, repose more dangerously, show pity more rarely, reform more slowly, die more desperately, and are punished more severely."[2] At the moment when Meyer was thus declaring against cloisters, John Heim, the Dominican reader, was exclaiming from the pulpit. "No; Christ did not, as the evangelicals teach, give satisfaction to his Father once for all. God must be daily reconciled with men by the sac-

---

[1] Cujus præsidio auxilioque præsentissimo, nos vestram dignitatem assidue commendamus. (Zw. Ep. p. 280.) [2] Langsamer gereiniget, verzweifelter stirbt härter verdammet. (Kirchhofer Reform. v. Bern. p. 48.)

rifice of the mass, and good works." Two citizens who were in the church, got up, and said, "It is not true." This led to great noise. Heim stood mute. Several urged him to continue, but he came down from the pulpit without finishing his discourse. The next day the great council, with one blow, struck both Rome and the Reformation, banishing from the town the two great controversialists, Meyer and Heim. "They are neither clear nor muddy,"[1] it was said of the Bernese, playing on the word Luther, which, in old German, means *clear*.[2]

But vain was the attempt to suppress the Reformation in Berne. It was making progress in every direction. The nuns of the monastery of the Isle had not forgotten Haller's visit. Clara May, and several of her friends, anxiously asking what they ought to do, wrote to the learned Henry Bullinger, who replied, "St. Paul enjoins young women not to make vows, but to marry; and not live in idleness, under a false semblance of piety. (1 Tim. v, 13, 14.) Follow Jesus in humility, charity, patience, purity, and honesty."[1] Clara, seeking help from above, resolved to follow this advice, and quit a life contrary to the Word of God, invented by man, and fraught with seduction and sin. Her father, Bartholomew, who had passed fifty years on battle fields and in councils, rejoiced when he learned his daughter's resolution. Clara quitted the convent.

The provost, Nicolas Watteville, whose whole interest bound him to the Roman hierarchy, and who, on the first vacancy in

[1] Dass sie weder luther nöch trüb seyen. (Kirchofer's Ref., v, Bern., p. 50.)
[2] Romish writers, in particular M. Haller, have quoted from Salat and T. Tschudi, enemies of the Reformation, a pretended letter of Zuinglius addressed at this time to Kolb, at Berne. It is as follows:—" Salvation and blessing from God our Lord. Dear Francis, move softly in the affair: throw the bear at first only one sour pear among several sweet ones—throw two, then three. After he has begun to eat, keep always throwing more, sour and sweet, pell-mell; at last shake out the whole bag, soft, hard, sweet, sour, and unripe. He will eat them all, and no longer allow any one to take them from him, or drive him away.—Zurich, Monday before St. George, 1525.
"Your servant in Christ, ULRICH ZUINGLIUS."
There are decisive reasons against the authenticity of this letter. I. In 1525, Kolb was pastor at Wertheimer. He did not come to Berne till 1527. (See Zw., Ep. p. 521.) M. Haller, it is true, substitutes 1527 for 1525, but very arbitrarily. The object of the correction, no doubt is easily seen; but unfortunately, M. Haller, in making it, contradicts Salat and Tschudi, who though they do not agree as to the day on which this letter was spoken of in the Diet, agree as to the year, both making it 1525. II. There is a difference as to the mode in which the letter was procured. One account is, that it was intercepted, another, that Kolb's parishioners communicated it to an inhabitants of the small cantons, who happened to be at Berne. III. The original is in German, whereas Zuinglius always wrote in Latin to his literary friends; besides, he addressed them as their *brother*, not as their *servant*. IV. Any reader of the letters of Zuinglius must see that his style is the most opposite possible to that of the pretended letter. Never would Zuinglius have written a letter to say so little; his epistles are usually long and full of news. To call the little pleasantry picked up by Salat a letter, is mere mockery. V. Salat deserves little confidence as a historian, and Tschudi appears to have copied him with slight variations. It may be that an inhabitant of the small cantons received from some inhabitant of Berne the letter of Zuinglius to Haller, (of which we have spoken in our second volume,) where Zuinglius very happily employs the comparison of the bear, which is met with in all the authors of that time. This may have suggested to some wit the idea of inventing this spurious letter and addressing it to Kolb as from Zuinglius. [3] Euerem Herrn Jesu nachfolget in Demuth. (Kirch. Ref, v. B. 60.)

Switzerland, must have risen to the episcopal bench, also renounced his honours, his benefices, and his hopes, to keep a pure conscience, and, breaking off all the ties by which the popes had tried to entwine him, he entered the state of marriage instituted by God from the beginning of the creation. Nicolas Watteville married Clara May, and his sister Margaret, the nun of Königsfeld, was, about the same time, united to Lucius Tscharner of Coire.[1]

CHAP. VIII

Basle—Œcolampadius—He goes to Augsburg—He enters the Convent—He returns to Sickingen—Returns to Basle—Ulric Von Hutten—His projects—Last Effort of Chivalry—Hutten dies at Uffnau.

Thus every thing gave intimation of the triumphs which the Reformation was shortly to gain in Berne. A city of no less importance, and at this time the Athens of Switzerland—Basle— began also to prepare for the great combat which signalises the sixteenth century.

Each town of the Confederation had its peculiar aspect. Berne was the city of great families; and there the question was apparently to be decided in favour of the party who should gain certain of the leading men of the city. At Zurich the ministers of the Word, as Zuinglius, Leo Juda, Myconius, Schmidt, drew after them a powerful community of citizens. Lucerne was the town of arms and military enlistments. Basle that of knowledge and printing. Erasmus, the head of the republic of letters in the sixteenth century, had fixed his residence in it, and, preferring the liberty which he here enjoyed, to the seductive invitations of popes and kings, had become the centre of a large circle of literary men.

But a humble, meek, and pious man, inferior in genius to Erasmus, was soon to exercise over the town a more powerful influence than that of the prince of schools. Christopher Utenheim, Bishop of Constance, in concert with Erasmus, sought to gather round him men fitted to accomplish a kind of intermediate Reformation. With this view he gave an invitation to Capito and Œcolampadius. In the latter there was somewhat of the monk, which often annoyed the illustrious philosopher. But Œcolampadius soon became enthusiastically attached to him, and perhaps would have lost all his independence in this close relation, had not Providence removed

[1] Zw Ep., Annotatio. p. 451. From this union the Tscharners of B. ine are descended.

him from his idol. In 1517, he returned to Weinsberg, his native town, and was shocked with the irregularities and profane jests of the priests. He has left us a fine memorial of the grave spirit which then animated him in his celebrated work "*on the Easter Merriment*," which appears to have been written about this time.[1]

Having been called, towards the end of 1518, to Augsburg, as preacher of the cathedral, he found this town still agitated by the famous interview which had taken place there in May, between Luther and the papal legate. It was necessary to take a part for or against: Œcolampadius, without hesitation, declared for the Reformer. This frankness soon raised up a keen opposition against him, and, being convinced that his timidity, and the weakness of his voice, would not allow him to succeed in the world, he began to look around, and fixed his eye on a neighbouring convent of monks of St. Bridget, celebrated for their piety, and their profound and liberal studies. Feeling the want of repose, leisure, rest, and prayer, he turned toward these monks, and asked them, "Can one live with you according to the Word of God?" They having assured him that this could be done, Œcolampadius crossed the threshold of the convent on the 23rd April, 1520, but under the express condition that he was free should ever the service of God call him elsewhere.

It was well that the future Reformer of Basle should, like Luther, know this monastic life, which was the highest expression of Roman Catholicism. But he found no repose: his friends blamed the step; and he himself declared openly that Luther was nearer the truth than his opponents. Hence Dr. Eck, and other Roman doctors, followed him with menaces even into his calm retreat.

At this time Œcolampadius was neither one of the Reformed, nor a follower of Rome. He wished a kind of purified Catholicism, which no where exists in history, but the idea of which has served many as a kind of stepping-stone. He set about correcting the statutes of his order by the Word of God. "I pray you," said he to the friars, "don't esteem your ordinances more than the commandments of the Lord." The monks replied, "We wish no other rule than that of the Saviour. Take our books, and mark, as in the immediate presence of Christ, whatever you find contrary to his Word." Œcolampadius began the task, but found it painfully wearisome. "Almighty God!" he exclaimed, "what abominations has not Rome approved in these statutes!"

No sooner had he pointed out some of these than the wrath of the friars began to be kindled. "Heretic," they exclaimed: "apostate, you deserve a dark dungeon till the end of your days." He was

[1] Herzog, Studien und Kritiken, 1840, p. 334.

excluded from the common prayers. But the danger was still greater from without. Eck and his people had not abandoned their projects. In three days he was told he was to be arrested. He went to the friars, and said to them, "Will you give me up to assassins?" The monks were speechless and irresolute. They were unwilling either to save or to destroy him. At this moment some friends of Œcolampadius arrived near the cloister with horses to conduct him to a place of safety. At this news the monks determined on allowing the departure of a brother who had brought trouble into their convent. "Adieu!" he said, and was free. He had been nearly two years in the cloister of St. Bridget.

Œcolampadius was saved: at length he again breathed. Writing to a friend he says: "I have sacrificed the monk and got back the Christian." But his flight from the convent and his heretical writings were every where known; every where also people stood aloof on his approach. He knew not what to do, when, in the spring of 1522, Sickingen offered him an asylum, which he accepted.

His spirit, which had been weighed down by monastic bondage, took a new spring amid the noble warriors of Ebernburg. "Christ is our liberty," exclaimed he, "and what men regard as the greatest misfortune—death itself—is to us true gain." He forthwith began to read the gospels and epistles to the people in German. "As soon as the trumpets resound," said he, "the walls of Jericho crumble away."

Thus, in a fortress on the banks of the Rhine, amid boisterous knights, the most modest man of his age anticipated that transformation of worship which Christendom was soon to undergo. Ebernburg, however, was too narrow for him; and he felt the want of other society than that of military men. The bookseller, Cratander, invited him to Basle. Sickingen gave his permission; and Œcolampadius, happy to revisit his old friends, arrived on the 16th November, 1522. After living for some time as a simple scholar, without public vocation, he was appointed vicar of the church of St. Martin; and perhaps it was this call to a humble and unknown employment[1] that decided the Reformation of Basle. Whenever Œcolampadius mounted the pulpit, an immense crowd filled the church.[2] At the same time the public lectures, given both by him and Pellican, were crowned with so much success, that even Erasmus was obliged to exclaim, "Œcolampadius triumphs."[3]

In fact, says Zuinglius, this meek but firm man, shed around him the sweet savour of Christ, and all who heard him made progress in

[1] Meis sumtibus non sine contemptu et invidia. (Œcol. ad Pirckh. de Eucharistia.)
[2] Dass er kein Predigt thate, er hatte ein mächtig Volk darinn,—says Peter Ryf, his contemporary. (Wirtz., v, 350.)   [3] Œcolampadius apud nos triumphat. (Eras, ad Zuin. Zw. Ep. p 312.)

the truth.[1] Often, indeed, the news spread that he would soon be obliged to leave both, and again commence his adventurous travels. His friends, particularly Zuinglius, were in great alarm; but the report of new successes gained by Œcolampadius, soon dissipated their fears, and strengthened their hopes. The fame of his labours even reached Wittemberg, and rejoiced Luther, who daily talked of him to Melancthon. Meantime the Saxon Reformer was not without uneasiness. Erasmus was at Basle, and Erasmus was the friend of Œcolampadius. Luther thought it his duty to put one whom he loved on his guard. "I much fear," he wrote, "that, like Moses, Erasmus will die in the plains of Moab, without conducting us into the land of promise." [2]

Erasmus had retired to Basle, as a quiet town, situated in the centre of the literary movement, and from the bosom of which he could, by means of the printing-press of Frobenius, act upon France, Germany, Switzerland, Italy, and England. But he did not like to be disturbed, and if he felt some jealousy at Œcolampadius, there was another man who inspired him with still greater alarm. Ulric Von Hutten had followed Œcolampadius to Basle. For a long time he had attacked the pope as one knight attacks another. "The axe," said he, "is already laid to the root of the tree. Germans, yield not at the first brunt of the battle; the die is cast—the enterprise is begun. Liberty for ever!" He had abandoned Latin, and now wrote only in German; for it was the people he wished to address.

His ideas were grand and noble. An annual assembly of bishops was, according to him, to regulate the affairs of the Church. A Christian constitution, and, above all, a Christian spirit, was to spread from Germany as formerly from Judea, over the whole world. Charles V was to have been the young hero destined to realise the golden age; but Hutten's hopes in him having been disappointed, he had turned to Sickingen, and asked from chivalry what the empire refused. Sickingen, at the head of the feudal nobility, had played a distinguished part in Germany; but the princes had shortly after besieged him in his castle of Landstein, and the new engines, cannon and bullets, had battered down those old walls which had been accustomed to other kinds of assault. The taking of Landstein had been the final defeat of chivalry, the decisive victory of artillery over lances and bucklers, the triumph of modern times over the middle ages. Thus, the last exploit of knighthood, was to be in favour of the Reformation—the first efforts of new weapons and wars was to be against it. The steel clad men who fell under

---

[1] Illi magis ac magis in omni bono augescunt. (Eras. ad Zwing. Zw. Ep. p. 812.)
[2] Et in terram promissionis ducere non potest. (L. Ep. ii, p. 353.)

the unexpected force of bullets, and lay among the ruins of Landstein, gave place to other knights. Other feats of arms were about to commence. A spiritual chivalry succeeded that of the Du Guesclins and Bayards, and those old broken battlements, those ruined walls, those aspiring heroes, proclaimed still more forcibly than Luther was able to do that it was not by such allies and such weapons that the gospel of the Prince of Peace would gain the victory.

With the downfall of Landstein and chivalry, had fallen all Hütten's hopes. Over Sickingen's dead body he bade adieu to all the glorious days of which his imagination had dreamed, and, losing all confidence in man, all he now asked was a brief obscurity and repose. He came to seek them in Switzerland beside Erasmus. These two men had long been friends; but the rude and boisterous knight, disdaining the judgment of others, always used to lay his hand on his sword, and, attacking right and left all whom he met, could seldom move in accordance with the delicate and timid Erasmus, with his refined manners, his smooth and polished address, his eagerness for approbation, and his readiness to make every sacrifice to obtain it, fearing nothing in the world so much as a dispute.

Hütten having arrived at Basle a poor sick fugitive, immediately inquired for his old friend. But Erasmus trembled at the thought of sharing his table with a man under the ban of the pope and the emperor, a man who would care for no one, borrow money of him, and doubtless bring after him a crowd of those "evangelists," of whom Erasmus was always becoming more afraid.[1] He refused to see him, and, shortly after, the magistrates of Basle begged Hütten to leave the town. Hutten, mortified and irritated against his timid friend, retired to Mulhausen, and published a violent philippic against Erasmus, who wrote a very clever reply. The knight had seized the sword with both hands, and brought it down with force upon his adversary; the scholar, dexterously slipping aside, had returned the strokes of the sword with strokes of his beak.[2]

Hutten behoved again to fly. He arrived at Zurich, where he met with a generous reception from the noble-minded Zuinglius. But cabals obliged him to quit this town also, and, after passing some time at the baths of Pfeffers, he repaired with a letter from the Swiss Reformer to the house of pastor John Schnepp, who dwelt in the little islet of Ufnau, on the Lake of Zurich. This poor minister received the poor exiled knight with the most touching

---

[1] Erasmus, in a letter to Melancthon, in which he tries to excuse himself, thus writes:—"Ille egens et omnibus rebus destitutus quærebat nidum aliquem ubi moveretur. Erat mihi gloriosus ille miles cum sua scabie in ædes recipiendus simulque recipiendus ille chorus titulo *Evangelicorum*." (Er. Ep. p. 949.) "In want, and every way destitute, was looking out for some place where he might nestle. That vainglorious soldier, with his itch, was to be received into the house, and with him the band named *Evangelicals*." [2] Expostulatio Hutteni—Erasmisoongia.

charity. It was in this peaceful and unknown retreat, after a most agitated life—banished by some, pursued by others, forsaken almost by all, after constantly combating superstition, yet, as it would seem, without even possessing the truth, Ulrick von Hutten, one of the most remarkable minds of the sixteenth century, died in obscurity towards the end of August, 1523. The poor pastor, who was skilful in the healing art, had in vain given him all his care. With him died chivalry. He left neither money, nor furniture, nor books—nothing in the world except a pen.[1] Thus was the hand of iron broken that had presumed to support the ark of God.

CHAP. IX.

Erasmus and Luther—Uncertainty of Erasmus—Luther to Erasmus—Work of Erasmus against Luther on Free Will—Three Opinions—Effect on Luther—Luther on Free Will—The Jansenists and the Reformers—Homage to Erasmus—Rage of Erasmus—The Three Days.

There was a man in Germany more formidable to Erasmus than the unfortunate knight; this was Luther. The moment had arrived when the two greatest wrestlers of the age were to measure their powers in close combat. The two Reformations at which they aimed were very different. While Luther desired an entire Reformation, Erasmus, a friend of the middle course, sought to obtain concessions from the hierarchy, which might again unite the two extreme parties. The vacillation and uncertainty of Erasmus disgusted Luther. He said to him, "You wish to walk on eggs without crushing them, and among glasses without breaking them."[1]

At the same time, to the vacillation of Erasmus, he opposed complete decision. "We Christians," said he, "ought to be sure of our doctrine, and know how to say yes or no without hesitating. To attempt to hinder us from affirming with perfect conviction what we believe, is to deprive us of faith itself. The Holy Spirit is not a sceptic.[2] He has written in our hearts a firm and powerful assurance, which makes us as certain of our faith, as we are of life itself."

These words at once tell us on which side strength lay. In order to accomplish a religious transformation, there must be a

---
[1] Libros nullos habuit, supellectilem nullam, præter calamum. (Zw. Ep. p. 313.)
[2] Auf Eyern gehen und keiner zutreten. (L. Op. xix, p. 11.)   [3] Der heilige Geist ist kein Scepticus. (Ibid. p. 8.)

fi̇ and living faith. A salutary resolution in the Church never will proceed from philosophical views and human opinions. To fertilise the earth after long drought, the lightning must pierce the cloud, and the reservoirs of heaven be opened. Criticism, philosophy, history even may prepare the paths for true faith, but cannot supply its place. In vain do you clean out your canals and repair your embankments, so long as the water descends not from the sky. All human sciences without faith are only canals without water.

Whatever might be the essential difference between Luther and Erasmus, the friends of Luther, and Luther himself, long hoped to see Erasmus united with them against Rome. Sayings which his caustic humour let fall were reported, and showed his disagreement with the most zealous friends of Catholicism. One day, for instance, when he was in England, he had a keen discussion with Sir Thos. More on transubstantiation. " Believe that you have the body of Christ," said More, " and you have it really." Erasmus made no answer. Shortly after he left the banks of the Thames, and More lent him his horse to the sea-side; but Erasmus took it with him to the continent. As soon as More knew of it, he reproached him in the keenest terms. Erasmus only answered by sending him the following stanza:—

> Of Christ's body, this you declared the creed:
> " Believe you have it, and you have indeed."
> Apply the doctrine to your missing steed;
> Believe you have it, and you have indeed.

Erasmus had appeared in this character not only in England and Germany. At Paris it was said, " Luther has only widened the opening of the door of which Erasmus had previously picked the lock." [2]

The situation of Erasmus was difficult. In a letter to Zuinglius he says, " I will not be unfaithful to the cause of Christ, at least in so far as the age will permit."[3] In proportion as he saw Rome bestirring herself against the Reformation, he, from prudential motives, drew off. He was applied to from all quarters—the pope, the emperor, kings, princes, the learned; and even his most intimate friends, urged him to write against the Reformer.[4] The pope wrote unto him—" No work would be more agreeable to

---

[1] " Quod mihi dixisti nuper de corpore Christi:
Crede quod habes et habes;
Hoc tibi rescribo tantum de tuo caballo:
Crede quod habes et habes."
(Paravicini, Singularia. p. 71.)
[2] Histoire Cathol. de notre temps, par S. Fontaine de l'ordre de St. Francois, Paris, 1562. [3] Quantum hoc seculum patitur. (Zw. Ep. p. 221.) [4] A Pontifice, a Cæsare, a regibus et principibus, a doctissimis etiam et carissimis amicis huc provocor. (Erasm. Zw. Ep. p. 308.)

God—none more worthy of yourself and your genius."[1] For a long time Erasmus resisted these solicitations; he could not disguise from himself that the cause of the Reformers was the cause of religion as well as of letters. Besides, Luther was an opponent with whom none were fond of engaging, and Erasmus thought he could already feel the redoubled and sturdy blows of the champion of Wittemberg. In reply to a theologian of Rome he wrote: "It is easy to say, 'Write against Luther;' but it is a task pregnant with danger."[2] Thus he would, and yet would not.

This irresolute conduct of Erasmus subjected him to the attacks of the most violent men of both parties. Luther himself found it difficult to reconcile the respect which he had for the learning of Erasmus with the indignation which he felt at his cowardice. He resolved to escape from this painful condition, and in April, 1524, wrote him a letter, which he gave to the care of Camerarius. "As yet," said he, "you have not received of the Lord the courage necessary to march with us to give battle to the papists. We bear with your weakness. If letters flourish, if they open to all the treasures of the Scriptures, it is a gift for which we are indebted, under God, to you—a magnificent gift, for which our thanksgivings ascend to heaven. But do not abandon the task which has been imposed on you, in order to pass into our camp. No doubt your eloquence and genius would be useful to us; but since your courage fails you, remain where you are. I could wish that our people would allow your old age to slumber peacefully in the Lord. The greatness of our cause has long transcended your powers. But, on the other hand, my dear Erasmus, desist from throwing at us so many handfuls of pungent salt, which you know so well how to disguise under flowers of rhetoric. It is more painful to be slightly bitten by Erasmus, than to be ground to death by all papists put together. Content yourself with being the spectator of our tragedy:[3] publish no book against me; I, on my part, will publish none against you."

Thus Luther, the man of war, asked for concord: it was Erasmus, the man of peace, who disturbed it.

Erasmus received this proceeding on the part of the Reformer as the greatest of insults, and if he had not already resolved to write against Luther, it is probable that he resolved now. He replied, "Perhaps Erasmus, by writing against you, will do more service to the gospel than some fools who write for you,[4] and who do not allow me to be any longer a mere spectator of this tragedy.

---

[1] Nulla te et ingenio. eruditione, eloquentiaque tua dignior esse potest. (Adrianus Papa, Ep. Er. p. 1202.)   [2] Res est periculi plena. (Er. Ep. p. 758.)   [3] Spectator tantum sis tragœdiæ nostræ. (L. Ep. ii, p. 501.)   [4] Quidam stolidi scribentes pro te. (Unschuldige Nachricht, p. 545.)

But he had other motives also.

Henry VIII of England, and the leading men of that kingdom, were extremely urgent that he should declare publicly against the Reformation. Erasmus, during a moment of courage, allowed the promise to be forced from him. Besides, his equivocal situation had become a continual torment to him : he loved repose, but the necessity he felt of continually vindicating himself troubled his life : he loved glory, but he was accused of fearing Luther, and of being too feeble to answer him : he was accustomed to the first place, but the little monk of Wittemberg had dethroned the mighty Erasmus. He behoved then, by a courageous act, to conquer back the place which he had lost. All ancient Christendom was imploring him to do so. Ability, and the greatest reputation of the age, were wanted to oppose the Reformation. Erasmus yielded.

But what weapon was he going to employ? Will he cause the thunders of the Vatican to roar? Will he defend abuses which are the disgrace of the papacy? Erasmus could not do so. The great movement by which men's minds were agitated, after the deathlike lethargy which had lasted for so many ages, filled him with joy, and he would have feared to trammel it. Not being able to appear as the champion of Roman Catholicism, in regard to the additions which it has made to Christianity, he undertook to defend it in what it has cut off. In his attack upon Luther, Erasmus selected the point in which Catholicism is blended with rationalism— the doctrine of free will, or of the natural power of man. Thus, while undertaking the defence of the Church, Erasmus pleased the men of the world; while battling for the pope, he battled also for the philosophers. It has been said that he was awkwardly trammeled by an obscure and useless question.[1] Luther, the Reformers, and their age, thought otherwise. We agree with them. "I must acknowledge," said Luther, " that in this combat you are the only one who has seized your opponent by the throat. I thank you with all my heart, for I like better to deal with that subject than with all those secondary questions of the pope, purgatory, and indulgences, with which, till this hour, the enemies of the gospel have pestered me.[2]

His own experience, and the attentive study of the Holy Scriptures and of St. Augustin, had convinced Luther that the actual powers of man so incline him to evil, that all he can do of himself is to attain to a certain external decency, altogether insufficient in the eyes of the Deity. At the same time, he had learned that

[1] On this subject M. Nisard says—Erasmi Revue des deux mondes, iii, p. 411,— "One feels humbled for our species, on seeing men capable of grappling with eternal truths, spending their lives in fencing with men of straw, like gladiators making war on flies." [2] L. Op. xix. p. 146.

God gives a true righteousness, by carrying on the work of faith through operation of the Holy Spirit.

This doctrine had become the principle of his religious life, the predominant idea in his theology, and the point on which the whole Reformation turned.

While Luther maintained that every thing good in man came from God, Erasmus took the side of those who thought that this good came from man himself. God or man . . . —good or evil . . .— these, surely, are not paltry questions; if these are such questions, they must be sought for elsewhere.

In the autumn of 1524, Erasmus published his famous work, entitled "*Disquisition on Free Will.*" No sooner had it appeared than the philosopher could scarcely credit his own courage. He trembled, while, with eyes fixed on the arena, he beheld the gauntlet which he had just thrown down to his opponent. The die is cast, "wrote he, with emotion, to Henry VIII," the book on *Free Will* has appeared. . . . . This, believe me, is a daring act. I expect to be stoned. . . . . But I console myself by the example of your majesty, whom the wrath of those people has not spared."[1]

His alarm soon increased to such a degree, that he bitterly regretted the step he had taken. "Why was I not allowed," he exclaimed, "to spend my age in the garden of the Muses! Here I am, at sixty, pushed violently forward into the arena, and instead of the lyre, holding the cestus and net. . . . ."
"I know," said he to the Bishop of Rochester, "that in writing on free will, I was not in my sphere. . . . . You congratulate me on my triumphs. . . . . Ah, I know not in what I triumph! The faction (the Reformation) is daily increasing.[2] Was it then my destiny that, at my age, I was to be transformed from a friend of the Muses into a miserable gladiator?" . . . .

It was much, doubtless, for the timid Erasmus to have taken the field against Luther. But still he was far from having given proof of great hardihood. He seems, in his book, to attribute little to the will of man, and to leave the greater part to divine grace; but, at the same time, he chose his arguments in such a way as to make it be believed, that man does all, and God does nothing. Not daring to express his thoughts distinctly, he affirms one thing, and proves another; leaving one at liberty to suppose that he believed what he proved, and not what he affirmed.

He distinguishes three opinions opposed in different degrees to that of Pelagius. "Some," says he, "think that man can neither

---

[1] Jacta est alea . . . . audax, mihi crede, facinus . . . . expecto lapidationem. (Er. Ep. p. 811.) [2] Quomodo triumphans nescio. . . . . Factio crescit in dies latius. (Ibid., p. 809.)

will nor begin, far less accomplish any thing that is good, without special and continual help from divine grace. This opinion seems probable enough. Others teach that the will of man has power only to do evil, and that grace alone performs in us any thing that is good; and, lastly, there are some who maintain that there never was any free will, either in man or angels, either in Adam or in us, whether before or after grace, but that God produces in man both good or evil, and that every thing which takes place, happens through absolute necessity.[1]

Erasmus, while seeming to admit the first of these opinions, employs arguments which militate against it, and which may be employed by the most decided Pelagian. Thus, while referring to the passages of Scripture, in which God presents man with a choice of good and evil, he adds, "Man then must will and choose; for it would be ridiculous to say to any one, Choose! if it were not in his power to do so."

Luther was not afraid of Erasmus. "Truth," said he, "is mightier than eloquence. The victory belongs to him who lisps the truth, and not to him who is eloquent in favour of falsehood."[2]

But when he received the work of Erasmus, he found the book so feeble, that he hesitated to answer it. "What!" said he to him, " so much eloquence in so bad a cause; one would say it was a man serving up mire and filth on gold and silver plate.[3] It is impossible to get hold of you any where. You are like an eel which slips between the fingers; or, like the Proteus of the poets, who changes in the very hand of the person who is trying to bind him."

Meanwhile, as Luther did not answer, the monks and scholastic theologians began to shout: "Ah! well, where is now your Luther? Where is the great Maccabeus? Let him enter the lists! Let him come forward! Ah! ah! he has at length found the man that was wanted for him. He now knows how to keep in the back ground. He has learnt to hold his tongue."[4]

Luther saw that he behoved to answer; but it was not till the end of 1525 that he began to prepare; and Melancthon having intimated to Erasmus that Luther would use moderation, the philosopher was quite astonished. "If I have written with moderation," said he, " it is my natural turn: but Luther has the indignation of the son of Peleus (Achilles). And how could it be otherwise? When a ship encounters a tempest, like that which has

---

[1] De libero arbitrio Διατριβή. (Erasmi Op. ix, p. 1215, sq.)　[2] Victoria est penes balbutientem veritatem, non apud mendacem eloquentiam. (L. Ep. ii, p. 200.)
[3] Als wenn einer in silbern oder guldern Schüsseln wollte mist und Unflath Auftragen. (L. Op. xix, p. 4.　[4] Sehet, sehet nun da zu! wo ist nun Luther. Ibid., p. 3.)

risen against Luther, what anchor, what ballast, what helm, would not be necessary to enable it to keep its course? Hence, if he answers me in a manner not in accordance with his character, these sycophants will exclaim that we understand one another."[1] We will see that Erasmus was soon to be disencumbered of these fears.

The doctrine of an election by God, the only cause of man's salvation, had always been dear to the Reformer; but, till now, he had only considered it in a practical point of view. In his reply to Erasmus, it presented itself to him in a speculative form; and he laboured to prove, by the arguments which seemed to him most conclusive, that God does every thing in the conversion of man, and that our heart is so alienated from the love of God, that every sincere inclination to good can only proceed from the regenerating agency of the Holy Spirit.

"To call our will a free will," said he, "is to do like princes, who string together a long series of titles, calling themselves the lords of such and such kingdoms, such and such principalities, and distant islands (as Rhodes, Cyprus, and Jerusalem), while they have not the least power over them." At the same time, Luther here makes an important distinction, which shows well that he did not participate in the third opinion which Erasmus had described and imputed to him. "The will of man," says he, "may be called a free will, not in relation to what is above it—that is to say, God, but in relation to what is beneath—that is to say, the kings of the earth.[2] When my goods, my fields, my house, my farm, are in question, I can act, make, and manage freely. But in things which regard salvation, man is captive; he is subject to the will of God, or rather to that of the devil."[3] Among all the teachers of free will," exclaims he, "show me a single one who has in himself strength sufficient to endure a little injury, a passionate attack, or even a look from his enemy, and to do it joyfully, then,—without even asking him to abandon his body, his goods, his honour, and all things,—I declare that you have gained your cause."[4]

Luther's eye was too piercing not to detect the contradictions into which his opponent had fallen. Accordingly he proceeded, in his reply, to enclose the philosopher in the net in which he had placed himself. "If the passages which you quote," said he, "prove that it is easy for us to do good, why do you dispute? What need have we of Christ and the Holy Spirit? Christ has done foolishly in shedding his blood to procure us a strength,

---

[1] Ille si hic multum sui dissimilis fuerit, clamabunt sycophantæ colludere nos. (*Er. Ep.* p. 819.) [2] Der Wille des Menschen mag. . . . . (L. Op. xix, p. 29.) [3] Ibid., p. 33. [4] Ibid.

which we already have from nature." In fact the passages quoted by Erasmus were to be interpreted in quite a different sense. This much debated question is clearer than at first sight it seems. When the Bible says to man, "Choose," it is because it presupposes the assistance of the grace of God, by which alone he can do what it commands. God, in giving the command, gives also the power to perform it. When Christ said to Lazarus, come forth, it was not because Lazarus could raise himself, but, because, in commanding him to come forth from the tomb, he gave him power to do so, and accompanied his word with creative power. He speaks, and it is done. Besides, it is quite true that the man whom God addresses must will; it is himself that wills, and not another; but still he can receive this will only from God. It must, no doubt, be in the man; and this command which God addresses to him, and which, according to Erasmus 'proves man's power, so reconcileable with the agency of God, that it is precisely the means by which this agency is carried on. God says to man, "Be converted," and while so saying, converts him.

But the view on which Luther especially dwelt in his reply was, that the passages quoted by Erasmus, are designed to teach men what they ought to do, and their incapability of doing it, but not at all to acquaint them with this fancied power which is assigned to them. "How often does it happen," says Luther, "that a father calls his little child to him, saying, 'My son, will you come? Come, come then!' in order the child may learn to cry for help, and allow itself to be carried by him." [1]

After combating the arguments of Erasmus in favour of free will, Luther defends his own against the attacks of his opponent. "Dear Diatribe," says he ironically, "mighty heroine, who pretend to have overthrown the word of the Lord in the gospel of St. John, '*Without me ye can do* NOTHING,' which you, however, regard as the strongest in my power, and call the *Achilles of Luther*, listen to me for a little. At all events, until you prove that this word *nothing* not only may, but must signify *some little thing*, all your high words, all your splendid illustrations, have no more effect than chips of straw would have in extinguishing an immense conflagration. What have we to do with the assertions—'*This may mean; that may be understood thus*—when you are bound to demonstrate that it *must* be so understood.' If you fail to do so, we take the declaration in its natural sense, and laugh at all your illustrations, your great preparations and pompous triumph." [2]

At length, in a second part, Luther shows, and always by Scripture, that it is the grace of God that does all. "In one

[1] L. Op. xix. p. 55.   [2] Ibid. p. 116.

word," says he at the end, "since Scripture uniformly opposes Christ to all that is not Christ; since it declares that whatever is not Christ and in Christ, is under the power of error, darkness, the devil, death, sin, and the wrath of God, it follows that all the passages of the Bible which speak of Christ are contrary to free will. Now, these passages are innumerable; the Sacred Volume is filled with them.[1]"

We see that the discussion between Luther and Erasmus is the same as that which, a century later, took place between the Jansenists and the Jesuits—between Pascal and Molina.[2] To what is it owing, that while the Reformation has had such mighty results, Jansenism, defended by the most distinguished geniuses, has been suppressed without force? It is because Jansenism went back to St. Augustin, and leant upon the fathers; whereas the Reformation went back to the Bible, and leant upon the Word of God. It is because Jansenism made a compromise with Rome, and wished to establish a medium between truth and error; the Reformation confided in God alone, cleared away the soil, removed all the human rubbish which had covered it for ages, and laid bare the primitive rock. To stop midway is useless labour; in all things it is proper to go forward to the end. Hence, while Jansenism has passed away, the destinies of the world are bound up with evangelical Christianity.

Luther, after keenly refuting the error, paid a brilliant, but perhaps somewhat sarcastic, homage to the person of Erasmus. "I confess," said he, "that you are a great man. Where were more learning, intellect, ability in writing and speaking ever seen? For myself I have nothing of the kind; there is only one thing from which I can derive any glory. . . . I am a Christian. May God raise you in the knowledge of the gospel, infinitely above me, so that you may surpass me as much in this respect, as you already do in every other."[3]

Erasmus was beside himself on reading Luther's reply; he would see nothing in his compliments but the honey of a poisoned cup, or the embrace of a serpent. He immediately wrote to the Elector of Saxony, demanding justice; and Luther having tried to appease him, he laid aside his ordinary habit, and as one of his most ardent apologists expresses it, began "to inveigh in a broken voice and grey hairs."[4]

Erasmus was vanquished. Moderation had been his forte, and he had now lost it. The energy of Luther he could only supply

---

[1] L. Op. xix, p. 143. [2] It is needless to say that I do not mean personal discussions between individuals, the one of whom died in 1600, and the other was not born till 1623.   [3] L. Op. xix, p. 146, 147.   [4] M. Nisard. Erasme, p. 419.

by rage. The wise man wanted wisdom. He replied, publicly, in his *Hyperapistes*, accusing the Reformer of barbarism, falsehood, and blasphemy. The philosopher even went the length of prophesying. "I prophesy," said he, "that no name under the sun will be more execrated than that of Luther." This prophecy, after a lapse of three centuries, was answered on the jubilee of 1817, by the enthusiastic acclamations of the whole Protestant world.

Thus, while Luther, with the Bible, placed himself at the head of his age, Erasmus, in opposing him, wished to occupy the same place with philosophy. Which of the two leaders has been followed? Both, no doubt. Nevertheless, the influence of Luther on the nations of Christendom has been infinitely greater than that of Erasmus. Even those who did not well understand the matter in dispute, seeing the conviction of one of the antagonists, and the doubts of the other, could not help believing that the former was in the right and the latter in the wrong. It has been said that the three last centuries, the sixteenth, seventeenth, and eighteenth, may be conceived as an immense battle of three days.[1] We willingly adopt the happy expression, but not the part which is assigned to each day. The same task is given to the sixteenth and to the eighteenth century. The first day and the last it is philosophy that breaks the ranks. The sixteenth century philosophical! Strange mistake. No; each of these days had a distinct and striking characteristic. The first day of battle, it was the Word of God and the Gospel of Christ that triumphed. Then Rome was defeated, as well as philosophy, in the person of Erasmus and her other representatives. The second day, we admit Rome, her authority, her discipline, and her doctrine re-appear, and are on the eve of triumphing, by the intrigues of a celebrated society and the power of the scaffold, as well as by some characters of great veracity and men of distinguished genius. The third day, human philosophy rises up in all its pride; and finding not the gospel but Rome on the field of battle, makes easy work, and soon carries all the entrenchments. The first day is the battle of God, the second the battle of the priest, and the third the battle of reason. What will be the fourth? The confused mêlée, we think, the furious battle of all the powers together, to terminate in the triumph of Him to whom the triumph belongs.

[1] Port Royal, by Sainte Beuve, vol. I, p. 28.

CHAP. X.

The Three Adversaries—Source of the Truth—Anabaptism—Anabaptism and Zuinglius—Constitution of the Church—Prison—The Prophet Blaurock—Anabaptism at St. Gall—An Anabaptist family—Dispute at Zurich—The limits of the Reformation—Punishment of the Anabaptists.

But the battle which the Reformation fought on the grand day of the sixteenth century was not one only: it was manifold. The Reformation had at once several enemies to combat. After protesting against the decretals and supremacy of the popes, next against the cold apophthegms of the rationalists, philosophers, and schoolmen; it at the same time stood up against the reveries of enthusiasm, and the hallucinations of mysticism—opposing to these three powers at once the sword and buckler of Divine revelation.

It must be admitted that there is a great resemblance, a remarkable unity in these three adverse powers. The false systems which in all ages are most opposed to evangelical Christianity, are always characterised by their making religious knowledge proceed from within the man himself. Rationalism makes it proceed from reason; mysticism, from some internal light; Roman Catholicism, from an illumination of the pope. These three errors seek the truth in man; evangelical Christianity seeks it wholly in God. While rationalism, mysticism, and Roman Catholicism admit a permanent inspiration in certain persons like ourselves, and thus open the door to all errors and all variations, evangelical Christianity recognises this inspiration only in the writings of the Apostles and Prophets, and alone exhibits that grand, and beautiful, and living unity, which flows always the same through all ages.

The work of the Reformation was to re-establish the rights of the Word of God, in opposition not only to Roman Catholicism, but also rationalism and to mysticism itself.

The fanaticism of the Anabaptists being extinguished in Germany by Luther's return to Wittemberg, re-appeared in force in Switzerland, threatening the edifice which Zuinglius, Haller, and Œcolampadius had built on the Word of God. Thomas Munzer, when obliged to quit Saxony in 1521, had arrived on the frontiers of Switzerland. Conrad Grebel, whose restless and ardent temper we have already mentioned, had become connected with him, as well as Felix Manz, son of a canon, and some other inhabitants of Zurich. Grebel had immediately tried to gain Zuinglius. In vain had Zuinglius gone farther than Luther. He saw a party rising that wished to go still farther than he. "Let us," said Grebel to him, "form a community of true believers; for to them alone the promise belongs; and let us establish a church in which there is no sin."[1] "We cannot," said Zuinglius, "introduce heaven upon earth, and Christ has taught us that we must allow the tares to grow among the wheat."[2]

Grebel, having failed with Zuinglius, was desirous to appeal to the people. "The whole Zurich community," said he, "must decide supremely on matters of faith." But Zuinglius dreaded the influence which radical enthusiasts might exercise over a large assembly. He thought that, except in unusual cases, where the people might be called to give in their adherence, it was better to confide religious interests to a college, which might be considered as the *elite* of the representatives of the Church. Consequently, the Council of Two Hundred, which exercised political supremacy in Zurich, was also intrusted with ecclesiastical power, under the express condition that they should conform in every respect to the rule of Holy Scripture. No doubt it would have been better to constitute the Church fully, and call upon it to name its own representatives, who should be intrusted only with the religious interests of the people; for he who is capable of managing the interests of the State may be very unfit to manage those of the Church, and *vice versa*. Nevertheless, the inconveniences were not so serious then as they might be at this time, as the members of the Grand Council had entered frankly into the religious movement. Be this as it may, Zuinglius, while appealing to the Church, avoided bringing it too much upon the stage, and preferred the representation system to the active sovereignty of the people.

This is what the States of Europe, after the lapse of three centuries, are doing in the political sphere. Repulsed by Zuinglius, Grebel turned in another direction. Roubli, superannuated pastor at Basle, Brödtlein, pastor at Zollekon, and Louis Herzer, gave him a cordial reception. They determined to form an independent community in the midst of the great community—a church in the midst of the Church. A new baptism was to enable them to reassemble their congregation, composed exclusively of true believers. "The baptism of infants," said they, "is a horrible abomination—a manifest impiety, invented by the evil spirit, and by Nicholas II, Pope of Rome.[3]

The council of Zurich taking the alarm, ordered a public discussion; and the Anabaptists refusing to abjure their errors, some Zurichers among them were imprisoned, and some strangers ban-

---

[1] Vermeintend ein Kirchen ze versammlen die one Sünd wär. (Zw. Op. ii, p. 231.)
[2] Zw. Op. iii, p. 362. [3] Impietatem manifestissimam, a cacodæmone, a Nicolao II, esse. (Hottinger, iii, p. 219.)

ished. But persecution only increased their fervour. "Not with words only," they exclaimed, "but with our blood are we ready to bear testimony to the truth of our cause." Some, girding themselves with cords or osier-twigs, went up and down the streets crying, "A few days, and Zurich will be destroyed. Woe to thee, Zurich! woe! woe!" Several used blasphemous expressions. "Baptism," they said, "is a bath for a dog: it is of no more use to baptise a child than to baptise a cat."[1] Simple and pious people were moved and amazed. Fourteen men, among them Felix Mantz and seven women, were seized and put on bread and water in the heretics' tower. After a fortnight's confinement, they succeeded in raising some planks during the night, and, assisting one another, made their escape. "An angel," they said, "had opened the prison and let them out."[2]

A monk who had escaped from his convent, George Jacob de Coire, surnamed Blaurock, because it seems he always wore a blue coat, joined them, and was, on account of his eloquence, called the *second St. Paul*. This bold monk went from place to place, by his imposing fervour constraining people to receive his baptism. One Sunday at Zollekon, while the deacon was preaching, the impetuous Anabaptist interrupting him, exclaimed in a voice of thunder. "It is written, *My house shall be called the house of prayer, but ye have made it a den of thieves*." Then lifting his staff which he had in his hand, he violently struck four blows.

"I am a door," exclaimed he, "whosoever will enter in by me will find pasture. I am a good shepherd. My body I give to the prison; my life I give to the sword, the scaffold, or the wheel. I am the beginning of baptism and of the bread of the Lord."[3]

Zuinglius still opposing the torrent of Anabaptism in Zurich, St Gall was soon inundated by it. Grebel arrived, and was received by the brethren with acclamation; and on Palm Sunday, having repaired with a number of his adherents to the banks of the Sitter, he baptised them.

The news immediately spread to the neighbouring cantons, and a great crowd flocked from Zurich, Appenzel, and divers other places, to "little Jerusalem."

Zuinglius was heart-broken at the sight of this agitation. He saw a storm bursting on those districts in which the seed of the gospel was just beginning to spring.[4] He resolved to oppose these disorders, and composed a treatise "on baptism,"[5] which the coun-

---

[1] Nutzete eben so viel als wenn man eine Katze taufet. (Füssl. Beytr. i, p. 243.)
[2] Wie die Apostel von dem Engel Gottes gelediget. (Bull. Chr. p. 261.)   [3] Ich bin ein Anfanger der Taufe und des Herrn Brodes. (Fussl. Beytr. i, p. 264.)
[4] Mich beduret seer das ungewitter. ... (Zw. to the Council of St. Gall, ii, p. 230.)
[5] Vom Touf, vom Widertouf, und vom Kindertouf. (Zw. Op. ii, p. 230.)

cil of St. Gall, to whom he dedicated it, ordered to be read in church before all the people.

"Very dear brethren in God," said Zuinglius, "the torrent which leaps from our rocks, soon washes down whatever it reaches. At first it is only small stones; but these are carried violently against larger ones, until the torrent becomes so powerful that it carries away every thing it meets, and leaves nothing behind it but screams and useless lamentations and fertile meadows turned into a desert. The spirit of disputation and self-righteousness acts in the same way: it excites disorders, destroys charity, and where it found fair and flourishing churches, leaves nothing behind it but flocks plunged into mourning and despair."

Thus spoke Zuinglius, the mountaineer of the Tockenburg. "Tell us the Word of God," exclaimed an Anabaptist who was in the church, "and not the word of Zuinglius." Confused voices were immediately heard. "Let him take away the book, let him take away the book," exclaimed the Anabaptists. They then rose and quitted the church, crying, "Keep the doctrine of Zuinglius: as for us, we will keep the Word of God."[1]

This fanaticism manifested itself by still more lamentable disorders. Under the pretext that the Lord commands us to become like children, these poor creatures began to leap in the streets, clapping their hands, to dance a jig together, to squat on the ground, and to roll one another on the sand. Some burnt the New Testament, saying, "The letter killeth, but the spirit giveth life," and, several falling into convulsions, pretended that they had revelations of the Spirit.

In a lonely house, situated near St. Gall, on the Müllegg, lived a farmer of eighty—John Schucker, with his five sons. They had all, as well as their servants, received the new baptism, and two of the sons, Thomas and Leonard, were distinguished for their fanaticism. On the 7th of February, 1526, (Shrove Tuesday) they invited a great number of Anabaptists to meet at their house, and the father caused a calf to be killed for the occasion. The viands, the wine, and the numerous assemblage, heated their imaginations; they passed the whole night in converse and fanatical gesticulations, convulsions, visions, and revelations.[2]

In the morning, Thomas, still agitated by the proceedings of the night, and having even, as it appears, lost his reason, took the bladder of the calf, put some of its gall into it, wishing thus to imitate the symbolical language of the prophets, and, approaching his brother Leonard, said to him in a grave voice, "Thus, bitter

[1] So wollen wir Gottes Wort haben. (Zw. to the Council of St. Gall, ii, p. 237.)
[2] Mit wunderbaren geperden und gesprächen, verzucken gesichten, und offenbarungen. (Bull. Chr, i, . 324.

is the death which you must endure." Then he added, "Brother Leonard, go down on your knees." Leonard knelt. Shortly after. "Leonard rise." Leonard rose up. The father, the brothers, and the other Anabaptists, looked on in astonishment, asking what God meant to do. Shortly Thomas resumed: "Leonard, kneel again." Leonard did so. The spectators alarmed at the dismal look of the poor wretch, said to him, "Think of what you are doing, and take care no mischief happen."—"Fear not," replied Thomas: "nothing will happen but the will of our Father." At the same time he suddenly seized a sword, and bringing it down with force on his brother, who was kneeling before him as a criminal before the executioner, he cut off his head, and exclaimed, "Now the will of the Father is done." All who were standing round started back in horror, and the farm resounded with cries and groans. Thomas, whose whole clothing was shirt and pantaloons, went off barefoot and bareheaded, out of the house, and ran towards St. Gall, making frantic gestures. He entered the house of burgomaster Joachim Vadian, and, with haggard looks and loud cries, said to him, "I announce to thee the day of the Lord." The fearful news spread through St. Gall, "He has, like Cain," it was said, "killed his brother Abel."[1] The culprit was seized. "It is true I did it," repeated he incessantly; "but God did it by me." On the 16th February this poor creature was beheaded by the hand of the executioner. Fanaticism had made its last effort. The eyes of all were opened; and, as an old historian says, the same stroke cut off the head of Thomas Schucker and that of Anabaptism in St. Gall.

It still reigned at Zurich. On the 6th November of the previous year, a public discussion had taken place to please the Anabaptists, who kept continually crying, that they were condemning the innocent without a hearing. The three following theses were proposed by Zuinglius and his friends as the subject of the conference, and victoriously maintained by them in the hall of conference.

"Children born of believing parents, are children of God, like those who were born under the Old Testament, and, consequently, they may receive baptism.

"Baptism is under the New what circumcision was under the Old Testament; consequently baptism must now be administered to children as circumcision was.

"The custom of baptising anew cannot be proved either from examples, or from passages of Scripture, or reasons derived from Scripture. Those who get themselves re-baptised, crucify Jesus Christ."

But the Anabaptists did not confine themselves to merely religious questions. They demanded the abolition of tithes, considering, said

[1] Glych wie Kain den Abel sinen bruder ermort hat! (Bull. Chr., i, p. 324.)

they, that they are not of divine institution. Zuinglius replied that on tithes depended the maintenance of churches and schools. He wished a complete religious reform; but he was determined not to allow the public order, or political institutions to be interfered with in the least degree. This was the limit where he saw written in the handwriting of God these words, "Hitherto shalt thou come, but no farther."[1] It was necessary to stop somewhere; and here Zuinglius and the Reformers stopped, in spite of the impetuous men who strove to hurry them still farther.

Still, though the Reformers stopped, they could not stop the enthusiasts who seemed placed beside them to bring out their wisdom and soberness. The Anabaptists did not think it enough to have formed a church. This church was in their eyes the true state. Were they cited before the courts, they declared that they would not recognise civil authority, which was only a remnant of paganism, and that they obeyed no other power but God. They taught that Christians were not permitted to exercise public functions, or bear the sword, and similar in that to certain irreligious enthusiasts who have appeared in our day, they regarded a community of goods as the *beau ideal* of humanity.[2]

Thus the danger increased: civil society was menaced, and arose to reject these destructive elements from its bosom. The government, in alarm, allowed themselves to be dragged into strange measures. Determined to make an example, they condemned Mantz to be drowned. On the 5th January, 1527, he was placed in a boat. His mother, who had formerly been the canon's concubine, and his brother, were among the crowd that accompanied him to the water-edge. "Persevere even to the end," exclaimed they to him. At the moment when the executioner made ready to throw Mantz into the lake, his brother melted into tears; but his mother stood by calm, with resolute heart, dry and sparkling eye, to witness the martyrdom of her son.[3]

The same day Blaurock was beaten with rods. As they were taking him out of the town, he shook his blue coat and the dust of his feet against it.[4] It appears that this poor man was, at a later period, burnt alive by the Roman Catholics of the Tyrol.

No doubt there was a spirit of revolt among the Anabaptists: without doubt the ancient ecclesiastical law, which condemned heretics to death, was still in force, and the Reformation could not, in one year or two, reform all errors. No doubt, moreover, the Catholic states would have accused the Protestant states of encouraging

---

[1] Job, xxxviii, 11.   [2] Füssl. Beytr., i, p. 229-258; ii, p. 263.   [3] Ohne das er oder die Mutter, sondern nur der Bruder geweinet. (Hott. Helv., K. Gesch, iii, p.385,
[4] Und schüttlet sinen blauen rock und sine schüch über die Statt Zurich. (Bull Chr., i. p. 382.)

disorder; but these considerations, while they explain the rigour of the magistrate, cannot justify it. Measures might have been taken against every assault made on the civil constitution; but religious errors, combated by religious teachers, ought to have had entire exemption from civil courts. Such opinions are not lashed away with the whip—they are not drowned when those who profess them are thrown into the water: they rise up from the bottom of the abyss, and the fire only kindles in their adherents greater enthusiasm and thirst for martyrdom. Zuinglius, whose sentiments on this head we have already seen, took no part in these severities.[1]

CHAP. XI.

Popish Immobility—Protestant Progression—Zuinglius and Luther—Zuinglius and the Lord's Supper—Luther's great Principle—Carlstadt's writings prohibited—Zuinglius's Commentary—The Suabian Syngram—Capito and Bucer—Need of unity in diversity.

Baptism, however, was not the only subject on which dissension was to arise. The doctrine of the Supper was to occasion it in a still graver form.

The human mind, freed from the yoke under which it had groaned for so many ages, availed itself of its freedom; and if Roman Catholicism had its rocks of despotism, Protestantism had cause to fear rocks of anarchy. The characteristic of Protestantism is movement, as that of Rome is immobility.

Roman Catholicism, which possesses in the papacy a means of incessantly establishing new doctrines, does indeed at first appear to have a principle eminently favourable to variations. This it has used to a large extent; and we see Rome, from age to age, producing or ratifying new dogmas. But when once its system was completed, Roman Catholicism became the champion of immobility. Its safety lies here. It is like one of those tottering buildings, from which nothing can be taken away without producing a ruin. Allow the priests of Rome to marry, or do away with the doctrine of transubstantiation, and the whole system is shaken, the whole edifice falls.

It is not so with evangelical Christianity. Its principle is much less favourable to variations, and much more favourable to motion and life. On the one hand, the only source of truth which it re-

[1] Quod homines seditiosi, reipublicæ turbatores, magistratuum hostes, justa Senatus sententia, damnati sunt, num id Zwinglio fraudi esse poterit? (Rod. Gualther Epist. ad lectorem, Op. 1544, ii.) Can it be any charge against Zuinglius, that seditious men, disturbers of the common weal and enemies of the magistrates, were condemned by a just sentence of the Senate?

cognises is one Scripture, standing alone, always the same from the beginning of the Church to its end; how then could it vary as the papacy has done. But, on the other hand, each Christian must go and draw for himself at this source. Hence arise motion and liberty. Thus evangelical Christianity, while it is in the nineteenth century what it was in the sixteenth, and also in the first, is at all times full of energy and activity, filling the world with researches, labours, Bibles, missionaries, light, salvation, and life.

It is a great error to rank and almost confound evangelical Christianity with mysticism and rationalism, and impute their vagaries to it. Movement is natural to evangelical Protestantism; it has an antipathy to immobility and death; but it is the movement of health and life that characterises it, and not the aberrations of the man who has lost his senses, or the agitations of disease. We are going to see this characteristic manifested in the doctrine of the Supper.

This was to be expected. This doctrine had received divers interpretations in the early days of the Church, and this diversity subsisted, until the period when the doctrine of transubstantiation and the scholastic theology began, at the same time, to exert an ascendancy over the middle ages. This ascendancy having been shaken, the ancient diversity behoved to re-appear.

Zuinglius and Luther, after having been developed apart, the former in Switzerland, the latter in Saxony, were one day to meet in presence of each other. They were animated by the same spirit, and, in many respects, by the same character. Both were full of love for truth and hatred for injustice: both were naturally violent; and in both this violence was tempered by sincere piety. But there was a feature in the character of Zuinglius which carried him farther onward than Luther. He loved liberty not merely as a man, but as a republican, a countryman of Tell. Accustomed to the decisions of a free state, he did not allow himself to be arrested by considerations before which Luther recoiled. He had, moreover, studied scholastic theology less than Luther, and in this way was less under trammels. Both ardently attached to their inmost convictions, both determined to defend them, and little accustomed to bend before the convictions of others, they were to meet, like two fiery steeds, which rush into battle, and suddenly encounter each other.

A practical tendency predominated in Zuinglius, and in the Reformation, of which he was the author; and this tendency was directed to two great results—to simplicity in worship, and to holiness in life. To bring worship into accordance with the wants of the mind, which seeks not external pomp, but things invisible, was the first want of Zuinglius. The idea of a corporal presence of Jesus Christ in the Supper—an idea, the source of all the ceremonies and all the superstitions of the Church, behoved to be abolished. But another longing of the Swiss Reformer led him to the same results. He found that the doctrine of Rome on the Supper, and even that of Luther, pre-supposed a certain magical influence prejudicial to sanctification. He feared that the Christian, in imagining that he received Jesus Christ in the consecrated bread, would not be so zealous in seeking to be united to him by heart-felt faith. "Faith," said he, "is not knowledge, opinion, imagination, it is a reality.¹ It brings with it a real union in things divine." Hence, whatever the enemies of Zuinglius may allege, it was not a leaning to rationalism, but a profoundly religious idea, that led him to the adoption of his peculiar views. The result of the labours of Zuinglius coincided with his tendencies In studying the Scriptures as a whole, as he was accustomed to do, and not merely in detached portions, and in having recourse to the classics, in order to solve any difficulties of expression, he came to be convinced that the word *is*, in the institution of the Supper, must be taken in the sense of *signifies;* and, as early as 1523, he wrote to a friend that the bread and wine, in the institution of the Supper, are only what the water is in baptism. "It were vain,' added he, " to plunge him who believes not, a thousand times in water. Faith, then, is the thing essentially required.²"

Luther at first set out from principles very much akin to those of the teacher of Zurich. "It is not the sacrament which sanctifies," said he, "it is faith in the sacrament." But the extravagances of the Anabaptists, whose mysticism spiritualised every thing, produced a great change in his views. When he saw enthusiasts, who pretended to a particular inspiration, breaking images, rejecting baptism, denying the presence of Christ in the Supper, he was alarmed: he had a kind of prophetical presentiment of the dangers which threatened the Church, if this ultra-spiritualist disposition gained the ascendancy, and he threw himself into a quite different path, like a pilot, who, seeing his bark leaning much over to one side and ready to upset, leans with all his weight on the other side, in order to establish the equilibrium.

From this time Luther attached a higher importance to the sacraments. He maintained that they were not only signs by means of which Christians are externally recognised, as Zuinglius held, but testimonials of the divine will, fitted to strengthen our

---

¹ Fidem rem esse, non scientiam, opinionem vel imaginationem. (Comment. de vera relig. Zw. Op. iii, p. 230.) ² Haud aliter hic panem et vinum esse puto quam aqua est in baptismo. (Ad. Wittenbachium Ep. 15th June, 1523.)

faith. More than this, Christ, according to him, had been pleased to impart to believers a full assurance of their salvation; and in order to seal this promise in the most effectual manner, had added his true body in the bread and wine. "In the same way," said he, "as iron and fire, which, however, are two distinct substances, are blended together in a furnace, so that in each of its parts there is at once iron and fire; in the same way, and *à fortiori*, the glorified body of Christ exists in all the parts of the bread."

Thus, on the part of Luther at this period, there was perhaps some return to scholastic theology. He had completely disconnected himself with it in the doctrine of justification by faith; but in the sacrament he abandoned only one point, that of transubstantiation, and kept the other, the corporal presence. He even went the length of saying, that he would rather receive only blood with the pope than receive only wine with Zuinglius.

The great principle of Luther was to withdraw from the doctrine and customs of the Church, only when the words of Scripture rendered it absolutely necessary. "Where has Christ ordered the host to be elevated and shown to the people?" asked Carlstadt. "And where has Christ forbidden it?" replied Luther. Here is the principle of the two Reformations. Ecclesiastical traditions were dear to the Saxon Reformer. If he separated from them in several points, it was only after severe struggles, and because it was necessary, first of all, to obey the Word. But when the letter of the Word appeared in harmony with tradition and the usage of the Church, he clung to it with immoveable firmness. Now, this is just what happened in the case of the Supper. He denied not that the word *is* might be taken in the sense pointed out by Zuinglius. He acknowledged, for instance, that it was necessary so to understand it in the words, "*That rock was Christ;*"[1] but he denied that it could have this meaning in the institution of the Supper.

In one of the later schoolmen, the one whom he preferred to all the others, Occam,[2] he found an opinion which he embraced. Like Occam, he abandoned the constantly repeated miracle, in virtue of which, according to the Romish Church, the body and blood are, on each occasion, after consecration by the priest, substituted for the bread and wine; and, like this doctor, he substituted for it an universal miracle, performed once for all,—that of the ubiquity or omnipresence of the body of Jesus Christ. "Christ,

---

[1] 1 Cor. x, 4. [2] Diu multumque legit scripta Occam cujus acumen antefere-bat Thomæ et Scoto. (Melanc. Vita Luth.) Often and long he read the writings of Occam, whose acumen he preferred to Aquinas and Scotus.

said he, "is present in the bread and wine, because he is present every where, and especially every where he chooses."[1]

The tendency of Zuinglius was quite different from that of Luther. He was less disposed to preserve a certain union with the universal Church, and maintain a connection with the tradition of past ages. As a theologian, he looked to the Scriptures alone, from which he wished to receive his faith freely, and immediately, without troubling himself with what others had previously thought. As a republican, he looked to his community of Zurich. It was the idea of the present Church that engrossed him, not the idea of the Church of other times. He dwelt particularly on these words of St. Paul, "Because there is but one bread,—we who are many are one body." And he saw in the Supper the sign of a spiritual communion between Christ and all Christians. "Whoever," he said, "conducts himself unworthily, becomes guilty towards the body of Christ, of which he forms part." This idea had a great practical influence; and the effects which it produced on the lives of many persons, confirmed Zuinglius in it.

Thus Luther and Zuinglius had insensibly withdrawn from each other. Perhaps, however, peace would have longer subsisted between them, had not the turbulent Carlstadt, who was coming and going between Germany and Switzerland, set fire to these opposite opinions.

A proceeding, taken to maintain peace, had the effect of kindling war. The council of Zurich, wishing to prevent all controversy, prohibited the sale of Carlstadt's writings. Zuinglius, who disapproved of the violence of Carlstadt, and blamed his mystical and obscure expressions,[2] then thought himself bound to defend his doctrine, whether in the pulpit or before the council, and soon after wrote pastor Albert of Reutlingen a letter, in which he said, "Whether or not Christ speaks of the Sacrament in the sixth chapter of John, it is very clear that he speaks of a mode of eating his flesh and drinking his blood, in which there is nothing corporeal."[3] He then endeavoured to prove that the Supper, by reminding believers, according to Christ's intention, of his body broken for them, procured for them that spiritual eating, which alone is truly salutary.

Still Zuinglius was as yet very averse to a rupture with Luther. He trembled to think that new dissensions should rend this new

---

[1] Occam und Luther. Studien und Kritiken, 1839, p. 69.   [2] Quod morosior est (Carlstadius) in cæremoniis non ferendis, non admodum probo. (Zw. Ep. p. 369.)
[3] A manducatione cibi, qui ventrem implet, transit ad verbi manducationem, quam cibum vocat cœlestem, qui mundum vivificet. (Zw. Op. iii, p. 573.) From the eating of food, which nourishes the body, he passed to the eating of what he calls heavenly food, which shall give life to the world.

society which was then forming in the midst of decayed Christendom. Luther did not feel in the same way. He hesitated not to class Zuinglius with the enthusiasts, with whom he had already broken so many lances. He did not reflect that if images had been removed at Zurich, it was legally and by public authority. Accustomed to the forms of the Germanic States, he had little acquaintance with the procedure of Swiss republics; and he inveighed against the grave Helvetic theologians, as against the Münzers and Carlstadts.

Luther having published his treatise against "*the heavenly prophets*," Zuinglius no longer hesitated, and published almost at the same time his *Letter to Albert*, and his *Commentary on True and False Religion*, dedicated to Francis I. He here said, "Since Christ, in the sixth chapter of John, attributes to faith the power of imparting eternal life, and uniting the believer with himself in the most intimate manner, what need have we of any thing else? Why should he afterwards have attributed this virtue to his flesh, while he himself declares that his flesh profiteth nothing? The flesh of Christ, in so far as it was put to death for us, is of immense benefit to us: for it saves us from perdition; but in so far as eaten by us does us no good."

The struggle commenced. Pomeranus, Luther's friend, rushed to battle, and attacked the evangelist of Zurich somewhat too disdainfully. Œcolampadius then began to blush at having so long combated his doubts, and preached doctrines which already wavered in his mind. He took courage, and wrote from Basle to Zuinglius. The dogma of the real presence is the fortress and strong tower of their impiety. So long as they keep this idol, it will be impossible to vanquish them. He then also entered the lists, by publishing a tract on the meaning of our Saviour's words, "*This is my body.*"[1]

The mere fact of Œcolampadius joining the Reformer produced an immense sensation, not only at Basle, but throughout Germany. Luther was deeply moved at it. Brentz, Schnepff and twelve other pastors of Suabia, to whom Œcolampadius had dedicated his book, and who had almost all been his pupils, felt the greatest pain. "At the very moment of separating from him for a just cause," said Brentz, in taking up the pen to answer him, "I honour and admire him as much as it is possible to do. The bond of love is not broken between us, because we are not agreed." Then he published, with his friends, the famous *Syngram of Suabia*, in which he replied to Œcolampadius firmly, but charitably and respectfully.

[1] He took the word *is* in its ordinary acceptation; but by *body* he understood a symbol of the body.

"If an emperor," said the authors of the *Syngram*, "give a baton to a judge, saying to him, 'Take! this is the power of judging,' the baton, doubtless, is only a simple symbol, but these words being added, the judge has not only the symbol of power—he has power itself." The true Reformed Churches may admit this comparison. The *Syngram* was received with acclamation; its authors were regarded as the champions of the truth; several theologians, and even laymen, wishing to share in their glory, began to defend the doctrine which was attacked, and made a rush at Œcolampadius.

Strasburg then came forward as a mediator between Switzerland and Germany. Capito and Bucer were friends of peace, and the question in debate was, according to them, of secondary importance; they therefore placed themselves between the two parties, sent George Cassel, one of their colleagues, to Luther, and besought him not to break the bond of brotherhood which united him to the teachers of Switzerland.

No where was Luther's character more strikingly manifested than in this controversy on the Supper. Never did he so fully manifest the firmness with which he kept to what he believed to be a Christian conviction, his fidelity in seeking a foundation for it only in Scripture, the sagacity of his defence, and his animated, eloquent, often over-powering argumentation. But never, also, did he more strikingly manifest the obstinacy with which he adhered to his own views, the little attention which he paid to the reasons o his adversaries, and the uncharitable readiness which led him to attribute their errors to the wickedness of their hearts and the wiles of the devil. "One or other," said he to the mediator of Strasburg; "the Swiss or we must be the ministers of Satan. . . ."

This was what Capito called "the madness of the Saxon Orestes," and the madness was followed by exhaustion. Luther's health was affected; one day he fainted away in the arms of his wife and his friends, and he was for a whole week, as it were, "in death and hell."[1] "He had," he said, "lost Jesus Christ, and was tossed to and fro by the tempest of despair. . . . . The world was mouldering away, and announcing by prodigies that the last day was at hand."

But the divisions of the friends of the Reformation were to have still more fatal consequences. The Roman theologians triumphed, especially in Switzerland, in being able to oppose Luther to Zuinglius. Still, after three centuries, the remembrance of these divisions furnish evangelical Christians with the precious fruit of unity in diversity. Even then the Reformers, by setting themselves in opposition to each other, showed that the feeling which

[1] In morte et in inferno jactatus. (L. Ep. iii, p. 132.)

animated them was not a blind hatred of Rome, and that truth was the first aim of their researches. Herein it must be acknowledged there is something noble. A conduct thus disinterested failed not to bear some fruit, and to force, even from enemies, a feeling of interest and esteem.

Nor is this all. We may here perceive that the Sovereign hand which disposes of all events, permits nothing without the wisest design. Luther, notwithstanding of his opposition to the papacy, was, in an eminent degree, conservative. Zuinglius, on the contrary, was inclined to a radical reformation. These two opposite tendencies were necessary. If only Luther and his adherents had appeared in the days of the Reformation, the work would have been too soon arrested, and the reforming principle would not have fulfilled its task. If, on the contrary, Zuinglius only had appeared, the thread would have been too suddenly snapped, and the Reformation would have been isolated from the ages which preceded it.

These two tendencies, which, on a superficial glance, may seem to have existed merely that they might oppose each other, had, on the contrary, a task to accomplish, and we are able to say, after a lapse of three centuries, that they fulfilled their mission.

CHAP. XII.

The Tockenburg—An Assembly of the People—Reformation—The Grisons—Discussion of Ilantz—Results—Reform at Zurich.

Thus the Reformation had struggles to maintain in every quarter. After combating with the rationalist philosophy of Erasmus, and the fanatical enthusiasm of the Anabaptists, it had still a struggle with itself. But its great struggle ever was with the papacy, and the attack which it had begun in the cities of the plain, it now continued on the remotest mountains.

On the heights of the Tockenburg, the sound of the gospel had been heard, and three ecclesiastics were prosecuted by order of the bishop on a charge of heresy. "Let them convince us, with the Word of God in their hand," said Miiitus, Döring, and Farer, " and we will submit, not only to the chapter, but to the least of the brethren in Jesus Christ; if not, we will not obey any one, not even the man highest in power."[1]

This was indeed the spirit of Zuinglius and the Reformation.

[1] Ne potentissimo quidem, sed soli Deo ejusque verbo. (Zw. Ep. p. 370.) Not to the most powerful even, but to God alone, and his Word.

Shortly after, a circumstance occurred which inflamed the minds of those living in these high vallies. An assembly of the people had been held on St. Catherine's day. The citizens were met, and two men of Schwitz, who had come to the Tockenburg on business, were at one of the tables: conversation went on; "Ulric Zuinglius," exclaimed one of them, "is a heretic and a robber!" Steiger, secretary of state, undertook the Reformer's defence; the noise drew the attention of the whole assembly. George Bruggman, the uncle of Zuinglius, who was sitting at another table, darted from his seat in a rage, exclaiming, "Certainly it is of Master Zuinglius they are speaking." All the guests rose and followed him, fearing a scuffle.[1] The tumult increasing, the bailie hastily assembled the council in the open street, and Bruggman was entreated for peace' sake to content himself with saying to these men, "If you do not retract, you yourselves are the parties guilty of falsehood and robbery." "Remember what you have just said, replied the men of Schwitz, "we too will remember it." They then mounted their horses, and galloped off by the road to Schwitz.[2]

The government of Schwitz sent a threatening letter to the inhabitants of the Tockenburg. All were in alarm. "Be strong and fearless,"[3] wrote Zuinglius to the council of his native district. "Dont let the lies which are retailed against me give you any uneasiness. There is not a clamourer but who can call me heretic, but do you abstain from insult, disorder, debauchery, and mercenary wars; assist the poor, protect the oppressed, and whatever be the insults poured upon you, put unshaken confidence in Almighty God."[4]

The exhortations of Zuinglius were successful. The council still hesitated, but the people assembled in their parishes, and came to an unanimous resolution, that the mass should be abolished, and that they would be faithful to the Word of God.[5]

The conquests were not less important in Rhetia, which Salandronius had been compelled to quit, but where Gomander boldly preached the gospel. The Anabaptists, it is true, preaching their fanatical doctrines in the Grisons, had at first greatly injured the Reformation. The people had been divided into three parties. Some had thrown themselves into the arms of these new prophets; others, looking on in silent astonishment, were disquieted by the schism. In fine, the partisans of Rome shouted triumph.[6]

[1] Totumque convivium sequi, grandem conflictum timentes. (Zw. Ep. p. 371.)
[2] Auf solches, ritten sie wieder heim. (Ibid., p. 374.) Macti animo este et interriti. (Ibid., p. 351.) [4] Verbis diris abstinete ... opem forte egenis ... spem certissimam in Deo reponatis omnipotente. (Ibid.) One of the dates of the letters, 14th und 23rd, 1524, must be erroneous, or a letter of Zuinglius to his fellow-mountaineers of the Tockenburg must be lost. [5] Parochiæ uno consensu statuerunt in verbo Dei manere. (Ibid. p. 423.) [6] Pars tertia papistarum est in immensum gloriantium de schismate inter nos facto. (Ibid., p. 400.) The third part consists of papists glorying immensely in our schism.

An assembly was held at Ilantz, in the country of the Grisons, for a discussion: the supporters of the papacy, on the one hand, and the friends of the Reformation on the other, drew together their forces. The vicar of the bishop endeavoured at first to evade the combat. "These discussions occasioning great expense," said he, "I am ready, in order to cover it, to deposit ten thousand florins; but I demand that an equal sum be deposited by the other party." "If the bishop has ten thousand florins at his disposal," exclaimed the burly voice of a peasant from amid the crowd, "it is from us he has extorted them; to give as much more to these poor priests would truly be too much." "We are poor people with empty purses," said Comander, pastor of Coire; "scarcely have we the means of buying soup: where should we find ten thousand florins?"[1] Every one laughed at this expedient, and nothing more was said of it.

Among those present were Sebastian Hofmeister and James Amman of Zurich, holding in their hands the Holy Scriptures in Hebrew and Greek. The vicar of the bishop demanded that strangers should be excluded. Hofmeister saw that this was aimed at him, and said, "We have come provided with a Greek and Hebrew Bible, in order that no violence may be done in any manner of way to the Scriptures. However, sooner than prevent the conference, we are ready to withdraw." "Ah," exclaimed the curate of Diutzen, looking at the books of the two Zurichers, "if the Greek tongue and the Hebrew tongue had never entered our country, there would be fewer heresies."[2] "St. Jerome," said another, "translated the Bible for us; we have no need of Jewish books." "If the Zurichers are excluded," said the banneret of Ilantz, "the community will interfere." "Well then," it was answered, "let them listen, but say nothing!" The Zurichers accordingly remained, and their Bible with them.

Then Comander standing up, read the first of the theses which he had published. It was—"The Christian Church springs from the Word of God. It must abide by this Word, and listen only to its voice." He proceeded to prove his proposition by numerous passages of Scripture. "He walked with a sure step," said an eye-witness,[3] "and set down his foot with the tramp of an ox." "We have too much of this," said the vicar. "When among his boon companions listening to the flute," said Hofmeister, "he does not find it too much."[4]

---

[1] Sie wären gute arme Gesellen mit lehren Secklen. (Füssl. Beytr. i. p. 358.)
[2] Wäre die Griechische und Hebraische Sprache nicht in das Land gekommen. (Ibid., p. 360.) [3] Satzte den Fuss wie ein müder Ochs. (Ibid., p. 362.) [4] Den Pfeiffern zuzuhören, die . . . wie den Fürsten hofierten. (Ibid.)

A man rose from the middle of the assembly and came forward, waving his arms, twinkling with his eyes, and knitting his brows,[1] and apparently out of his senses: he sprang towards Comander, and several thought he was going to strike him. It was a schoolmaster of Coire. "I have put down several questions for you in writing," said he to Comander, "answer them instantly." "I am here," said the Grison Reformer, to defend my doctrine; attack it, and I will defend it: if not, return to your place. I will answer you when I have done." The schoolmaster stood for a moment in suspense. "Very good," he at length said, and resumed his seat.

It was proposed to pass to the doctrine of the sacraments. The Abbot of St. Luke declared it was not without fear he approached such a subject, while the frightened vicar made the sign of the cross.

The schoolmaster, who had already desired to attack Comander, began with much volubility to maintain the doctrine of the sacraments, founding on the words, "This *is* my body." "Dear Berre," said Comander to him, "how do you understand the words, 'John is Elias'?" "I understand," replied Berre, who saw Comander's drift, "that he was truly and essentially Elias." "And why then," continued Comander, "did John Baptist himself say that he was not Elias?" The schoolmaster was silent, and at length said, "It is true." There was a general burst of laughter, even from those who had employed him to speak.

The Abbot of St. Luke delivered a long harangue on the Supper, and the conference was closed. Seven priests embraced the evangelical doctrine; full religious freedom was proclaimed, and the Romish ritual was abolished in several churches. "Christ," to use the words of Salandronius, "every where sprang up in these mountains like the tender grass in spring, and the pastors were like living springs which watered these high vallies.[2]

The Reformation made still more rapid strides at Zurich. The Dominicans, Augustins, and Capuchins were compelled to live together—the hell anticipated for these poor monks. Instead of these corrupt institutions, schools, an hospital, and a theological seminary, were founded. Knowledge and charity every where took the place of idleness and selfishness.

---

[1] Blintzete mit den Augen, rumpfete die Stirne. (Füssl, Beytr. i, p. 368.)
[2] Vita, moribus et doctrina herbescenti Christo apud Rhœtos fons irriguus. (Zw. Ep p. 485.)

CHAP. XIII.

Executions—Discussion at Baden—Rules of the Discussion—Riches and Poverty—Eck and Œcolampadius—Discussion—Part taken by Zuinglius—Boasting of the Romans—Insults of a Monk—End of the Discussion.

These victories of the Reformation could not be overlooked. Monks, priests, and prelates, transported with rage, felt that the ground was every where moving from under their feet, and that the Church was ready to give way before unparalleled dangers. The oligarchs of the cantons—the men of pensions and foreign enlistments, became aware that they could no longer delay, if they wished to save their privileges; and at the moment when the Church was in fear and beginning to sink, they offered her their arm of steel. A Stein and a John Hug of Lucerne united with a John Faber, and the civil authority rushed to the assistance of that hierarchical power which utters high sounding words of pride, and makes war on the saints.[1]

Public opinion had long been demanding a discussion. There was no other means of calming the people.[2] The Councils of Zurich had said to the Diet—"Convince us from Scripture, and we will yield to your invitations." It was every where repeated, "The Zurichers have given you a promise: if you can convince them by the Bible, why don't you do it? and if you cannot, why don't you conform to the Bible?"

The conferences held at Zurich had exercised an immense influence: it was necessary to oppose them with a conference held in a Romish town, taking all necessary precautions to secure the victory to the papal party.

It is true these discussions had been declared unlawful; but means were found to escape from this difficulty. "The only thing to be done," it was said, "is to arrest and condemn the pernicious doctrines of Zuinglius."[3] This being agreed, a stout champion was wanted, and Dr. Eck presented himself. He had no fear. His expression, according to Hofmeister, was, "Zuinglius has doubtless milked more cows than he has read books."[4]

The great Council of Zurich sent Dr. Eck a safe conduct to come to Zurich itself; but Eck replied that he would await the answer of the confederation. Zuinglius then offered to debate at St. Gall or Schaffhausen; but the Council, founding on an article of the

---

[1] Rev. xiii.   [2] Das der gmeir man, one eine offne disputation, nitt zū stillen was. (Bulling. Chr. i, p. 331.)   [3] Diet of Lucerne, 13th of March, 1526.   [4] Er habe wohl mehr Kühe gemolken als Bücher gelesen. (Zw. Op. ii, p. 405.)

federal compact, which bore, "that every person accused shall be tried in the place where he resides," ordered Zuinglius to withdraw his offer.

The Diet at length decreed that a conference should take place at Baden, and fixed it for the 16th May, 1526. This conference was to be important, for it was the result and seal of the alliance which had been made between the ecclesiastical power and the oligarchs of the confederation. "See," said Zuinglius to Vadian, "what the oligarchs and Faber dare at this hour to undertake."[1]

Accordingly, the decision of the Diet produced a great impression in Switzerland. It was not doubted that a conference, held under such auspices, would prove unfavourable to the Reformation. It was said at Zurich, "Do not the five cantons most devoted to the pope rule in Baden? Have they not already declared the doctrine of Zuinglius heretical, and employed sword and fire against it? Has not Zuinglius been burned in effigy at Lucerne, after being subject to all kinds of insult? Have not his writings been given to the flames at Friburg? Is not his death every where longed for? Have not the cantons which exercise sovereign rights in Baden declared that, should Zuinglius set foot on any part whatever of their territory, they would apprehend him?[2] Has not Uberlingen, one of their leaders, said, that his only wish in this world was to hang Zuinglius, were he himself to be the executioner on the last day of his life?[3] And has not Dr. Eck been crying for years that heretics must be attacked with fire and sword? What then will be this discussion, and what the issue of it, but just the death of the Reformer!

Such were the fears which agitated the committee appointed at Zurich to examine this affair. Zuinglius, who was a witness of their agitation, rose and said, "You know what was the fate of the valiant men of Stammheim at Baden, and how the blood of the Wirths dyed the scaffold . . . and we are invited to the very place of their execution. . . . Let the place of conference be Zurich, Berne, St. Gall, or even Basle, Constance, Schaffhausen; let it be agreed to discuss fundamental points only, employing only the Word of God. Let no judge be set over it; in that case, I am ready to appear."[4]

Meanwhile fanaticism bestirred herself, and made victims. A consistory, headed by this same Faber who challenged Zuinglius, on 10th May, 1526, (about eight days before the discussion of

[1] Vide nunc quid audeant oligarchi atque Faber. (Zw. Ep. p. 484.) [2] Zwingii in ihrem Gebiet, wo er betreten werde, gefangen zu nehmen. (Ibid., p. 422.) [3] Da wollte er gern all sein Lebtag ein Henker genannt werden. (Ibid., p. 454.) [4] Wellend wir ganz geneigt syn ze erschynen. (Ibid., p. 423.)

Baden,) condemned to the flames as a heretic an evangelical minister named John Hügle, pastor of Lindau,[1] who walked to execution singing the *Te Deum*. At the same time Peter Spengler, another minister, was drowned at Friburg by order of the Bishop of Constance.

From all quarters sinister rumours reached Zuinglius. His brother-in-law, Leonard Tremp, wrote him from Berne, "I beseech you, as you value your life, don't come to Baden. I know that the safe-conduct will be violated."[2]

It was confidently stated that a plan had been formed to carry him off, gag him, put him into a boat, and carry him to some unknown place.[3] In the view of these menaces and scaffolds, the council of Zurich decreed that Zuinglius should not go to Baden.[4]

The discussion being fixed for the 19th May, the combatants, the representatives of the cantons, and the bishops, began gradually to arrive. On the part of the Roman Catholics appeared, first of all, the warlike and vain-glorious Dr. Eck: on the part of the Protestants, the modest and gentle Œcolampadius. The latter was well aware of the perils of this discussion. As an old biographer expresses it,—like a timid stag pursued by raging dogs, he had long hesitated. At last he determined to repair to Baden. Previously, however, he put forward the solemn protestation, "I acknowledge no rule of judgment but the Word of God." At first he had earnestly desired that Zuinglius should share his dangers;[5] but he soon doubted not that if the intrepid teacher had appeared in this fanatical town, the rage of the Roman Catholics firing at his presence would have put them both to death.

The first thing done was to determine the laws of the combat. Dr. Eck proposed that the deputies of the Wallenstein should be appointed to pronounce a definitive judgment. This was just to anticipate the condemnation of the Reformation. Thomas Plater, who had come from Zurich to Baden to be present at the conference, was despatched by Œcolampadius to Zuinglius to obtain his opinion. Having arrived at night, he found some difficulty in gaining admission into the Reformer's house. "Unfortunate disturber," said Zuinglius to him, rubbing his eyes. "For six weeks now, (thanks to this discussion,) I have not been in bed.[6] .... What is your message?" Plater explained the proposals of Dr. Eck. "And who," replied Zuinglius, "would put these peasants

---

[1] Hunc hominem hæreticum damnamus, projicimus et conculcamus. (Hotting. Helv. K. Gesch, iii, p. 309.) This heretic we condemn, cast forth, and trample under our feet. [2] Caveatis per caput vestrum. (Zw. Ep. p. 483.) [3] Navigio captum, ore mox obturato, clam fuisse deportandum. (Osw. Myc. Vit. Zw.)
[4] Zwinglium Senatus Tigurinus Badenam demittere recusavit. (Ibid.) [5] Si periclitaberis, periclitabimur omnes tecum. (Zw. Ep. p. 312.) If you are in danger, we will all be endangered with you. [6] Ich bin in 6 Wochen nie in das Beth kommen. (Plater's Leben, p. 263.)

into a condition to comprehend such things? Verily the milking of cows would be more intelligible to them."¹

On 21st May, the conference commenced. Eck and Faber, accompanied by prelates, magistrates, and doctors, clothed in vestments of damask and silk, and decked with rings, chains, and crosses, repaired to the church.² Eck strutted proudly into a magnificently ornamented pulpit, while the humble Œcolampadius, in mean clothing, had to face his haughty opponent on a platform of rude construction. "The whole time the conference lasted," says the chronicler Bullinger, "Eck and his people were lodged at the curacy of Baden, making good cheer, leading a gay and scandalous life, and drinking much wine with which the abbot of Wettingen supplied them.³ Eck," it was said, "bathes at Baden—in wine." The evangelicals, on the contrary, made a poor appearance, and were laughed at as a band of mendicants. Their mode of life contrasted strikingly with that of the champions of the papacy. The host of the inn of the Pike, where Œcolampadius lodged, being desirous to see what he was doing in his room, stated, that, whenever he looked in, he saw him reading or praying. It must be confessed," said he, "that he is a very pious heretic."

The discussion lasted eighteen days, and, during the whole period, the clergy of Baden daily made a solemn procession, chanting litanies in order to obtain the victory. Eck was sole speaker in defence of the Romish doctrine. It was still the champion of the Leipsic discussion, with his German accent, his broad shoulders, and powerful lungs, an excellent public crier, with more in his exterior of the butcher than of the divine. He debated, according to his wont, with great violence, trying to wound his opponents by cutting expressions, and sometimes even mincing an oath.⁴ But the president never called him to order.

> Eck thumps the desk with feet and hands,
> And roars, and raves, and scolds, and bans.
> "What pope and cardinals propound
> I hold as creed, ay creed most sound."⁶

Œcolampadius, on the contrary, with a serene, noble, and patriarchal air, spoke so meekly, and, at the same time, with so much ability and courage, that even his adversaries, moved and transported, said, one to another, "Oh, if the tall yellow man were on our side."⁶ His equanimity, however, was occasionally disturbed on

¹ Sie verstunden sich bas auf Kuh mälken. (Plater's Leben, p. 263.) ² Mit Syden, Damast und Sammet bekleydet. (Bull. Chr., i, p. 351.) ³ Verbruchten vil wyn. (Ibid.) ⁴ So entwuscht imm ettwan ein Schwür. (Ibid.)
⁵ Egg zablet mit fussen und henden
Fing an schelken und schenden, etc.
(Contemporaneous Poetry of Nicolas Manuel of Berne.)
⁶ O were der lange gül man uff unser syten. (Bull. Chr., i, p. 353.)

seeing the enmity and violence of the hearers. "Oh!" said he, "with what impatience they listen to me; but God is not wanting to his own glory, and this is all that we seek."¹

Œcolampadius, having attacked the first thesis of Dr. Eck, which turned on the real presence, Haller, who had arrived at Baden after the commencement of the discussion, entered the lists against the second. Little accustomed to such conferences, of a timid disposition, trammelled by the orders of his government, and embarrassed by the looks of his avoyer, Gaspard Mullinen, Haller had not the proud confidence of his antagonist, but he had more real force. After Haller had finished, Œcolampadius again entered the lists, and pressed Dr. Eck so closely, that he was reduced to the necessity of only appealing to the usage of the Church. "Usage," replied Œcolampadius, "has only weight in our Switzerland according to the constitution; now, in matters of faith, the constitution is the Bible."

The third thesis, on the invocation of saints, the fourth, on images, and the fifth, on purgatory, were successively discussed. Nobody rose to dispute the truth of the two last theses, which turned upon original sin and baptism.

Zuinglius took an active part in the whole discussion. The Catholic party, who had four secretaries, had forbidden any other person, under pain of death, from taking any thing down in writing. But a student of the Valais, named Jerome Wälsch, who possessed a very retentive memory, fixed what he had heard in his mind, and, hastening home, wrote it down. Thomas Plater, and Zimmerman of Winterthur, daily carried these notes and letters from Œcolampadius to Zuinglius, and brought back the Reformer's answers. All the gates of Baden were guarded by soldiers, armed with halberts, and the two messengers were obliged, by divers excuses, to elude the interrogatories of the soldiers, who did not understand why these youths were continually returning to the town.³ Thus Zuinglius, though absent from Baden in body was present in mind.

He counselled and encouraged his friends, and refuted his enemies. "Zuinglius," says Oswald Myconius, "laboured more by his meditations, his vigils, and his counsels sent to Baden, than he could have done by debating personally in the midst of his enemies.⁴"

During the whole conference the Roman Catholics kept by an

¹ Domino suam gloriam, quam salvam cupimus ne utiquam deserturo. (Zw. Ep. p. 511. ² Man sollte einem ohne aller weiter Urtheilen, den Kopf abhauen. (Thom. Plateri, Lebens Beschreib., p. 262. ³ When I was asked, what do you come here for? I bring chickens to sell to the gentry who come to the baths; for chickens were given me at Zurich, and the guards could not understand how I could always get new ones so quickly. (Autobiography of Plater.) ⁴ Quam laborasset disputando vel inter medios hostes. (Osw. Myc. Vit. Zw.) See the various writings of Zuinglius relating to the discussion at Baden. (Op. ii, pp. 398—520.

agitation, sent letters in all directions, and shouted victory "Œcolampadins," exclaimed they, " conquered by Dr. Eck, and stretched out on the arena, has sung a palinode.[1] The reign of the pope is about to be every where re-established.[2]" These shouts were heard over all the cantons, and the people, ready to believe whatever they hear, credited all these boastings of the partisans of Rome.

The discussion being ended, the monk Murner, of Lucerne, who was surnamed, "the tom cat," came forward and read forty accusations directed against Zuinglius. "I thought," said he, "that the coward would come and answer: he has not appeared. Very well, by all the laws which govern things human and divine, I declare forty times that the tyrant of Zurich, and all his partisans, are disloyal subjects, liars, perjurers, adulterers, infidels, robbers, blasphemers, true gallows birds, and that every honest man must blush at being in any way connected with them." Such were the insulting terms which, at this early period, doctors, whom the Roman Catholic Church herself ought to have disclaimed, decorated with the name of "Christian polemics."

There was great agitation in Baden: the general feeling being that the Roman champions had made the loudest noise, but used the weakest arguments.[3] Œcolampadius and ten of his friends were all who signed the rejection of Eck's theses, whereas, eighty-four persons, among whom were the presidents of the discussion and all the monks of Wittemberg, adhered to them. Haller had left Baden before the end of the conference.

The majority of the Diet then decided that Zuinglius, the head of this pernicious doctrine, having refused to appear, and the ministers who had come to Baden having refused to be convinced, they were all cast out of the universal Church.[4]

CHAP. XIV

Consequences at Basle, Berne, St. Gall, and other places—Diet at Zurich—The Small Cantons—Menaces at Berne—Foreign Aid.

But this famous conference, due to the zeal of the oligarchs and clergy, was to prove fatal to both. Those who had then con-

[1] Œcolampadius victus jacet in arena prostratus ab Eccio, herbam porrexit. (Zw. Ep. p. 514.) [2] Spem concipiunt lætam fore ut regnum ipsorum restituatur. (Ibid., p. 513.) [3] Die Evangelische weren wol uberschryen, nicht aber uberdisputiert worden. (Hotting. Helv. K. Gesch. iii, p. 320.) [4] Von gemeiner Kylcheu ussgestossen. (Bull. Chr. p. 355.)

tended for the gospel, on returning to their firesides, were to fill their fellow-citizens with enthusiasm for the cause which they had defended; and two of the most important cantons of the Helvetic alliance were thenceforth to begin to break off all connection with the papacy.

It was on Œcolampadius, a stranger to Switzerland, that the first blows were to fall, and he returned to Basle not without some misgivings. But his disquietude was soon dissipated. His mild sentences had struck impartial witnesses more than the clamour of Dr. Eck, and he was received with acclamation by all pious men. The adversary, it is true, used every effort to exclude him from the pulpit, but in vain; he taught and preached more forcibly than before, and never had the people shown such thirst for the Word.[1]

Similar results followed at Berne. The conference of Baden, which was to have stifled the Reformation, gave it a new impulse in this canton, the most powerful in the whole Swiss confederation. No sooner did Haller arrive in the capital, than the little council summoned him to appear, and ordered him to celebrate mass. Haller demanded to be heard before the great council; and the people feeling bound to defend their pastor, flocked in crowds. Haller, alarmed, declared that he would sooner leave the town than be the cause of any disturbance. Tranquility being restored, the Reformer said, "If I am required to celebrate this ceremony, I resign my charge: the honour of God and the truth of his holy Word are dearer to my heart than any anxiety as to what I shall eat, or wherewithal I shall be clothed." Haller spoke these words with deep emotion; the members of the Council were affected; even some of his opponents shed tears.[2] Moderation proved still stronger than force. To give Rome some satisfaction, Haller was deprived of his office as canon, but was appointed preacher. His most violent enemies, Louis and Anthony Diesbach and Anthony Erlach, indignant at this resolution, immediately left the Council and the town, and renounced their right of citizenship. "Berne has had a fall," said Haller, "but it has risen with more power than ever." This firmness of the Bernese produced a great impression in Switzerland.[3]

But the consequences of the conference of Baden were not confined to Berne and Basle. While these things were taking place there, a movement, more or less similar, was taking place in several of the States of the confederation. The preachers of St. Gall, on their return from Baden, preached the gospel:[4] at the end of a conference, the images were removed from the parochial church of

---

[1] Plebe Verbi Domini admodum sitiente. (Zw. Ep. p. 518.)   [2] Tillier, Gesch v. Bern., iii, p. 242.)   [3] Profuit hic nobis Bernates tam dextre in servando Berchtoldo suo egisse. (Œcol. ad Zw. Ep. p. 518.) It was of great advantage to us that the Bernese acted so dexterously in keeping their Berthold.   [4] San Gallenses officiis

St. Lawrence, and the inhabitants sold their most valuable articles of dress, their jewels, their rings, their gold chains, to found houses of charity. The Reformation spoiled, but it was to clothe the poor, and the spoils were those of the Reformers themselves.[1]

At Mulhausen, the gospel was preached with new courage. Thurgovia and the Rheinthal always approximated more and more to Zurich. Immediately after the discussion, Zurzach carried off the images of its churches, and the district of Baden almost every where received the gospel.

Nothing can be better fitted than such facts to prove to which party the victory truly belonged. Accordingly Zuinglius, on looking around him, gave glory to God. "We are attacked in many ways," said he, "but the Lord is stronger not only than menaces, but also than wars themselves. In the town and canton of Zurich there is an admirable agreement in favour of the gospel. We will surmount all difficulties by prayers offered up in faith."[2] Shortly after addressing Haller, Zuinglius said to him, "Every thing here below follows its destiny. To the boisterous blast of the north succeeds a gentler breeze. After the broiling days of summer, autumn pours its treasures into our lap. And now, after severe combats, the Creator of all things, in whose service we are, opens the way for us into the heart of the enemy's camp. We are still able to receive Christian doctrine, that dove so long driven off, but which never ceased waiting to spy the hour of its return. Be thou the Noah to receive and save it. . . . ."

This same year Zurich had made an important acquisition. Conrad Pellican, guardian of the Franciscan convent at Basle, and professor of theology at twenty-four, had been invited, by the exertions of Zuinglins, to be professor of Hebrew at Zurich. "It is long," said he on arriving, "since I have renounced the pope, and desire only to live for Jesus Christ."[3] Pellican, by his energetical talents, became one of the most useful labourers in the work of the Reformation.

Zurich continuing to be excluded from the Diet by the Romish cantons, and wishing to take advantage of the better dispositions manifested by some of the confederates, in the beginning of 1527, summoned a Diet, to be held at Zurich itself. The deputies of Berne, Basle, Schaffhausen, Appenzell, and St. Gall, repaired to it. "We wish," said the deputies of Zurich, "that the Word of God which alone leads us to Christ crucified, should alone be preached, alone taught, alone magnified. We abandon all human doctrines, whatever may have been the ancient customs of our forefathers, certain

---

[1] Kostbare Kleider, Kleinodien, Ring, Ketten, etc. freywillig verkauft. (Hott. iii, p. 338.) [2] Fideli enim oratione omnia superabimus. (Zw. Ep. p. 519.) [3] Jamdudum papæ renuntiavi et Christo vivere concupivi. (Ibid., p. 455.)

that if they had had the light of the Divine word which we enjoy, they would have embraced it with more respect than we, their feeble descendants, do."[1] The deputies present promised to take the representations of Zurich into consideration.

Thus the breach which had been made in Rome became larger every day. The discussion of Baden was to have repaired all her losses, and thereafter, on the contrary, cantons which had been undecided were disposed to go hand in hand with Zurich. The inhabitants of the plain already inclined to the Reformation: and now she drew closer to the mountains, and invaded them, while the primitive cantons, which were in a manner the cradle, and are still in a manner the citadel of Switzerland, hemmed in by their high Alps, seemed alone firmly to maintain the doctrine of their fathers. These mountaineers, continually exposed to violent tempests, to avalanches, to the overflow of torrents and rivers, have to struggle all their lives against these formidable enemies, and to sacrifice every thing to preserve the meadow that pastures their flocks, and the hut which shelters them from the storm, but which the first inundation sweeps away. Accordingly, a conservative instinct is strongly developed in them, and has for ages been transmitted from generation to generation. To preserve what they have received from their fathers, is the only wisdom recognised in these mountains. These rude Helvetians accordingly struggled against the Reformation, which sought to change their faith and worship, as they struggle still against the torrents which dash down from their snowy peaks, or against the new political ideas which are established at their threshold in the cantons around them. They will be the last to lay down their arms before the double power which is already displaying its signals on all the surrounding hills, and more closely threatening these conservative districts.

Accordingly, at the period of which I speak, these cantons, still more irritated against Berne than against Zurich, and trembling when they saw this powerful State escaping from them, called a meeting of their deputies at Berne itself, eight days after the conference of Zurich. They called upon the council to depose the new teachers, to proscribe their doctrines, and to maintain the ancient and true Christian faith, as it had been confirmed by centuries and confessed by martyrs. "Assemble all the bailiwicks of the canton: if you refuse, we will take it upon ourselves." The Bernese felt irritated, and replied, "We are able enough to speak to our own constituents."

[1] Mit höherem Werth und mehr Dankbarkeit dann wir angenommen. (Zurich Archiv. Absch. Sonntag nach Lichtmesse.)

This reply only increased the wrath of the Waldstettes and those cantons which had been the cradle of the political liberty of Switzerland, alarmed at the progress which religious liberty was making, began even to look abroad for allies to destroy it. In combating the enemies of enlistments an appeal might be made to enlistments themselves, and if the oligarchs of Switzerland were insufficient, was it not natural to have recourse to the princes their allies? In fact, Austria, which had not been able to maintain its power in the confederation, was ready to interpose for the purpose of then strengthening the power of Rome. Berne heard with dismay that Ferdinand, brother of Charles V, was making preparations against Zurich, and against all the adherents of the Reformation.[1]

Circumstances were becoming more critical. A succession of events more or less unfortunate, the successes of the Anabaptists, the disputes with Luther about the supper, and others besides, seemed to have, in a great measure, compromised the Reformation in Switzerland. The discussion of Baden had disappointed the hopes of the friends of the papacy, and the sword which they had brandished against their enemies, had broken in their hands; but spite and anger had increased, and a new effort was prepared. Already, even the imperial power began to put itself in motion, and the Austrian bands, which had been forced to flee from the defiles of Morgarten and the heights of Sempach, were ready again to enter Switzerland, with colours flying, to give strength to tottering Rome. The moment was decisive. It was no longer possible to chime in with both parties, and be neither "muddy nor clear." Berne and other cantons, which had so long been hesitating, behoved to come to a determination. It was necessary to return promptly to the papacy, or rally with new courage under the standard of Christ.

A Frenchman, from the mountains of Dauphiny, by name William Farel, at this time gave a powerful impulse to Switzerland, determined the Reformation of Romish Helvetia, which was still in a profound sleep, and thus turned the balance throughout the confederation in favour of the new doctrines. Farel arrived on the field of battle like those fresh troops, which at the moment when the fate of arms is still uncertain, rush into the thickest of the fight, and carry the day. He prepared the way in Switzerland for another Frenchman, whose stern faith and powerful genius were to put a finishing hand to the Reformation, and render it a complete work. In this way, by means of these illustrious men, France took rank in the great movement which was agitating Christian society. It is time to turn our eye toward her.

[1] Berne to Zurich, Monday after Misericorde. (Kirchoff, B. Haller, p. 85.)

BOOK TWELFTH.

THE FRENCH.

1500—1526.

CHAP. I.

Universality of Christianity—Enemies of the Reformation in France—Heresy and Persecution in Dauphiny—A Gentleman's Family—The Family Farel—Pilgrimage to St. Croix—Immorality and Superstition—William desires to become a Student.

UNIVERSALITY is one of the essential features of Christianity. It is not thus with religions of human origin. They adapt themselves to certain nations, and to the degree of culture which they have attained. They keep these nations fixed at a certain point, or if by any extraordinary circumstance these nations rise in the scale, religion being left behind thereby becomes useless.

There was an Egyptian, a Greek, a Latin, and even a Jewish religion; Christianity is the only religion for the whole human race.

Its point of departure in man is sin—a characteristic which belongs not to a single tribe, but is the inheritance of humanity. Accordingly, satisfying the most universal and the most elevated wants of our nature, the gospel is received as coming from God by the most barbarous tribes, and the most civilised nations. It does not consecrate national peculiarities, as did the religions of antiquity; but neither does it destroy them as modern cosmopolism would do. It does better. It sanctifies, ennobles, elevates them to a holy unity by the new and living principle which it imparts to them.

The introduction of Christianity into the world has produced a great revolution in history. Till then there was only a history of particular nations; now there is a history of humanity The idea of an universal education of the human race, accomplished by Jesus Christ, has become the historian's compass—the key of history, and the hope of nations.

But Christianity not merely acts on all nations, it acts on all periods of their history.

At the moment when it appeared, the world was like a torch on the point of being extinguished. Christianity made it revive as a celestial light.

At a later period, the barbarians, rushing upon the Roman empire, had broken down and confounded every thing. Christianity, opposing the cross to this devastating torrent, thereby subdued the wild child of the north, and gave humanity a new form.

A corrupting element, however, was already hidden in the religion brought by intrepid missionaries to these rude tribes. Their faith came from Rome almost as much as from the Bible. This element rapidly increased: man was every where substituted for God, (an essential feature in the Romish Church,) and a renovation of religion became necessary. Christianity accomplished it at the period of which we write.

The history of the Reformation in the countries, which we have already surveyed, has shown how the new doctrine rejected the extravagances of the Anabaptists and the new prophets, but infidelity is the obstacle which it encounters, especially in the kingdom towards which we now turn. No where had bolder protests been taken against the superstitions and abuses of the Church. No where was there seen a more powerful developement of a certain love of letters, a love which, independent of Christianity, often leads to irreligion. France carried in her bosom at the same time two reformations, the one of man, the other of God. "Two nations are in thy womb, and two manner of people shall be separated from thy bowels."[1]

In France, not only had the Reformation to combat infidelity as well as superstition, there was a third enemy which it had not encountered, at least in so powerful a form among the Germanic nations,—I mean immorality. The disorders in the Church were great; debauchery sat upon the throne of Francis I and Catherine de Medicis, and the stern virtues of the Reformers irritated these "Sardanapaluses."[2] Every where, no doubt, but especially in France, the Reformation behoved to be not only doctrinal and ecclesiastical, but also moral.

The violent enemies whom the Reformation thus encountered at the very outset among the French, stamped it with a peculiar character. No where did it dwell so much in dungeons, and resemble primitive Christianity in faith and charity, and the number of its martyrs. If in the countries of which we have hitherto spoken, the Reformation was more glorious by its triumphs in those

[1] Genesis, xxv, 23.   [2] Sardanapalus (Henry II) inter scorta. (Calvini, Ep. M.S.)

to which our attention is now to be directed, it was rendered more glorious by its defeats. If elsewhere it can show more thrones and sovereign councils, here it can enumerate more scaffolds and meetings in the wilderness. Whoever knows what constitutes the true glory of Christianity on the earth, and the features which give it a resemblance to its Head, will, with a deep feeling of respect and love, study the history, the often times bloody history, which we are going to relate.

The most of the men who have shone on the stage of the world were born in the provinces, and there began to be developed. Paris is a tree which presents to the eye a great deal of blossom and fruit, but a tree whose roots spread far into the bowels of the earth in search of the nourishing juices which these assimilate. The Reformation also followed this law.

The Alps, which saw Christian and intrepid men appear in every canton, and almost in every valley of Switzerland, were in France also to throw their gigantic shadows over the childhood of some of the first Reformers. There were ages when they kept the treasure more or less pure in their high valleys, among the inhabitants of the Piedmontese districts of Luzerne, Angrogne, Peyrouse. The truth, which Rome had not been able to attack there, had spread from these valleys along the slopes and at the foot of these mountains in Provence and Dauphiny.

The year after the accession of Charles VIII, son of Louis XI, a sickly, timid child, Innocent VIII had encircled his brow with the pontifical tiara (1484). He had seven or eight sons by different mothers, and hence, according to an epigram of the time, Rome was unanimous in saluting him by the name of *Father*.[1]

There was at this time on all the slopes of the Alps of Dauphiny and along all the banks of the Durance, a tinge of ancient Vaudois principles. "The roots," says an ancient chronicler, "were constantly and every where setting out new saplings."[2] Bold men termed the Romish Church the Church of the evil ones, and maintained that it is as profitable to pray in a stable as in a church.

The priests, bishops, and legates of Rome sent forth a cry of alarm, and on the fifth of the calends of May, 1487, Innocent VIII, the father of the Romans, launched a bull at these humble Christians. "To arms," said the pontiff, "and trample these heretics under foot as venomous asps."[3]

---

[1] Octo nocens pueros genuit totidemque puellas.
Hunc merito poterit dicere Roma Patrem.
[2] In Ebredunensi archiepiscopatu veteres Waldensium hæreticorum fibræ repullularunt. (Raynald. Annales Ecclesiast. ad ann. 1487.) [3] Armis insurgant, eosque veluti aspides venenosos .... conculcent. (Bull of Innocent VIII, preserved at Cambridge. Ledger Histoire des Eglises Vaudoises, ii, p. 8.)

At the approach of the legate, followed by an army of eighteen thousand men, and a multitude of volunteers who wished to share the spoil, the Vaudois abandoned their dwellings, and withdrew to the mountains, to caverns, and the clefts of rocks, as birds fly away the moment the tempest begins to grumble. Not a valley, not a wood, not a rock escaped the persecutors; every where in this part of the Alps, and particularly in the direction of Italy, these poor disciples of Christ were tracked like deer. At length the satellites of the pope grew weary, their strength was exhausted, their feet could no longer climb the steep retreats of "the heretics," and their arms refused to strike.

In these Alpine countries, thus agitated by the fanaticism of Rome, about three leagues from the ancient town of Gap,[1] in the direction of Grenoble, not far from the flowery turf which carpets the flat top of the mountain of Bayard, at the bottom of mount Aiguille, and near the Col de Glaize, not far from where the Buzor takes its rise, there was, and still is, a group of houses half hid by trees, and which bears the name of Farel, or, in provincial dialect, Farean.[2] On an extensive terrace raised above the neighbouring huts, there stood one of those houses which are called mansion houses. It was surrounded by an orchard which was continued to the village. There, in those troublous times, lived, as it appears, a noble family of known piety, of the name of Farel.[3] In the year when the papacy displayed its greatest severities in Dauphiny, in the year 1489, was born, in this modest residence, a son, who was named William. Three brothers, Daniel, Walter, and Claude, and a sister, grew up with William and shared his sports on the banks of the Buzon, and at the foot of the Bayard.

There passed William's childhood and early youth. His father and mother were most devoted servants of the papacy. He says himself, "my father and mother believed everything;"[4] they accordingly brought up their children in all the observances of Rome.

God had endowed William Farel with rare qualities, fitted to give him an ascendancy over others. Of a penetrating intellect, a lively imagination, great sincerity and uprightness, and a greatness of soul which would not allow him, for any consideration, to betray the convictions of his heart, he had, moreover, an ardour

---

[1] Principal town in the High Alps. [2] Survey of Dauphiny, July, 1837, p. 35, n going from Grenoble to Gap, about a quarter of an hour after passing the last stage, about a stone cast to the right of the public road, is seen the village of the Farels. The terrace on which the house of Farel's father stood is still shown. It is now indeed only occupied as a hut, but we see, by its dimensions, that it is much larger than an ordinary house. The occupier of the hut bears the name of Farel. I owe this information to Mr. Blanc, pastor of Mens. [3] Gulielmum Farellum Delphinatem nobili familia ortum. (Bezæ Icones.) Calvin, in his letter to Cardinal Sadolet, mentions, as proof of Farel's disinterestedness, "his being sprung from so noble a house." (Opuscula, p. 148.) [4] Of the True Use of the Cross, by William Farel, p. 237.

a fire, an indomitable courage, an intrepidity which recoiled at no obstacle. But, at the same time, he had the faults which accompany these qualities, and his parents had frequent occasion to check his violence.

William entered with his whole soul into the superstitions views of his credulous family. "I am horrified," said he, "when I think of the hours, the prayers, and divine services which I have paid, and caused to be paid, to the cross and other such like things."[1]

Four leagues to the south of Gap, near Tallard, on a mountain which rises above the impetuous waters of the Durance, was a place in high repute, named St. Croix. When William was scarcely seven or eight years of age, his parents resolved to take him on a pilgrimage.[2] "The cross at this place," said they, "is made of the real wood on which Jesus Christ was crucified."

The family set out, and at length reached the venerated cross, before which they prostrated themselves. After considering the sacred wood and the copper of the cross, made, said the priest, of the basin in which our Lord washed his disciples' feet, the eyes of the pilgrims were directed to a little crucifix attached to the cross. "When the devils," resumed the priest, "make hail and thunder, this crucifix moves so that it seems to detach itself from the cross, as if wishing to rush against the Devil. It also throws out fiery sparks previous to bad weather: did it not do so the whole fruits of the earth would be destroyed."[3]

The pious pilgrims were deeply moved on being told of these great prodigies. "No one," continued the priest, "knows and sees any of these things, save I and this man . . ." The pilgrims turned round and saw a man near them of a strange exterior. "His very appearance caused fear," says Farel.[4] There were white specks on the balls of both his eyes—"whether they were real, or Satan only made a semblance of them." This extraordinary man whom the unbelieving called "the priest's sorcerer," being appealed to by the priest, immediately confirmed his statements.[5] A new episode completed the picture, and to superstition added a suspicion of criminal irregularities. "Lo, a young female, who had some other devotion than the cross, carrying an infant under her cloak. Then the priest came forward, and, taking the woman and the child, led them within the chapel. I venture to say, ne'er did dancer take a female and lead her off in better style. But the blindness was such that no regard was paid to this. Had they even acted indecently before us, we should still have deemed it

---

[1] Of the True Use of the Cross, by William Farel, p. 232. [2] I was very young and could scarcely read. (Ibid., p. 232.) My first pilgrimage was to the holy cross. (Ibid., p. 233.) [3] Ibid., pp. 235-239. [4] Ibid., p. 237. [5] Ibid., p. 238.

good and holy. It was too clear that the woman, and her gallant of a priest, well knew the miracle, and made it a cover to their intercourse."[1]

We have here a faithful picture of the religion and manners of France at the commencement of the Reformation. Morality and doctrine were equally poisoned, and a powerful revival was required for both. The greater the value men attached to external works, the farther they were removed from holiness of heart; dead ordinances had every where been substituted for the Christian life, and (strange, yet natural union) the most scandalous profligacy was seen united to the most superstitious devotion. Theft had been perpetrated before the altar, seduction at the confessional, poisoning in the mass, adultery at the foot of a cross: superstition, by destroying doctrine, had destroyed morality.

Still, there were numerous exceptions in Christendom during the middle ages. A faith, even though superstitious, may be sincere. Of this, William Farel is an instance. The same zeal that at a later period carried him to so many places to spread the knowledge of Jesus Christ, now drew him to every place where the church exhibited some miracle, or claimed some adoration. Dauphiny had its seven wonders, which had long worked upon the imagination of its inhabitants.[2] But there were also in the natural beauties with which it is surrounded objects that might well raise their souls to the Creator.

The magnificent chain of the Alps, those summits covered with eternal snow, those vast rocks which sometimes throw up their sharp peaks into the air, sometimes extend their broken ridges beyond the clouds, where they seem like some solitary island in the skies; all these sublimities of creation which were then elevating the soul of Ulric Zuinglius, in the Tockenburg, were also speaking powerfully to the heart of William Farel in the mountains of Dauphiny. He was thirsting for life, light, and knowledge: his aspirations were for something great .... he asked leave to study.

This was a great blow to his father, who thought that a young noble ought to know only his rosary and his sword. At this time the country was ringing with the fame of a young countryman of William Farel, from Dauphiny like himself named Du Terrail, but better known by the name of Bayard, who, at the battle of Tar, on the other side of the Alps, had given a signal display of courage. "Such sons," it was said, "are like arrows in the hand of a mighty man. Happy the man who has his quiver filled with them." Farel's father, accordingly, opposed his son's inclination for study. But

---

[1] True Use of the Cross, p. 235. Some of the words are softened.
[2] The burning spring, the pools of Sassenage, the manna of Briangon, etc.

the young man was inflexible. God designed him for nobler contests than those of Bayard. He continually returned to the charge, and at last the old gentleman yielded.[1]

Farel immediately devoted himself to his task with astonishing ardour. The masters whom he found in Dauphiny were of little use to him, and he had to struggle against the bad methods and trifling of his preceptors.[2] These difficulties only stimulated him, and he had soon surmounted them. His brothers followed his example. Daniel ultimately became a politician, and was employed in some important negotiations concerning religion.[3] Gautier gained the entire confidence of the Count of Furstemberg.

Farel, having learned all that could be learned in his province, and still feeling eager for knowledge, turned his eyes to another quarter. The university of Paris had long been renowned over the Christian world. He was desirous to see "this mother of all the sciences, this true light of the Church, which never suffers an eclipse, this pure and polished mirror of the faith which no cloud obscures, and no touch stains."[4] He obtained permission from his parents, and set out for the capital of France.

CHAPTER II.

Louis XII, and the Assembly of Tours—Francis and Margaret—The Literati—Lefevre—His teaching at the University—Lefevre and Farel meet—Doubts and Inquiries of Farel—First awakening—Prophecy of Lefevre—He teaches Justification by Faith—Objections—Irregularities in Colleges—Effects on Farel—Election—Holiness of Life.

One day, in the year 1510, or shortly after, the young stranger from Dauphiny arrived in Paris. The province life had made him an ardent follower of the papacy—the capital was to make him something different. The Reformation in France was not to come forth from a small town, as it did in Germany. All the impetus which agitate the population proceed from the metropolis. At the commencement of the sixteenth century various providential circumstances concurred to make Paris a kind of focus from which a spark of fire might easily escape. The youth from the neighbourhood of Gap, who now arrived, humble and unknown, was to receive this spark into his heart. Several others received it with him.

[1] Cum a parentibus vix impetrassem ad litteras concessum. (Farel, Natali Galeoto, 1527, M.S. Letters of the Consistory of Neufchatel.) [2] A præceptoribus præcipue in Latina lingua ineptissimis institutus. (Farelli Epist.) I had the silliest teachers, especially in Latin. [3] Life of Farel, M.S., at Geneva. [4] Universitatem Parisiensem matrem omnium scientiarum . . . . speculum fidei torsum et politum . . . . (Prima Apellat Universit. an, 1396, Bulæus, iv, p. 806.)

Louis XII, the father of his people, had just called a convocation of the French clergy at Tours. This prince seems to have anticipated the days of the Reformation; so much so, that, had this great revolution taken place during his reign, all France might perhaps have been Protestant. The assembly of Tours had declared that the king was entitled to make war on the pope, and execute the decrees of the Council of Basle. These decrees were the subject of general conversation in the colleges, as well as in the city and at court, and must have made a deep impression on young Farel's mind.

Two children were then growing up at the court of France. The one was a young prince of a tall and striking figure, who showed little moderation in his character, and recklessly followed any course that passion dictated. Hence the king was wont to say, "This great boy will spoil all."[1] This was Francis of Angoulême, Duke of Valois, and cousin to the king. Boisy, his preceptor, however, taught him to honour literature.

Beside Francis was his sister Margaret, two years older than he, "a princess," says Brantome, "of very great wit and ability, as well natural as acquired."[2] Accordingly, Louis XII had spared nothing on her education, and the most learned men in the kingdom hastened to acknowledge her as their patroness.

In fact, a body of distinguished characters already surrounded Francis and Margaret of Valois. William Budé, who, at twenty-three, given up to his passions, and especially to the chase, living only for his birds, horses, and dogs, had all at once stopped short, sold his equipage, and begun to study with the same ardour which had led him amid his hounds to scour the fields and forests,[3] the physician Cop, Francis Vatable, a wonder to the Jewish masters themselves for the extent of his knowledge of Hebrew, James Tusan, a celebrated Greek scholar, and other literati besides, encouraged by Stephen Poncher, Bishop of Paris, by Louis Ruzé, civil lieutenant, and by Francis of Luynes, and already patronised by the two young Valois, withstood the violent attacks of the Sorbonne, who regarded the study of Greek and Hebrew as the most dreadful heresy. At Paris, as in Germany and Switzerland, the re-establishment of sound doctrine, was to be preceded by the revival of letters. But in France, the hands which thus prepared the materials, were not to erect the edifice.

Among the teachers who then adorned the capital, was remarked a man of very small stature, of mean appearance, and humble origin,[4] whose intellect, learning, and powerful eloquence

---

[1] Mezeray, vol. iv, p. 127. [2] Brantôme Dames Illustres, p. 331. [3] His wife and children came to Geneva in 1540, after his death. [4] Homunculi unius neque genere insignis. (Bezæ Icones.) One little man of no family.

had an indescribable charm over his hearers. He was named Lefevre, and was born about 1455, at Etaples, a small place in Picardy. He had received only a rude, or as Theodore Beza calls it, a barbarous education; but his genius had supplied the place of teachers, and his piety, learning, and nobleness of character only shone with greater lustre. He had travelled much. It would even seem that the desire of extending his knowledge had taken him to Asia and Africa.[1] As early as 1493, Lefevre, who had taken his degree as doctor in theology, was a professor at the university of Paris. He forthwith obtained an eminent,—in the opinion of Erasmus,[2]—the first place.

Lefevre felt that he had a task to perform. Although attached to the observances of Rome, he proposed to combat the barbarism which prevailed at the university,[3] and began to teach the branches of philosophy with a clearness previously unknown. He laboured to revive the study of languages and of classical antiquity. He went still farther. He became aware that, when a work of revival is in question, philosophy and literature are insufficient. Therefore, leaving scholastics, which alone had for several ages occupied the school, he returned to the Bible, and brought back to Christendom the study of the Holy Scriptures and evangelical knowledge. He did not devote himself to barren researches: he went to the core of the Bible. His eloquence, frankness, and amiable manners, captivated all hearts. Grave, and full of unction in the pulpit, he lived on terms of gentle familiarity with his pupils. Glarean, one of them, writing to Zuinglius, says, "He is exceedingly kind to me. Full of candour and goodness, he sings, plays, and debates with me, and often laughs at the folly of this world."[4] Accordingly a great number of pupils from every country sat at his feet.

This man, with all his learning, submitted, with the simplicity of a child, to all the ordinances of the Church. He spent as much time in churches as in his study, so that an intimate connection might have been predicted between the old doctor of Picardy, and the young scholar of Dauphiny. When two natures, so much alike, meet, they draw to each other. In his pious pilgrimages young Farel soon remarked an old man, and was struck with his devoutness. He prostrated himself before the images, and, remaining long upon his knees, prayed with fervour, and devoutly repeated his hours. "Never," says Farel, "had I seen any singer of mass who

---

[1] See his Commentary on the Second Epistle to the Thessalonians, where there is a singular account of Mecca and its temple from a traveller. [2] Fabro, viro quo vix in multis millibus reperias vel integriorem vel humaniorem. (Er. Ep. p. 174.) Lefevre, than whom you will scarcely find a man among thousands of greater integrity or refinement. [3] Barbariem nobilissimæ academiæ.... incumbentem detrudi. Bezæ Icones.) [4] Supra modum me amat totus integer et candidus, mecum cantillat, ludit, disputat, ridet mecum. (Zw. Ep. p. 26.)

sang it with greater reverence."[1] This was Lefevre. William Farel immediately desired to approach him, and was overjoyed when this celebrated man kindly accosted him. William had gained his object in coming to the capital. From this time his greatest happiness was to converse with the doctor of Etaples, to hear him and his admirable lectures, and devoutly prostrate himself with him before the same images. Old Lefevre and his young pupil were often seen carefully decking an image of the Virgin with flowers, and far from all Paris, far from pupils and teachers, muttering together by themselves the fervent prayers which they addressed to Mary.[2]

The attachment of Farel for Lefevre being observed by several, the respect which was felt for the old doctor was reflected on his young disciple. This illustrious friendship brought the stranger of Dauphiny out of obscurity. He soon gained a name for zeal, and several rich and devout persons in Paris entrusted him with different sums for the maintenance of poor students.[3]

Some time elapsed before Lefevre and his pupil came to a clear view of the truth. It was not the hope of a rich benefice, nor a longing for a life of dissoluteness that attached Farel to the pope · these vulgarities were not made for such a soul. To him the pop was the visible head of the Church—a sort of god by whose commands souls were saved. If he heard a word uttered against his venerated pontiff, he gnashed his teeth like a raging wolf, and could have wished the thunder to strike the guilty individual, and thereby "completely sink and ruin him."—"I believe," said he, "in the cross, in pilgrimages, in images, vows, and bones. What the priest holds in his hands, puts in the box, encloses, eats, and gives to be eaten, is my only true God. I have no other, either in heaven or on the earth."[4]—"Satan," said he, on another occasion, "had lodged the pope, the papacy, and all that belongs to it, in my heart, so that even the pope had not so much of it in himself."

Thus, the more Farel seemed to seek God, the more his piety languished, and the more superstition increased in his soul; every thing went from bad to worse. He has himself described his state with great energy.[5] "Oh how I am horrified at myself, and my faults, when I think how great and wonderful the work of God in making it possible for man to be delivered from such an abyss."

But though he was delivered, it was only by degrees. At first he had read profane authors, but his piety, finding no nurture in them,

---

[1] Epistle of Farel to all lords, people, and pastors. [2] Floribus jubebat Marianum idolum, dum una soli murmuraremus preces Marianas ad idolum, ornari. (Farellus Pellicano, an. 1556.) [3] Manuscript at Geneva. [4] Farel, to all lords, etc. [5] (Quo plus pergere et promovere adnitebar, eo amplius retrocedebam. Far. Galeoto, M.S. Letters of Neufchatel.)

he began to meditate on the lives of the saints; foolish as he was, these lives made him become still more foolish.[1] He then attached himself to several teachers of the day, but, after coming to them unhappy, he left them miserable. He at length began to study the ancient philosophers, and expected Aristotle would teach him how to be a Christian: his hopes were still disappointed. Books, images, relics, Aristotle, Mary, and the saints, all were useless. This ardent soul passed from one human wisdom to another human wisdom, without ever finding wherewith to appease the hunger which was wasting him.

Meanwhile, the pope allowing the writings of the Old and New Testament to be called the *Holy Bible*, Farel began to read them, as Luther once did in the cloister of Erfurth, and he stood quite aghast,[2] on seeing that every thing on the earth was different from what the Holy Scriptures enjoin. Perhaps he was on the eve of arriving at the truth, but suddenly double darkness fell upon him, and he was plunged into a new abyss. "Satan suddenly arrived," says he, "in order that he might not lose his possession, and dealt with me according to his custom."[3] A fierce struggle between the word of God and the word of the Church then arose in his heart. When he met with any passages of Scripture opposed to the usages of Rome, he held down his eyes, blushed, and durst scarcely believe what he read.[4] "Ah," said he, fearing to fix his eyes on the Bible, "I don't well understand such things. I must give these Scriptures another meaning than they seem to have: I must keep to the interpretation of the Church and the view of the pope!"

One day when he was reading the Bible, a doctor having entered, rebuked him sharply. "No man," said he, "should read the Holy Scriptures till he has learned philosophy, and finished his course of arts." This was a preparation which the apostles had not demanded; but Farel believed it was. "I was," says he, "the unhappiest of men, shutting my eyes that I might not see."[5]

Thenceforth there was in the young Dauphinist a revival of Romish fervour. The legends of the saints excited his imagination. The more severe the monastic rules were, the greater his inclination for them. Carthusians dwelt in gloomy cells in the midst of woods. He visited them with respect, and took part in their abstinences. "I employed myself entirely night and day," says he, "in serving the devil, according to the man of sin—the pope. I had my Pantheon in my heart, and so many intercessors, so many saviours, so many gods, that I might well have been taken for a popish register."

---

[1] Quæ de sanctis conscripta offendebam, verum ex stulto insanum faciebant. (Far. Galeoto, M.S. Letters at Neuchâtel.)   [2] Farel to all lords, etc.   [3] Ibid.
[4] Oculos demittens, visis non credebam. (Farel Galeoto.)   [5] Oculos a luce avertebam.

The darkness could not become greater, the star of the morning was soon to rise, and it was at Lefevre's word that it was to appear. In the doctor of Etaples there were already some rays of light: a feeling within told him that the Church could not remain in the state in which it then was; and often, at the very moment when he was returning from mass, or rising up from before some image, the old man turned to his young pupil, and, grasping his hand, said to him with a grave tone, "My dear William, God will renovate the world, as you shall see."[1] Farel did not perfectly understand these words. Lefevre, however, did not confine himself to mysterious expressions. A great change which then took place in himself, was to produce a similar change in his pupil.

The old doctor was engaged in a work of vast labour. He was carefully collecting the legends of the saints and martyrs, and arranging them according to the order of their names in the Kalendar. Two months were already printed, when one of those rays which come from above beamed upon his soul. He could not withstand the disgust which childish superstitions begot in a christian heart. The grandeur of the word of God made him sensible of the wretchedness of these fables. They now appeared to him nothing better than "sulphur to kindle the fire of idolatry." He abandoned his task, and throwing away the legends, turned with affection to the second volume. The moment when Lefevre, quiting the marvellous tales of the saints, laid his hand upon the word of God, is the commencement of a new era in France, and the beginning of its Reformation.

In fact, Lefevre on returning from the fables of the Breviary began to study the Epistles of St. Paul. The light grew rapidly in his heart, and he immediately put his pupils in possession of that knowledge of the truth, which we find in his Commentaries.[3] Strange to the school and to the age were those doctrines which were then heard in Paris, and which the press diffused over the Christian world. We easily conceive that the young scholars who listened to them were struck, moved, changed, and that thus, even before the year 1512, the dawn of a new day was prepared for France.

The doctrine of justification by faith, which at one blow overthrew the subtilties of the schoolmen, and the observances of the

---

[1] Farel to all lords, etc. See, also the letter to Pellican. Ante annos plus minus quadraginta, me manu apprehensum ita alloquebatur:—"Guilelme, oportet orbem immutari et tu videbis!" About forty years ago, less or more, having taken me by the hand, he thus addressed me, "William, the world must be changed, and you shall see it. [2] Farel to all lords, etc. [3] The first edition of his Commentaries on the Epistles of St. Paul, is dated, I believe in 1512. There is a copy in the Royal Library at Paris. I quote from the second edition. The learned Simon says, (Observations on the New Testament,) that "James Lefevre must be placed among the ablest commentators of his age." We would go still farther.

papacy, was openly announced in the bosom of the Sorbonne. "It is God alone," said the doctor, and the halls of the University must have been astonished when they re-echoed these strange words, " It is God alone, who by his grace through faith justifies unto eternal life.[1] There is a righteousness of works, and there is a righteousness of grace; the one comes from man, the other from God; the one is earthly and transient, the other is divine and eternal; the one is the shadow and the sign, the other is the light and the truth; the one gives the knowledge of sin in order that we may flee from death, the other gives knowledge of grace that we may obtain life."[2]

"What then," it was asked, on hearing doctrines which contradicted those of four previous centuries, "was there ever a single man justified without works?"—" A single man," replied Lefevre, " innumerable men. How many among people of bad lives have ardently desired the grace of baptism, having only faith in Christ, and have if they died immediately after, entered the mansions of the blessed without works!"—" But some will say, if we are not justified by works, it is in vain for us to do them." The doctor of Paris replied, and perhaps the other Reformers would not have entirely approved of the reply; "Certainly not it is not in vain. If I hold a mirror turned toward the sun, it receives the sun's image. The more it is polished and cleaned, the more brilliant the image is, but if it is soiled the brilliancy is lost. It is the same with justification in those who lead an impure life." Lefevre in this passage, as St. Augustine in several, perhaps does not distinguish sufficiently between justification and sanctification. The doctor of Etaples reminds us somewhat of the bishop of Hippo. Those who lead an impure life, have never had justification, and consequently they cannot lose it. But perhaps Lefevre meant, that when the Christian falls into some fault, he loses the impression of his salvation, not salvation itself. In that case there is nothing to object to his doctrine.

Thus a new life and a new doctrine had penetrated the university of Paris. The doctrine of faith, which a Pothinus and an Irenæus preached of old in Gaul again resounded. Thenceforth there were two parties and two classes of people in this great school of Christendom. The lessons of Lefevre, the zeal of his scholars formed a very striking contrast with the scholastic lectures of the greater part of the teachers, and the fickle giddy lives of the greater part of the students. In colleges, to learn to play parts in comedy, to deck

---

[1] Solus enim Deus est qui hanc justitiam per fidem tradit, qui sola gratia ad vitam justificat æternam, (Fabri Comm. in Epp. Pauli, p. 70.) [2] Illa umbratili vestigium atque signum. hæc lux et veritas est. (Ibid.)

in putting on grotesque dresses, and acting farces in the streets, than in studying to become acquainted with the oracles of God. These farces often attacked the honour of grandees, princes, and the king himself. The parliament interposed about the time of which we speak, calling the principals of several colleges before it, and forbidding these indulgent masters to allow such comedies to be performed in their houses.[1]

But these disorders were suddenly corrected by a more powerful dissuasive than the decrees of Parliament. Jesus Christ was taught. Rumour was loud on the benches of the university, and the students began to occupy themselves almost as much with evangelical doctrines, as with the subtleties of the school, or with comedies. Several of those whose lives were not the most irreproachable, stood out for *works*, and perceiving that the doctrine of faith condemned their conduct, maintained that St. James was opposed to St. Paul. Lefevre determined to defend the treasure which he had discovered, and demonstrated the agreement of the two apostles. "Does not St. James say (chap. i,) that every good and perfect gift cometh from above? Now who denies that justication is the perfect gift, the crowning grace? . . . When we see an individual breathe, we regard it as a sign of life. Thus works are necessary but only as signs of a living faith, which justification accompanies.[2] Do Collyriums or purifications give light to the eye? No; it is the power of the sun. Very well; these purifications and these collyriums are our works. The only ray which the sun darts from above is justification itself."[3]

At these lectures, Farel was an eager listener. This doctrine of salvation by grace had soon an indescribable charm for him. Every objection gave way, all struggle ceased. No sooner had Lefevre broached the doctrine, than Farel embraced it with his whole soul. He had had enough of toils and wrestlings to know that he could not save himself. Accordingly, as soon as he saw in the word, that God saves gratuitously, he believed. "Lefevre," says he, "drew me off from my false idea of merit, and taught me that every thing comes by grace: this I believed as soon as it was told me."[4] Thus by a sudden and decisive conversion like that of St. Paul, was brought to the faith, this Farel who as Theodore Beza expresses it, not being deterred by threatenings, or insults, or blows, won for Jesus Christ, Montbelliard, Neufchatel, Lausanne, Aigle, and lastly Geneva.[5]

[1] Crevier History of the University, V, p. 95. [2] Opera signa vivæ fidei, quam justificatio sequitur. (Fabri Comm. in Epp. Pauli, p. 73.) [3] Sed redius desuper a sole vibratus, justificatio est. (Ibid. p. 73.) [4] Farel to *all* lords.
[5] Nullis difficultatibus fractus, nullis minis, convitiis, verberibus denique indictis territus. (Bezæ Icones.)

Meanwhile, Lefevre continuing his lectures and taking pleasure like Luther, in employing contrasts, and paradoxes, which cover great truths, extolled the grandeur of the mystery of redemption. "Ineffable exchange, exclaimed he, innocence is condemned and the guilty is acquitted; blessing is cursed, and he who was cursed is blest; life dies and death receives life; glory is covered with confusion, and he who was confounded is covered with glory."[1] The pious doctor penetrating still farther, perceived that all salvation emanates from the love of God. "Those who are saved," said he, "are so by election, by grace, by the will of God, and not by their own will. Our election, our will, our works, are without efficacy; the election of God alone is most powerful. When we are converted, our conversion does not make us the elect of God, but the grace, the will, the election of God convert us."[2]

But Lefevre did not stop at doctrines. While he rendered glory to God, he demanded obedience from man, and urged the obligations flowing from the high privileges of the Christian. "If thou art of the Church of Christ, thou art of the body of Christ, thou art filled with the divinity; for the fulness of the Godhead dwells in him bodily." Oh! if men could comprehend this privilege, how carefully they would maintain purity, chastity, and holiness, and account all the glory of the world disgrace in comparison of the inward glory which is hidden from the eye of sense.[3]

Lefevre felt that the teacher of the Word holds a high office, and he exercised it with unshaken fidelity. The corruption of the period, and particularly that of the clergy, excited his indignation, and was made the subject of severe lectures. "What a shame," said he, "to see a bishop entreating people to drink with him, making gaming his only study, handling the dice and cornet, taking up his time with birds and dogs, constantly hunting and shouting after beagles and hares, entering houses of debauchery.[4] . . . O, men, more deserving of punishment than Sardanapalus himself!"

---

[1] O ineffabile commercium! . . . (Fabri Comm. 145 verso.) O ineffable intercourse. [2] Inefficax est ad hoc ipsum nostra voluntas, nostra electio; Dei autem electio efficacissima et potentissima, etc. (Fabri Com. p. 89, verso.) [3] Si de corpore Christi, divinitate repletus es. (Ibid., p. 176, verso.) [4] Et virgunculas gremio tenentem, cum suavlis sermones miscentem. (Ibid., p. 208.)

CHAP. III.

Farel and the Saints—The University—Conversion of Farel—Farel and Luther—Other Disciples—Date of the Reformation in France—The different Reformation spontaneous—Which is the first ?—Place due to Lefevre.

Thus spake Lefevre. Farel listened, thrilled with delight, received all, and threw himself into the new path suddenly opened before him. There was, however, a point of his old creed which, as yet, he was unable to yield; this was the Saints and the Invocation of them. The best intellects often have these remains of darkness, and retain them after their illumination. Farel listened with astonishment, when the illustrious doctor declared that Christ alone was to be invoked. "Religion," said Lefevre, "has only one foundation, one aim, one head, Jesus Christ, who is blessed for ever. He alone trode the wine-press ; and therefore we do not take our name from St. Paul, Apollos, or St. Peter. The cross of Christ alone opens heaven, and alone shuts the gate of hell." On hearing these words, there was a great struggle in Farel's soul. On the one hand he saw the multitude of the saints with the Church ; on the other, Jesus Christ alone was his Master. Sometimes he leant to the one side, and sometimes to the other. It was his last error and his last combat; he hesitated, he still felt attached to the venerated men, at whose feet Rome falls prostrate. At length the decisive blow was given from on high. The scales fell from his eyes. Jesus alone appeared worthy of adoration. "Then," says he, "the papacy was entirely overthrown : I began to detest it as diabolical, and the holy word of God had the first place in my heart." [1]

Public events hastened the progress of Farel and his friends. Thomas De Vio, who, at a later period, had a wrestle with Luther at Augsburg, having in one of his works advanced that the pope was absolute monarch of the Church, Louis XII laid the work before the university, in the month of February, 1512. James Allman, one of the youngest doctors, a man of profound genius and an indefatigable student, in a full assembly of the faculty of theology, and amid great applause, read a refutation of the assertions of the cardinal.[2]

What impression must not such addresses have produced on Lefevre's young scholars! Could they hesitate, when the university seemed impatient of the papal yoke? If the main body began to move, must not they hasten on in front as pioneers?

[1] Farel. To all lords, etc.   [2] Crevier Hist. of the Un. v, p. 81.

"It was necessary," says Farel, "that the papacy should fall in my heart by little and little; for it did not come down at the first stroke."[1] He contemplated the abyss of superstition into which he had been plunged. Arrested on its banks, he once more, with uneasiness, surveyed all its depths, and recoiled with a feeling of terror. "Oh, how much I am horrified at myself and my faults!" he exclaimed.[2] "O Lord," continued he, "if my soul had served thee with a living faith as thy faithful servants have done; if it had prayed and honoured thee as much as my heart did the mass, and served this magic morsel, giving it all honour!" Thus the youth of Dauphiny deplored his past life, and repeated, with tears, like St. Augustine of old, "Too late have I known, too late have I loved thee."

Farel had found Jesus Christ, and having arrived in port, was happy to rest, after long tempests.[3] "Now," said he, "every thing presents itself in a new light.[4] The Scriptures are made clear, the Prophets are opened, the Apostles shed great light upon my soul.[5] A voice, hitherto unknown, the voice of Christ my Shepherd, my Master, my Teacher, speaks to me with power."[6] He was so changed, that instead of the murderous heart of a ravening wolf, he returned, he said, calmly as a meek and lovely lamb, with a heart entirely withdrawn from the pope, and devoted to Jesus Christ.[7]

Escaped from this great evil, he turned towards the Bible,[8] and began the diligent study of Greek and Hebrew.[9] He constantly read the Holy Scriptures, and always with deeper affection, God enlightening him from day to day. He still continued to attend the old worship in the churches. But what did he find in it? Innumerable cries and chants, and words pronounced without meaning.[10] Accordingly, often in the midst of the multitude, who were thronging towards an image or an altar, he exclaimed, "Thou alone art God: thou alone art wise: thou alone art good.[11] Nothing is to be taken from thy holy law, nothing added to it; for thou art the Lord alone, who willest and oughtest to command."

Thus, in his eyes, all men and all teachers fell from the heights on which his imagination had placed them; he no longer saw any thing in the world but God and his word. The persecutions which the other teachers of Paris employed against Lefevre, lost them

---

[1] Farel. To all lords, etc. [2] (Ibid.) [3] Animus per varia jactatus, verum nactus portum, soli hæsit. (Farel Galeoto.) [4] Jam rerum nova facies. (Ibid.) [5] Notior scriptura, apertiores prophetæ, lucidiores, apostoli. (Ibid.) [6] Agnita pastoris, magistri et præceptoris Christi vox. (Ibid.) [7] Farel. To all lords, etc. [8] Lego sacra ut causam inveniam. (Farel Galeoto.) [9] Life of Farel. MS. of Geneva and Choupard. [10] Clamores multi, cantiones innumeræ. (Farel Galeoto.) [11] Vere tu solus Deus! (Ibid.)

his good opinion. But shortly Lefevre himself, his beloved guide, was nothing to him but a man. He always loved and revered him, but God only became his master.

Of all the Reformers, Farel and Luther, perhaps, are those whose spiritual developments we know best, and who had to endure the greatest conflicts. Keen and ardent, men of attack and battle, they had to maintain violent struggles before they obtained peace. Farel is the pioneer of the Reformation in Switzerland; he throws himself into the thicket; he takes his axe and hews down the secular forests. Calvin comes at a later period, as does Melancthon, from whom, no doubt, he differs in regard to disposition, but with whom he shares the character of theologian and organiser. These two men, the one in the graceful, the other in the stern class of character, somewhat resemble the lawgivers of antiquity. They build up, constitute, and make laws in the countries which the two previous Reformers had gained. Still, if Luther and Farel have some features in common, it must be acknowledged that the latter is only an inferior resemblance. Besides his superior genius, Luther had, in every thing which concerned the Church, a moderation, a wisdom, a knowledge of the past, a comprehensiveness of view, and even an organising power, which exist not to the same degree in the Reformer of Dauphiny.

Farel was not the only young Frenchman in whom new light then arose. The doctrines, which proceeded from the mouth of the illustrious doctor of Etaples, were working in the minds of the multitude who followed his lessons. In his school were formed brave soldiers, who on the day of battle were to fight on to the very foot of the scaffold. They listened, compared, and discussed, arguing keenly on both sides. It is not improbable, that among the small number of scholars who defended the truth, was young Peter Robert Olivetan, born at Noyon, towards the end of the fifteenth century, who, at a later period, translated the Bible into French, after the translation of Lefevre; and appears to have been the first to bring the doctrines of the gospel under the notice of a young kinsman, also a native of Noyon, and afterwards the most distinguished leader of the Reformation.[1]

Thus, before 1512, at a time when Luther had not yet acquired any distinction in the world, and was setting out to Rome on a concern of monks, at a period when Zuinglius had not even begun to devote himself zealously to sacred literature, and was crossing the Alps with the confederates to fight for the pope, Paris and France heard the delivery of those vital truths, out of which the Reformation was to spring, and minds fitted to propagate them

[1] Biog. Uni., Art. Olivetan. Hist. du Calvinisme, par Maimbourg, p. 53.

were receiving them with holy avidity. Hence, Theodore Beza, speaking of Lefevre of Etaples, hails him as the individual, "who courageously began the revival of the pure religion of Jesus Christ;"[1] and he remarks that, "in the same way as the school of Isocrates was anciently seen to furnish the best orators, so, from the audience of the doctor of Etaples, proceeded several of the most distinguished men of their age and of the Church."[2]

The Reformation in France, therefore, was not a foreign importation. It had its birth on the French soil; it germinated in Paris: it had its first roots in the university itself, which formed the second power in Roman Christendom. God placed the principles of the work in the honest hearts of men of Picardy and Dauphiny, before its commencement in any other country. We have seen that the Swiss Reformation was independent of the German Reformation. The French Reformation was, in its turn, independent of both. The work began at once in these different countries without any communication with each other; as in a battle, all the different forces composing the army move at the same instant, though the one does not tell the other to march, because one and the same command, proceeding from the commander-in-chief, is heard by all. The time was accomplished, the people were prepared, and God began the renovation of his Church in all quarters at once. Such facts demonstrate that the great revolution of the sixteenth century was a Divine work.

If regard is had only to dates, it must be acknowledged that the honour of commencing the work belongs neither to Switzerland nor to Germany, although these two countries only have hitherto claimed it. The honour truly belongs to France. This is a fact which we purpose to establish, because it seems to have been hitherto overlooked. Without dwelling on the influence which Lefevre exerted, directly or indirectly, over several individuals, and in particular, perhaps over Calvin himself, let us attend to that which he had over one of his pupils, over Farel, and to the energetic activity which this servant of God thenceforth displayed. After this, how can we resist the conviction, that even though Zuinglius and Luther should never have appeared, there would have been a movement of Reform in France? It is impossible, no doubt, to calculate what would have been its extent; it must even be acknowleged that the rumour of what was going on beyond the Rhine and the Jura, animated, and at a later period quickened, the pace of the French Reformers. Still, they were the first whom the blast of the heavenly trumpet in the sixteenth century awoke, and

---

[1] Et purioris religionis instaurationem fortiter agressus. (Bezæ Icones.)
[2] Sic ex Stapulensis auditorio præstantissimi viri plurimi prodierint. (Ibid.)

they were the first who appeared equipped and arrayed on the field of battle.

Nevertheless, Luther is the great workman of the sixteenth century, and, in the most extensive sense, the first Reformer. Lefevre is not a complete Reformer, like Calvin, Farel, and Luther. He is of Wittemberg and Geneva, but has also a tinge of the Sorbonne: he is the first Catholic in the Reform movement, and the last of the reformed in the Catholic movement. He remains to the last a kind of go-between—a somewhat mysterious mediator, designed to remind us, that though there is apparently an impassable abyss between the old and the new things, there is still a connection between them. Repulsed and persecuted by Rome, he is still attached to Rome by a feeble thread, which he is unwilling to break. Lefevre of Etaples has a place of his own in the theology of the sixteenth century. He is the link which connects ancient with modern times—the individual in whom the transition is made from the theology of the middle ages to the theology of the Reformation.

CHAP. IV.

Character of Francis I—Beginning of Modern Times—Liberty and Obedience—Margaret of Valois—The Court—Brigonnet, Count of Montbrun—Lefevre applies to the Bible—Francis I and his " Sons "—The Gospel brought to Margaret—A Conversion —Adoration—Character of Margaret.

Thus the whole university was in motion. But the Reformation in France was not to be merely the work of learned men. It was to be established among the grandees of the world, and even at the court of the king.

Young Francis of Angoulême, cousin-german of Louis XII, and his son-in-law, had succeeded him. His beauty, his address, his bravery, his love of pleasure, made him the first chevalier of his time. He aspired, however, to something higher: he wished to be a great and even a good king, provided every thing could bend to his sovereign will. Valour, love of letters, and gallantry: these three words sufficiently express the character of Francis and the spirit of his age. At a later period, two other illustrious kings, Henry IV, and in particular Louis XIV, presented the same features. These princes wanted what the gospel gives; and although the nation has never been without elements of holiness and Christian elevation, it may be said that these three great monarchs of modern France stamped their own character on their subjects, or rather, their own character was a faithful representation of the character of their subjects. Had the gospel entered France through the most illustrious of the Valois, it would have given to the nation what it has not—a spiritual tendency, a Christian holiness, an understanding in divine things, and would thus have made it complete in that which contributes most to the power and greatness of kingdoms.

Under the reign of Francis I, France and Europe passed from the middle ages to modern times. The new world, which was in embryo when this prince mounted the throne, then grew up and entered into possession. Two classes of men exercised an influence over the new society. On the one hand arose the men of faith, who were at the same time the men of wisdom and holiness, and close beside them the writers of the court, the friends of worldliness and disorder, who, by the licentiousness of their principles, contributed as much to the corruption of manners, as the former class did to their reformation.

Had not Europe, in the days of Francis I, seen the Reformer arise, and had she, by a severe judgment of Providence, been given up to infidel innovators, it was all over both with her and with Christianity. The danger was great. For some time, these two classes of combatants the adversaries of the pope, and of Jesus Christ, were confounded together. Both calling for liberty, seemed to make use of the same arms against the same enemies. Amid the turmoil of the battle-field, an inexperienced eye might have been unable to distinguish between them. Had the Reformers allowed themselves to be hurried along by the Literati, all was lost. The enemies of the hierarchy passed rapidly to the extreme of impiety, and were pushing Christian society into a frightful abyss. The papacy itself contributed to this dreadful catastrophe, by its ambition and disorders hastening the destruction of those remains of truth and life which had continued in the Church. But God raised up the Reformation, and Christianity was saved. The Reformers who had cried 'Liberty!' shortly after shouted 'Obedience!' The very men who had overturned the throne on which the Roman pontiff delivered his oracles, prostrated themselves before the word of God. The separation was now precise and decisive: even war was declared between the two divisions of the army. The one had wished liberty only for themselves, the other had claimed it for the word of God. The Reformation became the most formidable enemy of this infidelity, for which Rome often manifests some degree of indulgence. The Reformers, after restoring liberty to the Church, restored religion to the world. Of the two gifts, the latter was at this time the more necessary.

For a time, the friends of infidelity hoped to count among their number Margaret of Valois, Duchess of Alençon, whom Francis. loved exceedingly, always, as Brantôme says, calling her his little pet.[1] The same tastes and the same talents existed in the brother and the sister. Margaret, handsome like Francis, joined the mild virtues which captivate to the strong qualities which form great characters. In the world, at festivities, at the court of the king, as well as at that of the emperor, she shone as a queen, charmed, astonished, and conquered all hearts. Passionately fond of literature, and endowed with rare talents, she retired to her study, and there gave herself up to the pleasures of thinking, writing, and acquiring knowledge. But her strongest wish was to do good and prevent evil. When ambassadors, after being received by the king, went to pay their respects to Margaret, "they were," says Brantôme, " exceedingly delighted, and carried back glowing descriptions of her to their country." [2]

This celebrated princess was always of the strictest morals, but while many people placed strictness in word, and freedom in act. Margaret did the contrary. Irreproachable in her conduct, she was not perfectly so in respect of her writings. In place of being surprised at this, perhaps the wonder ought rather to be, that one so corrupt as Louisa of Savoy, had a daughter so pure as Margaret. While journeying over the country in the train of the court, she employed herself in depicting the manners of the time, and, in particular, the corruption of priests and monks. Brantôme says, " I have heard it told by my grandmother, who always travelled with her in her sedan, how she and her maid of honour held the writing-desk." [3] Such, according to some, was the origin of the Heptameron; but highly-distinguished modern critics are convinced that Margaret was a stranger to this collection, sometimes more than frivolous, and that Despériers, valet de chambre to the queen, was its author.[4]

This Margaret, so beautiful, so talented, and living in the heart of a polluted atmosphere, was to be one of the first who was to be

---

[1] Vie des Dames illustres. (P. 333. Ed. Hagen, 1740.)   [2] Ibid., p. 337.
[3] Ibid., p. 346.   [4] This is proved by one of the most distinguished critics of our day, M. Ch. Nodier, in the Revue des Deux Mondes, tom. xx, where he says, *inter alia* p. 350, " Despérier is the real and almost sole author of the Heptameron. I have no hesitation in declaring that I have no doubt of this, and that I am entirely of the opinion of Bouistuan, who had no other inducement to *omit or conceal* the name of the Queen of Navarre. If, as I think, Margaret composed some of the tales, (the most decent, doubtless, of those in the Heptameron) it must have been in early life, immediately after her marriage with the Duke d'Alençon (1509). The circumstance mentioned by Brantôme, that the queen-mother, and Madame of Savoy, "being young," wished to "imitate Margaret," is a proof of this. To this testimony we may add that of De Thou, who says, "Si tempora et *juvenilem aetatem* in qua scriptum est respicias non prorsus damnandum, certe gravitate tantæ heroinæ et extrema vita minus dignum. (Thuan. ri v. 117.) Brantôme and De Thou are unexceptionable witnesses.

carried along by the religious movement which then began to agitate France. But, in the midst of a court so dissolute, and the licentious tales which amused it, how could the Duchess of Alençon be reached by the Reformation? Her elevated soul felt wants which the gospel alone could satisfy: grace acts every where, and Christianity, which even before an apostle had appeared in Rome, had adherents in the house of Narcissus and in the court of Nero,[1] soon penetrated, at its revival, to the court of Francis I. Some ladies of the court addressed the princess in the language of faith, and the sun which was then rising in France shed some of its earliest rays on an illustrious head, by which they were immediately reflected on the Duchess of Alençon.

Among the most distinguished nobles of the court was William de Montbrun, son of Cardinal Briçonnet of St. Malo, who had entered the Church after he became a widower. Count William, who was passionately attached to literature, also took orders, and became successively bishop of Lodeva and of Meaux. Sent twice to Rome as ambassador, he returned to Paris without having been seduced by the charms and pomp of Leo X.

When he returned to France, the movement was universally spread. Farel, master of arts, was teaching in the celebrated college of Cardinal Lemoine, one of the four principal houses of the theological faculty of Paris, and equal in rank to the Sorbonne. Two countrymen of Lefevre, Arnaud and Gerald Roussel, and others besides, enlarged this circle of free and noble spirits. Briçonnet, who had just quitted the festivities of Rome, was astonished at what had taken place in Paris during his absence. Thirsting for knowledge, he renewed his old relations with Lefevre, and shortly after passed precious hours with the doctor of Sorbonne, Farel, the two Roussels, and their other friends.[2] Full of humility, this illustrious prelate was willing to be instructed by the humblest individuals, but above all by our Lord himself. "I am in darkness," said he, "waiting for the interposition of divine grace, of which I have deprived myself by my demerits." His spirit was, as it were, dazzled by the lustre of the gospel. He dared not to look up on its unparalleled refulgence. "All eyes united," he adds, "are insufficient to receive the light of this sun."[3]

Lefevre had referred the bishop to the Bible; he had shown him as it were, the guiding thread which always conducts to the origi-

[1] Rom., xvi, 11; Phil., iv, 22.   [2] Hist. de la Revocat. de l'Edit. de Nantes, vol. i, p. 7.   Maimbourg, Hist. du Calv. p. 12.   [3] These words of Briçonnet are taken from the MS. of the Bibliotheque Royale, entitled "Letters of Margaret Queen of Navarre" and marked S. F. 337. This MS., which I found great difficulty in deciphering I will repeatedly have occasion to quote. The quotations are given in the language of the time.

nal truths of Christianity, to which it was antecedent to all schools, sects, ordinances, and traditions; he had shown him the powerful means by which the religion of Jesus Christ is renewed. Briçonnet read the Scriptures. "The sweetness of divine food is so great," said he, "that the longing of the mind for it becomes insatiable; the more it is tasted, the more it is desired."[1] The simple and mighty truths of salvation filled him with rapture; he found Christ, he found God himself. "What vessel," he exclaimed, "is capable of receiving the full amount of inexhaustible sweetness? But the lodging is enlarged according to the desire which is felt to receive the good guest. Faith is the chamber which alone can lodge him, or to speak more properly, which makes us lodge in him." At the same time the good bishop was grieved to see this doctrine of life, which the Reformation was restoring to the world, in so little esteem at court, in the city among the people; and he exclaimed, "O singular, most worthy, and by my fellows little relished innovation! . . ."

Thus did evangelical sentiments pave a way for themselves amidst the giddy, dissolute, and literary court of Francis I. Several individuals who belonged to it, and enjoyed the full confidence of the king, as John Du Bellay, Budé, Cop, the court physician, and even Petit, the king's confessor, seemed favourable to the sentiments of Briçonnet and Lefevre. Francis, who was fond of letters, and invited into his domains learned men who were inclined to "Lutheranism," and who "expected," says Erasmus, "thus to adorn and distinguish his reign more magnificently than he could have done by trophies, pyramids, or the most gorgeous buildings," was himself influenced by his sister, Briçonnet, and the Literati of his court and university. He attended the discussions of the learned—took pleasure in hearing their conversation at table, and called them "his sons." He prepared the way for the Word of God, by founding chairs for the study of Hebrew and Greek. Accordingly, Theodore Beza, on placing his portrait at the head of those of the Reformers, says, "O pious beholder, shudder not at the view of his adversary. Must not a share in this honour belong to him who, after banishing barbarism from the world, firmly fixed in its place three languages and sound literature, to form as it were porticos to the new edifice which was soon to be raised?"[2]

But at the Court of Francis I, there was an individual in particular who seemed prepared for the evangelical influence of the

[1] MS. of the Bibliotheque Royale, S. E. 337.
[2] Neque rex potentissime pudeat . . . . quasi atrienses hujus ædis futuras. (Bezæ Icones.)—Disputationibus eorum ipse interfuit. (Flor. Ræmundi, Hist. de ortu hæresium, vii, p. 2.)

doctor of Etaples and the bishop of Meaux. Margaret, undecided and wavering in the midst of the dissolute society around her, sought support, and found it in the Gospel. Turning towards the new truth which was re-animating the world, she enhaled it with delight as an emanation from heaven. Some ladies of her court informed her of what was taught by the new teachers. She obtained their works and small treatises, called, in the language of the times, "Tracts." She heard the expressions "Primitive Church, pure Word of God, worship in spirit and in truth, christian liberty which shakes off superstition and human traditions, and attaches itself to none but God."[1] Shortly after, this princess became personally acquainted with Lefevre, Farel, and Roussel: she was struck with every thing about them,—their zeal, their piety, and their manners, but her principal guide in the way of faith was the bishop of Meaux, with whom she had long been intimate.

Thus was accomplished amid the brilliant court of Francis I, and the dissolute family of Louisa of Savoy, one of those conversions of the heart which, in every age, are produced by the Word of God. Margaret afterwards embodied in verse the different movements of her soul at this important era in her life. By this means we are able to discover some traces of the path which she then traversed. We see that she was deeply penetrated with a conviction of sin, and that she bewailed the levity with which she had treated the scandals of the world. She exclaims—

> What depth of punishment can possibly suffice
> E'en for a tenth part of the guilt which on me lies?

This corruption of which she had so long been unconscious, every where met her view, now that her eyes were opened.

> Within, well do I feel I have the root;
> Without are branch, and flower, and leaf, and fruit.[2]

Still, amid the alarm which she felt at the state of her soul, she discovered that the God of peace had drawn near to her.

> My God, to me thou hast drawn nigh,
> Although a naked worm am I.

Ere long the love of God in Christ was shed abroad in her heart.

---

[1] Maimbourg. Hist. du Calvinisme. [2] Marguerites de la Marguerite des princesses. (Lyon, 1547.) Tom. i, Miroir de l'Ame Pecheresse, p. 15. The copy I have used apparently belonged to the Queen of Navarre herself: some notes in it are said to be by her own hand. It belongs to one of the author's friends. [3] Ibid. p. 18, 19.

"My Father, then, ... but who? yea the Eternal,
Always unseen, immutable, immortal,
Who will forgive by grace each sin of mine;
Therefore, O Lord, I cast me as a criminal
Before thy sacred feet, O sweet Emanuel;
Have pity then on me, Father divine.
Thou art the altar, thou the sacrifice—
Thou didst for us what doth indeed suffice,
Since God declares, 'tis pleasing in his eyes."

Margaret had found faith, and her soul became enraptured with holy transport,—

"Word divine! Christ Jesus! Lord!
Only Son of the Eternal God—
The first and last, and all-renewing
Bishop and King, in might triumphing,
From death, by death delivering.
Man is by faith made son of God,
And just and pure, kind like his Lord.
Man is by faith made free from stain;
And man by faith in Christ doth reign,
By faith I Christ possess, all riches gain."

From this period a great change had been effected in the Duchess of Alençon—

"Myself poor, ignorant, impotent,
In Christ am rich, wise, and puissant."

Still the power of evil was not destroyed. She felt in her soul a disagreement, a struggle which astonished her—

"Noble in mind, yet nature's slave,
Offspring of heaven, child of the grave;
Throne of God, yet vessel of sin;
Immortal, rottenness within,
Nourished by God, on earth I feed,
Fleeing bad, yet loving evil deed.
Reason I love, yet justice shun,
And till my course on earth is done,
In strife like this my days must run."

Margaret, seeking for some natural emblem which might express the wants and affections of her soul, took, says Brantome, that of the flower of the marigold, " which, by its corolla and leaves, has the greatest affinity with the sun, and follows it wherever it goes."[5] She added the following device:—

---

[1] Marguerites de la Marguerite des princess. Oraison à J. C., p. 143. [2] Ibid. Discord de l'Esprit et de la Chair, p. 73. [3] Ibid. Miroir de l'Ame, p. 22.
[4] Ibid. Discord de l'Esprit et de la Chair, p. 71. [5] Vie des Femmes Illustres, p. 83.

'Non inferiora secutus'—
'I follow not the things below.'

"To testify," adds the courtly writer, "that she directed all her actions, thoughts, wishes, and affections to this great Sun, which was God; on this account she was suspected of Luther's religion."[1]

In fact, the princess soon experienced the truth of the words, that "*All who will live godly in Christ Jesus will suffer persecution.*" Margaret's new opinions were spoken of at court, and caused a great explosion. What! even the king's sister belong to those people! It might have been thought for some time that it was all over with Margaret. She was denounced to Francis I. But the king, who was very fond of his sister, affected to think there was nothing in it, while Margaret's own character gradually weakened opposition. Every one loved her; for, says Brantome, "She was very good, mild, gracious, charitable, of easy access, a great almsgiver, despising no one, and gaining all hearts by the good qualities which she had in her."[2]

Amid the corruption and levity of this age, the mind rests with delight on this choice soul which the grace of God could reach under all this vanity and worldly grandeur. But her character as woman did not allow her to go farther. If Francis I had had the convictions of his sister, he would doubtless have carried them fully out. The timid heart of the princess trembled before the wrath of her king. She was continually agitated between her brother and her Saviour, unwilling to sacrifice either the one or the other. She cannot be regarded as a Christian who had fully attained to the liberty of the children of God, but is a perfect type of those superior minds so numerous in all ages, especially among females, who, while powerfully drawn towards heaven, are, however, unable to disengage themselves entirely from earthly ties.

Still, as she is, she is one of the remarkable characters of history. Neither Germany nor England presents us with a Margaret of Valois. The star is, no doubt, somewhat dimmed, but there is a surpassing softness in its light, and even at the time of which I am now speaking, this light is easily discerned. It was not till a late period, when the angry look of Francis I betokened mortal hatred to the gospel, that his sister in alarm put a veil upon her faith. At present she lifts her head in the midst of this corrupt court, and appears in it as a bride of Jesus Christ. The respect which was paid to her, the high opinion entertained of her intellect and her heart, pleaded the cause of the gospel before the Court of France better than any preacher could have done. This mild female influence gave access to the

[1] Vie des Femmes Illustres, p. 33   [2] Ibid.

new doctrine. Perhaps to this period may be traced the leaning of the French nobility to Protestantism. Had Francis also followed his sister—had the whole nation been thrown open to Christianity, the conversion of Margaret might have proved the salvation of France. But while the nobility received the Gospel, the throne and the people still adhered to Rome. It was ultimately a great misfortune to the Reformation to have had Condés and Navarres in its bosom.

CHAPTER V.

Enemies of the Reformation—Louisa—Duprat—Concordat at Bologna—Opposition of the Parliament and the University—The Sorbonne—Beda—His character—His Tyranny—Berquin, the most learned of the nobles—The Leaders of the Sorbonne—Heresy of the three Magdalenes—Luther Condemned at Paris—The Sorbonne addresses the King—Lefevre quits Paris for Meaux.

Thus the gospel was already making illustrious conquests in France. In Paris, Lefevre, Briçonnet, Farel, Margaret, joyfully yielded to the movement which was beginning to shake the world. Francis I himself at this time seemed more attracted by the charms of literature, than repulsed by the severity of the gospel. The friends of the word of God were cherishing the fondest hopes: they were thinking that the heavenly doctrine would circulate without opposition throughout their native land, when a formidable opposition was formed at the Sorbonne and the Court. France, which was, during three centuries, to signalise herself in the cause of Roman Catholicism by her persecutions, rose up with pitiless severity against the Reformation. If, in the seventeenth century it was a bloody victory, in the sixteenth it was a fearful struggle. Nowhere, perhaps, did the Reformed Christians find more merciless foes than on the very spots where they raised the standard of the gospel. In Germany, the enemy manifested his rage in other States, and in Switzerland he manifested it in other Cantons; but in France, the parties met face to face. A dissolute female, and an avaricious minister then stood at the head of a long list of enemies of the Reformation.

Louisa of Savoy, the mother of the king and of Margaret, notorious for her amours, despotic in her wishes, and surrounded by a female Court whose licentiousness was the commencement of a long series of immoralities and scandals in the Court of France, naturally arrayed herself against the word of God. She was the more to be dreaded in consequence of the almost unlimited influence which she always possessed over her son. But the gospel found a still more formidable adversary in Louisa's favourite, Anthony Duprat, for whom she procured the appointment of chancellor of the kingdom. This man, whom a contemporary historian calls the most vicious of all bipeds,[1] was still more avaricious than Louisa was dissolute. Having at first enriched himself at the expense of justice, he afterwards wished to enrich himself, at the expense of religion, and entered into orders that he might obtain possession of the richest benefices.

Luxury and avarice were thus the characteristics of these two personages, who being both devoted to the pope, sought to hide the scandals of their life in the blood of heretics.[2]

One of their first acts was to deliver the kingdom to the ecclesiastical domination of the pope. The king, after the battle of Marignan, met with Leo X at Bologna, where was concluded the famous Concordat, in virtue of which, these two princes shared between them the spoils of the Church. They deprived Councils of their supremacy in order to give it to the pope, and churches of the appointment to bishopricks and benefices to give it to the king. Then Francis I, holding up the train of the pontiff's mantle, appeared in the cathedral church of Bologna, to ratify the negotiation. He felt the injustice of the Concordat, and turning to Duprat, whispered in his ear, "There is enough in it to damn us both."[3] But what cared he for his salvation? All he wanted was money and an alliance with the pope.

The Parliament offered a vigorous resistance to the Concordat. The king caused its deputies to wait for several weeks at Amboise, till one day, as he rose from table, he ordered their attendance, and then said to them, "There is a king in France, and I don't understand that a senate exists in it as at Venice." Thus saying, he ordered them to depart before sunset. Evangelical liberty had nothing to hope from such a prince. Three days after, Trémouille, the grand chamberlain, appeared in parliament, and ordered that the Concordat should be registered.

The university was now agitated. On the 18th March, 1518, a solemn procession, all the students and bachelors attending in their gowns, walked to the church of St. Catherine des Ecoliers, to supplicate the Diety for the preservation of the liberties of the Church and of the kingdom.[4] "Then were seen colleges closed, and scholars in armour walking over the town in large bands, threatening, and sometimes maltreating personages of note, while engaged, by command of the king, in publishing and executing the said Concordat."[5] At last, however, the university tolerated

---

[1] Bipedum omnium nequissimus. (Belcarius, xv, p. 435.) [2] Sismondi. Hist. des Français. [3] Matthieu, i, p. 16. [4] Crevier, v, p. 110. [5] Fontaine Hist. Cathol. Paris, 1562. p. 16.

its execution, but without revoking the enactments by which it had declared its opposition, " and thereupon," says Correro, the ambassador of Venice, " the king began liberally to distribute bishoprieks on the solicitation of the ladies of the court, and give offices to his soldiers; so that a traffic in bishoprieks and offices was carried on at the court of France, in the same way as at Venice a traffic is carried on in pepper and cinnamon." [1]

While Louisa and Duprat were preparing to destroy the gospel by the destruction of the liberties of the Gallican Church itself, in another direction a fanatical and powerful party was formed against the Bible. Christian truth has always had two great enemies— the dissoluteness of the world, and the fanaticism of priests. Scholastic Sorbonne and a licentious court were to go hand in hand against the confessors of Jesus Christ. In the early days of the Church, infidel Sadducees and hypocritical Pharisees were the bitterest enemies of Christianity, and they are so at all times. The darkness of the School soon sent forth the most pitiless adversaries of the gospel. At their head was Noel Bedier, commonly called Beda, a Picard by birth, and syndic of the Sorbonne, who has been described as the greatest bawler and the most factious spirit of his time. Trained in the dry sentences of scholastics, having grown up among the theses and antitheses of the Sorbonne, venerating every distinction of the School far more than the word of God, he was transported with rage against those whose audacious mouths dared to utter other doctrines. Of a restless spirit, unable to give himself any repose, always longing for new pursuits, he was the plague of all who were near him. Trouble was his element; he seemed made to create storms; when he had no opponents, he attacked his friends. An impetuous quack, he made the town and the university echo with ignorant and violent declamations against literature, against the innovations of the time, and against all who were not at his beck eager enough in suppressing them. Several laughed when they heard him, but others gave credit to the speeches of the blustering orator, while the violence of his character secured him a tyrannical ascendancy in the Sorbonne. He behoved ever to have some opponent to contend with, some victim to drag to the scaffold. Accordingly, he had found heretics before they actually existed, and had demanded that Merlin, Vicar-General of Paris, should be burnt for having attempted to justify Origen. But when he saw the new teachers appear, he bounded like the wild beast which suddenly comes upon a prey which it can easily devour. " In our Beda are three thousand monks," said the prudent Erasmus.[2]

[1] Raumer. Gesch. Europ. i, p. 270. (Eras. Ep. p. 373.)   [2] In uno Beda sunt tria millia monachorum.

Still his very excesses injured his cause. "What!" said the wisest men of the age, "is it on such an Atlas that the Romish Church is to repose?"[1] What causes the fire but the follies of Beda?"

In fact, the same blustering oratory which struck terror into the feeble-minded, disgusted generous minds. At the court of Francis I, was a gentleman of Artois, named Louis Berquin, who was then about thirty years of age, and unmarried. The purity of his life,[2] his profound knowledge, which procured him the title "of the most learned of the nobility,"[3] the frankness of his disposition, his tender care of the poor, and the unbounded attachment which he showed to his friends, distinguished him among his equals.[4] The rites of the Church, fasts, feasts, and masses, had not a stricter observer;[5] in particular, he manifested a perfect horror at every thing that was called heresy. It was a marvellous thing to see so much devotion at the court.

It seemed impossible that any thing could dispose such a man in favour of the Reformation. There were, however, two features in his character which were destined to bring him to the gospel. He had a thorough disgust at every thing like dissimulation, and as he never wished to wrong a single individual, so he could not bear to see any body wronged. Hence the tyranny of Beda and other fanatics, their trickery and persecution, filled him with indignation; and, as he did nothing by halves, wherever he went, in the city and at the court, "even among the most distinguished of the kingdom,"[6] he inveighed with the utmost vehemence against the tyranny of these doctors, and attacked, "even in their hives," says Theodore Beza, "those odious hornets which were at that time the terror of the world.[7]

Nor was this enough. Opposition to injustice led Berquin to enquire after truth. He felt a desire to know that Holy Scripture, so much loved by the men against whom Beda and his partizans were raging, and no sooner did he begin to read, than it won his heart. Berquin was immediately brought into communication with Margaret, Briçonnet, Lefevre, and all who loved the Word, and from converse with them derived the purest enjoyment. He felt that he had some other thing to do than to oppose the Sorbonne. He could have wished to make all France acquainted with the convictions of his own soul. He accordingly began to write and translate into French

---

[1] Talibus Atlantibus nititur Ecclesia Romana. (Eras. Ep. p.1113.) Such the Atlas on whose shoulders the Roman Church is borne? [2] Ut ne rumusculus quidem impudicitiæ sit unquam in illum exortus. (Ibid., p. 1278.) [3] Gaillard Hist. de Francois Ier. [4] Mirere benignus in egenos et amicos. (Er. Ep. p. 1238.) [5] Constitutionum ac rituum ecclesiasticorum observantissimus . . . . (Ibid.)
[6] Actes des Martyrs de Crespin, p. 103. [7] Ut maxime omnium tunc metuendos crabrones in ipsis eorum cavis . . . . (Bezæ Icones.)

several Christian works. It seemed to him that every one ought to acknowledge and embrace the truth as promptly as he himself had done. The impetuosity which Beda displayed in the cause of human traditions, Berquin displayed in the service of the word of God. Younger than the syndic of Sorbonne, less prudent, less able, his strength lay in a noble eagerness for truth. They were two powerful wrestlers, about to try which could throw down the other. But Berquin had something else in view than to give Beda fall. Accordingly Theodore Beza says, "that France would perhaps have found in Berquin another Luther, could he have found, in Francis I another Elector."[1]

Numerous obstacles were to trammel his efforts. Fanaticism ever meets with followers: it is a fire which increases as it goes. The monks and ignorant priests followed in the train of the syndic of the Sorbonne. An *esprit de corps* reigned in this company under the direction of certain intriguers and fanatics who knew adroitly how to avail themselves of the nonentity or vanity of their colleagues, in order to make them share in their enmities. At each sitting these leaders were the only spokesmen, over-awing the others by their violence, or reducing feeble and moderate men to silence. No sooner did they make a proposal than they exclaimed with threatening accents, "Now we shall see who they are that belong to the faction of Luther."[2] Did any one give utterance to equitable sentiments, Beda, Lecouturier, Duchesne, and their whole band, seemed horrified, and exclaimed all at once, "It is worse than Luther." This manœuvre was successful. The timid, who like better to live in peace than to dispute, those who are ready to abandon their own sentiments for their individual advantage, those who do not understand the simplest questions, those, in fine, who are always driven from their position by clamour, were dragged along by Beda and his tribe. Some remained mute, others shouted, all gave implicit submission to the power which a proud and tyrannical spirit exercises over vulgar souls. Such was the condition of this company, which was regarded as so venerable, and which was then the most impassioned enemy of evangelical Christianity. A glance at the most celebrated bodies would often be sufficient to set a just value on the war which they wage against truth.

Thus the university which, under Louis XII, had applauded the attempts at independence by Almain, again plunged all at once into fanaticism and servility under Duprat and Louisa of Saxony. If we except the Jansenists, and some other teachers, we nowhere

[1] Gallia fortassis alterum esset Luterum nacta. (Bezæ Icones.) [2] Hic inquiunt apparebit qui sint Lutheranæ factionis. (Er. Ep. p. 889.)

find a true and noble independence in the Gallican clergy. All they have done has been to oscillate between servility towards the court and servility towards the pope. If, under Louis XII or Louis XIV, there was some appearance of liberty, it was because their master of Paris was then contending with their master of Rome. This explains the sudden change to which we have just referred. The university and the bishops ceased to remember their rights and their duties the moment the king ceased to demand it of them.

Beda had long been irritated against Lefevre. The fame of the doctor of Picardy enraged his fellow-countryman and offended his pride. He could have wished to shut Lefevre's mouth. Once already had Beda attacked the doctor of Etaples; and, little skilled as he was in discerning evangelical doctrines, he had attacked his colleague on a point which, strange as it may seem, well nigh brought Lefevre to the scaffold.[1] Lefevre had maintained that Mary, the sister of Lazarus, Mary Magdalene, and the woman that was a sinner, of whom St. Luke speaks (Luke, xvii), were three different individuals. The Greek fathers had distinguished between them, but the Latin fathers had confounded them. This dreadful *heresy* of the three Magdalenes, set Beda, and all his host, in motion. Christendom was aroused. Fisher, Bishop of Rochester, one of the most distinguished prelates of that age, wrote against Lefevre, and the whole Church decided against an opinion now received by all Roman Catholics. Lefevre, who had been previously condemned by the Sorbonne, was prosecuted as a heretic by the Parliament, when Francis I, who was delighted at the opportunity of striking a blow at the Sorbonne and humbling monkery, rescued him from the hands of his persecutors.

Beda, indignant at being deprived of his victim, determined to take his measures better next time. Luther's name was beginning to make a noise in France. The Reformer, after the Leipsic discussion with Dr. Eck, had agreed to submit to the decision of the universities of Erfurth and Paris. The zeal which the university had displayed against the Concordat doubtless made him hope that he would find impartial judges in its bosom. But times had changed; and the more decision the faculty had shown against the encroachments of Rome, the more it was bent on displaying Rome's orthodoxy. Beda thus found it quite inclined to enter into his views.

On the 20th January, 1520, the censor of the French nation purchased twenty copies of Luther's conference with Dr. Eck for the purpose of distributing them among the members of the company who were to report on this affair. More than a year was

[1] Gaillard Hist. de François I*r*, iv, p. 228.

employed in the investigation. The Reformation of Germany was beginning to make an immense sensation in France. The universities which were then institutions of true catholicity, and which were attended by crowds of students from all the countries of Christendom, brought Germany, France, Switzerland, and England into closer and readier connection in regard to theology and philosophy, than is the case at the present day. The noise which Luther's work had made at Paris, strengthened the hands of the Lefevres, Briçonnets, and Farels. Each of his victories animated them with courage. Several of the doctors of Sorbonne were struck with the admirable truths which they found in the writings of the monk of Wittemberg. Candid confessions were made; but, at the same time, fierce opposition was aroused. "All Europe," says Crevier, "were anxiously awaiting the decision of the university of Paris." The struggle seemed doubtful; but, at last, Beda carried the day. In April, 1521, the university decided that Luther's works should be publicly committed to the flames, and that their author should be compelled to recant.

Nor was this enough. Indeed, the disciples of Luther had crossed the Rhine still more rapidly than his writings. "In a short time," says the jesuit Maimbourg, "the university was filled with strangers, who, because they knew a little of Hebrew, and a good deal of Greek, acquired a reputation, insinuated themselves into the houses of persons of quality, and used an insolent liberty in interpreting the Bible." [1] The faculty named a deputation to present its complaints to the king.

Francis I, caring little for the quarrels of theologians, continued his round of amusements, and conducting the gentlemen and ladies of the court of his mother and sister from chateau to chateau, gave himself up to all sorts of dissipation, far away from the annoying gaze of the citizens of his capital. He thus travelled over Brittany, Anjou, Guienne, Angoumois, and Poiton, claiming the same service in villages and forests as if he had been at Paris in the Chateau des Tournelles. There were tournays, combats, masquerades, sumptuous entertainments, tables covered with dainties, "by which," says Brantôme, "those of Lucullus were far surpassed." [2]

For a moment, however, he interrupted the round of his pleasures to receive the grave deputies of the Sorbonne. But he saw only learned men in those whom the faculty denounced to him as heretics. Would a prince, who boasted that he had taken the kings of France *out of leading strings*, lower his head before some fanatical doctors? "I am not willing," replied he, "that those people be

---

[1] Histoire du Calvinisme, p. 10.   [2] Vie des Hommes Illustres. i, p. 326.

molested. To persecute those who teach, would be to prevent men of talent from coming into the kingdom."[1]

The deputation retired in a rage. What was to be the result? The evil was increasing from day to day; already men were beginning to call heretical opinions " sentiments of men of genius;" the devouring flame was spreading into the most secret recesses. The conflagration would blaze, and throughout France the edifice of faith would tumble with a crash.

Beda and his faction, unable to obtain scaffolds from the king, had recourse to more hidden persecution. There was no kind of annoyance to which the evangelical doctors were not subjected. There were constantly new reports and new denunciations. Old Lefevre, tormented by these ignorant zealots, sighed for repose. The pious Briçonnet, who ceased not to express his veneration for the doctor of Etaples,[2] offered him an asylum. Lefevre left Paris, and repaired to Meaux. This was a first advantage gained over the gospel, and it was thenceforth seen that if the faction could not succeed in gaining the aid of the civil power, it had a secret fanatical police, by means of which it could surely attain its end.

CHAP. VI.

Briçonnet visits his Diocese—Reformation—The Reformers Prosecuted at Paris—
Philibert of Savoy—Correspondence of Margaret and Briçonnet.

Thus Paris began to take part against the Reformation, and trace the first lines of that enclosure which was destined for nearly three centuries to hedge in the capital from the reformed worship. God had been pleased that the first rays of the Reformation should appear in Paris, but men immediately exerted themselves in extinguishing them; the spirit of the Sixteen was already fermenting in the metropolis, and other towns of the kingdom were about to welcome the light which the capital spurned away.

Briçonnet, on returning to his diocese, had displayed the zeal of a Christian and a bishop. He had visited all his parishes, and assembling the deans, curates, vicars, church-wardens, and the principal parishioners, had made himself acquainted with the doctrine and lives of the preachers. At the collecting season, he was told, the Franciscans of Meaux began their course; a single preacher

[1] Maimbourg, p. 11. [2] Pro innumeris beneficiis, pro tantis ad studia commodis. (Epist. Dedicat. Ep. Pauli.) For innumerable favours, for so great help in study.

went over several parishes in one day, repeating the same sermon at each place, not in order to nourish the souls of his hearers, but to fill his belly, his purse, and his convent.[1] The wallet once filled, the end was attained, the preachers concluded, and the monks did not again appear in the churches till another begging season arrived. The only business of these shepherds is to clip the wool off their flocks.[2]

On the other hand, the curates, for the greater part, spent their incomes at Paris. "Oh!" said the pious bishop on finding a presbytery which he came to visit empty, "are not those traitors who thus abandon the warfare of Christ?"[3] Briçonnet resolved to remedy these evils, and convened a meeting of all his clergy on 13th October, 1519. But these worldly priests, who cared little for the remonstrances of their bishop, and for whom Paris had so many charms, took advantage of a custom, in virtue of which they could present one or more vicars to feed their flocks in their absence. Out of one hundred and twenty-seven vicars, Briçonnet found only fifteen whom he approved.

Worldly curates, imbecile vicars, monks who thought only of their belly. Such was the condition of the Church. Briçonnet denied the use of the pulpit to the Franciscans,[4] and persuaded that the only method of filling his bishopric with good ministers, was to form them himself, he determined on founding a school of theology at Meaux, and placing it under pious and learned teachers. It was necessary to find them. They were furnished by Beda.

In fact, this fanatical man and his company gave themselves no rest, and complaining bitterly of the toleration of the government, declared that they would make war on the new doctrines with it, without it, or against it. It was in vain that Lefevre had quitted the capital. Did not Farel and his friends remain? Farel, it was true, did not mount the pulpit, for he was not a priest, but at the university, in the town, with the professors, priests, students, and citizens, he boldly maintained the cause of the Reformation. Others animated by his example, were always becoming more open in spreading the word of God. Martial Mazurier, a celebrated preacher and president of the college of St. Michael, used no disguise in painting the disorders of the times in the darkest yet truest colours, and it seemed impossible to withstand the power of his eloquence.[5] The rage

[1] Ea solum doceri quœ ad cœnobium illorum ac ventrem explendum pertinerent. (Acta Mart. p. 334.)   [2] MS. of Meaux. I am indebted to the kindness of M. Ladevze, pastor of Meaux, for the copy of the MS. which is there preserved.   [3] Ibid.
[4] Eis in universa diocesi sua prædicationem interdixit. (Acta. Mart. p. 334.)
[5] Frequentissimas de reformandis hominum moribus conciones habuit. (Lannoi, Savarræ Gymnasii Hist. p. 261.)

of Beda and his theological partisans knew no bounds. "If we tolerate these innovators," said he, "they will gain possession of the whole body, and it will be all over with our lectures, our traditions, our places, and the respect shown to us by France and all Christendom."

The theologians of the Sorbonne proved the strongest. Farel, Mazurier, Gerard Roussel, and his brother Arnand, soon saw their activity every where paralysed. The bishop of Meaux urged his friends to come and join Lefevre, and these excellent men hounded by the Sorbonne, and hoping that, beside Briçonnet, they might be able to form a holy phalanx for the triumph of the truth, accepted the invitation of the bishop and repaired to Meaux.[1] Thus the gospel light gradually withdrew from the capital where providence had kindled its first rays. *This is the condemnation, that light is come into the world, and men have loved the darkness rather than the light, because their deeds are evil.*[2] It is impossible not to perceive, that Paris at this time drew down upon itself the judgment which these words of our Saviour express.

Margaret of Valois deprived successively of Briçonnet, Lefevre, and their friends, felt uneasy when she saw herself alone in the midst of Paris, and the licentious court of Francis I. She was on intimate terms with Philibert of Savoy, a young princess, her mother's sister. Philibert, whom the king, in order to seal the Concordat, had given in marriage to Julian the Magnificent, brother to Leo X. had after her marriage gone to Rome, where the Pope, overjoyed at the illustrious alliance, had expended a hundred and fifty thousand ducats in giving her sumptuous fetes.[3] In 1516, Julian, when in command of the army of the Pope, died, leaving his widow at the age of eighteen. She became attached to Margaret, who by her talents and her virtues had great influence on all around her. The grief of Philibert opened her heart to the voice of religion. Margaret imparted to her whatever she read, and the widow of the lieutenant general of the Church began to relish the soothing doctrine of salvation. But Philibert was too inexperienced to support her friend Margaret, who often felt humbled in thinking of her great weakness. If the love which she bore to the king, and the fear she had of displeasing him, led her into some act contrary to her conscience, she was immediately troubled in her soul, and turning again in sadness toward the Lord, she found in him, a master, a brother, more merciful and more soothing to her heart than Francis himself. At such a time she thus addressed her Saviour.

[1] They were obliged to quit Paris by the persecution raised against them at Paris. Vie de Farel, par Choupard. [2] John, iii, 19. [3] Guichenon, Hist. én. de Savoie, ii, p. 180.

> O gentle brother ! who when thou mightest chide
> Thy erring sister, call'st her to thy side ;
> For murmur, injury, and great offence,
> Dost give her grace and love, as recompence.
> Too much, alas ! yea far too much, my brother,
> In me is no desert of such a treasure.

Margaret, seeing all her friends retiring to Meaux, turned a sad look towards them amid the festivities of the Court. Every one seemed to abandon her. Her husband, the duke D'Alençon, was setting out for the army: her young aunt Philiberte, for Savoy. The duchess turned towards Briçonnet, and thus wrote him:

"Monsieur De Meaux,—Knowing that only one is necessary, I address myself to you, praying you to supplicate heaven to guide, agreeably to its holy will, M. D'Alençon, who, by command of the king, is setting out as a lieutenant-general of the army, which, I fear, will not be disbanded without war. And thinking that, independent of the public good of the kingdom, you have a good title in whatever touches his salvation and mine, I ask your spiritual aid. To-morrow my aunt sets out from Nemours for Savoy. I am obliged to occupy myself with many things which give me many fears. Wherefore, if you know that master Michael could undertake a journey, it would give me a consolation which I ask only for the glory of God." [2]

Michael D'Arande, whose assistance Margaret requested, was one of the members of the evangelical society of Meaux who, at a later period, exposed himself to many dangers in preaching the gospel.

The pious princess was alarmed when she saw the formidable opposition which was rising and increasing against the truth. Duprat and the men in power, Beda and those of the Sorbonne, filled her with dismay. Briçonnet, in order to strengthen her, says in his reply, "War is what our gracious Saviour says in the gospel he had brought upon the earth ; it was also fire . . . . great fire, by which the terrestrial is transformed into the divine. I desire with all my heart to aid you, Madam ; but, from my own nothingness, expect no more than the will. Whoso hath faith, hope, and love, has all that is necessary, and has no need of aid or assistance . . . God is all in all, and out of him is nothing to be found. In contending, have a stout heart . . . . and love unspeakable . . . . The war is carried on through love. Jesus demands the heart: unhappy the man who is estranged from him. He who fights in person is certain of victory. He often falls who fights by others." [3]

---

[1] Miroir de l'âme pécheresse. Marguerites de la Marguerite, etc., i, p. 36.
[2] Lettres de Marguerite, reine de Navarre. (Bibl. Royale Manuscript, S.F., 337. 1521.) [3] Ibid., 12th June, 1521.

The Bishop of Meaux began himself to know what it is to fight for the word of God. Theologians and monks, indignant at the asylum which he gave to the friends of the Reformation, violently accused him; so that his brother, the Bishop of St. Malo, came to Paris to examine the affairs.[1] Margaret was so much the more touched by the consolation which Briçonnet offered her, and replied with an offer of her assistance.

Writing him, she says, "If in any thing you think I can be of service to you or yours, rest assured that any trouble I may take will be my comfort. May eternal peace be given you, after those long wars which you carry on for the faith, and in which you desire to die.

"Ever your daughter, MARGARET."[2]

It is to be lamented that Briçonnet did not die in the struggle. Nevertheless he was then full of zeal. Philiberte of Nemours, respected by all for her sincere devotion, her liberality towards the poor, and the great purity of her manners, read with keen and increasing interest, the evangelical writings sent her by the Bishop of Meaux. "I have all the tracts which you sent me," wrote Margaret to Briçonnet, "my aunt of Nemours has had her share. I will send her the last, for she is in Savoy at the marriage of her brother, which is no small loss to me; wherefore, I pray you to have pity on me in my solitude." Unhappily, Philiberte did not live long enough to declare decidedly in favour of the Reformation. She died in 1524, at the castle of Virieu le Grand, in Bugey, at the age of twenty-six.[3] This was a sad blow to Margaret. Her friend, her sister, she who could entirely understand her, was taken from her. Perhaps, there was only one other death, that of her brother, at which she felt greater agony than now.

> So many tears bedew my eyes,
> They veil my view of earth and skies,
> And like a spring incessant rise.

Margaret feeling how weak she was in resisting grief and the seductions of the court, begged Briçonnet to exhort her to the love of God. The bishop replied, "Our mild and gracious Lord, who wills, and who alone can do what he powerfully wills, is, in his infinite goodness, visiting your heart, exhorting it to love him with its own self. No other than he, madam, has power to do so: you must not expect light from darkness, nor heat from cold. By attracting he inflames, and by inflaming enlarges the heart, inducing it to follow him. Madam, you ask me to have pity upon you be-

---

[1] MS. de Meaux. [2] MS. Bib. Roy., S. F. 227. [3] Guichemon Hist. de la Maison de Savoie, ii, p. 181. [4] Hymn after the king's death. (Marguerites,i, p. 473.

cause you are alone. I do not understand this statement. He who lives in the world and has his heart in it remains alone. Excess and evil are companions. But she whose heart is asleep to the world, and awake to the meek and gracious Jesus, her true and faithful husband, is truly alone, living necessarily in Him alone, and yet is not alone, because not abandoned by Him who fills and keeps all. Pity I cannot and must not have for such solitude, which is more to be esteemed than the whole world, from which I am assured that the love of God has saved you, so that you are no longer its child. Madam, remain alone in Him alone who was pleased to suffer a painful and ignominious death and passion.

"Madam, recommending myself to your good graces, I beg you will be pleased no longer to use expressions similar to those in your last. Of God alone are you the daughter and spouse; no other father must you claim. . . . I exhort and admonish you to be to him as good a daughter as he is a good Father, ... and though you should not be able to attain to this, I beg he would be pleased to increase your strength that you may wholly love and serve him."[1]

Nothwithstanding of these words, Margaret was not yet comforted. She bitterly regretted the spiritual guides of whom she had been deprived; the new pastors whom it was sought to impose upon her in order to gain her back, had not her confidence, and after all that the bishop said she felt herself alone in the midst of the court. All around her seemed dark and desert. In a letter to Briçonnet, she says—" Just as a sheep in a strange land, wandering unacquainted with its pasture, not knowing the new shepherds, naturally raises its head to get a view of the nook where the chief shepherd was wont to give it sweet nurture, am I constrained to beg your charity. Come down from the high mountain, and, among all this people estranged from the light, look in pity on the blindest of all the flock. MARGARET."[2]

The Bishop of Meaux, in his answer, continuing the figure of a wandering sheep, proceeds to represent the mysteries of salvation under the figure of a forest. "The sheep," says he, " going into the forest, being led by the Holy Spirit, is forthwith enraptured with the richness, beauty, straightness, length, breadth, depth, and height, the invigorating and odoriferous fragrance of this forest; and after looking all around, sees only *Him in all, and all in Him;*[3] and, moving along with rapid step, finds it so pleasant that the journey is like life, joy, and consolation."[4] The bishop next represents the sheep vainly seeking the extremity of the forest (a figure of the soul trying to fathom the mysteries of God) falling in with high

[1] MS., S.F., 337, Bib. Roy., 10th July.   [2] Ibid   [3] All in Christ.   [4] MS., S.F., Bib. Roy.

mountains which it attempts to climb, but everywhere finds "infinitude, inaccessible and incomprehensible." Then he shows her the path by which the soul in quest of God surmounts these difficulties; he shows her how the sheep in the midst of mercenaries finds "the nook of the Great Shepherd." "By means of faith," says he, "it begins the flight of contemplation;" everything is made smooth, everything is explained, and it begins to sing, "I have found him whom my soul loveth."

Thus spoke the bishop of Meaux. At this time, burning with zeal, he wished to see France renewed by the gospel.[1] Often, in particular, his mind turned to the three great personages who seemed to preside over the destinies of his countrymen. He thought that if the royal family was enlightened, the whole people would be so; and that the priests, aroused to jealousy, would at length quit their death-like state. "Madam," wrote he to Margaret, "I pray God most humbly, that he would be pleased by his goodness, to kindle a fire in the hearts of the king, madam, and yourself, so that you three may burn with a brilliant flame which will enkindle the rest of the kingdom, and specially that order by the coldness of which all others are frozen."

Margaret did not share these hopes. She speaks neither of her brother nor her mother; it was a subject which she dared not touch; but replying to the bishop, in January, 1522, (her heart dulled by the indifference and worldliness which surrounded her,) she says to him, "The time is so cold, the heart so frozen"—and she signs—"Your frozen, thirsty, and famishing daughter.

"MARGARET."

This letter did not discourage Briçonnet, but it made him enter into himself, and there feeling how much he who wished to quicken others stood in need of being quickened, he commended himself to the prayers of Margaret and Madame de Nemours. "Madam," wrote he with great simplicity, "I beg you by your prayers to awaken a poor slumberer."[2]

Such, in 1521, were the views exchanged at the court of the king of France—strange views, doubtless, which, after a lapse of more than three centuries, a manuscript of the Royal Library of Paris has revealed. Was this influence of the Reformation in so high a quarter advantageous to it, or was it hurtful? The arrow of truth penetrated to the court, but perhaps only served to awaken the slumbering ferocious beast, to stir up its rage, and make it pounce with greater fury on the humblest of the flock.

[1] Studio veritatis aliis declarandæ inflammatus. (Act. Mart., p. 334.)   [2] MS. Bibl. Royale.

CHAP. VII.

First beginnings of the Church of Meaux—The Scriptures in French—The Tradesmen and the Bishop—Evangelical Harvest—The Epistles of St. Paul sent to the King—Lefevre and Roma—The Monks before the Bishop—The Monks before the Parliament—Briçonnet yields.

In fact, the time was approaching when the storm was to burst on the Reformation. Previously, however, it was to shed some additional seeds and reap some grain. This town of Meaux, made famous a century and a half afterwards by the sublime defender of the Gallican system against the despotic pretensions of Rome, was destined to become the first town in France in which a renovated Christianity was to establish its empire. It was at this time the field on which the cultivators were bestowing labour and seed, and where they were already laying down some sheaves. Briçonnet, less asleep than he said he was, animated, inspected, and directed everything. His fortune equalled his zeal; never did man make a nobler use of his wealth, and never did such noble devotedness seem destined from the outset to bear such excellent fruit. Transported to Meaux, the pious teachers of Paris thenceforth acted with new freedom. There was an emancipation of the Word, and the Reformation in France moved rapidly forward. Lefevre forcibly expounded that gospel with which he would fain have filled the world. "It is necessary," said he, "that kings, princes, nobles, people, all nations, think only of Jesus Christ,[1] and aspire to him. Each priest must resemble the angel that St. John saw in the Apocalypse, flying through the midst of heaven, holding in his hand the eternal gospel, and carrying it to every people, tongue, and kindred, and nation. Come pontiff, come kings, come generous hearts. . . . . Nations awaken to the light of the gospel, and breathe life eternal?[2] The word of God is sufficient."[3]

Such, in fact, was the motto of this school,—" *The Word of God is sufficient*." The whole Reformation is comprehended in this sentence. "To know Christ and his word," said Lefevre, Roussel, Farel, "is the alone living, the alone universal theology. He who knows this, knows all."[4]

The truth produced a deep impression in Meaux. First separate meetings were held, next conferences, and at last the gospel was

---

[1] Reges, principes, magnates omnes et subinde omnium nationum populi, ut nihil aliud cogitent. . . . . ac Christum. . . . . (Fabri. Comment. in Evang. Præfat.)
[2] Ubivis gentium expergiscimini ad Evangelii lucem. . . . . . (Fabri. Comment. in Evang. Præfat.) [3] Verbum Dei Sufficit. (Ibid.) [4] Hæc est universa et sola vivifica Theologia. . . . . Christum et verbum ejes esse omnia. (Ibid. in Ev. Johan. p. 271.)

preached in the churches. But a new exertion which was made gave a still more formidable blow to Rome.

Lefevre wished to enable the Christians of France to read the Holy Scriptures. On the 30th October, 1522, he published the French translation of the four Gospels; and on the 6th November, that of the other books of the New Testament. On the 12th October, Collin, at Meaux, published a volume containing the whole of the books thus translated; and in 1525, a French version of the Psalms.[1] Thus began in France almost at the same time as in Germany, the preaching and dissemination of the Scriptures in the vulgar tongue—a procedure which was three centuries afterwards to be carried to so great an extent over the whole world. In France, as on the other side of the Rhine, the Bible had a decisive influence. Experience had taught many Frenchmen that when they sought to know divine things, doubt and obscurity appeared on every side. How many moments, and perhaps years, in their lives, during which they have been tempted to regard the most certain truths as illusions! We must have light from above to illumine our darkness! Such was the sigh of many souls at the period of the Reformation. With such desires, many received the sacred books from the hands of Lefevre. They were read in families and in the closet; and conversations on the Bible became frequent; Christ appeared to their long bewildered spirits as the sun and centre of all revelations. There was no more need of demonstrations to prove to them that the Scriptures were from the Lord. This they knew, for it had transformed them from darkness to light.

Such was the progress by which distinguished individuals in France arrived at the knowledge of God. But there were other methods more simple, and if the thing be possible, more vulgar, by which many of the people attained to the truth. The population of Meaux consisted almost entirely of mechanics and people trading in wool. "In many," says a chronicler of the sixteenth century, "was engendered so ardent a desire to know the way of salvation, that artisans, carders, spinners, and combers, employed themselves while engaged in manual labour, in conversing on the word of God, and deriving comfort from it. In particular, Sundays and festivals were employed in reading the Scriptures and enquiring after the good-will of the Lord."[2]

Briçonnet was delighted at seeing piety thus substituted for superstition in his diocese. "Lefevre, aided by the reputation of his great learning," says a contemporary historian,[3] "was able by his plausible discourse so to cajole and circumvent master William Bri-

[1] Le Long, Biblioth. sacrée, 2d Edit., p. 42. [2] Act. des Mart., p. 182. [3] Hist. Cath. de Temps, par Fontaine, de l'Ordre de St. François. Paris, 1562.

çonnet as to have him entirely devoted to him, so much so that it has never since been possible to purge the town and diocese of Meaux of this mischievous doctrine, even to this day, when it has marvellously increased. It is a great pity that this good bishop, who, till then, had been so devoted to God and the Virgin Mary, should have been so perverted."

Still all were not so entirely devoted as the Franciscan whom we have just quoted, represents. The town was divided into two parties. On the one side were the monks of St. Francis and the friends of the Romish doctrine; on the other, Briçonnet, Lefevre, Farel, and all who loved the new doctrine. An individual in ordinary life, named Leclerc, was one of the most servile adherents of the monks; but his wife and two sons, Peter and John, had eagerly received the gospel. John, who was a carder of wool, soon distinguished himself among the new Christians. James Pavanne, a young scholar of Picardy, "a man of great sincerity," whom Briçonnet had attracted to Meaux, showed great zeal for the Reformation. Meaux had become a focus of light. Persons who had occasion to visit it often heard the gospel and brought it back to their homes. The Holy Scriptures were searched, not in the town only, but also, says a chronicler, "several of the villagers did likewise, so that that diocese began to exhibit an image of the renovated Church."

The environs of Meaux being covered with rich crops at the season of harvest, great numbers of labourers flocked to it from the surrounding countries. When reposing at noon from their fatigues, they conversed with the inhabitants of the district, who spoke to them of other crops and other harvests. Several peasants from Thiérache, and especially from Landouzy, after they returned home persevered in the doctrine which they had heard, and shortly after there was formed in that place an evangelical church, which is one of the oldest in the kingdom.[1] "The fame of this great boon circulated over France," says the chronicler.[2] Briçonnet himself preached the gospel from the pulpit, and endeavoured everywhere to disseminate what he calls "that infinite, sweet, cheerful, true, and only light, which dazzles and illumines every creature who receives it, and which, in illuminating, dignifies him with the filial adoption of God."[3] He prayed his flock not to lend an ear to those who wished to turn them aside from the word. "Even," said he, "should an angel from heaven preach any other gospel unto you, do not listen to him." Sometimes he was seized with melan-

---

[1] These facts are taken from old papers, much defaced, found in the church of Landouzy-la-Ville (Aisne), per M. Colany, when he was pastor there. [2] Actes des Mart., p. 182. [3] MS., Bibl. Royale, S.F., No. 337.

choly thoughts. He was not sure of himself. He recoiled in dismay when thinking of the fatal effects which might result from his unfaithfulness, and, forewarning his people, said to them—"Should even I, your bishop, change my discourse and doctrine, do you beware of changing with me."[1] At the time nothing gave intimation of such a disaster. "Not only was the word of God preached," says the chronicler, "it was practised; all works of charity and love were practised, manners were reformed, and superstitions brought into disrepute."[2]

Always full of the idea of gaining the king and his mother, the bishop sent to Margaret "the Epistles of St. Paul, translated and magnificently illuminated," begging her very humbly to present it to the king; "This from your hands," added he, "cannot but be agreeable. It is a royal dish," continued the good bishop, "nourishing without corrupting, and curing all diseases. The more we taste it, the more we hunger for it, with uncloying and insatiable appetite."[3]

What dearer message could Margaret receive? . . . . She thought the moment favourable. Michael d' Arande was at Paris, detained by command of the queen mother, for whom he was translating portions of the Holy Scriptures.[4] But Margaret would have wished Briçonnet himself to present St. Paul to her brother, and wrote to him, "You would do well to come here, for you know the confidence which the king and she place in you."[5]

Thus the word of God was at this time (1522, 1523) placed under the eyes of Francis I, and Louisa of Savoy. They were brought into contact with that gospel which they were at a later period to persecute. It does not appear that the Word made any salutary impression upon them. The Bible was then making much noise, and a feeling of curiosity made them open it; but it was no sooner opened than shut.

Margaret herself had difficulty in struggling with the worldliness which surrounded her on every side. Her affection for her brother, the obedience which she owed to her mother, and the flattery which she received at court, all seemed to conspire against the love which she had vowed to Jesus Christ. Christ was single against a number. The soul of Margaret, assailed by so many foes, and stunned by the noise of the world, sometimes turned aside from its Lord. Then recognising her fault, the princess shut herself up in her chamber, and giving herself up to grief, sent forth sounds

---

[1] Hist. Cathol. de Fontaine. [2] Actes des Martyrs, p. 182. [3] MS. of the Bibliotheque Royale, S. F., No. 337. [4] Par le commandment de Madame a quy il a lyvre quelque chose de la saincte Escripture qu'elle desire parfaire. (Ibid.) By command of Madame, to whom he has delivered some portion of the Holy Scriptures, which she is desirous to peruse. [5] Ibid.

very different from those jovial strains with which Francis and the young nobility associated in his debaucheries and festivities, caused the palace to resound.

> Left you I have my pleasure to follow;
> Left you I have for a choice most hollow;
> Left you I have—but ah! whither to go?
> Away where nought is but cursing and woe.
> Left you I have a friend constant and true,
> And then, to conceal your love from my view,
> Have leagued with all that is hostile to you.

Then Margaret, turning towards Meaux, wrote in her anguish, "I return to you, to M. Fabry, (Lefevre) and all your band, begging you to obtain from ineffable mercy by your prayers, an awakening for a poor drooping slumbering creature .... from her deep and deadly lethargy." [2]

Thus Meaux had become a focus of light. The friends of the Reformation gave themselves up to flattering illusions. Who could oppose the gospel if the power of Francis I paved the way for it? The corrupting influence of the court would then be changed into a holy influence, and France acquire a moral force which would make her the benefactress of the nations.

On the other hand the friends of Rome became alarmed. Among the most distinguished of those at Meaux was a Jacobin monk named De Roma. One day when Lefevre, Farel, and their friends were conversing with him and some other adherents of the papacy, Lefevre could not refrain from expressing his hopes. "The gospel," said he, "is already gaining the hearts of the grandees and people, and soon diffusing itself over all France, it will every where bring down the inventions of men." The old doctor had become animated, his eyes which had become dim sparkled, his trembling voice was again full toned. One would have said it was old Simeon thanking the Lord for having seen his salvation. The friends of Lefevre shared his emotion, and his opponents were dumb with astonishment. . . . All at once De Roma started up, and with the voice of a tribune of the people, exclaimed, "Then I and all the other monks will preach a crusade: we will stir up the people; and if the king permits the preaching of your gospel, we will make his own subjects chase him from his own kingdom." [3]

Thus a monk dared to enter the lists with a royal knight. The Franciscans applauded the words. The future predicted by the old doctor must not be allowed to be realised. Already the friars are day after day returning with diminished alms. The alarmed

---

[1] Les Marguerites, i, p. 40.   [2] MS. in the Biblio. Royale, S. F., No. 337.
[3] Farel. Epitre au Duc de Lorraine. Gen. 1634.

Franciscans spreading themselves among families, exclaimed "These new teachers are heretics; the holiest observances they attack, the most sacred mysteries they deny! . . . ." Then becoming more emboldened, the most irritated of them come forth from their cloisters, repair to the episcopal palace, and being admitted to the presence of the prelate, exclaim, "Crush this heresy, or the plague which already devastates this town of Meaux will soon spread over the kingdom."

Briçonnet was concerned, and for a moment at a loss how to deal with this attack; but he yielded not; he had too much contempt for these coarse monks and their selfish clamour. He mounted the pulpit, justified Lefevre, and called the monks Pharisees and hypocrites. Still this opposition produced trouble and an internal struggle in his soul; he tried to reassure himself by reflecting that these spiritual combats were necessary. "By this battle," said he, in his somewhat mystical language, "we reach a death, quickening and, at the same time, mortifying life; in living, we die, in dying, we live."[1] The path would have been safer, if hastening towards the Saviour, like the apostles, when tossed by the winds and waves, he had exclaimed, "Master, save us, we perish."

The monks of Meaux, furious at being repulsed by the bishop, resolved to carry their complaints to a higher quarter. They had a power of appeal. If the bishop will not yield, they can compel him. Their leaders set out for Paris, and came to an understanding with Beda and Duchesne. They hastened to the Parliament, and there denounced the bishop and the heretical teachers. "The town," said they, "and the whole neighbourhood are affected with heresy, and it is the episcopal palace itself that sends forth the polluted streams."

Thus, the cry of persecution against the gospel began to be heard in France. The priestly and the civil power, the Sorbonne and the Parliament, took up arms, arms that were to be dyed in blood. Christianity had taught that there are duties and rights anterior to all civil associations, had emancipated religious thought, founded liberty of conscience, and produced a great revolution in society; for antiquity, which saw the citizen every where, and man nowhere, had made religion simply an affair of state. But no sooner had these ideas been given to the world than the papacy had corrupted them. For the despotism of the prince, it had substituted the despotism of the priest. It had often even stirred up the prince and the priest against the Christian people. A new emancipation was required, and it took place in the sixteenth century. In all places where the Reformation was established, it broke the yoke of Rome, and religious thought was again set free. But there is in human nature such a love of domineering over the truth, that among many Protestant nations the Church disengaged from the arbitrary power of the priest, is in our days on the point of again falling under the yoke of the civil power, and doomed, like its ruler, to vibrate incessantly between these two despotisms, to pass ever and anon from Caiaphas to Pilate, and Pilate to Caiaphas.

Briçonnet, who was held in high estimation at Paris, easily justified himself. But it was in vain he sought to defend his friends. The monks were not willing to return to Meaux empty handed. If the bishop is to escape, his brethren must be sacrificed. Of a timid character, not much disposed to abandon his riches and his rank for Jesus Christ, already alarmed and filled with sadness, false counsels led him still further astray. It was suggested to him that, if the evangelical doctors quitted Meaux, they could carry the Reformation elsewhere. An agonising struggle took place in his heart. At length worldly prudence prevailed; he yielded, and on the 12th April, 1526, issued an injunction, depriving these pious teachers of liberty to preach. This was Briçonnet's first fall.

Lefevre was the person principally aimed at. His commentary on the four Gospels, and especially his "epistle to Christian readers," which preceded it, had increased the rage of Beda and his band. They denounced the work to the faculty. "Does he not presume," said the blustering syndic, "to recommend the reading of the Holy Scriptures to all the faithful? Do we not read in it that whoso loves not the word of Christ is not a Christian;[1] and that the word of God is sufficient for eternal life?"

In this accusation Francis I saw only a cabal of theologians. He named a commission, and Lefevre, having justified himself before it, came off from the attack with the honours of war.

Farel, who had fewer protectors at Court, was obliged to quit Meaux. It appears that he at first repaired to Paris,[2] and that having attacked the errors of Rome without reserve, he could no longer remain, but was obliged to retire into Dauphiny, whither his heart was bent on carrying the gospel.

[1] Qui verbum ejus hoc modo non diligunt, quo pacto hi Christiani essent. (Præf. Comm. in Evang.) How can those who do not love his word in this way be Christians? [2] "Farel, after living as long as he could at Paris." (Bezæ Hist. Eccl., i, 6.)

CHAP VIII.

Lefevre and Farel Persecuted—Difference between the Lutheran and Reformed Churches—Leclerc puts up his Pancartes—Leclerc Branded—Zeal of Berquin—Berquin before the Parliament—Francis I saves him—Apostacy of Mazurier—Fall and Grief of Pavanne—Metz—Chatelain—Peter Toussaint becomes attentive—Leclerc breaks Images—Condemnation and Torture of Leclerc—Martyrdom of Chatelain—Flight.

Lefevre intimidated, Briçonnet beginning to backslide, Farel constrained to flee!—this was a first victory. The Sorbonne already thought themselves masters of the movement. The doctors and monks were congratulating themselves on their triumph. This however, was not enough: blood had not flowed. They accordingly set to work, and blood—since blood it must have—was soon to gratify the fanaticism of Rome.

The evangelical Christians of Meaux, seeing their leaders dispersed, sought mutually to edify each other. John Leclerc, a carder of wool, whom the discourses of the teachers, the reading of the Bible and of several religious books, had instructed in Christian doctrine,[1] was distinguished by his zeal and his readiness in expounding Scripture. He was one of those men whom the Spirit of God[2] fills with courage, and soon places at the head of a religious movement. The church of Meaux was not long in regarding him as its pastor.

The idea of an universal priesthood, an idea to which the first Christians were so much alive, had been restored in the sixteenth century, by Luther.[3] But this idea seemed then to remain theoretical in the Lutheran church, and became a living reality only in the Reformed churches. The Lutheran churches (and in this they agree with the Anglican church) seemed to hold a middle place between the Church of Rome and the Reformed Church. Among the Lutherans everything proceeded from the pastor or the priest, and nothing was good in the church that did not come organically through its heads. But the Reformed Churches, while holding the divine institution of the ministry, which some sects overlook, approximated nearer to the primitive condition of the apostolic communities. From the period of which we speak, they recognised and proclaimed, that Christian flocks were not simply to receive what the priest gives; that the members of the church, as well as

---

[1] Aliis pauculis libellis diligenter lectis. (Beza Icones.) Having carefully read some other short treatises. [2] Animosæ fidei plenus. (Ibid.) Fall of ardent faith. [3] Volume second.

its leaders, possess the key of the treasury from which these draw their instructions, since the Bible is in the hands of all; that the grace of God, the spirit of faith, wisdom, consolation, and light, are not given to the pastor merely; that each is called to use the gift which he has received, for the common advantage; that often even a certain gift necessary for the edification of the church may be refused to the minister and granted to a member of his flock. Thus the passive state of the churches was exchanged for a state of general activity. It was in France especially that this revolution was accomplished. In other countries the Reformers are almost without exception pastors and doctors. But in France the men of learning are in close union with the men of the people. There God takes for his first workmen a doctor of the Sorbonne and a carder of wool.

Carder Leclerc now began to go from house to house confirming the disciples. But not stopping at these ordinary labours, he wished to see the edifice of the papacy crumbling to pieces, and France, from amid its ruins, turning with a shout of joy towards the gospel. His somewhat immoderate zeal reminds us of that o' Hottinger at Zurich, and Carlstadt at Wittemberg. He accordingly drew up a proclamation against the Antichrist of Rome, in which he announced that the Lord was about to destroy it by the breath of his mouth. Then he boldly posted up his "Pancartes" on the very gate of the cathedral.[1] Forthwith all was confusion around the ancient edifice. The faithful were astonished, the priests enraged. What! a man employed in carding wool to attack the pope? .... The Franciscans were beside themselves, and demanded that this once, at least, a dreadful example should be made. Leclerc was thrown into prison.

His trial was concluded in a few days, under the very eyes of Briçonnet, who was obliged to see and endure it all. The carder was condemned to be beaten with rods three days in succession through the streets of the town, and then branded on the forehead. Shortly after, this sad spectacle was exhibited. Leclerc, with his hands tied and back bare, was led through the streets, and the executioners let fall upon his body those blows which he had brought upon himself by attacking the bishop of Rome. An immense crowd followed the procession, the course of which might have been traced by the blood of the martyr. Some uttered cries of rage against the heretic; others, by their silence even, gave him unequivocal marks of their tender compassion; a female with eye and tongue encouraged the poor sufferer. It was his mother.

[1] This heretic wrote Pancartes, which he posted up on the doors of the great church of Meaux (MS. of Meaux.) See also Bezæ Icones, Crespin, Actes des Martyrs, etc.

At length, on the third day, after the bloody procession was finished, Leclerc was taken to the ordinary place of execution. The executioner prepared the fire, heated the iron, the impress of which was to be burnt into the evangelist, and approaching him, branded him in the forehead as a heretic. A cry was heard, but it proceeded not from the martyr. His mother, who was present at the frightful spectacle, torn with grief, had a violent struggle within herself. The enthusiasm of faith was struggling in her heart with the love of the mother, and she exclaimed in a voice which made all her adversaries tremble, "Live Jesus Christ and his ministers."[1] Thus this Frenchwoman of the sixteenth century fulfilled the command of the Son of God—"He who loves son more than me is not worthy of me." Such boldness at such a moment deserved exemplary punishment; but the Christian mother had filled the priests and soldiers with amazement. All their fury was restrained by an arm more powerful than their own. The crowd giving way with respect, allowed the mother of the martyr, with lingering pace, to regain her humble dwelling. Even the monks and town-officers stood motionless as she passed. "Not one of her enemies," says Beza, " dared to lay a hand upon her." Leclerc having been released, retired to Rosay in Brie, a small town, six leagues from Meaux, and afterwards repaired to Metz, where we shall again meet with him.

The enemy triumphed. " The cordeliers having reconquered the pulpit, scattered about their lies and silly tales as usual."[2] But the poor mechanics of the town, deprived of the hearing of the Word at regular meetings, " began to assemble in secret," says our chronicler, " after the example of the sons of the prophets, in the time of Ahab, and the Christians of the primitive church; and according as opportunity offered, met one day in a house, and another day in some cave, or occasionally, also, in a vineyard or forest. Then he of their number who was best read in the Holy Scriptures, exhorted them. This done, they prayed together with great courage, supporting themselves with the hope that the gospel would be received in France, and that the tyranny of Antichrist would come to an end."[3] No power is capable of arresting the truth.

Still one victim was not sufficient. The first victim of persecution was a worker in wool; the second was a gentleman of the court. It was necessary to strike terror into the nobles as well as the people. The doctors of the Sorbonne at Paris were not the persons to allow themselves to be outstripped by the Franciscans

---

[1] Beze Hist.Eccl., p. 4. Crespin Hist. des Martyrs, p. 92.   [2] Actes des Martyrs, p. 183.   [3] Ibid.

of Meaux. Berquin, "the most learned of the nobles," had continued to gain new courage from the Scriptures, and after attacking "the hornets of the Sorbonne" in some epigrams, had openly accused them of impiety.[1]

Beda and Duchesne, who had not ventured to reply in their usual style to the witty sallies of a gentleman of the king, changed their view of the matter as soon as they discovered that these attacks were backed by serious convictions. Berquin had become a Christian, and his destruction was resolved. Beda and Duchesne, having seized some of his translations, found matter in them sufficient to burn more than one heretic. "He maintains," said they, "that it is unbecoming to invoke the Virgin in place of the Holy Spirit, and to call her the source of all grace.[2] He attacks the custom of calling her *our hope, our life*, and says that these titles are applicable only to the Son of God." There was more than this. Berquin's study was like a bookseller's shop, from which corrupting books were circulated all over the kingdom. In particular, the *Common Places* of Melancthon, written with so much elegance, made a deep impression on the literati of France. The pious gentleman living only amid folio volumes and *tracts*, had from Christian charity, became a translator, corrector, printer, and bookseller. . . . . It was necessary to arrest this formidable torrent at its very source.

Accordingly one day when Berquin was quietly at his studies in the midst of his beloved books, his house was suddenly surrounded by armed police, who knocked violently at the gate. It was the Sorbonne and its agents, who, fortified with the authority of the Parliament, came to pay him a domiciliary visit. Beda, the formidable syndic, was at their head, and never did inquisitor better fulfil his duty: he made his way with his satellites into the library of Berquin, declared the mission with which he said he was entrusted, and ordering his people to have an eye upon Berquin, commenced his search. Not a book escaped his piercing glance; and by his orders an exact inventory of the whole was taken. Here a treatise of Melancthon, there a writing of Carlstadt! Here heretical books translated from Latin into French by Berquin, there others of his own composition. All the works which Beda seized with the exception of two, were filled with Lutheran errors. He left the house with his booty, more elated than ever general was with the spoils of conquered nations.[3] Berquin saw that a violent storm was about to burst upon his head, but his courage

---

[1] Impietatis etiam accusatos, tum voce tum scriptis. (Bezæ Icones.) He had accused them of impiety, both verbally and in writing. [2] Incongrue beatam Virginem invocari pro Spiritu Sancto. (Erasmi Ep. 1279.) [3] Gaillard Hist. de François I, iv, 241. Crevier, Univ. de Paris, v, p. 171.

failed not. He despised his adversaries too much to fear them. Meanwhile Beda lost no time. On the 13th May, 1523, the Parliament issued a decree, bearing that all the books seized at the house of Berquin should be submitted to the Theological Faculty. The opinion of the company was not long delayed. On the 25th June they condemned the works to the fire as heretical, with the exception of the two which we have mentioned, and ordered Berquin to abjure his errors. The Parliament sanctioned the decision.

The gentleman appeared before this formidable body. He knew that a scaffold was probably behind; but like Luther at Worms he stood firm. In vain did the Parliament order him to recant. Berquin was not one of those who "*fall away*" after being "*made partakers of the Holy Ghost.*" "*He who is begotten of God keepeth himself, and that wicked one toucheth him not.*"[1] Every fall proves that the conversion was only apparent or partial. The conversion of Berquin was real. He answered firmly to the court before which he appeared. The Parliament, more severe than the Diet of Worms had been, ordered its officers to apprehend the accused and carry him to the Conciergerie. This was on the 1st August, 1523. On the 5th August the Parliament remitted the heretic into the hands of the bishop of Paris, in order that this prelate might take cognisance of the affair, and assisted by doctors and counsellors, pronounce due sentence on the culprit. He was transferred to the prison of the officiality.[2]

Thus Berquin passed from tribunal to tribunal, from prison to prison. Beda, Duchesne, and their company kept hold of their victim: but the court had always a grudge at the Sorbonne, and Francis was more powerful than Beda. There was a feeling of indignation among the nobility. Did these monks and priests forget what the sword of a gentleman was worth? "Of what is he accused?" said they to Francis. "For blaming the custom of invoking the Holy Spirit. But Erasmus and many others also blame this. And for such trifles must an officer of the king be put in prison?[3] The blow is aimed at letters, true religion, the nobility, chivalry, the very crown." The king was pleased once more to provoke an outcry from all the company. He gave letters of liberation to the council, and on the 8th August an officer presented himself at the prison of the officiality bearing an order from the king to set Berquin at liberty.

It was a question whether the monks would yield. Francis who had foreseen that some difficulty might be made, had said to

---

[1] Hebrews, vi, 4; 1 John, v, 18.   [2] Ductus est in carcerem, reus hæreseos periclitatus. (Erasm. Ep. 1270. Crevier, Gaillard, loc. cit.)   [3] Ob hujusmodi nænias. (Er. Ep. 1279.)

the officer entrusted with his orders, "If you meet with resistance, I authorise you to break open the door." These words were clear. The monks and the Sorbonne yielded, swallowing the affront; and Berquin, set at liberty, appeared before the king's council, and was acquitted.[1] Thus Francis had humbled the church. Berquin imagined that under his reign France might be emancipated from the papacy, and had thoughts of renewing the war. With this view he entered into correspondence with Erasmus, who immediately recognised in him a good man.[2] But "remember," said the philosopher, who was always timid and temporising, "that it is unnecessary to provoke the hornets; peacefully enjoy your studies.[3] Above all, do not mix me up with your affair; that would not be useful either to me or to you."[4]

This refusal did not discourage Berquin: if the most powerful genius of the age withdraws, he will trust in God, who never fails. The work of God is to be done with men or without them. "Berquin," says Erasmus himself, "was somewhat like the palm tree: he stood up and showed a bold front to whosoever sought to terrify him."[5]

This was not the case with all who had received the gospel doctrine. Martial Mazurier had been one of the most zealous preachers. He was charged with having preached very erroneous doctrines,[6] and even with having committed certain acts of violence, while he was at Meaux." "This Martial Mazurier, being at Meaux," says a manuscript of this town, which we have already quoted, " going to the church of the reverend fathers, the Cordeliers, and seeing the statue of St. Francis standing at the outside of the door of the convent, where at present a St. Roche is placed, threw it down and broke it." Mazurier was seized, and sent to prison,[7] when he suddenly fell into profound reveries, and deep anguish. It was the morality rather than the doctrine of the gospel, that had drawn him into the ranks of the Reformers, and morality left him without strength. Terrified at the scaffold which awaited him, thinking that in France the victory would be decidedly in favour of the Romish party, he easily convinced himself that he should gain more influence and honour by returning to the papacy. He therefore recanted, and caused doctrines to be preached in his parish the opposite of those which he was accused of having taught:[8] at a later period connecting himself with the most fanati-

[1] At judices, ubi viderunt causam esse nullius momenti, absolverunt hominem. (Er. Ep. 1279.) But the Judges seeing that the case was of no moment, acquitted him.   [2] Ex epistola visus est mihi vir bonus. (Ibid.)   [3] Sineret crabrones et suis se studiis oblectaret. (Ibid.)   [4] Deinde ne me involveret suæ causæ. (Ibid.)   [5] Ille, ut habebat quiddam cum palmā commune, adversus deterrentem to'lebat animos. Probably an allusion to Pliny, Nat. Hist., xvi, 42.   [6] Histoire l'Université par Crévier, v, p. 203.   [7] Gaillard, His. de François 1st, v, p. 234.
[8] "Being a dexterous man, he escaped condemnation," says Crevier, v, p. 203.

cal doctors, and in particular with the celebrated Ignatius Loyola, he showed himself one of the most ardent supporters of the papal cause.[1] From the days of the Emperor Julian, apostates, after their faithlessness, have always proved the most pitiless enemies of the doctrines which they had for a time professed.

Mazurier soon found an opportunity of exercising his zeal. Young James Pavanne had also been cast into prison. Martial hoped that by causing his fall he might hide his own. The youth, amiable manners, learning, and integrity of Pavanne excited a strong interest in his favour, and Mazurier imagined that he would himself be less guilty if he could drag Master James into similar guilt. He repaired to his dungeon, and began his manœuvres. He pretended to have gone farther than he in the knowledge of the truth. "You err, James," he often repeated to him, "you have not seen the bottom of the sea: you know only the surface of the waves and billows."[2] Sophisms, promises, threats, nothing was spared. The unhappy youth seduced, agitated, shaken, at last yielded to these perfidious attacks, and publicly recanted his pretended errors the day after Christmas 1524. But from that time a spirit of despondency and grief from the Almighty was upon Pavanne. His sighs were incessant. "Ah," repeated he, "nothing remains to me but a life of bitterness." Sad reward of faithlessness!

There were however, among them who received the word of God in France, men of a more intrepid spirit than Pavanne and Mazurier. Towards the end of 1523, Leclerc had quitted Metz and gone into Lorraine, where, says Theodore Beza, he had followed the example of St. Paul at Corinth, who, while making tents, persuaded both Jews and Greeks.[3] Leclerc, while following his trade of wool-carder, taught the people of his own class. Several among them had been truly converted. Thus this humble artisan laid the foundations of a church which afterwards became celebrated.

Leclerc was not alone at Metz. Among the ecclesiastics of the town was an Augustin monk of Tournay, a doctor of theology, named John Châtelain, who had been brought to the knowledge of God,[4] by his intercourse with the Augustins of Antwerp. Châtelain had gained the respect of the people by the austerity of his manners,[5] and the doctrine of Christ preached by him in his chasuble and stole, had appeared to those inhabitants of Metz less strange, than when it came to them from the poor artisan who

---

[1] Cum Ignatio Loyolâ init amicitiam. (Launoi Navarrœ gymnasii historia, p. 621.)
[2] Actes des Martyrs, p. 99.   [3] Acts, xviii, 3, 4.   Apostoli apud Corinthios exemplum sectus. (Bezæ Icones.)   [4] Vocatus ad cognitionem Dei. (Act. Mart. p. 180.)   [5] Gaillard, Hist. de François 1er, v, p. 232.

quitted the comb with which he was carding wool, to explain a translation of the gospel in French.

Evangelical light, thanks to the zeal of these two men, was beginning to be diffused throughout the town. A very devout female of the name of Toussaint, of burgher parentage, had a son called Peter, to whom, when amusing himself beside her, she often addressed grave words. Every where, at this time, even in the houses of the citizens, something extraordinary was expected. One day the child, occupying himself with the diversions of his age, was riding through his mother's room on a long staff. She was conversing with some friends on religious matters, and said to them with emotion, "Antichrist will soon come in great power, and destroy those who shall have been converted by the preaching of Elias."[1] These words, which were often repeated, struck the child, who called them to mind at a later period. Peter Toussaint was full grown at the time when the doctor of theology and the wool-carder were preaching the gospel at Metz. His parents and friends, astonished at his youthful genius, hoped to see him one day occupying a distinguished place in the Church. One of his uncles, his father's brother, was primicier of Metz. This was the first dignity in the chapter.[2] Cardinal John of Lorrain, son of Duke René, who had a large establishment, had a great love for the uncle and nephew. The latter, notwithstanding of his youth, had just obtained a canonicate, when he began to give attention to the gospel. Might it not be that the preaching of Châtelain and Leclerc was that of Elias? Already, indeed, Antichrist was everywhere arming against it. But what then? "Let us," said he, "lift our heads toward the Lord, who will come and will not tarry."[3]

The gospel doctrine made its way into the first families of Metz. A person of considerable rank, the Chevalier d' Esch, an intimate friend of the primicier, had just been converted.[4] The friends of the gospel were delighted. "The knight, our good master, . . ." repeated Peter; " if however," added he, with a noble candour, "it is lawful to have a master on earth."[5]

Thus Metz was on the eve of becoming a focus of light when the imprudent zeal of Leclerc suddenly arrested its slow but sure progress, and raised a storm which well nigh ruined this rising Church. The great body of the lower classes continued to practise their old superstitions, and Leclerc's heart was grieved when he

---

[1] Cum equitabam in arundine longa, memini sæpe audisse me a matre, venturum Antichristum cum potentia magna, perditurumque eosqui essent ad Eliæ prædicationem conversi. (Tossanus Farrello, 4 Sept., 1525, MS. of the consistory of Neuchâtel.)
[2] Ibid., 21st July, 1525. [3] Levemus interim capita ad Dominum qui veniet nostra et non tardabit . . . (Ibid. 4th Sept., 1525.) [4] Clarissimum illum equitem . . . . cui multum familiaritis et amicitiæ, cum primuerio Metensi, patruo meo. (Ibid., 2nd August, 1524.) [5] Ibid., 21st July, 1525.

saw the city given up to idolatry. A great festival was at hand. About a league from the town was a chapel containing images of the virgin, and the most celebrated saints of the country, and to whom on a certain day all the inhabitants of Metz were accustomed to make a pilgrimage in order to worship the images, and obtain the pardon of their sins.

The eve of the festival having arrived, the pious and intrepid soul of Leclerc was violently agitated. Has not God said, "Thou shalt not bow down to their gods, nor serve them, nor do after their works; but thou shalt utterly overthrow them, and quite break down their images"?[1] Leclerc thought that this command of God was addressed to him, and, without consulting either Chatelain or Esch, or any of those who he might have suspected would oppose his scheme, in the evening, at nightfall, he went out of the town, and repaired to the chapel. There, seated in solemn silence beside these statues, he spent some time in meditation. He might indeed flee away; but . . . . to-morrow, within a few hours, a whole city, bound to worship God only, would be prostrated before these blocks of wood and stone. A struggle similar to that which so often took place in the breasts of the primitive Christians, now took place in the soul of the wool-carder. What matters it that these images are those of male and female saints, and not those of the gods and goddesses of Paganism? Does not the worship which the people pay to these images belong to God only? Like Polyeuctes beside the idols of the temple, his heart shudder and his courage is inflamed:

> Ne perdons plus de tems, le sacrifice est prêt,
> Allons-y du vrai Dieu soutenir l'intérêt,
> Allons fouler aux pieds ce fondre ridicule,
> Dont arme un bois pourri ce peuple trop crédule;
> Allons en eclairer l'aveuglement fatal,
> Allons briser ces dieux de pierre et dè métal;
> Abandonnons nos jours à cette ardeur céleste,
> Faisons triompher Dieu . . . qu'il dispose du reste.[2]

In fact, Leclerc stands up, approaches the images, lifts them, breaks them, and indignantly scatters the fragments before the altar. He doubted not that it was the Spirit of the Lord which inspired him to do so, and Beza is of the same opinion.[3] After this Leclerc returned to Metz, which he re-entered at day-break, being perceived by some persons at the moment when he was going through the gate of the town.[4]

---

[1] Exod., xx, 4; xxiii, 24. [2] Polyeucte par Pierre Corneille. What many admire in verse, they condemn in history. [3] Divini Spiritus afflatu impulsus. (Bezæ Icones.) [4] Mane apud urbis portam deprehensus.

Meanwhile, every thing was in motion in the ancient city. The bells were ringing, the trades assembled, and the whole town, headed by the canons, the priests, and the monks, went out in procession, repeating prayers and singing hymns to the saints whom they were going to worship, with crosses and banners in full display, while instruments of music responded to the chant of the faithful. At length, after walking more than an hour, the procession reached the place of pilgrimage. But what was the astonishment of the priests when presenting themselves, with the censer in their hand, they see the images which they came to worship mutilated, and their remains strewing the ground. They start back in dismay, and publicly announce the act of sacrilege. All at once the hymns cease, the instruments are mute, the colours are lowered, and the whole multitude are indescribably agitated. The canons, curates, and monks, strive to inflame the minds of the people, urging them to make a search for the culprit, and demand his death.[1] The cry is heard from all sides, "Death, death to the perpetrator of the sacrilege!" They return to Metz precipitately and without order.

Leclerc was known to all: he had repeatedly called images idols. Besides, had he not been seen at day-break on his way back from the chapel? Being apprehended, he immediately confessed the crime, and urged the people to worship God only. But this language increased the fury of the multitude, who would on the instant have dragged him to death. When taken before the judges, he boldly declared that Jesus Christ, God manifest in the flesh, ought alone to be worshipped. He was condemned to be burnt alive, and was led off to the place of execution.

Here a dreadful scene awaited him. The cruelty of his persecutors prepared every thing that could add to the horrors of his execution. Near the scaffold they were heating pincers to minister to their rage. Leclerc, calm and firm, stood unmoved amid the savage yells of the monks and people. They began by cutting off his right thumb; then, seizing the hot pincers, they pulled off his nose; then, still using the same instrument, they laid hold of both his arms, and, after breaking them in several places, seized him by the breast.[2] While the cruelty of his enemies was thus venting itself upon his body, his mind was at peace. Solemnly and with loud voice, he repeated the words of David,[4] "*Their idols are silver and gold, the work of men's hand. They have mouths, but they speak*

---

[1] Totam civitatem concitarunt ad auctorem ejus facinoris quærendum. (Act. Mart. Lat. p. 189.) [2] Naso candentibus forcipibus abrepto, iisdemque brachio utroque, ipsis que mammis crudelissime perustis. (Bezæ Icones.) MS. de Meaux; Crispin, etc. [3] Altissima voce recitans. (Bezæ Icones.) [4] Psalm cxv, 4-9.

not; eyes have they, but they see not. They have ears, but they hear not; noses have they, but they smell not. They have hands, but they handle not, neither speak they through their throat. They that make them are like unto them; so is every one that trusteth in them. O Israel, trust thou in the Lord, he is their help and their shield." His enemies, on seeing such strength of soul, were amazed, while believers felt strengthened.[1] The people who had manifested so much rage, were astonished and moved.[2] After these tortures, Leclerc was burnt at a slow fire, as his sentence bore. Such was the death of the first martyr for the gospel in France.

But the priests of Metz were not satisfied. In vain had they tried to shake Chatelain. "He is deaf like the adder," they said, " and refuses to hear the truth."[3] He was seized by the people of the Cardinal of Lorraine, and carried to the castle of Nommeny.

There he was degraded by the officials of the bishop, who took off his vestments, and scratched his finger with a bit of glass, saying, " By this scratching we deprive you of the power of sacrificing, consecrating, and blessing, which you received by the laying on of hands."[4] Afterwards, putting a layman's dress upon him, they remitted him to the secular power, which condemned him to be burnt alive. The pile was soon prepared, and the minister of Christ was consumed by the flames. "Lutheranism, nevertheless, spreads in all the district of Metz," say the authors of the History of the Gallican church, while approving greatly of these severities.

From the moment the storm had burst upon the Church of Metz, there was great distress in the house of Toussaint. His uncle, the primicier, without taking any active part in the persecutions of Leclerc and Chatelain, shuddered when the thought of his nephew belonging to these people. The alarm of his mother was greater still. There was not a moment to be lost; all who had lent an ear to the gospel were threatened in their liberty and their life. The blood the inquisitors had shed, only increased their thirst, and new scaffolds were about to be erected. Peter Toussaint, the Chevalier d'Esch, and several others, quitted Metz in all haste, and took refuge in Basle.

[1] Adversariis territis, piis magnopere confirmatis. (Bezæ Icones.) [2] Nemo qui non commoveretur, attonitus. (Act. Mart. Lat. p. 189.) [3] Instar aspidis serpentis aures omni surditate affectas. (Ibid., p. 183.) [4] Utriusque munus digitos lamina vitrea erasit. (Act des Mart., Lat. p. 66.) He scratched the fingers of both hands with a bit of glass.

CHAP. IX.

Farel and his brothers—Farel driven from Gap—He preaches in the fields—Chevalier Anemond of Coct—The Minorite—Anemond quits France—Luther to the Duke of Savoy—Farel quits France.

Thus the storm of persecution raged at Meaux and at Metz. The north of France repudiated the God, and for a time the gospel withdrew. But the Reformation only changed its place. The south eastern provinces became the theatre of it.

Farel, who had taken refuge at the foot of the Alps, there displayed great activity. To him it was a small matter to enjoy domestic happiness in the bosom of his family. The rumour of what had taken place at Meaux and at Paris, had inspired his brothers with a kind of terror; but an unknown power attracted them to the new and unknown truths with which William entertained them. With the impetuosity of his zeal he urged them to be converted to the gospel,[1] and David, Walter, and Claude, were at length gained to the God whom their brother preached. They did not at the first moment abandon the worship of their ancestors; but when persecution arose they boldly sacrificed friends, goods, and country for liberty to worship Jesus Christ.[2]

The brothers of Luther and Zuinglius appear not to have been as decidedly converted to the gospel. The French reformation had from the beginning a more friendly and domestic character.

Farel did not confine himself to his brothers; he announced the truth to his relatives and friends at Gap, and in its neighbourhood. It would even appear, if we can credit a manuscript, that, availing himself of the friendship of certain ecclesiastics, he preached the gospel in several churches;[3] but other authorities assure us that at this time he did not mount the pulpit. Be this as it may, the doctrine which he professed made a great noise. The multitude and the clergy wished to put him to silence. "A new and strange heresy!" said they. "Can it be that all pious observances are vain? He is neither monk nor priest. He has no right to act the preacher."[4]

All the civil and ecclesiastical powers of Gap were soon united against Farel. He was evidently an agent of the sect which was everywhere spoken against. "Let us," it was said, "cast far from

---

[1] MS. de Choupard. [2] Farel, a gentleman of rank, possessed of good means, all of which he lost for religion, as did also his three brothers. [3] He preached the gospel publicly with great freedom. [4] MS. de Choupard. Hist. des Éveq. de Nismes, 1738.

us this firebrand of discord." Farel was summoned to appear, treated harshly, and violently banished from the town.[1]

He did not, however, abandon his native district. Did not the fields, the villages, and the banks of the Durance, the Guisanne, and the Isere contain many souls which had need of the gospel? And if he there ran some risk of danger, did not those forests, and caves, and steep rocks which he had so often visited in his youth, offer him an asylum? He began to go up and down the country, preaching in houses and amid lonely pastures, taking shelter in woods and on the brinks of torrents.[2] It was a school in which God was training him for other labours. "Crosses, persecutions, and the machinations of Satan, of which I had been forewarned, have not been wanting," said he, " they are far too strong for me to withstand them, but God is my father; he has furnished, and will furnish, me with all the strength I require.[3] A great number of the inhabitants of these districts received the truth from his mouth. Thus the persecution which had driven Farel from Paris and from Meaux, spread the Reformation throughout the provinces of the Saône, the Rhone, and the Alps. In all ages this scripture is fulfilled, " *Therefore they that were scattered abroad went everywhere preaching the word.*"[4]

Among the French who were then gained to the gospel, was a gentleman of Dauphiny, Chevalier Anemond of Coct, a younger son of auditor de Coct, lord of Chastelard. Quick, ardent, easily moved, pious hearted, an enemy of relics, processions, and the clergy, Anemond received the evangelical doctrine with great readiness, and soon was entirely devoted to it. He could not endure forms in religion, and would willingly have abolished all the ceremonies of the church. To him the religion of the heart, internal adoration, alone was true. "Never," said he, " has my spirit found any rest in externals. A summary of Christianity is contained in these words, " *John baptized with water, but you will be baptized with the Holy Spirit: there must be a new creature.*"[5]

Coct, who had all the vivacity of a Frenchman, spoke and wrote sometimes in Latin, and sometimes in French. He read and quoted the *Donat*, Thomas Aquinas, Juvenal, and the Bible. He spoke in short sentences, and passed abruptly from one idea to another. Always in motion, wherever a door appeared open to the gospel, or a celebrated doctor was to be heard, there he was to be found. By his warm-heartedness he gained the love of all with whom he was

[1] "He was expelled with great rudeness as well by the bishop as by the people of the town." (Ibid.) [2] Olim errabundus in sylvis, in nemoribus, in aquis. (Farel ad Capit. de Bucer., Basil 25 Oct. Letter MS. of Neuchâtel.) I formerly wandered up and down in woods, and groves, and among waters. [3] Non defuere crux, persecutio et Satanæ machinamenta. (Farel Galeoto.) [4] Acts, viii, 4.
[5] Nunquam in externis quievit spiritus meus. (Coctus Farello, MS. of the Consistory of Neuchâtel.)

brought into connection. "He is a man of distinguished truth and learning," said Zuinglius, at a later period, "but he is still more distinguished for his piety and affability."[1] Anemond is a kind of type of many Frenchmen of the Reformation. Vivacity, simplicity, zeal amounting to imprudence, such were some of the characteristics of his countrymen who embraced the gospel. In the other extreme of the French character we find the grave figure of Calvin, who forms a striking contrast to the fickleness of Coct. Calvin and Anemond are the two opposite poles, between which all the religious world in France vibrates.

No sooner had Anemond been instructed by Farel in the knowledge of Jesus Christ,[2] than he himself sought to gain souls to this doctrine of spirit and life. His father was dead: his elder brother, of a harsh and haughty temper, repulsed him with disdain. Laurence the youngest of the family, and who had a great affection for him, seemed only, partially, to comprehend him. Anemond seeing himself repulsed by his own family, turned his activity elsewhere.

Till now the revival of Dauphiny had been confined to laymen. Farel, Anemond, and their friends, longed to see a priest at the head of the movement. At Grenoble there was a curate, a minorite, named Peter de Sebville, an eloquent preacher, and an honest good hearted man, who consulted not with flesh and blood, and whom God was gradually drawing to himself.[3] Sebville soon perceived that there was no infallible teacher but the word of God, and abandoning doctrines supported only by human testimony resolved in spirit to preach the word "clearly, purely, holily."[4] These three words express the whole Reformation. Coct and Farel were delighted when they heard this new preacher of grace raise his eloquent voice in their province, and they thought that their presence would thenceforth be less necessary.

The more the revival extended, the more violent the opposition became. Anemond, desirous to know Luther and Zuinglius and the countries in which the Reformation had commenced, and indignant at seeing the truth repulsed by his fellow-citizens, resolved to bid adieu to his country and his family. Having made a will disposing of his property, (which was then in possession of his eldest brother, lord of Chatelard,) in favour of his brother Laurence,[5] he quitted Dauphiny and France, and hastening with his usual impetuosity from the south over countries then difficult to pass, he crossed

---

[1] Virum est genere, doctrinaque clarum, Ita pietate humaniteque longe clariorem (Zw. Ep. 319.)   [2] In a letter to Farel, (2nd Sept., 1524,) he subscribes himself "your humble son."   [3] Pater cœlestis animum sic tuum ad se traxit. (Zuinglius Sebvillæ. Ep., p. 820.)   Our heavenly Father so draws your mind to himself.   [4] Nitide, pure, sancteque prædicare in animum inducis. (Ibid.)   [5] "My brother, Anemond Coct, the knight, on leaving the country, made me his heir." (MS. Letters of the Library of Neuchâtel.)

Switzerland, and scarcely stopping at Basle, arrived at Wittemberg beside Luther. This was shortly after the second Diet of Nuremberg. The French gentleman accosted the Saxon doctor with his ordinary vivacity. He spoke enthusiastically of the gospel, and with earnestness explained the plans which he had formed for the propagation of the truth. Saxon gravity smiled at the southern imagination of the knight,[1] and Luther, though he had some prejudices against the French character, was won and carried away by Anemond. He was moved to think how this gentleman had come for the gospel from France to Wittemberg.[2] "Of a surety," said the Reformer to his friends, "this French knight is an excellent, learned, and pious man."[3] The young gentleman produced the same impression on Zuinglius and Luther.

Anemond seeing what Luther and Zunglius had done, thought that if they would take possession of France and Saxony, nothing could resist them, and hence when he could not persuade them to go thither, he urged them to consent at least to write. In particular, he begged Luther to address a letter to Duke Charles of Savoy, brother of Louisa and Philibert, uncle of Francis I and Margaret. "This prince," said he to the doctor, "takes a great interest in piety and true religion,[4] and likes to talk of the Reformation with some persons of his court. He is fitted to comprehend you, for his motto is '*Nihil deest timentibus Deum*.'[5] This motto is also yours. Struck at alternately by the Empire and by France; humbled, grieved, always in danger, his heart is in want of God and his grace. All he requires is a powerful impulse. Were he gained to the gospel, he would have an immense influence over Switzerland, Savoy, and France. Do write him."

Luther was wholly German, and would have found himself ill at ease out of Germany. Still animated by a truly catholic spirit, he gave his hand as soon as he saw brethren—wherever there was a word to be delivered, he took care to have it heard. Occasionally he wrote on the same day to the extremities of Europe, the Low Countries, Savoy, and Livonia.

"Certainly," replied he to Anemond's request, "the love of the gospel in a prince is a rare gift, and an inestimable jewel."[6] He addressed a letter to the duke, which was probably carried by Anemond as far as Switzerland.

"Will your highness pardon me," wrote Luther, "if I, a humble

---

[1] Mere ardens in Evangelium, says Luther to Spalatin. (Ep. ii, p. 340.) "Sehr brünstig in der Herrlichkeit des Evangelii," are his words to the Duke of Savoy. (Ibid., p. 401.) [2] Evangelii gratia huc profectus e Gallia. (Ibid.) [3] Hic Gallus eques .... optimus vir est, eruditus ac pius. (Ibid.) [4] Ein grosser Liebhaber der wahren Religion und Gottseligkeit. (Ibid. p. 401.) [5] Nothing is wanting to those who fear God. (Hist. Gen. de la Maison de Savoie par Guichenon, ii, p. 228.)
[6] Eine seltsame Gabe und hohes Kleinod unter den Fursten. (L. Ep. ii, p. 401.

and despised individual, dare to address you, or rather will your Highness be pleased to impute this boldness to the glory of the gospel? For I cannot see this splendid luminary rise and shine in any quarter, without exulting with joy. . . . . My desire is, that my Lord Jesus may win many souls by the example of your most serene Highness. Wherefore I wish to tell you of our doctrine. . . . We believe that the commencement of salvation, and the sum of Christianity, is faith in Christ, who by his blood alone, and not by our works, has expiated sin, and destroyed the dominion of death. We believe that this faith is a gift of God, and that it is created by the Holy Spirit in our hearts, and not found by our own exertion. For faith is a living thing,[1] which begets man spiritually, and makes him a new creature."

Luther next proceeded to the consequences of faith, and showed how we cannot possess it unless the scaffolding of false doctrines and human works which the church had so laboriously reared, were forthwith thrown down. "If grace," said he, "is gained by the blood of Christ, it is not by our own works. Wherefore all works and cloisters are useless, and these institutions must be abolished as being against the blood of Jesus Christ, and leading men to confide in their own works. Incorporated with Jesus Christ, it now only remains for us to do that which is good, because having become good trees, we ought to testify it by good fruits.

"Gracious Lord and Prince," says Luther in concluding, "may your Highness, who has begun so well, continue to spread this doctrine not by the power of the sword, which would do harm to the gospel, but by calling into your states teachers who preach the Word. It is by the breath of his mouth that Jesus will destroy Antichrist, in order that, as Daniel expresses it, he may "be broken without hand." (Dan., viii, 25.) Therefore, most serene Prince, may your Highness revive the spark which has begun to burn in you. May a fire come forth from the house of Savoy, as of old from the house of Joseph.[2] May all France be as stubble before the fire: may it burn, and crackle, and purify, so that this illustrious kingdom may bear in truth the name of *most Christian kingdom*, which till this hour it owes only to the torrents of blood shed in the service of Antichrist!"

Such was Luther's effort to spread the gospel in France. It is not known what effect the letter produced upon the Prince; but it does not appear that he ever showed any desire so detach himself from Rome. In 1522 he prayed Adrian VI to be godfather to his first son, and at a later period the pope promised the second a

---

[1] Der Glaube ist ein lebendig Ding . . . . (L. Ep. ii, p. 402.) The original Latin is lost. [2] Das ein Feuer von dem Hause Sophoy ausgehe. (Ibid., p. 406.)

cardinal's hat. Anemond after attempting to see the court and Elector of Saxony,[1] for which purpose he had received a letter from Luther, returned to Basle more determined than ever to sacrifice his life for the gospel. In his ardour he wished he were able to shake all France. "All that I am," said he, "and all that I shall be; all that I have, and all that I shall have, I wish to devote to the glory of God."[2]

At Basle Anemond found his countryman Farel. Anemond's letters had produced in him an eager desire to see the Reformers of Switzerland and Germany. Farel moreover required a sphere of activity, in which he could more freely display his powers. He therefore quitted that France which had nothing but scaffolds to give to the preachers of the pure gospel. Taking by roads and concealing himself in the woods, he succeeded, though with difficulty, in escaping the hands of his enemies. He frequently lost his way. "By my powerlessness in these petty things," saith he, "God means to teach me what my powerlessness is in great things."[3] At length in the beginning of 1524, he arrived in Switzerland. It was here he was to spend his life in the service of the gospel, and it was at this time that France began to send into Helvetia those generous evangelists who were to establish the Reformation in *Romane* Switzerland, and give it a new and powerful impulse throughout the Confederation, and the whole world.

CHAP. X.

Catholicity of the Reformation—Friendship of Farel and Œcolampadius—Farel and Erasmus—Altercation—Farel calls for a Discussion—Theses—Scripture and Faith —Discussion.

A fine feature in the Reformation is its catholicity. Germans come into Switzerland—Frenchmen go into Germany—at a later period Englishmen and Scotchmen repair to the Continent, and teachers from the Continent to Great Britain. The Reformation of the different countries began almost independently of each other; but no sooner do they begin than they shake hands. There is but one faith, one spirit, one Lord. I think it was not well done hitherto to write the history of the Reformation only for one country. The work is one, and Protestant churches, from their origin, form one body, "fitly joined together."[4]

[1] Vult videre aulam et faciem Principis nostri. (L. Ep. ii, p. 340.) [2] Quidquid sum, habeo, ero, habebove, ad Dei gloriam insumere meus est. (Coct. Ep. MS. of Neuchatel.) [3] Voluit Dominus per infirma haec, docere quid possit homo in majoribus. (Farel Capitoni., ibid.) [4] Eph. iv, 16.

At this time a French church, saved from the scaffold, was formed at Basle by several refugees from France and Lorraine. They had spoken about Lefevre, Farel, and the events at Meaux, and hence when Farel arrived in Switzerland he was already known as one of the most devoted champions of the gospel.

He was immediately introduced to Œcolampadius, who had been for some time returned to Basle. Seldom have two more opposite characters met. Œcolampadius, charmed by his mildness, Farel carried away by his impetuosity; but from the first moment these two men felt united for ever.[1] It was the second union of a Luther and a Melancthon. Œcolampadius received Farel into his house, gave him a modest chamber, a frugal table, and introduced him to his friends. The learning, piety, and courage of the young Frenchman, soon won all hearts. Pellican, Imeli, Wolfhard, and other ministers of Basle, felt strengthened in the faith by his energetic discourses. Œcolampadius was at this time in very low spirits. "Alas!" said he to Zuinglius, "I speak in vain, and see not the least ground for hope. Perhaps I should have had more success among the Turks."[2] . . . . "Ah!" added he with a deep sigh, "I blame nobody but myself." But the more he saw of Farel, the more his heart revived and the courage which was thus imparted to him became the basis of an imperishable affection. "Oh my dear Farel," said he to him, "I hope the Lord will make our friendship immortal! and if we cannot be united here below, our joy will only be the greater when we meet beside the Saviour in heaven."[3] Pious and touching thoughts! The arrival of Farel was evidently assistance sent to Switzerland from above.

But while this Frenchman was delighted with Œcolampadius, he recoiled coldly, and with a noble disdain, from a man at whose feet all the nations of Christendom did homage. The prince of scholars—he from whom a word and a look were objects of ambition—the master of the age, Erasmus, was disregarded by Farel. The young man from Dauphiny had refused to go and do homage to the old sage of Rotterdam, because he despised the men who are never more than half-way on the side of truth, and who, while aware of the dangers of error, are full of deference for those who propagate it. Thus in Farel was seen that decision which became one of the distinguishing characteristics of the Reformation in France and French Switzerland, and which has sometimes been stigmatised as rudeness, exclusiveness, intolerance. A discussion

---

[1] Amicum semper habui a primo colloquio. (Farel ad Bulling. 27th May, 1566.) He was even my friend after our first interview. [2] Fortasse in mediis Turcis felicius docuissem. (Zw. et Ecol. Ep., p. 200.) [3] Mi Farelle, spero Dominum conservaturum amicitiam nostram immortalem; et si hic conjungi nequimus, tanto beatius alibi apud Christum erit contubernium. (Ibid., p. 201.)

had taken place in regard to the commentaries of Lefevre, between the two greatest doctors of the period, and there never was a party where those present did not either take part with Erasmus against Lefevre, or for Lefevre against Erasmus.[1] Farel had not hesitated to take part with his master. But what had especially excited his indignation was the cowardice of the philosopher of Rotterdam in regard to evangelical Christians. Erasmus shut his door against them. Very well. Farel won't knock at it. This cost him but a small sacrifice, convinced, as he was, that Erasmus wanted the basis of all true theology, piety of heart. "The wife of Frobenius," he said, "has more theology than he." Indignant at Erasmus for having written to the pope, stating how he ought to proceed in order "to extinguish the fire raised by Luther," he declared loudly that Erasmus wished to stifle the gospel.[2]

Young Farel's independence irritated the illustrious scholar. Princes, kings, doctors, bishops, popes, reformers, priests, men of the world, all considered themselves happy in coming to pay him their tribute of admiration. Luther himself had showed some deference for his person, and this exiled stranger from Dauphiny presumed to brave his power. This insolent freedom gave more chagrin to Erasmus than the homage of the whole world gave him joy. Accordingly he omitted no opportunity of discharging his bad humour at Farel: besides, in attacking so decided a heretic, he washed himself, in the eyes of the Roman Catholics, of the suspicion of heresy. "Never," said he, "have I seen a more false, virulent, and seditious man.[3] His heart is full of vanity, his tongue full of malice."[4] But the wrath of Erasmus did not stop at Farel: it broke out against all the French refugees at Basle whose frankness and decision had annoyed him. They showed that they had little respect of persons. When the truth was not frankly professed, they cared little for the man, how great soever his genius might be. They perhaps wanted somewhat of the mild temper of the gospel, but their fidelity had in it something of the strength of the old prophets. We love to meet with men who refuse to bend to what the world worships. Erasmus, astonished at this proud disdain, complained to everybody. Writing to Melancthon he says, "What! shall we reject pontiffs, and bishops, only to have more cruel tyrants, scabbed madmen, for such France has sent us?"[5] "Some Frenchmen," wrote he to the pope's secretary in presenting him with his book on *Free Will*, "are still madder than the Germans themselves. They have always in their mouths these

[1] Nullum est pene convivium . . . . (Er. Ep., p. 179.)   [2] Consilium quo sic extinguatur incendium Lutheranum. (Ibid.)   [3] Quo nihil vidi mendacius, virulentius, et seditiosius. (Ibid., p. 798.)   [4] Acidæ linguæ et vanissimus. (Ibid., p. 2129.)   [5] Scabiosos . . rabiosos . . . nam nuper nobis misit Gallia. (Ibid., p. 350.)

five words—*Gospel, Word of God, Faith, Christ, Holy Spirit*—and yet I doubt not it is the spirit of Satan that impels them."[1] Instead of *Farellus* he often wrote *Fallicus*, thus designating one of the frankest men of his age by the epithet of cheat or deceiver.

The spirit and wrath of Erasmus were at their height, when he was told that Farel had called him a *Balaam*. Farel thought that Erasmus, like that prophet, allowed himself, perhaps without knowing it, to be seduced by presents to speak against the people of God. The learned Dutchman, unable to contain himself, resolved to call the audacious Frenchman to account: and one day when Farel was talking on Christian doctrine with several friends, Erasmus, bluntly interrupting him, said, "Why do you call me Balaam."[2] Farel, astonished at first at the bluntness of the question, soon recovered himself, and replied that it was not he who had so called him. Pressed to name the culprit, he mentioned Du Blet of Lyons, like himself a refugee at Basle.[3] "It may be he is the person who said it," replied Erasmus, "but it was you who taught him to say it." Then ashamed at having lost his temper, he quickly turned the conversation. "Why," said he to Farel, "do you maintain that the saints are not to be invoked? Is it because the Holy Scriptures do not command it?" "Yes," said the Frenchman. "Very well," replied the scholar, "I challenge you to prove by Scripture that it is necessary to pray to the Holy Spirit." Farel made this simple and true reply, "If he is God he must be invoked."[4] "I left off the discussion," says Erasmus, "for it was drawing to night."[5] Thenceforth every time that the name of Farel came under his pen, it was to reproach him as a hateful being, to be shunned at all hazards. The letters of the Reformer, on the contrary, are full of moderation in regard to Erasmus. Even in the hottest temperament, the gospel is milder than philosophy.

At Basle, the Reformed doctrine had already many friends in the Council and among the people, but the professors of the University combated it with all their might. Œcolampadius and Stor, pastor of Liestal, had maintained theses against them. Farel thought it his duty in Switzerland also to make a public profession of the great principle of the Evangelical school of Paris and Meaux—*the sufficiency of the Word of God*. He asked permission of the University to maintain theses, "rather," he added modestly, "that I may be corrected if I am wrong, than to teach others."[6] The University refused.

---

[1] Non dubitem quin agantur spiritu Satanæ. (Er. Ep., p. 350.) [2] Diremi disputationem . . . (Ibid., p. 804.) [3] Ut diceret negotiatorem quemdam Dupletum hoc dixisse. (Ibid., p. 2129.) [4] Si Deus est, inquit, invocandus est. (Ibid., p. 804.) [5] Omissa disputatione, nam imminebat nox. (Ibid.) We have only the account of this conversation given by Erasmus, who himself tells us, that Farel also gave an account of it which differed greatly from his. [6] Damit er gelehrt werde, ob er irre. (Füssli Beytr. iv, p. 244.)

Farel then addressed the Council, and the Council announced that a Christian man named William Farel, having by the inspiration of the Holy Spirit prepared certain articles conformable to the gospel,[1] permission was given him to maintain them in Latin. The University prohibited every priest and student from appearing at this discussion, but the Council issued a contrary order.

The following are some of the thirteen propositions which Farel posted up:—

"Christ has given us the most perfect rule of life: no man is entitled to take from it or to add to it.

"To be guided by other precepts than those of Christ, leads directly to impiety.

"The true ministry of priests is to devote themselves to the administration of the Word: they have no higher office.

"To deprive the glad tidings of Christ of their certainty, is to destroy them.

"He who hopes to be justified by his own power and his own merits, erects himself into a God.

"Jesus Christ, whom all things obey, is our polar star, and the sole star which we ought to follow." [2]

Thus this "Frenchman" presented himself at Basle.[3] A mountaineer of Dauphiny, brought up in Paris at the feet of Lefevre, came to this celebrated University of Switzerland, under the eye of Erasmus, and boldly expounded the great principles of the Reformation. Two ideas were contained in Farel's theses. The one was the duty of returning to the Holy Scriptures; the other the duty of returning to faith; two things which the papacy, in the famous bull of Unigenitus, at the beginning of the eighteenth century, has decidedly condemned as heretical and impious, and which, closely connected with each other, in fact overturn the system of the papacy. If faith in Christ is the beginning and end of Christianity, it is to the word of Christ we must attach ourselves, and not to that of the Church. More than this: if faith unites souls, where is the necessity for an external bond of union? Do crosses, bulls, and tiaras constitute this sacred unity? Faith unites in a spiritual and true unity all those in whose hearts it fixes its abode. Thus vanished at one blow the triple delusion of meritorious works, human traditions, and a spurious unity. This is the whole of Roman Catholicism.

The discussion commenced in Latin.[4] Farel and Œcolampadius explained and proved their articles, repeatedly challenging their

[1] Aus Eingiessung des heiligen Geistes ein christlicher Mensch und Bruder. (Fussli Beytr. iv, p. 244.) [2] Gulielmus Farellus Christianis lectoribus, die Martis post Reminiscere. (Ibid., p. 247.) Fussli does not give the Latin text. [3] Schedam conclusionum a Gallo illo. (Zw. Ep., p. 333.) [4] Schedam conclusionum Latine apud nos disputatam. (Ibid.)

opponents to reply, but none of them appeared. The sophists (so Œcolampadius styles them) made a great bluster, but hidden in their obscure retreats.[1] Accordingly the people began to despise the cowardice of the priests, and to detest their tyranny.[2]

Thus Farel obtained a place among the defenders of the Reformation. People were delighted to see a Frenchman combining so much learning and piety. The greatest triumphs were anticipated. " He is strong enough by himself alone," it was said, "to destroy all the Sorbonne."[3] His candour, sincerity, and frankness, gained all hearts.[4] But in the midst of his activity, he forgot not that it was in his own soul his mission behoved to commence. The mild Œcolampadius, and the ardent Farel, entered into a paction in virtue of which they bound themselves to exercise humility and meekness in their ordinary conversation. These intrepid men knew how to train themselves for peace even on the very battle field. The impetuosity of a Luther and a Farel were however necessary virtues. Some effort must be made, when the end in view is to displease the world, and renovate the Church. The men of our day too often forget a truth which the meekest men of that day recognised. "Some," said Œcolampadius to Luther in introducing Farel to him, "some could wish that this zeal against the enemies of the truth were more moderate; but I cannot help seeing in this very zeal an admirable virtue, which, if seasonably displayed, is no less necessary than gentleness."[5] Posterity has confirmed the judgment of Œcolampadius.

In the month of May, 1524, Farel, with some friends from Lyons, visited Schaffhausen, Zurich, and Constance. Zuinglius and Myconius gave a glad welcome to this exile of France. Farel remembered it all his days. On his return to Basle he found Erasmus and his other enemies at work, and received orders to quit the town. In vain did his friends loudly testify their disapprobation of such an abuse of power. He behoved to quit the soil of Switzerland, which was hereafter doomed to great disasters. " Such," said Œcolampadius, " is the way in which hospitality is understood by us, true sons of Sodom."[6]

Farel, while at Basle, had continued upon intimate terms with Chevalier d'Esch, who resolved to accompany him. They accordingly set out furnished with letters to Capito and Luther, to whom the doctor of Basle recommended Farel as " the William who had

[1] Agunt tamen magnos interim thrasones, sed in angulis lucifugæ. (Zw. Ep. p. 333.) [2] Incipit tamen plebs paulatim illorum ignaviam et tyrannidem verbo Dei agnoscere. (Ibid.) [3] Ad totam Sorbonnicam affligendam si non et perdendam. (Œcol. Luthero, Ep., p. 200.) [4] Farello nihil candidius est. (Ibid.)
[5] Verum ego virtutem illam admirabilem et non minus placiditate, si tempestive fuerit, necessariam. Ibid.) [6] Adeo hospitum rationem habemus, veri Sodomitæ. (Zw. Ep., p. 454.)

laboured so much in the work of God."[1] At Strasburg, Farel formed an intimate friendship with Capito, Bucer, and Hedio, but he appears not to have gone as far as Wittemberg.

CHAP. XI.

New Campaign—Calling of Farel to the Ministry—An advanced post—Lyons an Evangelical Focus—Sebville at Grenoble—Conventicles—Preaching at Lyons—Maigret in Prison—Margaret intimidated.

God usually removes his servants from the field of battle to bring them back stronger and better armed. Farel and his friends in Meaux, Lyons, and Dauphiny, driven from France by persecution, had become imbued, in France and Germany, with the spirit of the oldest Reformers: and now like an army at first scattered by the enemy, but instantly rallied, they were about to turn round and march forward in the name of the Lord. These friends of the gospel did not only reappear on the frontiers; in France itself they resumed courage, and prepared to renew the attack. The trumpets now sounded the reveillé: the soldiers buckled on their armour, and formed themselves in bands to multiply their blows: the leaders were preparing for the onset—the watchword " Jesus, his word and his grace"—more powerful than the flourish of martial music at the moment of battle, filled men's hearts with equal enthusiasm. All was ready in France for a second campaign, which was to be signalised by new victories, and by new and greater reverses.

Montbeliard at this time demanded a labourer. Duke Ulric of Wittemberg, young, violent, and cruel, dispossessed of his estates in 1519, by the Suabian league, had taken refuge in this county, the only one of his dominions remaining to him. He saw the Reformers in Switzerland : his misfortunes proved salutary, and he felt a relish for the gospel.[2] Œcolampadius informed Farel that a door was opened in Montbeliard, and Farel hastened secretly to Basle.

Farel had not regularly entered the ministry, but at this period we find in him all that was necessary to constitute a minister of the Lord. He did not throw himself into the service of the church thoughtlessly and of his own accord. " Looking at my littleness," he says, " I should not have dared to preach, waiting until my

---

[1] Gulielmus ille qui tam probe navavit operam. (Zw. et Œcol. Ep., p. 175.)
[2] A prince who had a knowledge of the gospel. (Farel Summaire.'

Lord should send a fitter person.[1] But God gave me a triple call. He was no sooner arrived at Basle than Œcolampadius, touched with the wants of France, besought him to devote himself to it. "See," said he to him, "how little Jesus Christ is known by all who speak the French language. Will ye not give them some instruction in their mother tongue, that they may the better understand the Holy Scriptures?"[2] At the same time he received a call from the people of Montbeliard, and the prince consented.[3] Was not this triple call from God? . . . . "I did not think," says he, "it could be lawful for me to resist. According to God I obey."[4] Concealed in the house of Œcolampadius, struggling with the responsibility which was offered to him, yet obliged to yield to the clear manifestation of the will of God, Farel accepted the charge, and Œcolampadius commended him to it, calling on the name of the Lord,[5] and giving his friend counsels full of wisdom. "The more you are inclined to violence," said he to him, "the more ought you to exercise yourself in gentleness—temper your lion courage with dove-like gentleness."[6] Farel answered this appeal with all his soul.

Thus Farel, of old an ardent follower of the ancient church, was going to become a servant of God in the new Church. If Rome demands, to the validity of an ordination, the laying on of the hands of a bishop descended by uninterrupted succession from the apostles, it is merely because she places human tradition above the word of God. In every church where the authority of the Word is not absolute, it is necessary to have recourse to another authority. And then, what more natural than to look to the most venerated ministers of God, for what they know not how to find in God himself? If they speak not in the name of Jesus Christ, is it not something at least to speak in the name of St. John and St. Paul? He who speaks in the name of antiquity, is stronger than the rationalist who speaks only in his own name. But the Christian minister has a still higher authority: he preaches not because he descends from St. Chrysostom and St. Peter, but because the word which he announces descends from God himself. The idea of succession, how respectable soever it may appear, is only a human system substituted for the system of God. In the ordination of Farel there was no human succession. Nay more, there was not in it a thing which is necessary in the Lord's flocks, among whom *everything must be done in order, God being not a God of confusion.* He had no ordination by the Church. But extraor-

[1] Summaire, c'est à dire, Briève Déclaration de G. Farel, in the Epilogue.
[2] (Ibid.) [3] Being required and demanded by the people, with the consent of the prince. [4] (Ibid.) [5] With invocation in the name of God. (Ibid.)
[6] Leoninam magnanimitatem columbina modestia frangas. (Œcol. Ep., p. 198.)

dinary times justify extraordinary things. At this memorable period God himself interposed. By marvellous dispensations he consecrated those whom he called to the renovation of the world, and this consecration is well worth that of the Church. There was in Farel's ordination the infallible word of God given to a man of God to carry it to the world—the call of God and the people, and the ordination of the heart. Perhaps there is not a minister of Rome or Geneva who has been more legitimately ordained to the holy ministry. Farel set out for Montbeliard accompanied by D'Esch.

Farel was thus placed as an advanced post. Behind him were Basle and Strasburg, to support him by their counsels and printing presses. Before him stretched the provinces of Franche-Comté, Burgundy, Lorraine, Lyonnais, and the rest of France, where men of God were beginning to struggle against error in the midst of profound darkness. He immediately began to preach Christ, and to entreat the faithful not to allow themselves to be turned from the Holy Scriptures by threats or guile. Farel was at Montbeliard like a general on a height, with a piercing eye taking in the whole field of battle, urging those who are actually engaged, rallying those whom the impetuosity of the attack has thrown into disorder, and by his own courage inflaming those who remained behind.[1] Erasmus immediately wrote to his Roman Catholic friends that a Frenchman escaped from France was making a great disturbance in those regions.[2]

Farel's lessons were not in vain. One of his countrymen writing to him says, "Everywhere we see men springing up and spending their labour and their whole life in doing what they can to extend the gospel of Jesus Christ."[3] The friends of the gospel blessed the Lord that the Sacred Word was daily shining throughout Gaul with a brighter lustre.[4] The enemy was alarmed. "The faction," wrote Erasmus to the bishop of Rochester, "is every day extending more and more, being propagated in Savoy, Lorraine, and France."[5]

For some time Lyons seemed to be the centre of the evangelical movement within the kingdom, as Basle was beginning to be out of it. Francis I, going into the South on a campaign against Charles V, had arrived there with his mother, his sister, and his court. Margaret had with her several individuals devoted to the gospel.

[1] This comparison was made by a friend of Farel during his stay at Montbeliard. .... Strenuum et oculatum imperatorem, qui iis etiam animum facias qui in acie versantur. (Tossanus Farello, MS. of the Consist. Neuchatel, 2 Sept., 1524.)
[2] Tumultuatur et Burgundia nobis proxima, per Phallicum quemdam Gallum qui e Gallia profugus. (Er. Ep., p. 809.) [3] Suppullulare qui omnes conatus adferant, quo possit Christi regnum quam latissime patere. (MS. Neuchatel, 2 Aug., 1524.)
[4] Quod in Galliis omnibus sacrosanctum Dei verbum in dies magis ac magis elucescat. (Ibid.) [5] Factio crescit in dies latius, propagata in Sabaudiam, Lothoringiam, Franciam. (Er. Ep., p. 809.)

"All others she left behind," says a letter of this period.[1] While Francis I sent through Lyons 6000 troops, and 1500 lances of French nobility, to join 14,000 Swiss, in order to repel the invasion of Provence by the imperialists—while this great city resounded with the noise of arms, the trampling of horses, and the sound of trumpets, the friends of the gospel were marching to more peaceful conquests. They wished to attempt at Lyons what they had been unable to accomplish at Paris. It might be that away from the Sorbonne and the Parliament, the word of God would have greater freedom. It might be that the second city of the kingdom was destined to become, with regard to the gospel, the first. Was it not here that, nearly four centuries before, worthy Peter Waldo began to spread the Divine word? He had at that time shaken France. Now that God had fully prepared the emancipation of his church, might not larger and more decisive success be anticipated? Accordingly the men of Lyons, though it is true they were not in general, as in the twelfth century, the "poor," began boldly to wield "the sword of the Spirit, which is the word of God."

Among the persons about Margaret was her almoner, Michel d'Arande. The Duchess caused the gospel to be publicly preached in Lyons. Master Michel preached it loudly and purely to a large audience, attracted partly by the interest which the glad tidings excited wherever they are published, and partly also by the respect in which the preaching and the preacher were held by the beloved sister of the king.[2]

Anthony Papillon, a man of very cultivated mind, an elegant scholar, a friend of Erasmus, and "the first in France well-learned in the gospel,"[3] also accompanied the princess. He had at Margaret's request translated Luther's work on monastic vows, "which brought him into much trouble with those Parisian vermin," says Sebville.[4] But Margaret had protected this learned man when attacked by the Sorbonne, and had procured him the office of First Master of Requests to the Dauphin, with a place in the Great Council.[5] He aided the gospel not less by his devotedness than by his prudence. A merchant named Vaugris, and especially a gentleman named Anthony Du Blet, a friend of Farel, were at the head of the Reformation in Lyons. The latter, possessed of great activity, served as a link to connect the Christians scattered over those districts and placed them in communication with Basle. While the warriors of Francis I only passed through

---

[1] De Sebville à Coct, 28 Dec., 1524. (MS. de Neuchatel.) [2] Elle a ung docteur appelé Maître Michel Eleymosinarius, lequel ne prêche devant elle que purement l'Evangile. (Ibid.) She has a doctor called Master Michael, the Almoner, who preaches before her only the pure gospel. (Ibid.) [3] Ibid. [4] Ibid. [5] Ibid.

Lyons, the spiritual soldiers of Jesus Christ stopped there with Margaret. Allowing the former to carry war into Provence and the plains of Italy, they began in Lyons itself to fight the battle of the gospel.

But they did not confine themselves to Lyons. They looked all around them. The campaign commenced in several quarters at once. The Christians of Lyons, by their words and their labours, encouraged all who confessed Christ in the surrounding provinces. They did more. They sent and preached it where it was not yet known. The new doctrine ascended the Saône, and an evangelist trod the rough and narrow streets of Mâcon. Michel d'Arande himself, almoner to the king's sister, went thither in 1524, and, by the aid of Margaret's name, obtained liberty to preach in this town,[1] which, at a later period, was to be full of blood, and whose *leaps* were to pass into a by-word.

After climbing in the direction of the Rhone, the Christians of Lyons, ever on the out-look, climbed in the direction of the Alps. At Lyons there was a Dominican named Maigret, who had been obliged to quit Dauphiny where he had preached the new doctrine with decision. He urgently asked that some one should go and encourage his brethren of Grenoble and Gap. Papillon and Du Blet went.[2] A violent storm had just burst on Sebville and his preaching. The Dominicans had moved heaven and earth. Furious at seeing so many evangelists, Farel, Anemond, Maigret, escape them, they would fain have annihilated those within their reach.[3] They had accordingly called for the apprehension of Sebville.[4]

The friends of the gospel in Grenoble were in dismay. Must Sebville also be taken from them? Margaret interceded with her brother. Several of the most distinguished persons of Grenoble, among others, the king's advocate, avowed or secret friends of the gospel, exerted themselves in behalf of the evangelical cordelier, and at length their united efforts rescued him from the fury of his enemies.[5]

But if Sebville's life was safe, his mouth was shut. "Be silent," he was told, " or the scaffold awaits you." Writing to Anemond de Coct, he says, "Silence is imposed upon me under pain of death."[6] These menaces of the enemy alarmed even those of

---

[1] Arande preaches at Mascon. (Sebville a Coct, MS. of Neuchatel.) [2] There were two great personages at Grenoble. (Ibid.) The title of *Messire*, given to Du Blet, indicates a person of rank. I presume that the term *negociator*, which is elsewhere given to him, refers to his activity. It is possible, however, he may have been one of the great merchants of Lyons. [3] Conjicere potes ut Macretum et me in Sebivillam exarserint. (Anemond a Farel, 7 Sept., 1524, MS. Neuchatel.) You may guess that after Maigret and me their rage burnt against Sebville.
[4] The Thomists wished to proceed against me by inquisition and imprisonment. (Letter of Sebville. Ibid.) [5] Had it not been for certain secret friends, I had been placed in the hands of the Pharisees. (Ibid.) [6] Ibid.

whom the best had been hoped. The king's advocate, and other friends of the gospel, now showed nothing but coldness:[1] several returned to the Romish ritual, pretending to worship God in the secrecy of their heart, and to give the external rites of Catholicism a spiritual meaning—a sad delusion, which leads from infidelity to infidelity. No hypocrisy can thus be justified. The unbeliever by means of his system of myths and allegories, will preach Christ from the Christian pulpit: and the follower of some abominable superstition among the heathen will be able, with a little intellect, to find in it the symbol of a pure and elevated idea. In religion the first thing is truth. Some of the Christians of Grenoble, among them Amedeus Galbert, and a cousin of Anemond, continued firm in the faith.[2] These pious men met in secret with Sebville sometimes at the house of one or other of them, and *talked* together of the gospel. They repaired to some distant retreat, or went during the night to the house of a brother. They hid themselves to pray to Jesus Christ, as robbers do to commit crimes. More than once the humble assembly was disturbed by false alarms. The enemy connived at their secret conventicles, but they had sworn that the faggot would do justice to whoever should dare to discourse publicly of the word of God.[3]

It was in these circumstances that Messires Du Blet and Papillon arrived at Grenoble. Seeing that Sebville's mouth was shut, they exhorted him to come and preach Christ at Lyons. The Lent of the following year was to present a favourable occasion for preaching it to a numerous crowd. Michael d'Arande, Maigret, and Sebville prepared to fight at the head of the gospel phalanxes. Every preparation was thus made for a brilliant manifestation of the truth in the second city of France. The rumour of this evangelical Lent spread as far as Switzerland. " Sebville is set free, and will preach this Lent, at St. Paul's at Lyons," wrote Anemond to Farel.[4] But a great disaster, carrying affliction into every part of France, prevented this spiritual combat. It is in peace that the gospel makes its conquests. The defeat of Pavia, which took place in the month of February, frustrated this bold plan of the Reformers.

Meanwhile, without waiting for Sebville, Maigret, at Lyons, preached salvation by Christ alone, notwithstanding of the keen opposition of priests and monks.[5] In these discourses there was no longer any question as to the worship of creatures, the saints, the virgin, and the power of the priests. The great mystery of

---

[1] Non solum tepidi sed frigidi. (MS. Neuchatel.) Not only lukewarm, but cold.
[2] Tuo cognato, Amedeo Galberto exceptis. (Ibid.) [3] But to speak it publicly is to court the flames. (Ibid.) [4] The Saturday of Quatre-Temps., Dec. 1524. (Ibid.) [5] In truth Maigret has preached at Lyons in spite of priests and monks. (Ibid.)

godliness, "God manifest in the flesh," was alone proclaimed. The ancient heresies of the paupers of Lyons, it was said, have reappeared in a worse form than ever. Notwithstanding of this opposition, Maigret continued his ministry. The faith which animated his soul expressed itself in powerful language. It is of the nature of truth to embolden the heart which has received it. However Rome was to prevail at Lyons as at Grenoble. In presence of Margaret, Maigret was arrested, dragged along the streets, and cast into prison. Vaugris, a merchant, who at this time left the town on a journey into Switzerland, spread the news as he passed along. They produced astonishment and despondency. One idea, however, calmed the fears of the Reformed: "Maigret is seized," it was said; "but *Madam d' Alençon is there, thank God!*"[1]

This hope was soon disappointed. The Sorbonne had condemned several of the propositions of this faithful minister.[2] Margaret, whose situation was always becoming more difficult, saw at once an increase in the hardihood of the friends of the Reformation, and in the hatred of its powerful enemies. Francis I began to feel impatient at the zeal of the evangelists. He saw in these fanatics what he deemed it right to suppress. Margaret, thus suspended between her desire of being useful to her brethren, and her inability to save them, sent an intimation to them not to throw themselves into new dangers, seeing that she would write no more to the king in their favour. The friends of the gospel thought that this resolution was not irrevocable, "God give her grace," said they, "to say and write only what is necessary to poor souls."[3] But if this human resource fails them, Christ remains. It is good for the soul to be left without help in order that it may lean on Christ alone.

CHAP. XII.

The French at Basle—Encouragement of the Swiss—Fear of disunion—Translations and Printing Presses at Basle—Bibles and Tracts circulated in France.

Meantime the efforts of the friends of the gospel were paralysed. The great were beginning to be hostile to Christianity. Margaret was afraid: dreadful news were about to cross the Alps, and blow after blow to throw the kingdom into mourning, leaving only one thought—to save the king, to save France. But if the Christians

---

[1] MS. Neuchatel. [2] Gaillard, Hist. de Francois 1er. iv, p. 233. [3] Pierre Toussaint à Farel, Basle, 17th Dec. 1524. (MS. Neuchatel.)

of Lyons were arrested in their labours, were there not at Basle soldiers who had escaped from the battle, and were ready to begin anew. The exiles of France have never forgotten her. Driven from their country for nearly three centuries by the fanaticism of Rome, we see their latest descendants carrying to the towns and fields of their fathers the treasures of which the pope deprives them. At the moment when the soldiers of Christ in France, in despondency, threw down their arms, the refugees of Basle prepared for the combat. Seeing the monarchy of St. Louis and Charlemagne tottering in the hands of Francis I, will they not feel called to aspire to *a kingdom which cannot be moved?*" [1]

Farel, Anemond, d'Esch, Toussaint, and their friends, formed in Switzerland an evangelical society with the view of delivering their country from spiritual darkness. Letters were received from all quarters informing them that the thirst for the word of God was growing in France. [2] It was necessary to take advantage of this— to water and sow seed during seed time. Œcolampadius and Oswald Myconius ceased not to encourage them in it. They gave their hand, and inspired them with their faith. The Swiss schoolmaster, in January 1525, wrote to the French knight : "Banished as you are from your country by the tyranny of antichrist, your very presence in the midst of us proves that you have acted with courage in the cause of the gospel. The tyranny of the Christian bishops will soon make the people regard them only as liars. Remain firm. The time is not distant when we shall enter the haven of rest, whether tyrants strike us or be themselves struck,[3] and then all will be well with us, provided we be faithful to Jesus Christ."

These encouragements were precious to the French refugees; but a blow proceeding from these same Christians of Switzerland and Germany who sought to strengthen them, tore their hearts to pieces. Scarcely escaped from the faggot, they were in dismay when they saw the evangelical Christians beyond the Rhine disturbing the repose which they enjoyed by lamentable dissensions. The discussion on the Supper had begun. Moved and agitated, feeling strongly how much need there was of charity, the French would have given every thing to effect a reconciliation between these divided spirits. This became their ruling thought. At the period of the Reformation, none had so much need of Christian unity as they. Of this, at a later period, Calvin was a proof. "Would to God," said Peter Toussaint, "that I were able, with all my blood, which indeed is not worth much, to purchase peace, concord, and union in Jesus Christ."[4]

[1] Heb. xii, 28. [2] Gallis verborum Dei sitientibus. (Coctus Farello, 2 Sept. 1524. MS. Neuchatel.) [3] Non longe abest enim, quo in portum tranquillum perveniamus. (Osw. My<unk>. to Anemond de Coct., Ibid.) [4] 21st Dec. 1525. (MS. Neuchatel.)

The French, possessed of a clear and ready judgment, immediately perceived that this new discussion would arrest the work of the Reformation. "Everything would go on much better than at present if we were agreed. There are many people who would willingly come to the light, but when they see these divisions among the clergy, they know not what to do."[1]

The French were the first who thought of taking steps for reconciliation. "Why," they wrote to Strasburg, "not send a Bucer, or some other learned man, to Luther? The longer we wait, the greater the dissension will become." These fears only increased.[2] At length, seeing their efforts useless, these Christians, in grief, turned their eyes away from Germany, and fixed them earnestly on France.

France, the conversion of France, thenceforth exclusively engrossed the heart of these generous men, whom history, which has inscribed on her pages the names of so many individuals vainly puffed up with their own glory, has not even mentioned. Thrown upon a foreign land, they there flung themselves upon their knees, and daily, in the solitude of their retreat, invoked God in behalf of the land of their fathers.[3] Prayer! Such was the power by which the gospel was spread over the kingdom, and the great instrument to which the Reformation owed her conquests.

But these Frenchmen were not only men of prayer; never did an evangelical army number soldiers more ready to devote their persons in the hour of battle. They saw the importance of diffusing the Holy Scriptures and pious books in their country, still immersed in the darkness of superstition. A spirit of enquiry circulated over the whole kingdom; it was necessary to give it wings. Anemond, always prompt in action, and Michael Bentin, another refugee, resolved to unite their zeal, their talents, their means, and their labours. Bentin wished to establish a printing press at Basle, and the knight, in order to turn to profit the little that he knew of German, proposed to translate the best works of the Reformation into French. In the joy which their project inspired, they exclaimed, "Would to God that France were completely filled with gospel volumes, so that everywhere in the cottages of the poor, and the palaces of the great, in cloisters and presbyteries, and in the inner sanctuary of the heart, a powerful testimony might be borne to Jesus Christ."[4]

[1] 21st Dec., 1525. (MS. Neuchatel.) [2] Multis jam Christianis Gallis dolet quod a Zwinglii aliorumque de Eucharistia sententia, dissentiat Lucherus. (Tossanus Farello, 14th July, 1525.) Many Christians in France are now grieved that Luther differs from Zuinglius and others on the subject of the Eucharist. [3] Quam sollicite quotidianis precibus commendem. (Ibid., 2nd Sept., 1525, Neuchatel.) How anxiously I commend them to God in my daily prayers. [4] Opto enim Galliam Evangelicis voluminibus abundare. (Coctus Farello, MS. Neuchatel.) I would have France to abound in gospel volumes.

Such an enterprise required friends, and the refugees had nothing. At this time Vaugris was at Basle, and Anemond, on his departure, sent by him a letter to the brethren of Lyons, several of whom were rich in worldly goods, and who, though oppressed, were always faithful to the gospel. He asked them to send him some assistance.[1] But this was not enough. The French wished to establish several presses in Basle, which working night and day might inundate France with the word of God.[2] At Meaux and Metz, and other places besides, were men rich enough and powerful enough to aid in this enterprise. No man could address Frenchmen with so much authority as Farel. To him, therefore, Anemond turned.[3]

It does not appear that the knight's scheme was realised; but the work was done by others. The presses of Basle were constantly employed in printing French books. These were sent to Farel, who was unremitting in introducing them into France. One of the first productions sent by this Religious Tract Society was the Exposition of the Lord's Prayer by Luther. The merchant Vaugris, wrote Farel, "We sell the tract of the Pater at four deniers of Basle, by retail; but wholesale we sell 200 for two florins, which is not so much."[4]

From Basle, Anemond sent Farel all the useful books which appeared there, or arrived from Germany; one of these was a Treatise on the Training of Christian Ministers, and another on the Education of Children.[5] Farel examined these writings. He composed, translated, or procured others to translate into French. He appeared to be at once all action, and all study. Anemond urged on and superintended the press; and these epistles, these prayers, these books, all these flying sheets were the means of regenerating the age. While dissipation came forth from the throne, and darkness from the steps of the altar, these unobserved writings sent over the nation rays of light and seeds of holiness.

But it was the word of God, above all, that the evangelical merchant of Lyons demanded in the name of his countrymen. This people of the sixteenth century, hungering for intellectual food, were to receive in their own tongue those ancient monuments of the first ages of the world, and enhale the new breath of primitive humanity, together with those holy oracles of gospel times in

---

[1] Ut pecuniæ aliquid ad me mittant. (Coctus Farello MS. Neuchatel.) [2] Ut prœla multa erigere possimus. (Ibid.) [3] An censes inveniri posse Lugduni Meldæ, aut alibi in Galliis qui nos ad hæc juvare velint. (Ibid.) [4] Vaugris à. Farel; Bâle, 29th August, 1524. (MS. Neuchatel.) [5] Mitto tibi librum de instituendis ministris Ecclesiæ cum libro de instituendis pueris. (Ibid.) I send you book on training ministers of the Church with a book on the training of children.

which the fulness of the Christian revelation is displayed. Vaugris wrote to Farel, "I pray you, if it be possible, to get a translation of the New Testament by some man able to make it. It would be a great boon to France, Burgundy, and Savoy. And if it was necessary to have a French letter (printing types,) I would cause it to be procured from Paris or Lyons. If good ones can be got at Basle, so much the better."

Before this time the books of the New Testament in French, but in detached parts, had been published by Lefevre at Meaux. Vaugris wished that some one would revise the whole, and superintend a complete edition. Lefevre undertook the task, and published it, as we have already said, on the 12th October, 1524. An uncle of Vaugris, named Conrard, a refugee at Basle, immediately procured a copy of it. On the 18th November, Chevalier de Coct, at the house of a friend, saw the book, and was overjoyed. "Haste and get it reprinted," said he, "for I doubt not that a very great number will be disposed of."[1]

Thus the word of God was presented to France in opposition to the traditions of the Church, which Rome still ceases not to offer to her. "How is it possible," asked the Reformers, "to distinguish between what is human in tradition, and what is divine, unless by the Scriptures of God? The sentences of Fathers, the decretals of the heads of the Church cannot be the rules of our faith. They show us what was the opinion of those ancient teachers; but the word alone informs us what is the truth of God. We must make every thing submit to Scripture."

Such was the principal means by which these writings were diffused. Farel and his friends entrusted the books to some dealers or hawkers, simple and pious men, who, bearing their precious burden, went from town to town, village to village, and house to house, in Franche-Comté, Lorraine, Burgundy, and the neighbouring provinces, knocking at every door. These books were given them at a low price, "in order that they might feel desirous to sell them."[2] Thus, as early as 1524, there was in Basle for the benefit of France, a Bible and Religious Tract Hawking Society. It is an error to suppose that these take their date from our age. In their essential idea they go back not only to the period of the Reformation, but to the first ages of the Church.

[1] MS. Neuchatel.   [2] Vaugris à Farel. (Ibid.)

CHAP. XIII.

Progress at Montbeliard—Opposition and Disturbance—Toussaint quits Œcolampadius—The day of the Bridge—Death of Anemond—Successive Defeats.

The attention which Farel gave to France did not make him overlook the places in which he lived. Having arrived at Montbeliard, towards the end of July, 1524, he had there scarcely sown the seed, than, as Œcolampadius expresses it, the first-fruits of the harvest began to appear. Farel, quite delighted, wrote of it to this friend. "It is easy," replied the teacher of Basle, " to introduce some dogmas into the ears of the hearers, but to change the heart is God's own work."[1]

Chevalier de Coct, delighted with the news, repaired, with his ordinary vivacity, to Peter Toussaint. "I set out, to-morrow, on a visit to Farel," said he hastily. Toussaint, who was more calm, wrote to the evangelist of Montbeliard: "Take care; the cause that you maintain is a great cause; it must not to defiled by human counsels. The powerful promise you their favour, their assistance, mountains of gold. . . . . But to trust in these things is, to desert Jesus Christ and walk in darkness."[2] Toussaint was finishing his letter when the Chevalier entered. He took it, and set out for Montbeliard.

He found the whole town in great agitation. Several of the great in alarm, and eyeing Farel disdainfully, said, "What does this poor wretch mean? Would to God he had never come! He cannot remain here, for he would involve us all in his ruin." These nobles, who had taken refuge at Montbeliard with the duke, feared that the noise which the Reformation everywhere made would draw upon them the attention of Charles V, and Ferdinand, who would chase them from their last asylum. But Farel met with the greatest resistance from the clergy. The guardian of the Franciscans of Besançon had hastened to Montbeliard, and had formed a plan of defence with the clergy of the place. On the following Sunday, Farel had scarcely begun his sermon when they interrupted him, calling him a liar, and a heretic. Immediately the whole assembly was in a stir. They rose up, and called for silence. The duke hastened up, caused both the guardian and Farel to be apprehended, and ordered the former either to prove his accusations, or to retract them. The guardian preferred the latter

---

[1] Animum autem immutare, divinum opus est. (Œcol. Ep., p. 200.) [2] . . A quibus si pendemus, jam a Christo defecimus. (MS. Neuchatel.)

alternative, and an official report was published on the whole affair.¹

This attack aroused Farel still more. He thought himself thenceforth bound to show no delicacy in unmasking these selfish priests; and drawing the sword of the word, he dealt vigorous blows. He was more disposed to imitate Jesus, when he drove the money-changers from the temple, and overthrew their tables, than when the prophetical spirit bore this testimony to him: "*He shall not strive nor cry, neither shall any one hear his voice in the streets.*" Œcolampadius was alarmed. In these two men were perfect types of two diametrically opposite characters, and yet both worthy of admiration. "You have been sent," wrote Œcolampadius to Farel, " to draw men gently to the truth, and not to drag them with violence; to bring glad tidings, and not to curse. Physicians have recourse to amputation, only when other remedies are useless. Conduct yourself as a physician, and not as an executioner. I do not hold it enough for you to be mild towards the friends of the word. You must also gain its enemies. If the wolves are driven away from the sheepfold, let the sheep at least hear the voice of the Shepherd. Pour oil and wine into wounds, and conduct yourself as an evangelist, and not as a tyrant."²

The noise of these doings spread over France and Lorraine, and alarm began to be felt in the Sorbonne and by the Cardinal, at this union of the refugees in Basle and Montbeliard. It was wished to break up an alliance that gave uneasiness; for error knows no greater triumph than to win over deserters. Already, Martial Mazurier and others had given the Gallican papacy the joy produced by shameful defection; but if they could succeed in seducing one of these confessors of Christ, who had taken refuge on the banks of the Rhine, after having suffered much for the name of the Lord, how great a victory to the pontifical hierarchy! She accordingly prepared her batteries, and singled out the youngest as the object of attack.

The primicier, the Cardinal of Lorraine, and all who belonged to the numerous circles which met at the house of this prelate, deplored the sad fate of Peter Toussaint, who had given them so many hopes. He is at Basle, it was said, in the very house of Œcolampadius, living with one of the leaders of heresy. They wrote to him with earnestness, as if his eternal salvation had been at stake. These letters tormented the poor young man the more,

---

¹ Der Christliche Handel zu Mümpelgard, verloffen mit gründlicher Wahrheit. Quod Evangelistam, non tyrannicum, legislatorem præstes. (Ecol. Ep., p. 206.)

that he could not help seeing in them an affection which he valued.[1] One of his relations, probably the primicier himself, called upon him to go to Paris or Metz, or any place he pleased, provided it was away from the Lutherans. This relative, who was aware of all that Toussaint owed him, did not doubt that he would immediately obey his orders; and hence, when he saw his efforts unavailing, his affection was transformed into violent hatred. At the same time, this refusal on the part of the young refugee, exasperated against him all his family and all his friends. His mother, "who was under the power of the Court,"[2] was applied to. The priests surrounded her, frightened her, and persuaded her that her son had done things which could not be spoken of without horror. The mother, in despair, wrote her son a touching letter, as he expresses it, "full of tears," in which, in the most heart-rending manner, she depicted to him all her misfortunes. "Ah! wretched mother," said she, "ah! unnatural son: cursed be the breast that nursed, and the knees that bore you!"[3]

Poor Toussaint was in consternation. What was he to do? Return to France he could not. To quit Basle for Zurich or Wittemberg, out of the reach of his family, would have encreased their sorrow. Œcolampadius suggested a middle course. "Quit my house," said he.[4] He, in fact, did quit Œcolampadius, with a heart full of sadness, and went to live with an ignorant and obscure priest,[5] well fitted to restore confidence to his relations. What a change for Toussaint! It was only at table he met his host. There they ceased not to debate on matters of faith; but as soon as the meal was finished, Toussaint hastened again to shut himself up in his chamber, and there alone, free from noise and dispute, he carefully studied the word of God. "The Lord is my witness," said he, "that in this valley of tears I have only one wish, and it is to see the kingdom of Christ extended, so that all may with one mouth glorify God.[6]

One circumstance occurred which consoled Toussaint. The enemies of the gospel were always becoming stronger in Metz. At his urgent request, Chevalier d'Esch set out, in the course of January, 1525, to strengthen the evangelical Christians of that town; he crossed the forest of the Vosges, and arrived at the

---

[1] Me in dies divexari legendis amicorum litteris qui me . . . ab instituto remorari nituntur (Tossanus Farello, 2nd Sept., 1524. (MS. Neuchatel.) I am daily tormented by the letters of my friends who are striving to divert me from my purpose.   [2] Jam capulo proxima. (MS. Neuchatel.)   [3] Litteras ad me dedit plenas lacrymis quibus maledicit et uberibus quæ me lactavunt, etc. (MS. Neuchatel.)   [4] Visum est Œcolampadio consultum . . . ut a se secederem. (Ibid.)   [5] Utor domo cujusdam sacrificuli. (Ibid.)   [6] Ut Christi regnum quam latissime pateat. (Ibid.)

place where Leclerc had yielded up his life, carrying with him several books, with which he had been furnished by Farel.[1]

Lorraine was not the only quarter to which the French refugees turned their eyes. Chevalier de Coct received a letter from one of Farel's brothers, in which the state of Dauphiny was pourtrayed in the darkest colours. He took care not to show it, for fear of alarming the weak; and contented himself with praying earnestly to God, that he would give the assistance of his mighty hand.[2] In December, 1524, a messenger from Dauphiny, named Peter Verrier, charged with commissions for Farel and Anemond, arrived on horseback at Montbeliard. The Chevalier, with his usual vivacity, resolved to return to France. "If Peter has brought money," wrote he to Farel, "take it. If he has brought letters to me, open them, take a duplicate, and then send them. Nevertheless, don't sell the horse, but return it, for perhaps I may want it. I am induced to go secretly into France by the way of Jacobus Faber, (Lefevre) and Arandius. Write me your opinion."[3]

Such was the confidence between these two refugees; the one opened the letters of the other, and received his money. It is true that De Coct owed thirty-six crowns to Farel, whose purse was always open to his friends. There was more zeal than prudence in the knight's desire to return to France. He had too little prudence not to expose himself to certain death. Of this Farel doubtless convinced him. He quitted Basle and returned to a small town, where he had "great hopes of having the German language, God assisting."[4]

Farel continued to evangelise Montbeliard. His soul was vexed within him, when he saw the majority of the inhabitants addicted to the worship of images. It was, according to Farel, a renewal of the ancient idolatry of Paganism.

Meanwhile, the exhortations of Œcolampadius, and the fear of compromising the truth, might long have restrained him, but for an unforeseen circumstance. One day, towards the end of February, (it was the feast of St. Anthony) Farel was walking near the banks of a small stream which crosses the town, beneath the high rock on which the citadel stands, when, on arriving at the bridge, he met a procession, which was advancing, repeating prayers to St. Anthony, and having at its head two priests, with an image

---

[1] Let him return to Metz, where the enemies of God are daily rising against the gospel. (MS. Neuchatel. 17th Dec., 1524.) [2] Accepi ante horam a fratre tuo epistolam quam hic nulli manifestavi; terrentur enim infirmi. (Coctus Farello, 2nd Sept., 1524.) An hour ago I received a letter from your brother, which I have not shown to any one, for the weak are terrified, [3] Coct à Farel, Dec., 1524. (MS. Neuchatel. [4] Coct à Farel, Jan., 1525. (MS. Neuchatel.)

of the Saint. Farel thus found himself suddenly brought face to face with these superstitions without having sought them. A violent struggle took place in his soul. Will he give way? Will he hide himself? Would not this be cowardly unbelief? These dead images, carried on the shoulders of ignorant priests, made his blood boil. Farel came boldly forward, seized the holy hermit out of the arms of the priests, and threw it from the bridge into the river. Then, turning towards the astonished people, he exclaimed, "Poor idolaters, will you never leave off your idolatry?"[1]

The priests and the people stood still in amazement. A religious dread seemed to chain the multitude. But the stupor soon ceased. "The image is drowning," exclaimed one of the crowd, and then to stupor and silence succeeded transports and cries of fury. The crowd were going to rush on the sacrilegious man, who had thrown the object of their adoration into the water. But Farel, we know not how, escaped their rage.[2]

There is ground, we are aware, to regret, that the Reformer allowed himself to be betrayed into this act, which rather arrested the progress of the truth. No man should think himself entitled violently to attack any proceeding by public authority. Still, in the zeal of the Reformer, there is something more noble than that cold prudence so common in the world, which recoils before the least danger, and fears to make the least sacrifice for the advancement of the kingdom of God. Farel was not ignorant that he ran the risk of losing his life, like Leclerc. But the testimony of his conscience, urging him to seek only the glory of God, took away all his fears.

After the day at the bridge, a characteristic feature in Farel's history, the Reformer was obliged to conceal himself, and soon after to quit the town. He took refuge in Basle, beside Œcolampadius; but he always regarded Montbeliard with the affection which a servant of God invariably feels for the first-fruits of his ministry.[3]

At Basle, sad news awaited Farel. He was a fugitive, and his friend Anemond de Coct was seriously ill. Farel immediately sent him four gold crowns; but a letter from Oswald Myconius, of 25th March, informed him of the knight's death. "Let us live," wrote Oswald, "so as to gain the rest, into which we hope that the spirit of Anemond has already entered."[4]

---

[1] Revue du Dauphiné, tom. ii, p. 38. (MS. of Choupard.) [2] Kirchhofer, in his life of Farel, gives this as an uncertain tradition. But it is related by Protestant writers even, and seems to me, in accordance with the character of Farel and the fears of Œcolampadius. We must admit the foibles of the Reformers. [3] Ingens affectus, qui me cogit Mumpelgardum amare. (Farelli Ep.) [4] Quo Anemundi spiritum jam pervenisse speramus. (Myconius Farello. MS. Neuchatel.)

Thus Anemond, still young, full of activity, full of strength, desirous by every means to evangelise France, qualities which made him worth a host, descended to a premature grave. *God's ways are not our ways.* It was not long since, near Zurich, also, another knight, Ulric von Hutten, had breathed his last. There are some features of resemblance between the German and the French knight, but the piety and Christian virtues of the latter place him far above the witty and dauntless enemy of priests and monks.

Shortly after the death of Anemond, Farel, unable to remain at Basle, from which he had once been banished, repaired to Strasburg, to his friends, Capito and Bucer.

Thus, at Montbeliard and at Basle, as at Lyons, blows were given to the Reformation. Among the most devoted combatants some were carried off by death, others by persecution or exile. In vain did the soldiers of the gospel try all means of assault; they were everywhere repulsed. But if the forces which they had concentrated, first at Meaux, then at Lyons, and then at Basle, were successively scattered, there still remained here and there combatants who, in Lorraine, at Meaux, at Paris even, struggled more or less openly to maintain the word of God in France. If the Reformation saw its masses broken, there still remained isolated soldiers. It was against them that the Sorbonne, and the Parliament, were going to turn their rage. They wished that on the soil of France there should not remain one of the noble men who had undertaken to plant the standard of Jesus Christ, and at this time unheard of misfortunes seemed to conspire with the enemies of the Reformation, and lend them a strong hand to finish their work.

CHAP. XIV.

Francis taken at Pavia—Reaction against the Reformation—Louisa consults the Sorbonne—Commission against the Heretics—Briçonnet denounced—Appeal to the assembled Parliament — Fall — Reconciliation—Lefevre accused—Condemnation and flight—Lefevre at Strasburg—Louis de Berquin incarcerated—Erasmus attacked—Schuch at Nantz—His martyrdom—Contest with Caroli—Sadness of Pavanne—His Faggot Pile—A Christian hermit—Concourse at Nôtre-Dame.

During the latter days of Farel's residence at Montbeliard, great events had taken place on the theatre of the world. Lannoy and Pescaire, the generals of Charles V, had retreated from France on the approach of Francis I, who had passed the Alps, and proceeded to blockade Pavia. On 24th February, 1525, he was attacked by Pescaire. Bonnivet, La Tremouille, La Palisse, and

Lescure, had been slain near the king. The Duke D'Alençon, the husband of Margaret, and first prince of the blood, had fled with the rear guard, and gone to die of grief and shame at Lyons. Francis, thrown from his horse, had surrendered his sword to Charles de Lannoy, viceroy of Naples, who received it with bended knee. The king of France was the emperor's prisoner. The captivity of the king seemed the greatest of misfortunes. "Of every thing am I stript save human life," wrote the king to his mother. But no one felt a deeper grief than Margaret. The glory of her country compromised, France without a monarch, and exposed to the greatest dangers, her beloved brother the captive of his proud enemy, her husband dishonoured and dead . . . . What woes! But she had a Comforter; and while, to console her, her brother repeated, "All is lost but honour," she could say—

"But Jesus, brother, Jesus, Son of God!"[1]

France, the princes, parliament, and the people, were in consternation. Soon, as in the first centuries of the Church, the calamity which had befallen the country was imputed to the Christians, and from all quarters fanatical voices demanded blood as a means of warding off still greater misfortunes. The moment was favourable. It was not enough to have driven the evangelical Christians from the strong position which they had taken up. It was necessary to take advantage of the general terror to strike when the iron was hot; and to make this opposition, which was becoming so formidable to the papacy, a *tabula rasa* throughout the whole kingdom.

At the head of the conspiracy of these clamourers was Beda, Duchesne, and Lecouturier. These irreconcilable enemies of the gospel flattered themselves that they should easily obtain from the public terror the victims who had hitherto been refused them. They immediately set every engine at work — conversation, fanatical sermons, complaints, menaces, defamatory writings, in order to stir up the wrath of the realm, and especially of its leaders. They threw fire and flames at their opponents, and overwhelmed them with the most scurrilous abuse.[2] All means were good. They picked out some words here and there, left out what might have explained the quotation, substituted their own expressions for those of the teacher whom they impugned, and retracted or added according as they wished to blacken their adversaries.[3] This is the testimony of Erasmus himself.

[1] Les Marguerites de la Marguerite, p. i, p. 29.
[2] Plus quam scurrilibus con- viciis debacchantes . . . . (Eras. Francisco Regi, p. 1108.)
[3] Pro meis verbis supponit sua, prætermittit, addit . . . . (Ibid., p. 887.)

Nothing excited their rage so much as the fundamental doctrine of Christianity and of the Reformation — Salvation by grace. "While I see," said Beda, "three men, otherwise possessed of such penetrating genius, Lefevre, Erasmus, and Luther, uniting in a conspiracy against works of merit, and laying the whole weight of salvation on faith only,[1] I am no longer astonished that thousands of men, seduced by these doctrines, come and say, 'Why should I fast and make a martyr of my body?' Let us banish from France this odious doctrine of grace. There is in this neglect of merit a fatal delusion of the devil."

Thus the syndic of the Sorbonne attempted to combat faith. He was to find support in a debauched court, and another portion of the nation more respectable, but not less opposed to the gospel, I mean those grave men of strict morals, who, given up to the study of the law and legal forms, see in Christianity only a system of legislation in the church, only a moral police, and who, unable to reconcile the doctrine of the spiritual incapacity of man, the new birth, and justification by faith, with their engrossing ideas of jurisprudence, regard them as fantastic imaginations, dangerous to the public morals, and the prosperity of the state. This hostile tendency to the doctrine of grace was manifested in the sixteenth century by two very different extremes: in Italy and Poland by the dogmas of Socinus, of an illustrious family of lawyers in Sienna, and in France by the persecuting decrees and faggot piles of the Parliament.

Parliament, in fact, despising the great truths of the gospel which the Reformers announced, and thinking themselves obliged to do something in the fearful calamity which had befallen the nation, addressed a strong remonstrance to Louisa of Savoy on the conduct of the government in regard to the new doctrine. "Heresy," it said, "has raised its head in the midst of us; and the king, by not causing scaffolds to be erected for it, has brought down on the kingdom the wrath of heaven."

At the same time the pulpits resounded with complaints, menaces, and maledictions; prompt and exemplary punishment was demanded. Martial Mazurier held a distinguished place among the preachers of Paris, and seeking, by his violence, to make his old connections with the adherents of the Reformation to be forgotten, declaimed against the "hidden disciples of Luther. "Know you," exclaimed he, "the rapidity of this poison? Know you its strength? Ah! let us tremble for France! It acts with inconceivable energy; and in a short time can put thousands of souls to death."[2]

[1] Cum itaque cerneram tres istos .... uno animo in opera meritoria conspirasse. (Natalis Bedæ Apologia adversus clandestinos Lutheranos, f.l. 41.) [2] Mazurius contra occultos Lutheri discipulos declamat, ac recentis veneni celeritatem vimque denunciat. (Launoi, regii Navarræ gymnasii historia, p. 621.)

It was not difficult to excite the regent against the adherents of the Reformation. Her daughter Margaret, the great personages of the court, Louisa of Savoy herself,—Louisa, always so devoted to the Roman pontiff—were denounced by certain fanatics as favouring Lefevre, Berquin, and other innovators? Had she not read their tracts and translations of the Bible? The queen mother wished to clear herself of these insulting suspicions. She had already sent her confessor to the Sorbonne to ask by what means heresy might be extirpated. "The detestable doctrine of Luther," she had caused be said to the faculty, " is every day gaining new adherents." The faculty had smiled on receiving this message. Previously their representations had been refused to be listened to, and now they were humbly begged to call a council on the affair. At length they had in their power that heresy which they had long been desirous to stifle. Noel Beda was appointed to reply to the regent. The fanatical syndic did so. "Since the sermons, discussions, and books, in which we have so often opposed this heresy, have not had the effect of arresting it, an ordinance should be passed prohibiting all the writings of the heretics. Force and constraint must be employed against the *person* even of these false teachers. Those who resist the light must be subdued to it by *punishment* and *terror*.[1]

Louisa had not even waited for their answer. Scarcely had Francis I fallen into the hands of Charles V, than she had written to the pope to ask his pleasure in regard to heretics. It was of importance to the politics of Louisa to secure the favour of a pontiff who was able to raise Italy against the conqueror of Pavia, and she was ready to purchase it at the price of a little French blood. The pope, delighted at being able to exercise severity, in the kingdom of his most Christian majesty, against a heresy which he was unable to arrest either in Switzerland or Germany, immediately ordained that the inquisition should be introduced into France, and addressed a brief to the Parliament. At the same time Duprat, whom the pontiff had made a cardinal, and to whom he had given the archbishopric of Sens, and a rich abbey, sought to return the favour of the court of Rome by displaying indefatigable hatred against the heretics. Thus the pope, the regent, the doctors of the Sorbonne, the parliament, the chancellor, the ignorant and fanatical portion of the nation, all together and at once, conspired the ruin of the gospel and the death of its confessors.

The Parliament took the lead. Nothing less than the first body in the kingdom was required to carry on the campaign against this doctrine. Besides, as the public safety was concerned, was it not

[1] Histoire de L'Université, par Crevier, v, p. 196.

their business? The Parliament, then, carried away by holy zeal and fervour against these innovators,[1] issued a decree, ordaining "that the bishop of Paris, and other bishops, should be held bound to lend their assistance to Messieurs Philip Pot, President of Requests, and Andrew Verjus, Counsellor, and Messieurs William Duchesne and Nicolas Leclerc, Doctors in Theology, in framing and conducting the process against such as should be found infected with the doctrine of Luther."

"And in order that it might appear that these commissaries were more under the authority of the Christian church than the Parliament, his Holiness was pleased to send his Brief, (20th May, 1525,) approving of the said named commissioners."

"Following upon this, all who were declared Lutherans by the bishops or judges of the Church, deputed to this effect, were given over to the secular arm, that is to say, to the said Parliament, which therefor condemned them to be burnt alive."[2] So says a manuscript of the period.

Such was the dreadful inquest appointed during the captivity of Francis I, against the evangelical Christians of France, for the sake of public safety. It was composed of two laymen, and two ecclesiastics. One of the latter was Duchesne, next to Beda, the most fanatical doctor in the company. Shame had not allowed them to put their leader upon it, but his influence was thus only better secured.

Thus the machine was wound up: its springs were in good order, and every blow which it struck would be mortal. The question was, against whom should the first attack be directed? Beda, Duchesne, Leclerc, assisted by Philip Pot, president, and Andrew Verjus, counsellor, deliberated on this important question. Was there not the Count of Montbrun, the old friend of Louis XII, the ex-ambassador to Rome, Briçonnet, bishop of Meaux? The Committee of public safety met at Paris, in 1525, thought that by beginning with a man of his high rank, they would be sure to spread terror over the kingdom. This reason was sufficient, and this venerable bishop was served with a charge.

Far from allowing himself to be intimidated by the persecution of 1523, Briçonnet had persisted, as well as Lefevre, in opposing the popular superstitions. The more eminent his place in the Church and in the State, the more fatal his example, and therefore the more necessary to obtain from him a striking recantation, or inflict a blow more striking still. The committee of inquest

---

[1] De la Religion Chretienne en France, par de Lezeau. MS. Bibliotheque St. Genevieve á Paris. [2] The Manuscript of the Library of St. Genevieve at Paris, from which I have taken this fragment, bears the name of Lezeau, but in the catalogue it bears that of Lefevre.

hastened to collect the charges against him. They stated the
kind reception which the bishop had given to heretics—that eight
days after the guardian of the Cordeliers had preached at Meaux in
the church of St. Martin, conformably to the instructions of the
Sorbonne, to reestablish sound doctrine, Briçonnet himself had
mounted the pulpit, had replied to him, and treated the preacher
and the other cordeliers, his colleagues, as false prophets and
hypocrites. Not content with this public affront, he had made
his official prepare a charge, summoning the guardian to appear in person.[1] .... It would even appear from a manuscript of the time, that the bishop had gone still farther, and that
in the autumn of 1524, accompanied by Lefevre of Etaples, he
had travelled, during three months, over his diocese, and burnt
all the images except the crucifix. This bold procedure, which
would show that Briçonnet combined great hardihood with much
humility, cannot, if it is true, subject him to the blame attached
to other destroyers of images. When he reformed these superstitions, he was at the head of the Church, and acted within the
sphere of his rights and duties.[2]

Be this as it may, Briçonnet was to have guilt enough in the
eyes of the enemies of the gospel. He had not only attacked the
Church in general, he had attacked the Sorbonne itself, that company whose supreme law was its own glory and preservative. Accordingly it was delighted on hearing of the inquest directed against
its enemy. John Bochart, one of the most celebrated advocates of
the time supporting the charge against Briçonnet before the Parliament, exclaimed, raising his voice "Against the Faculty, neither
bishop of Meaux, nor any other individual, can raise the head or
open the mouth. Neither is the Faculty under any obligation to
go and dispute, to carry and state its reasons before the said
bishop, who must not resist the wisdom of this holy company,
which he must consider to be aided by God."[3]

In consequence of this requisition, the Parliament, on the 3rd
Oct., 1525, issued a decree in which, after ordering the personal
apprehension of all those who were specified, it ordained that the
bishop should be interrogated by James Menager and Andrew

[1] Hist. de L' Université, par Crevier, v, p. 204. [2] In the library of the pastors of Neuchatel there is a letter of Sebville containing the following passage:—" I notify to you that the bishop of Meaux, in Brie, near Paris, *cum Jacobo Fabro stapulensi*, three months ago in visiting the bishopric, burnt *actu* all the images except the crucifix, and are personally summoned to Paris, the month of March next, to answer *coram suprema curia et universitate.*" I am rather inclined to think this fact authentic, though Sebville was not on the spot, and neither Mezeray, Daniel, nor Maimbourg, speaks of it. These Roman Catholics, who are very brief, might, besides, have motives for passing it in silence, considering the issue of the process. Besides, Sebville's statement agrees with all the facts known to us. The matter is doubtful.

[3] Crevier Hist. de L'Université, v, p. 204.

Verjus, counsellors of the court, on the facts with which he was charged.[1]

This decree of the Parliament terrified the bishop. Briçonnet, ambassador at Rome to two kings—Briçonnet a bishop and prince, the friend of Louis XII and Francis I, about to be subjected to the interrogatives of two counsellors of the court . . . . He who had hoped that God would kindle in the heart of the king, his mother, and his sister, a flame which would communicate itself to all the kingdom, saw the kingdom turning against himself, in order to extinguish the flame which he had received from heaven. The king is a prisoner, his mother is moving at the head of the enemies of the gospel, and Margaret, dismayed at the disasters which have fallen on France, dares not turn aside the blows which are going to strike her dearest friends, and first of all that spiritual father who has so often consoled her; or if she dares, she has not the power. Recently she had written Briçonnet a letter full of pious ejaculations—" Oh may the poor dead heart feel some spark of the love in which it longs to burn to ashes!"[2] Now there was literally a question of being burnt to ashes. This mystic language was now out of place. He who would confess his faith, must brave the scaffold. The poor bishop, who had hoped so much to see an evangelical Reformation spread gradually, and peacefully, was in fear and trembling when he saw that it must now be purchased at the expence of life. The dreadful thought, perhaps, had never before occurred to him, and he started back in anguish and dismay.

Briçonnet, however, had still a hope that he would be permitted to appear before the assembled Chambers of Parliament, this being due to a personage of his rank, and in that august and numerous court he would find (he was sure of it) generous hearts, who would understand his language, and undertake his defence. He accordingly petitioned the court to grant him this indulgence. But his enemies had likewise foreseen what the issue of such an audience might be. Had not Luther been seen at Worms before the Germanic Diet, shaking the most resolute hearts? Eager to keep away every chance of escape, they did their work so well, that the Parliament, by a decree of the 25th Oct., 1525, confirming the former one, refused Briçonnet's application.[3]

Here, then, was the bishop of Meaux sent away, like the most obscure priest, before Masters James Menager and Andrew Verjus. These two lawyers, docile instruments of the Sorbonne, could not be moved by the elevated views to which the whole chamber might have been sensible. They were matter of fact men. Has

---

[1] Maimbourg Hist. du Calvinisme, p. 14. No. 337. [3] Maimbourg Hist. du Calv. p. 15.   [2] MS. Biblioth. Royale, S. F.

the bishop been, or has he not been, at variance with the Company?
This was all they asked. Briçonnet's condemnation was therefore
certain.

While the sword was thus suspended by the Parliament over the
head of the bishop, the monks, priests, and doctors, were not losing
their time. They perceived that a recantation by Briçonnet would
serve their purpose better even than his execution. His death
would inflame all those who shared his faith: but his apostacy
would be a very great discouragement. To work, then! He was
visited and urged. Martial Mazurier in particular laboured to
make him fall, as he had fallen himself, and he was not without
arguments which might seem specious to Briçonnet. Was he
willing to leave his place? Might he not, by remaining in the
Church, use his influence over the king and the Court, to do good of
which it was impossible to foresee the extent? What would become
of his old friends, when he was no longer in power? How much
might his resistance compromise a reform which, in order to
be salutary and durable, must operate by the legitimate influence
of the clergy! How many would be shocked by his resistance to
the Church, how many, on the contrary, should he attract by yielding! . . . There was a wish like his own for reform. Everything
was insensibly leading to it. At court, in the city, in the provinces,
everywhere, there was an advance. Could he feel glad at heart,
while annihilating this fair prospect! . . . . In reality he was not
asked for any sacrifice of doctrine, but only to submit to the order
established in the Church. Was it well, when France was overwhelmed with so many disasters, to stir up new troubles? "In
the name of religion, in the name of your country, in the name of
your friends, in the name of the Reformation itself—yield." By
such sophisms, the noblest causes are lost.

Meanwhile every one of these words made some impression on
the bishop. The tempter, who would have made our Saviour fall
in the desert, presented himself under specious forms, and Briçonnet, instead of exclaiming with his Master, " Get thee behind me,
Satan," listened, received, weighed these discourses. After this it
was all over with his fidelity.

Briçonnet had never, like a Farel or a Luther, entered fully into the movement which was then regenerating the Church. There
was in him a certain mystical tendency, which enfeebles the mind,
and deprives it of the firmness and courage which a faith founded
on the word of God alone can give. The cross, which he behoved
to take up in order to follow Jesus Christ, was too heavy.[1] Shaken,
frightened, stupified, distracted,[2] he tottered and stumbled over

[1] Crucis statim oblatæ terrore perculsus. (Bezæ Icones.) (Ibid.)
[2] Dementatut.

the stone which was craftily thrown in the way . . . He fell. Instead of throwing himself into the arms of Jesus Christ, he threw himself into those of Mazurier,[1] and by a shameful recantation sullied the glory of a noble fidelity.[2]

Thus fell Briçonnet, the friend of Lefevre and of Margaret: thus the first supporter of the gospel in France, denied the glad tidings of grace in the guilty thought, that if he remained faithful to them, he would lose his influence on the Church, the Court, and France. But what was presented to him as the salvation of his country, became, perhaps, its ruin. What would have happened if Briçonnet had had the courage of a Luther? If one of the first bishops of France, dear to the king, dear to the people, had mounted the scaffold, and had there, like the little ones in the estimation of the world, sealed the truth of the gospel by a courageous confession, and a Christian death, might not France have been moved, and the blood of the bishop of Meaux, becoming like that of the Polycarps and Cyprians, the seed of the Church, might not those countries, so illustrious in so many respects, have been seen emerging from the long spiritual darkness in which they are still plunged?

Briçonnet, as a matter of form, underwent the interrogatory before Masters James Menager and Andrew Verjus, who declared that he had sufficiently exculpated himself from the crime with which he was charged. He was then brought to repentance, and assembled a synod in which he condemned the books of Luther, retracted all that he had taught contrary to the doctrine of the Church, reestablished the worship of saints, laboured to bring back those who had abandoned the worship of Rome, and wishing to leave no doubt as to his reconciliation with the pope and the Sorbonne, he, on the eve of Corpus Christi, held a solemn fast, and ordered a pompous procession, in which he appeared in person, giving pledges of his faith, by his magnificence and all sorts of devotion.[3]

Briçonnet is, perhaps, the most celebrated instance of backsliding which the Reformation presents. Nowhere do we see a man so far engaged in the Reformation, and so sincerely pious, turn so suddenly against it. Still it is necessary to form a distinct idea both of his character and his fall. Briçonnet was on the side of Rome, and Lefevre was on the side of the Reformation. They are both of the *juste-milieu*, and properly do not belong to any of the two parties, but the one is of the *centre-droit*, the other of the *centre-gauche*. The doctor of Etaples inclines towards the Word, the bishop of Meaux towards the Hierarchy; and when these two men

---

[1] Ut episcopus etiam desisteret suis consiliis effecit. (Launoi, Regii Navarræ Gymnasii Hist., p. 621.) [2] Nisi turpi palinodia gloriam hanc omnem ipse sibi invidisset. (Bezæ Icones.) [3] Mezeray, ii, p. 981. Daniel, v, p. 644. Moreri, article Briçonnet.

who approximate each other are obliged to decide, the one arrays himself with Rome, and the other with Jesus Christ. At the same time we cannot believe that Briçonnet was altogether faithless to the convictions of his faith. Even after his recantation the Roman doctors never had full confidence in him. He acted as did, at a later period, the bishop of Cambray, to whom he has more than one feature of resemblance. He thought he could submit externally to the pope, while he continued inwardly subject to the Divine Word. This is a weakness incompatible with the principles of the Reformation. Briçonnet was one of the heads of the mystic, or quietest school in France, and we know that one of its first principles always was to accommodate itself to the church in which it happened to be, be that church what it might.

The guilty fall of Briçonnet went to the heart of his old friends, and was the sad forerunner of those deplorable apostacies which, in another age, the spirit of the world so often obtained in France. This personage who, in regard to the Reformation, seemed to hold the reins in his hand, was suddenly thrown out of the chariot, and the Reformation was thenceforth to pursue its course in France without head, without human guide, in humility and obscurity. But the disciples of the gospel raised their head, and thenceforth looked with still firmer faith to the heavenly head whose fidelity they knew could not be shaken.

The Sorbonne triumphed: a great stride had been made towards the annihilation of the Reformation in France. It was necessary to hasten without longer delay to another victory. Lefevre was the first after Briçonnet. Accordingly Beda had immediately directed his attacks against this distinguished teacher, by publishing against him a book containing such gross calumnies, that, as Erasmus expresses it, "Smiths and cobblers might have pointed to them with their finger." What especially excited his wrath was the doctrine of justification by faith, which Lefevre had first proclaimed in Christendom. This was the point to which Beda incessantly returned, the article which, according to him, subverted the Church. "What!" said he, "Lefevre affirms that whosoever ascribes to himself the power of obtaining salvation, will perish, while he who, divesting himself of all strength, throws himself entirely into the arms of Jesus Christ, will be saved. . . . Oh! what heresy thus to preach the impotence of merit. . . . . What infernal error! what pernicious doctrine of the devil! Let us oppose it with all our might!"[1]

The doctor of Etaples was immediately subjected to the perse-

---

[1] Perpendens perniciosissimam demonis fallaciam. . . . . Occurri quantum valui. (Nat. Bedæ Apolog. adv. Lutheranos, fol. 42.)

cutting machinery which produced retraction or death. They hoped to see Lefevre sharing the fate either of the poor wool-carder Leclerc, or of the distinguished bishop Briçonnet. His accusation was soon drawn up, and a decree of the Parliament, (28th Aug., 1525,) condemned nine propositions drawn from his Commentaries on the Gospel, and classed his translation of the Holy Scriptures among the prohibited books.[1]

This was only the prelude. Of this the learned doctor was aware. From the first symptom of persecution he had felt that, in the absence of Francis I, he would fall under the attacks of his enemies, and that the moment was come to observe the command of the Lord, "*When they persecute you in this city, flee ye into another.*"[2] Lefevre quitted Meaux, where, since the fall of the bishop, he had drunk bitterness, and seen all his activity paralysed, and withdrawing from his persecutors, he shook off the dust of his feet against them, "not to wish them any ill, but as a sign of the ills which await them, for he says somewhere, in the same way, as this dust is shaken from our feet, are they shaken from the face of the Lord."[3]

The persecutors had missed their victim, but they consoled themselves with thinking that France, at least, was delivered from the parent of heretics.

Lefevre, a fugitive, arrived under a borrowed name at Strasburg. He at once frankly joined the friends of the Reformation. How great his joy at hearing that gospel publicly taught, which he had been the first to bring forward in the Church. "Here is my faith!" This, indeed, was what he had wished to be able to say. Gerard Roussel, one of those evangelical men, who, like the doctor of Etaples, did not attain to a complete emancipation, had, also like him, been obliged to quit France. They, together, attended the lectures of Capito and Bucer;[4] with these faithful teachers they had special interviews;[5] and the rumour even spread that they had been sent for this purpose by Margaret, the king's sister.[6] But reverence for the ways of the Lord, occupied Lefevre more than polemics. Turning his eye upon Christendom, filled with astonishment at the great things which were then taking place, his heart stirred with gratitude and full of expectation, he fell on his knees, and prayed the Lord "to perfect what he then saw commencing."[7]

A joyful meeting awaited him at Strasburg. His son Farel,

---

[1] J. Lelong Biblioth. Sacrée, 2nd part, p. 44.   [2] Matth., x, 14, 23.   [3] Quod excussi sunt a facie Domini sicut pulvis ille excussus est a pedibus. (Faber in Ev. Matth., p. 40.)   [4] Faber stapulensis et Gerardus Rufus, clam e Gallia profecti, Capitonem et Bucerum audierunt. (Melch. Adam. Vita Capitonis, p. 90.)   [5] De omnibus doctrinæ præcipuis locis cum ipsis disseruerint. (Ibid.)   [6] Missi a Margaretha regis Francisci sorore. (Ibid.)   [7] Farel à Tous Seigneurs, Peuples, et Pasteurs.)

whom persecution had separated from him for nearly three years, had arrived there before him. The old doctor of the Sorbonne found in this young pupil a man in the full vigour of life, a Christian in the full energy of faith. Farel respectfully clasped the wrinkled hand which had guided his first steps, and felt an undescribable joy in again finding his father in an evangelical town, and in seeing him surrounded with believing men. They together attended the pure lessons of illustrious teachers; they communicated at the Lord's Supper, administered agreeably to the institution of Jesus Christ, and received touching evidence of the charity of their brethren. "Do you remember," said Farel to him, "what you once said to me when we were both plunged in darkness?" "William, God will renovate the world, and you shall see it . . . Here is the commencement of what you then spoke to me." "Yes," replied the old man. "Yes, God is renewing the world. O, my son! continue boldly to preach the holy gospel of Jesus Christ."[1]

Lefevre, doubtless from an excess of prudence, wished to remain at Strasburg *incognito*, and had taken the name of Anthony Peregrine, while Roussel took that of Solnin. But the illustrious old man could not be concealed. The whole town, even the very children, soon bowed respectfully to the old French doctor.[2] He did not live by himself, but at the house of Capito, with Farel, Roussel, Vedaste, whom every body praised for his modesty, and one Simon, a recent Jewish convert. The houses of Capito, Œcolampadius, Zninglius, and Luther, were thus a kind of inns. Such was the strength of brotherly love in those times. There were many other Frenchmen in this town on the banks of the Rhine, and they here formed a church, in which Farel often preached the doctrine of salvation. This Christian society alleviated their exile.

While these brethren thus enjoyed the asylum which brotherly charity had opened to them, those who were at Paris or in other parts of France, were exposed to great dangers. Briçonnet had recanted—Lefevre had left. This, doubtless, was something to the Sorbonne; but they were still waiting for the punishments which they had advised. . . . There was an individual who irritated them still more than Briçonnet and Lefevre. This was Louis de Berquin. The gentleman of Artois, of a more decided character than his two masters, let no opportunity pass of assailing the theologians and monks, and unmasking their fanaticism.

[1] Quod et pius senex fatebatur: meque hortabatur pergerem in annuntiatione sacri Evangelii. (Farellus Pellicano Hotting. H. L. vi, p. 17.) [2] Nam latere cupiunt et tamen pueris noti sunt. (Capito Zwing. Ep., p. 439.) For they would be hid, and yet the children know them.

Residing by turns at Paris and in the country, he collected the works of Erasmus and Luther, and translated them.[1] He also himself composed controversial writings. In short, he defended and propagated the new doctrines with all the zeal of a new convert. He was denounced by the bishop of Amiens. Beda supported the complaint; and the parliament caused him to be thrown into prison. "This one," it is said, "will not escape like Briçonnet or Lefevre." In fact, he was kept under bars and bolts. In vain did the prior of the Carthusians, and others besides, implore him to offer an apology. He declared distinctly that he would not yield in a single point. "Then," says a chronicler, "it seemed that nothing remained but to take him to the fire."[2]

Margaret, in consternation at what had happened, trembled at the thought of seeing Berquin dragged to the scaffold, which the bishop had so disgracefully escaped. She dared not to penetrate into his prison; but she tried to send him some words of consolation; and it may have been for him the princess made the touching complaint of the prisoner, when addressing the Lord, he exclaims—

> Oh! surety, safety, access, refuge sure
> Of the afflicted, Judge of the orphan-poor,
> Treasure of consolations that endure !
> These bars of iron, draw-bridge, portal gate,
> By which I here am held in sad estate,
> Exclude all friends who sorrow at my fate ;
> But here or there, where'er my prison be,
> No bar, no lock, can keep me far from thee,
> For by my side thou art perpetually.[3]

But Margaret did not confine herself to this. She immediately wrote to her brother, soliciting him to interfere in Berquin's behalf; happy if she could in time deliver him from the hatred of his enemies.

While waiting for their victim, Beda resolved to make the enemies of the Sorbonne and the monks tremble, by humbling the most celebrated of them. Erasmus had attacked Luther; but no matter. If they succeed in destroying Erasmus, à fortiori, the ruin of Farel, Luther, and their associates, will be inevitable. The surest way of striking an object is to take aim beyond it. When once a foot was on the neck of the philosopher of Rotterdam, who should escape the vengeance of Rome? Already, Lecouturier, commonly called, from the translation of his name into Latin, Sutor, had taken the first step by launching at Erasmus from his solitary Carthusian cell a most violent philippic in which he called

---

[1] Erasm. Ep., p. 923. [2] Actes des Martyrs, p. 103. [3] Marguerites de la Marguerite, i, p. 445.

his opponents theologasters and little asses, and imputed to them scandals, heresies, and blasphemies. Handling subjects, which he did not at all understand, he reminded one, says Erasmus cuttingly, of the old adage, "*Ne sutor ultra crepidam.* Let the cobbler only mend his shoes."

Beda hastened to the support of his colleague. He told Erasmus not to write any more,[1] and himself taking the pen, which he ordered the first writer of the age to lay down, he made a selection of all the calumnies which the monks had invented against the distinguished philosopher, translated them into French, and made a book of them, which he circulated at Court, and in the city, trying to arouse all France against him.[2] This book was the signal of attack. From all quarters an assault was made on Erasmus. Nicholas d'Ecmond, an old Carmelite of Lorraine, every time he mounted the pulpit, exclaimed, "There is no difference between Erasmus and Luther, unless it be that Erasmus is the greater heretic;"[3] and wherever the Carmelite was, at table, travelling by land or water, he called Erasmus a heresiarch and falsifier.[4] The faculty of Paris, moved by these brawlers, prepared a censure of this illustrious author.

Erasmus was in consternation. Such, then, is the result of all his management, and even of his hostility against Luther. More than any other had he placed himself in the breach; and it was now wished to treat him like a stepping-stone, and trample him under foot, the more readily to reach the common enemy. He revolts at the thought. He suddenly wheels round, and has no sooner attacked Luther in front, than he turns on the fanatical doctors, who had struck him from behind. Never was his correspondence more active. Looking all around him, his quick eye immediately discovers in what hands his lot is placed. He hesitates not. He will carry his complaints and cries to the foot of the Sorbonne, the parliament, the king, the emperor himself. Addressing those of the theologians of the Sorbonne, from whom he still hoped for some impartiality, he says, "Who has caused this immense fire of Luther? who has stirred it up but Beda with his violence?[5] In war, a soldier who has behaved well, receives reward from his generals; but all the reward I am to receive from you, the generals of the war, is a book of calumnies by the Bedas and the Lecouturiers!"

"What!" he wrote to the parliament of Paris, "I was combating

---

[1] Primum jubet ut desinam scribere. (Erasm. Ep., p. 921.) First he tells me I must give over writing. [2] Ut totam Galliam in me concitaret. (Erasm. Ep., p. 886.) [3] Nisi quod Erasmus esset major hæreticus. (Ibid., p. 915.) [4] Quoties in conviciis, in vehiculis, in navibus. (Ibid.) [5] Hoc gravissimum Lutheri incendium, unde natum, unde hac progressum, nisi ex Beddaicis intemperiis. (Erasm. Ep., p. 887.)

these Lutherans, and while fighting a fierce battle by orders of the emperor, the pope, and other princes, to the peril even of my life, Lecouturier and Beda attack me from behind with furious libels. Ah! had not fortune carried off from us king Francis, I would have besought that avenger of the muses against this new invasion of the barbarians.[1] But now it is for you to lay an arrest on this injustice! . . . ."

No sooner did he descry the possibility of getting a letter to reach the king, than he wrote him also. His penetrating eye could see in those fanatical doctors of the Sorbonne the germs of the league—the predecessors of those three priests who were one day to establish the *sixteen* against the last of the Valois. His genius gave a prediction to the king of the crimes and misfortunes which his descendants were to know but too well. "They put faith in front," said he; "but they aim at tyranny, even over princes. They march with a sure step, though under ground. Should the prince refuse to be at their beck in every thing, they will forthwith declare, that he may be deposed by the Church, that is, by some false monks and some false theologians, conspiring against the public peace."[2] Erasmus, in writing to Francis I, could not have touched a better string.

Lastly, to make still more sure of escaping from his enemies, Erasmus invoked the protection of Charles V himself. "Invincible emperor," said he, "men who, under pretext of religion, wish to procure a triumph for their belly and their despotism,[3] are raising horrible clamour against me. I fight under your banners, and those of Jesus Christ. Let your wisdom, and your power give peace to the Christian world. . . . ."

Thus the prince of literature made application to all the great ones of the world. The danger was averted from his head; the princes of the world interposed, and the vultures were obliged to abandon a prey which they already thought within their talons. They then turned their eyes in another direction, seeking other victims, and did not miss them.

It was in Lorraine that blood was first again to flow. From the first days of the Reformation there was a copartnery of zeal between Paris and the country of the Guises. If Paris reposed, Lorraine set to work, and then Paris began anew, waiting till new supplies reached Nancy or Metz. The first blows seemed to fall

---

[1] Musarum vindicem adversus barbarorum incursiones. (Ibid., p. 2070.) [2] Nisi princeps ipsorum voluntati per omnia paruerit, dicetur fautor haereticorum et destitui poterit per ecclesiam. (Ibid., p. 1118.) If the prince do not in all things comply with their wishes it will be said he is a favourer of heretics, and may be deposed by the church. [3] Simulato religionis prætextu ventris tyrannidisque suæ, negotium agentes. (Ibid., p. 962.)

upon an excellent man, one of the refugees of Basle, a friend of Farel and Toussaint. At Metz, the Chevalier d'Esch had been unable to escape the suspicions of the priests. It being known that he was connected with the evangelical Christians, he was made prisoner at Pont-à-Mousson, five miles from Metz, on the banks of the Moselle.[1] This news caused great grief to the French refugees, and also to the Swiss themselves. "O, heart, full of innocence!" exclaimed Œcolampadius. "I have confidence in the Lord, that he will preserve this man for us, whether in life to announce his name as a preacher of righteousness, or in death to confess him as a martyr."[2] But, at the same time, Œcolampadius disapproved of the vivacity, the impetuosity, the zeal, in his opinion zeal without prudence, which distinguished the French refugees. "I wish," said he, that my dear French lords would not hasten to return into their country until they have carefully examined all things, for the devil is everywhere laying his snares. Nevertheless, may they obey the Spirit of Christ, and may this Spirit never abandon them."[3]

In fact, there was ground to tremble for the chevalier's fate. There was double hatred in Lorraine. Friar Bonaventure Renel, provincial of the cordeliers, confessor of Duke Anthony the Good, a forward man of indifferent morals, allowed this feeble prince, who reigned from 1508 to 1544, great liberty in his pleasures, and persuaded him, almost as a kind of penance, to destroy all innovators without mercy. This prince, so well counselled by Renel, used often to say, "It is enough for each to know the Pater and Ave-Maria; the greatest doctors are the cause of the greatest troubles."[4]

Towards the end of 1524 it was learned at the court of the Duke, that a pastor named Schuch was preaching a new doctrine in the town of Saint-Hippolyte, situated at the foot of the Vosges. "Let them return to order," said Anthony *the Good;* "if not, I march against the town and fill every place with fire and blood."[5]

The faithful pastor resolved to sacrifice himself for his sheep; he repaired to Nancy, where the prince resided. Immediately on his arrival, he was cast into a pestilential prison, under the guard of coarse and cruel men. Friar Bonaventure then, at length, saw the heretic in his prison. He presided at the inquest, and addressed him as "Heretic! Judas! Devil!" Schuch, calm and collected, made no answer to those insults; but holding in his hand his Bible, all covered with notes which he had written in it,

---

[1] Noster captus detinetur in Bundamosa quinque millibus a Metis. (Œcol. Farello Ep., p. 201.) [2] Vel vivum confessorem, vel mortuum martyrem servabit. (Ibid. [3] Nollem carissimos dominos meos Gallos properare in Galliam. (Ibid.) [4] Actes des Martyrs, p. 97. [5] Ibid., p. 95.

he meekly and forcibly confessed Jesus Christ crucified. Suddenly becoming animated, he stood up boldly, raised his voice, as if under an impulse from the Spirit above, and looking the judges in the face, denounced to them dreadful judgments from God.

Friar Bonaventure and his companions, amazed and transported with rage, rushed upon him with loud cries, tore the Bible, in which he read his denunciations, out of his hands; and, like mad dogs, says the chronicler, " unable to gnaw at his doctrine, they burnt it in their convent."[1]

The whole court of Lorraine rung with the obstinacy and audacity of the minister of St. Hippolyte, and the Prince, curious to hear the heretic, resolved to be present at his last appearance; but, in secret, concealed from every eye. The interrogatories having been put in Latin, he could not comprehend them; but he was struck at seeing the minister with a firm countenance, apparently neither vanquished nor astonished. Anthony the Good, astonished at this obstinacy, rose up, and, on going away, said, " Why debate any more? He denies the sacrament of the mass; let sentence be pronounced upon him."[2] Schuch was immediately condemned to be burnt alive. On learning his sentence, he raised his eyes to heaven, and said calmly, " I was glad when they said unto me, Let us go into the house of the Lord."[3]

On the 19th of August, the whole town of Nancy was in movement. The bells were ringing the death of a heretic. The sad procession began to move. The road lay in front of the convent of the Cordeliers, who, joyous, and on the alert, had met at the gate. At the moment when Schuch appeared, father Bonaventure, pointing to the images sculptured on the front of the convent, exclaimed, " Heretic, give honour to God, his mother, and the saints!"—"O, hypocrites!" replied Schuch, looking up at those pieces of wood and stone, " God will destroy you, and bring your impostures to light. . . . ."

The martyr having arrived at the place of execution, the first thing done was to burn his books in his presence; then he was summoned to recant, but he refused, saying, " Thou, O God, hast called me, and will confirm me unto the end."[4] He then began to repeat, aloud, the fifty-first Psalm, " Have mercy upon me, O God! according to thy loving kindness." After mounting the scaffold, he continued to repeat the psalm, until the smoke and flames choked his voice.

---

[1] Actes des Martyrs, p. 97. [2] Gaillard Hist. de François I, iv. p. 233. [3] Psalm cxxii. 1. [4] Eum auctorem vocationis suæ atque conservatorem ad extremum usque spiritum recognovit. (Acta Mart., p. 202.) Him he acknowledged even to the last breath as the author and preserver of his country.

Thus, the persecutors of France and Lorraine saw their triumphs again begun. At length attention was paid to their advice. The heretical ashes thrown to the winds at Nancy, were a challenge to the capital of France. What! Were Beda and Lecouturier to be the last to show their zeal for the pope? Let flames answer flames, and soon let heresy, swept from the soil of the kingdom, be driven entirely beyond the Rhine!

Before succeeding, Beda had to fight a battle half in earnest, half in mockery, with one of those men with whom the struggle with the papacy is only a game of intellect, not a matter of the heart.

Among the learned men whom Briçonnet had drawn into his diocese, was a doctor of Sorbonne, named Peter Caroli, a vain, giddy man, as full of bluster and chicanery as Beda himself. Caroli saw in the new doctrine the means of producing an effect, and of thwarting Beda, whose ascendancy he could not endure. Accordingly, on his return from Meaux to Paris, he made a great sensation by carrying into all the pulpits what was called "The new mode of preaching." An incessant struggle now commenced between the two doctors. It was blow for blow, and wile for wile. Beda summons Caroli before the Sorbonne, and Caroli, to repay the honour hands him over to the Officiality. The faculty proceeds with its inquest, and Caroli intimates an appeal to the Parliament. He is interdicted from taking his turn in the chair, and he preaches in all the churches of Paris. He is expressly excluded from all the pulpits, and he publicly expounds the Psalms in the college of Cambray. The faculty prohibits him to continue this exercise, and he asks permission to finish the exposition of the twenty-second Psalm, which he had commenced. At length his request is refused, and he placards the college gates with the following notice : . "*Peter Caroli, desirous to obey the orders of the sacred faculty, ceases to teach. He will resume his lectures, (when it shall please God,) at the verse where he stopped:* THEY PIERCED MY HANDS AND MY FEET." Thus Beda had at last found his match. Had Caroli defended the truth in earnest, the fire would soon have done him justice; but he had too profane a spirit to be put to death. How was it possible to execute a man who put his judges out of countenance? Neither the Officiality, nor the Parliament, nor the Council, could ever judge his cause definitively. Two men like Caroli, would have worn out the activity of a Beda; but the Reformation did not see two.[1]

This annoying contest ended, Beda set himself to more serious affairs. Happily for the syndic of Sorbonne there were men who

---

[1] Gerdesius, Historia sæculi xvi, renovati, p. 52. D'Argentré, Collectio Judiciorum de novis erroribus, ii, p. 21. Gaillard Hist. de Francois 1er. iv, p. 238.

furnished better subjects for persecution than Caroli. It is true, Briçonnet, Erasmus, Lefevre, and Berquin, had escaped him; but since he cannot reach great personages, he will content himself with humble ones. The poor youth, James Pavanne, since his abjuration at Christmas, 1524, had always been sighing and weeping. He was seen with a melancholy air, his eye fixed on the ground, inwardly groaning, and keenly reproaching himself for having denied his Saviour and his God.[1]

Pavanne was no doubt one of the most modest and inoffensive of men. But no matter. He had been at Meaux at this time; no more was required. The cry was raised, "Pavanne has relapsed: *The dog has returned to his vomit, and the sow that was washed, to her wallowing in the mire.*" He was forthwith seized, cast into prison, and taken before the judges. This was the very thing that young Master James longed for. He felt comforted so soon as he was in irons, and recovered strength to make a full confession of Jesus Christ.[2] The cruel smiled to see that this time nothing could deprive them of their victim: no recantation, no flight, no powerful protector. Neither the mildness of the young man, nor his candour and courage, nothing could soften his adversaries. He looked at them with love: for, in throwing him into chains, they had restored him his tranquillity and joy. But this tender look only hardened their heart the more. His accusation was quickly drawn up, and the Place de Grève soon saw a scaffold erected, on which Pavanne died joyfully, by his example strengthening all who in this great city openly or secretly believed in the gospel of Jesus Christ.

This was not enough for the Sorbonne. If those in humble life are sacrificed, quality must be redeemed by number. The flames of the Place de Grève have spread terror over Paris and France; but a new pile, kindled in some other place, will double the terror. It will be spoken of at court, in colleges, and the workshops of the people. Such examples will show better than all edicts, that Louisa of Savoy, the Sorbonne, and the Parliament, are determined to sacrifice every remaining heretic to the anathemas of Rome.

In the forest of Livry, three leagues from Paris, not far from the place where stood the ancient abbey of the Augustins, lived a hermit, who, having met in his wanderings with some individuals from Meaux, had received the gospel into his heart.[3] The poor

---

[1] Animi factum suum detestantis dolorem, sæpe declaraverit. (Acta Mart., p. 203.)
[2] Puram religionis Christianæ confessionem add t. (Ibid.) [3] The seed of Faber and his disciples, taken from the granary of Luther, budded in the foolish mind of a hermit who lived near the town of Paris. (Hist. Catholique de notre temps par

hermit had found himself very rich in his retirement, when one day, along with his coarse loaf, which public charity gave him, he had brought back with him Jesus Christ and his grace. Thereupon he understood how it was better to give than receive. He went from house to house in the surrounding villages, and had no sooner opened the doors of the poor peasants, whom he visited in their humble huts, than he spoke to them of the gospel, of the complete pardon which it gave to agonised souls, and which was better than absolutions.[1] The good hermit of Livry was soon known in the environs of Paris. He was sought after in his poor hermitage, and became a gentle and fervent missionary to the poor of the district.

A report of the doings of the new evangelist were not long of reaching the ears of the Sorbonne and the tribunals of Paris. The hermit was apprehended, dragged from his hermitage, from his forest, and from the places which he daily traversed, thrown into a dungeon in the great city which he had always shunned, there tried, convicted, and condemned to be "exemplarily punished with the punishment of slow fire."[2]

It was resolved, in order to make the example more striking that he should be burnt alive in the square of Notre Dame, in front of this celebrated basilisk and majestic symbol of Roman Catholicism. The whole clergy assembled, and great pomp was displayed as on the most solemn festivals.[3] The wish would have been to assemble all Paris around this pile, "the great bell of the temple of Notre Dame, ringing," says a historian, "with full peal, to warn the whole people of the town."[4] In fact, the people thronged into the square through all the streets that opened into it. The deep tones of the bell arrested the workman in his shop, the scholar in his studies, the merchant in his traffic, and the soldier in his idleness. The whole square was already filled by an immense crowd, while the people still kept flocking. The hermit arrayed in the clothing assigned to obstinate heretics, his head and feet bare, had been brought before the gates of the cathedral. Calm, firm, and collected, his only answer to the exhortations of the confessors, who presented the crucifix to him, was to declare, that his hope was solely in the pardon of God. The doctors of the Sorbonne, who were in the front seat of the spectators, seeing his constancy, and the effect which it produced upon the people, cried aloud, "He is damned: they are taking him to hell fire."[5]

Meanwhile the large bell continued to peal, and its sounds, stun-

---

[1] Who, in the village which he frequented, under colour of asking alms, held heretical discourses. (Hist. Catholique de notre temps par S. Fontaine, Paris, 1562.)
[2] Ibid. [3] With great ceremony. (Histoire des Egl. Ref.par Theod. de Beza, l, p. 4.) [4] Ibid. [5] Ibid.

ning the ears of the people, increased the solemnity of this sad festival. At last the bell was silent, and the martyr having replied to the last questions of his enemies, that he wished to die in the faith of the Lord Jesus Christ, was, as his sentence bore, "burnt with a slow fire." Thus died peacefully on the pavement of Notre Dame, amid the shouts and agitation of a whole people, under the towers reared by the piety of Louis the Young, one whose name even history has not preserved—"the hermit of Livry."

CHAP. XV.

A Scholar of Noyon—Character of young Calvin—Early Education—He is devoted to Theology—The bishop gives him the tonsure—He quits Noyon because of the Plague—The Reformation creates new languages—Persecution and terror—Toussaint put into prison—Persecution gives new strength—Death of Du Blet, Merlin, and Papillon—God saves the Church—Project of Margaret—Departure for Spain.

While in France men were thus putting the confessors of Jesus Christ to death, God was preparing more powerful confessors. Beda, in dragging to execution a modest scholar, a humble hermit, almost thought he was dragging with him the whole Reformation. But Providence has resources which the world knows not. The gospel, like the fabulous bird, carries in it a principle of life which the flames cannot consume. It rises from its ashes. It is often at the very moment when the storm is at its height, when the thunder seems to have struck down the truth, and when the darkness of night covers it, that a sudden gleam shines forth, and announces a great deliverance. At this time, when all human powers in France were arming for the total destruction of the Reformation, God was preparing an instrument, feeble in appearance, which should one day maintain his rights, and defend his cause with an intrepidity more than human. Amid the persecution and faggot piles, which succeed and press close on each other, ever since Francis was the prisoner of Charles, let us cast an eye on a child who should afterwards be called to place himself at the head of a great army, in the holy wars of Israel.

Among the inhabitants of the town and the colleges of Paris, who heard the sounds of the great bell, was a young student of sixteen, of middle stature, of a pale complexion, with piercing eyes, and an animated expression betokening an intellect of uncommon sagacity.[1] His dress remarkable at once for its cleanness and per-

[1] Statura fuit mediocri, colore subpallido et nigricante, oculis ad mortem usque limpidis, quique ingenii sagacitatem testarentur. (Bezæ Vita Calvini.)

fect simplicity, indicated order and modesty.[1] This young man, named John Cauvin or Calvin, was then studying at the college of La Marche, under Mathurin Cordier, a regent celebrated for his probity, his erudition, and the talents he had received for instructing youth. Brought up in all the superstitions of the papacy, the scholar of Noyon was blindly submissive to the Church, devoted with docility to its observances,[2] and persuaded that the heretics richly deserved the flames which had consumed them. The blood which then flowed in Paris only served in his eyes to magnify the crime of heresy. But though naturally of a timid temper, which he himself has called soft and pusillanimous,[3] he had that integrity and generosity of heart which dispose the possessor to sacrifice every thing for the convictions once acquired. Accordingly, in vain was his youth struck with these frightful spectacles, in vain on the Place de Grave and the square of Notre Dame did murderous flames consume the faithful disciples of the gospel; the remembrance of their horrors could not hinder him from one day entering this new path, where apparently he could only expect imprisonment and the scaffold. In the character of young Calvin already appeared traits which announced what he was to become. The strictness of his morals was a prelude to the strictness of his doctrine, and in the student of sixteen might have been recognised a man who would take in earnest whatever he should receive, and who would require from others what he himself felt it quite simple to do. Quiet and grave during the lectures, in the hours for recreation, taking no part in the amusements and follies of his fellow-students, but keeping himself apart;[4] impressed with horror at sin, he occasionally censured their irregularities sharply and even with some degree of bitterness.[5] Accordingly a canon of Noyon assures us that his fellows had surnamed him the *accusative*.[6] He was among them the representative of conscience and duty, so far was he from being what some slanderers have wished to make him. The pale hue, the piercing eye of the student of sixteen already inspired his comrades with more respect, than the black gown of their teachers, and this child of Picardy, of little stature and timid air, who came daily to take his seat on the benches of the college of La Marche, was even now, without

---

[1] Cultu corporis neque culto neque sordido sed qui singularem modestiam deceret. (Bezæ Vita Calvini.) [2] Primo quidem quum superstitionibus Papatus magis pertinaciter addictus essem. (Calv. Præf. ad Psalm.) [3] Ego qui natura timido, molli et pusillo animo me esse fatcor. (Ibid.) [4] Summam in me ri us affectabat gravitatem et paucorum hominum consuetudine utebatur. (Rœmundi Hist. Hæres. vii, 10.) He affected the greatest gravity in his manners, and cultivated the society only of a few individuals. [5] Severus omnium in suis sodalibus censor. (Bezæ Vita Calv.)
[6] Annales de l'Eglise de Noyon, par Levasseur, Chanoine, p. 1158.

thinking it, by the gravity of his speech and deportment, a master and a Reformer.

It was not in these respects only that the boy of Noyon was above his fellow-students. His great timidity sometimes prevented him from manifesting the hatred which he felt for vanity and vice, but he was already devoting to study the whole strength of his intellect and his will. On seeing him, one might have had presentiment of a man who would wear out his life in exertion. He comprehended every thing with inconceivable facility; he ran in his studies, when his fellows only crept on slowly; and engraved deeply on his young genius what others took much time to learn superficially. Hence his masters were obliged to take him out of the class, and make him pass by himself to new studies.[1]

Among his fellow-students were the young De Mommors, belonging to the first nobility of Picardy. John Calvin was intimately connected with them, especially with Claude, who was at a later period abbot of St. Eloi, and to whom he dedicated his Commentary on Seneca. Calvin had gone to Paris in the company of these young nobles. His father, Gerard Cauvin, a notary apostolic, procurator-fiscal of the county of Noyon, secretary to the bishopric, and procurator of the Chapter,[2] was a judicious and able man. By his talents he had obtained those offices which were sought by the first families, and gained the esteem of all the gentlemen of the district, in particular of the illustrious family of Mommor.[3] Gerard lived at Noyon.[4] He had married a young lady of Cambray, of remarkable beauty, and retiring piety, named Jean Lefranq. She had already given him a son named Charles, when on the 10th July, 1509, she had a second son who was named John, and baptised in the church of St. Godebert.[5] A third son named Anthony, who died in early life, and two daughters, completed the family of the procurator-fiscal of Noyon.

Gerard Cauvin, living in intimate relation with the heads of the clergy and nobles of the province, wished his son to receive the same education as those of the best families. John, who had shown

[1] Exculto ipsius ingenio quod ei jam tum erat acerrimum, ita profecit ut cæteris sodalibus in grammatices curriculo relictis ad dialecticos et aliarum quas vocant artium studium promoveretur. (Beza.) [2] Levasseur, Annales de l'Egl. Cath. de Noyon, p. 1151. Drelincourt, Defense de Calvin, p. 193.) [3] Erat is Gerardus non parvi judicii et consilii homo, ideoque nobilibus ejus regionis plerisque carus. (Beza.)
[4] In the place where the stag inn now stands. (Desmay, Doctor of the Sorbonne.) Vit. de Jean Calvin, heresiarch, p. 30. Levasseur, Ann. de Noyon, p. 1157.
[5] The calumnies and absurd stories as to Calvin's person, began early. Levasseur, who was at a later period Dean of the Canons of Noyons, relates that at his birth "before the child was born, a great number of flies came forth : an undoubted omen that he was one day to be an evil speaker and calumniator." (Annales.) These absurdities, and all others of the same kind invented against the Reformer, refute themselves without our taking the trouble to do it. In our day those of the Romish doctors who are not ashamed to employ the weapons of calumny, make a selection among those low and ridiculous tales, not venturing to repeat them all. All, however, are of equal value.

precocious talents, was brought up with the sons of the house of Mommor. He was like one of themselves, and received the same lessons as young Claude. In this family he learnt the first elements of literature and life, and had thus a higher culture than that which he seemed destined to receive.[1] At a later period he was sent to the college of Capettes, founded in the town of Noyon.[2] The boy had few recreations. Sternness, which was one of the features in the character of the son, was in the father also. Gerard brought him up strictly. John, from his most tender years, behoved to bend under the inflexible rule of duty. He was early trained to this, and in this way the influence of the father counteracted that of the family of Mommor. Calvin, of a timid disposition and somewhat rustic nature, as he himself describes it,[3] rendered still more timid by the severity of his father, shunned the splendid apartments of his patrons, and loved to dwell alone in the shade.[4] His young soul was thus formed in retirement for great thoughts. It appears that he sometimes went to Pont l'Evêque, near Noyon, where his grandfather dwelt in a cottage,[5] and where other relations besides, who afterwards changed their name from hatred to the heresiarch, then gave a kind welcome to the son of the procurator-fiscal. But young Calvin's time was especially devoted to study. While Luther, who was to act upon the people, was brought up as a child of the people, Calvin, who was to act chiefly as a theologian, as a thinker, and to become the legislator of the renovated church, received from infancy a more liberal education.[6]

At an early period a spirit of piety was disclosed in the heart of the child. An author relates that they had accustomed him, when a child, to pray in the open air, under the vault of heaven, and this contributed to keep a feeling of the Divine presence alive in his heart.[7] But though Calvin may from infancy have heard the voice of God in his heart, there was not a person in Noyon more strict than he in the observance of ecclesiastical rules. Hence Gerard, struck with this disposition, conceived the design of devoting his son to theology.[8] This prospect, doubtless, contributed to give his soul that grave form, that theological character which distinguished him at a later period. His mind was of a description to receive strong impressions, and to familiarise itself

---

[1] Domi vestræ puer educatus, iisdem tecum studiis educatus primam vitæ et litterarum disciplinam familiæ vestræ nobilissimæ acceptam refero. (Calv. Præf. in Senecam ad Claudium.) [2] Desmay Remarques, p. 31. Drelincourt, Defense, p. 158. [3] Ego qui natura subrusticus. (Præf. ad Psalm.) [4] Umbram et otium semper amavi . . . latebras captare. (Ibid.) [5] "The report is, that his grandfather was a cooper." (Drelincourt, p. 36. Levasseur Ann. de Noyon, p. 1151.) [6] Henry, das Leben Calvins, p. 29. [7] Calvin's Leben von Fischer, Leipzig, 1794. The author does not give his authority for the fact. [8] Destinârat autem eum pater ab initio theologiæ studiis, quod in illa etiam tenera ætate mirum in modum religiosus esset. (Beza.)

from youth with the most elevated thoughts. The report that he was at this time one of the boys of the choir has no foundation, according to the testimony of his enemies themselves. But they confidently assert, that when he was a boy he was seen in processions bearing a sword with a cross guard, to represent a cross,[1] a presage, they add, of what he was one day to be. The servant of the Lord says in Isaiah, "The Lord has made my mouth like a sharp sword." The same may be said of Calvin.

Gerard was poor. The education of his son cost him much, and he desired to attach him to the church irrevocably. The Cardinal of Lorraine had, at the age of fourteen, been appointed coadjutor to the bishop of Metz. It was then common to give offices and ecclesiastical revenues to children. Alphonso of Portugal was made a cardinal at eight, by Leo X; and Odet of Chattilon, by Clement VII, at eleven. At a later period the celebrated mother Angelica, of Port Royal, was appointed coadjutress of the monastery at seven. Gerard, who died a good catholic, was in the good graces of the bishop of Noyon, Messire Charles de Hangest, and his vicars-general. Accordingly the chaplain of Gesine having resigned his office, the bishop, on the 21st May, 1521, gave the living to John Calvin, who was then about twelve. This was communicated to the Chapter twelve days after. On the eve of Corpus Christi, the bishop, in due form, cut the hair of the boy,[2] and by this ceremony of the tonsure, John entered the clerical order, and became capable of being admitted to holy orders, and of possessing benefice, without residence.

Thus Calvin was called, as a child, to make upon himself an experiment of the abuses of the Church of Rome. There was not a tonsured individual in the kingdom more in earnest in his piety than the chaplain of Gesine, and the grave child was perhaps himself astonished at the work performed by the bishop and his vicars-general. But in his simplicity he had too much veneration for these high personages, to allow himself to entertain the least suspicion as to the legitimacy of his tonsure. He had held the office for two years when Noyon was visited by a dreadful plague. Several canons applied to the Chapter for permission to quit the town. Many of the inhabitants had been struck by the "great death," and Gerard began to be afraid that the plague might in a moment bereave him of his son John, the hope of his life. The young Mommors were going to prosecute their studies at Paris. This was the very thing which the procurator-fiscal had ever desired for his son. Why should he separate John from his

---

[1] Levasseur, Ann. de Noyon, p. 1159, 1173.   [2] Desmay, Vie de Calvin, p. 31.
Levasseur, p. 1158.

fellow-students? Accordingly on the 5th August, 1523, he presented a petition to the Chapter, requesting leave for the young chaplain "to go wherever should seem to him good during the plague, without forfeiture of his living." This was granted till the feast of St. Remy.[1] John Calvin thus quitted the paternal roof at the age of fourteen. It requires great effrontery in slander to attribute his departure to other causes, and thus boldly encounter the disgrace which justly recoils on the promoters of charges whose falsehood has been so completely demonstrated. Calvin, it would seem, alighted in Paris at the house of one of his uncles, Richard Cauvin, who lived near the church of St. Germain-l'Auxerrois. "Thus fleeing the plague," says the canon of Noyon, "he was to catch it elsewhere."

In the metropolis of literature, a new world opened on the young student. He availed himself of it, set himself to study, and made great progress in Latin. He familiarised himself with Cicero, and learned of this great master to use the language of the Romans with a facility, purity, and grace which excited the admiration even of his enemies. But at the same time he found in this language riches which he was at a later period to transfer to his own.

Till now Latin had been the only literary language. It was, and to our day has remained, the language of the Church. It was the Reformation which created, or at least everywhere emancipated modern languages. The exclusive character of the priests had ceased: the people were called to learn and know. In this fact alone there was an end to the language of the priest, and the introduction of the language of the people. It was no longer to the Sorbonne merely, it was no longer to some monks, some ecclesiastics, that new ideas were to be addressed. It was to the noble, the citizen, the mechanic. All were to be preached to, and what is more, all were going to preach—carders of wool and knights, as well as curates and doctors. A new tongue, then, was required, or, at least, the vulgar tongue must undergo an immense transformation—a great emancipation. Drawn from the common uses of life, it must receive from renovated Christianity its patent of nobility. The gospel which had so long slept, was awake: it spoke, it addressed the whole nation, and everywhere enkindled the most generous affections. It opened the treasures of heaven, to a generation which was thinking only of the petty interests here below. It moved the masses. It spoke to them of God, of man, of good and evil, of the pope, of the Bible, of a crown in heaven, and, it might be, a scaffold upon

---

[1] The priest, and vicar-general Desmay, (Jean Calvin, heresiarque, p. 32,) and canon Levasseur, (Ann. de Noyon, p. 1160,) declare they had found this in the records of the Chapter of Noyon. These Romish authors thus refute the inventions or mistakes of Richelieu and other authors.—See the preface.

earth. The popular idiom, which till now had been only the language of chroniclers and troubadours, was called by the Reformation to act a new part, and consequently to undergo new developments. Society saw a new world begin, and this new world must have new languages. The Reformation freed the French language from the swaddling bands in which it had till then been wrapt up, and enabled it to reach the age of majority. Thenceforth this language was in full possession of those exalted rights which relate to the things of mind and the blessings of heaven, and of which it had been deprived under the tutelage of Rome. No doubt the people form their own language. It is they who form those happy words—those figurative and energetic expressions, which give language so much vivacity and life. But there are resources which lie beyond their reach, and can only come from men of intellect. Calvin being called to discuss and prove, gave the language connections, relations, shades, transitions, and dialectic forms which it did not previously possess.

All these elements were already at work in the head of the young student of the college La Marche. This youth, who was to be so mighty in wielding the human heart, was also to conquer the language which he was called to employ. Protestant France was formed, at a later period, on the French of Calvin, and Protestant France was the best informed part of the nation. From it came forth those families of literati and high magistracy which had so powerful an influence on the culture of the people: from it came forth Port Royal,[1] one of the greatest instruments which contributed to form French prose and even French poetry, and which having attempted to carry into the Gallican catholicism the doctrine and language of the Reformation, failed in the one project, but succeeded in the other. For Roman Catholic France had to come and learn of its Jansenist and Reformed opponents, how to wield those weapons of language without which she could not combat them.[2]

Meantime, while thus in the college of La Marche was being formed the future reformer of religion and even of language, all was in agitation around the youthful and the grave student, who, as yet, took no part in the great movement which was stirring society. The flames which had consumed the hermit and Pavanne, had spread terror over Paris. But the persecutors were not satisfied; a system of terror was put in operation throughout France. The friends of the Reformation durst no longer correspond with

---

[1] A. Arnauld, grandfather of Mother Angelica and of all the Arnaulds of Port Royal, was a Protestant.—See Port Royal, by Sainte-Beuve. [2] Etude Literaire sur Calvin, par M. A. Sayous, Geneva, 1839. It has just been followed by other studies on Farel, Viret, and Beza.

each other, lest their letters being intercepted, should mark out for the vengeance of the tribunals both themselves and those to whom they were addressed.[1] One man, however, ventured to carry news from Paris and France to the refugees of Basle by sewing unsigned letters into his doublet. He escaped the platoons of arquebusiers, all the marshalmen of the different communes, the scrutiny of the provosts and lieutenants, and arrived at Basle without the mysterious doublet having been torn up. His statements struck Toussaint and his friends with terror. "It is dreadful to hear of the great cruelties which are there done,"[2] exclaimed Toussaint. A short time before had arrived at Basle, with the officers of justice at their heels, two monks of St. Francis, one of whom, named John Prevost, had preached at Meaux, and been afterwards cast into prison at Paris.[3] What they told of Paris and Lyons, called forth the deepest sympathy in the refugees. "May our Lord send thither his grace!" wrote Toussaint to Farel. "I assure you I sometimes feel myself in great anguish and tribulation."

Still these excellent men did not lose courage. In vain were all the parliaments on the watch, in vain did the spies of the Sorbonne and of the monks come into churches, colleges, and even private families, to pry into every evangelical word that might be pronounced, in vain did the king's gens d'armes arrest on the roads every thing that seemed to bear the stamp of the Reformation. These Frenchmen, whom Rome and her partizans tracked and crushed, had faith in a better future, and already hailed the end of this Babylonish captivity, as they termed it. "At length," said they, "the seventieth year will come, the year of deliverance, and liberty of mind and conscience will be given us."[4] But the seventy years were to last for three centuries, and it was only after unheard of disasters that their hopes were to be realised. It was not, however, from men that the refugees hoped any thing. "Those who have begun the dance," said Toussaint, "will not stop by the way." But they believed that the Lord "knew those that were his, and would himself work out a mighty deliverance."[5]

Chevalier d'Esch had in fact been delivered. Having escaped from the prisons of Pont-a-Mousson, he had hastened to Strasburg. There, however, he did not remain long. Toussaint had immediately written to Farel, "For the glory of God try and get the Knight, our good master,[6] to return as quickly as may be: for the other brethren have great need of such a captain." In fact the

---

[1] Nobody dares write me. (Toussaint a Farel, 4th Sept. 1525. MS. Neuchatel.)
[2] Ibid. [3] Ibid., 21st July, 1525. [4] Sane venit annus septuagesimus et tempus appetit ut tandem vindicemur in libertatem spiritus et conscientiæ. (Ibid.)
[5] Sed novit Dominus quos elegerit. (Ibid.) [6] "Si nos magistrum in terris habere deceat," he adds. (Ibid.)

French refugees had new fears. They trembled lest this dispute on the Lord's Supper, which had distressed them so much in Germany, should cross the Rhine, and bring new sorrows into France. Francis Lambert, the monk of Avignon, after being at Zurich and Wittemberg, had come to Metz, but there was not complete confidence in him. It was feared that he might bring Luther's sentiments, and by useless controversies, "monstrous," Toussaint calls them, arrest the progress of the Reformation.[1] Esch then returned to Lorraine, but it was to be exposed anew to great dangers, " with all those who then sought the glory of Jesus Christ."[2]

Toussaint was not of a character to send others to the battle, without going himself. Deprived of daily intercourse with Œcolampadius, confined to the society of a coarse priest, he had sought the presence of Christ, and his courage had increased. If he could not retire to Metz, might he not at least go to Paris? The piles of the hermit and Pavanne were still smoking, it is true, and served to warn off from the capital all who had a similar faith. But if the colleges and streets of Paris were terror-struck, so that no person now dared to pronounce the word Gospel or Reformation, was not this a reason for repairing thither? Toussaint quitted Basle, and came within that enclosure where fanaticism had taken the place of festivities and dissipation. He sought, while advancing in Christian studies, to connect himself with the brethren in the colleges, and especially in that of Cardinal Lemoine, where Lefevre and Farel had taught.[3] But he was not long at liberty to do so. The tyranny of the commissioners of the parliament, and the theologians, reigned supreme in the capital, and every one who displeased them was by them accused of heresy.[4] A duke and an abbot, whose names are not given, denounced Toussaint as a heretic, and one of the king's serjeants arrested the youth from Lorraine, and threw him into prison. Separated from all his friends, and treated as a criminal, Toussaint felt his wretchedness the more keenly. " O Lord," exclaimed he, " take not thy Spirit from me ; for, without him, I am only flesh and blood, and a sink of iniquity." While his body was in fetters, he thought of all those who were still combating freely for the gospel. There was Œcolampadius, his father, he " whose work we are in the Lord;"[5] there was Lefevre, whom he thought, doubtless on account of his age, "incapable of bearing the burden of the gospel;"[6] Roussel, "by whom

---

[1] Vereor ne aliquid monstri alat. (Tossanus Farello, 27th Sept., 1525.)
[2] Audio etiam equitem periclitari, simul et omnes qui illic Christi gloriæ favent. (Ibid., 27th Dec., 1525.) [3] Fratres qui in collegio Cardinalis Monachi sunt te salutant. (Ibid.) [4] Regnante hic tyrannide commissariorum et theologorum. (Ibid.) [5] Patrem nostrum cujus nos opus sumus in Domino. (Ibid.) This letter is without date, but appears to have been written shortly after Toussaint's deliverance, and shows what his thoughts were at this period. [6] Faber impar est oneri evangelico ferendo. (Ibid.)

he hoped that the Lord would perform great things;"[1] Vaugris, who displayed all the charity "of the most affectionate brother" in order to deliver him from his enemies;[2] in fine, there was Farel, to whom he wrote, "I commend myself to your prayers, that I may not fall in this combat."[3] Oh! how all the names of these beloved men alleviated the bitterness of his imprisonment! Indeed he was not ready to fall. Death, it is true, threatened to overtake him in this city, in which the blood of a multitude of his brethren was to be poured out like water,[4] while the friends of his mother, and his uncle, the primicier of Metz, and the Cardinal Lorraine, made him the most splendid offers.[5] . . . . "I despise them," he replied. "I know that it is a temptation from God: I would rather be hungry, I would rather be a door-keeper in the house of the Lord, than dwell with great riches in the palaces of the ungodly."[6] At the same time he made an open profession of his faith: "I glory," said he, "in being called a heretic by those whose life and doctrine are opposed to Jesus Christ."[7] This interesting and intrepid young man signed his letters, "Peter Toussaint, unworthy of being called a Christian."

Thus, in the absence of the king, new blows were struck at the Reformation. Berquin, Toussaint, and many others, were in prison: Schuch, Pavanne, and the hermit of Livry, had been put to death: Farel, Lefevre, Roussel, and a great many more, defenders of sound doctrine, were in exile. The lips of the eloquent were mute. The light of the gospel day was becoming more and more overcast, and the storm incessantly growling, bent, shook, and threatened as it were to root up the still tender tree which the hand of God had planted in the soil of France.

Nor was this all. To the humbler victims who had been sacrificed, more illustrious were to succeed. The enemies of the Reformation in France, not having been able to succeed when they began at the top, had become resigned to begin at the bottom, but with the hope of rising step by step in condemnation and death, until they should reach the highest pinnacles. This inverted course succeeded. Scarcely were the ashes with which persecution had covered the Place-de-Grave and the pavement of Notre Dame, been dispersed, when new blows were struck. Messire Anthony Du Blet, that excellent man, that merchant of Lyons, fell under the attacks of the enemies of the truth, with another disciple, François Moulin, though we do not know the details of his death.[8] They

---

[1] Per Rufum magna operabitur Dominus. (Tossanus Farello, 27th Dec., 1525.)
[2] Fidelissimi fratris officio functum. (Ibid.) [3] Commendo me vestris precibus, ne succumbam in hac militia. (Ibid.) [4] Me periclitari de vita. (Ibid.)
[5] Offerebantur hic mihi conditiones amplissimæ. (Ibid.) [6] Malo esurire et objectus esse in domo Domini . . . . (Ibid.) [7] Hæc, hæc gloria mea quod habeor hæreticus ab his quorum vitam et doctrinam video pugnare cum Christo. (Ibid.) [8] Periit Franciscus Molinus ac Dubletus. (Erasm. Ep., p. 1109.)

went farther still, and took a higher aim. There was an illustrious personage, one they could not reach in person, but they could strike her in those who were dear to her. This was the Duchess D'Alençon. Michael d' Arande, chaplain to the king's sister, for whom Margaret had dismissed all her other preachers, and who preached the pure gospel before her, became the object of attack by the persecutors, and was threatened with imprisonment and death.[1] Almost at the same time Anthony Papillon, for whom the princess had procured the office of first Master of Requests to the Dauphin, died suddenly, and the universal rumour, even among the enemy, was, that he had been poisoned.[2]

Thus persecution extended in the kingdom, and always drew nearer to Margaret. After the forces of the Reformation, concentrated at Meaux, Lyons, and Basle, had been dispersed, the isolated combatants, who had here and there maintained her cause, were cut off in detail. A few efforts more, and the French soil will be purged of heresy! Silent manœuvres, secret wiles, succeed to clamour and the scaffold. The war will be carried on in open day, but at the same time also in darkness. If fanaticism employs the tribunal and the scaffold for the ignoble, it will reserve poison and the poniard for the great. The teachers of a celebrated society have only too much patronised the use of it, and even kings have fallen under the daggers of the assassin. But if Rome has always had Scides, it has also seen Vincent Pauls and Fenelons. These blows, struck in darkness and silence, were well fitted to spread universal terror. To this perfidious course, to these fanatical persecutions within, were joined fatal defeats without. The whole kingdom was veiled in mourning. There was not a family, especially among the nobility, in which tears did not flow for a father, a husband, or a son left on the plains of Italy,[3] or one where the heart did not tremble for the liberty or life of one of its members. The great reverses which had overtaken the kingdom, diffused a leaven of hatred against the heretics. The people, the parliament, the Church, the throne, even lent a hand.

Was it not enough that the defeat of Pavia had deprived the Duchess D'Alençon of her husband, and cast her brother into prison? Must she see the gospel torch, in whose soft light she had always rejoiced, extinguished, perhaps, for ever? The news from Spain increased the general grief. Chagrin and sickness were endangering the life of the haughty Francis I. If the king continues

Erasmus, in his letter addressed to Francis I, (July, 1526,) mentions those who, during he captivity of the prince, had become victims of the fanatics of Rome.
[1] Periclitatus est Michael Arantius. (Erasm. Ep., p. 1109. [2] " Periit Papilio non sine gravi suspicion veneni," says Erasmus. (Ibid.) [3] Gaillard Hist. de Francois I, tom. ii, p. 255.

prisoner, if he dies, if the regency of his mother continues for many long years, is it not all over with the Reformation? "But, though all seems lost," said the young scholar of Noyon at a later period, "God saves and guards his church in a miraculous manner."[1] The Church of France, which was travailing as in birth, was to have a time of refreshing before new sorrows, and, in order to give it to her, God employed a feeble woman who never declared decidedly in favour of the Reformation. She was then thinking more of saving the king, and the kingdom, than of delivering obscure Christians, who, however, put great hope in her.[2] But under the glare of worldly affairs, God often conceals the mysterious means by which he governs his people. A noble project was formed in the breast of the Duchess D'Alençon:—to cross the sea or the Pyrenees to rescue Francis I from the hands of Charles V. Such is henceforth the aim of her life.

Margaret de Valois intimated her design, and France hailed her with a shout of gratitude. Her great talents, the reputation which she had acquired, the love which she had for her brother, and that which Francis had for her, were, in the eyes of Louisa and Duprat, a counterbalance for her attachment to the new doctrine. All turned their eyes towards her as the only person capable of delivering the kingdom from the peril in which it was placed. Let Margaret herself, then, go to Spain; let her speak to the mighty Emperor and his ministers; and let her employ the admirable talents, which Providence has bestowed upon her, in the deliverance of her brother and her king.

Meanwhile very various feelings filled the hearts of the nobles and the people when they saw the Duchess D'Alençon, placing herself amid the hostile councils and fierce soldiery of the Catholic king.

Every one admired the courage and devotedness of this young female, but without participating in them. The friends of the princess had fears for her, which were well nigh realised. But the evangelical Christians were full of hope. The captivity of Francis I had brought unparalleled severities on the friends of the Reformation, and it was thought that his liberation might put an end to them. To open the gates of Spain to the king, was to shut those of the officialities and castles into which the servants of the word of God were thrown. Margaret strengthened herself in a design on which her whole soul was bent, by all these different motives:

[1] Nam habet Deus modum, quo electus suos mirabiliter custodiat, ubi omnia perdita videntur. (Calvin., Ep. Rom. xi, 2.) For God has a way in which he wonderfully preserves his elect when all seems lost. [2] .... Beneficio Illustrissimæ Ducis Alençoniæ. (Toussaint to Farel.)

MARGARET'S DEPARTURE FOR SPAIN. 377

No height of heaven can bar my way,
Nor depth beneath my soul dismay;
E'en Hell must own my Saviour's sway![1]

Her weak female heart was strengthened by the faith which gives the victory over the world, and her resolution was unmoved. Every thing was prepared in haste for this important and dangerous voyage.

The archbishop of Embrun, since Cardinal of Tournon, and the president De Selves, were already at Madrid to negotiate the deliverance of the king. They were made subordinate to Margaret, as was also the Bishop of Tarbes, since Cardinal De Graṁmont. Full powers were given to the princess alone. At the same time Montmorency, who at a later period was so hostile to the Reformation, was sent in all haste into Spain in order to obtain a safe-conduct for the king's sister.[2] The emperor made difficulties. He said it was for his ministers alone to arrange the affair. "One hour of conference," exclaimed Selves, "between your majesty, the king, my master, and the Duchess D'Alençon, will advance the treaty more than a month of discussion between lawyers."[3]

Margaret, impatient to arrive because of the sickness of the king, set out without a safe-conduct, with an imposing retinue.[4] She quitted the court, and passed through Lyons, proceeding towards the Mediterranean. As she was on the way, Montmorency returned with letters from Charles, who guaranteed her liberty for three months only. She arrived at Aigues-Mortes,[5] and here the sister of Francis I embarked in the vessel prepared for her. Led by God into Spain rather to deliver humble Christians from oppression than to bring the mighty monarch of France out of captivity, Margaret committed herself to the billows of the same sea which had borne her captive brother after the disastrous battle of Pavia.

[1] Marguerites de la Marguerite, i, p. 125.   [2] Memoirs de du Bellay, p. 124.
[2] Garnier, Histoire de France, tom. xxiv.   [3] To test to the quick the will of the said Emperor, ... Madam Margaret, Duchess of Alençon, very notably accompanied by several ambassadors. (Les Gestes de Françoise de Valois, par E. Dolet, 1540.   [5] Jam in itinere erat Margarita, Francisci soror . . . . e fossis Marianis solvens, Barcinonem primum, deinde Cæsar Augustam appulerat, (Belcarius, Rerum Gallic. Comment.

END OF THE THIRD VOLUME.

William Collins & Co., Printers, Glasgow.

www.ingramcontent.com/pod-product-compliance
Lightning Source LLC
Chambersburg PA
CBHW030356230426
43664CB00007BB/617